AAT

Technician

NVQ Level 4

Units 17 and 18
Business and Personal Taxation
(Finance Act 1998)

WORKBOOK

117X/S99

British Library Cataloguing-in-Publication Data

A catalogue record for this book is available from the British Library.

Published by AT Foulks Lynch Ltd
Number 4
The Griffin Centre
Staines Road
Feltham
Middlesex
TW14 0HS

ISBN 0 7483 4117 X

Acknowledgements

We are grateful to the Association of Accounting Technicians, the Association of Chartered Certified Accountants, the Chartered Institute of Management Accountants and the Institute of Chartered Accountants in England and Wales for permission to reproduce past examination questions. The answers have been prepared by AT Foulks Lynch Ltd. The copyright to the questions remains with the examining body.

CONTENTS

PREFACE

This is the 1999 edition of the AAT NVQ workbook for the Revised Standards of Units 17 and 18 - Business and Personal Taxation. It is based on Finance Act 1998 which will be assessed by the AAT up to June 2000. The workbook includes the sample devolved simulation provided by the AAT.

The workbook has been produced to complement our Units 17 and 18 textbook and it contains numerous practice questions and tasks designed to reflect and simulate the work place environment. These are arranged to match the chapters of the textbook, so that you can work through the two books together.

The workbook also contains practice devolved assessments to prepare you completely for the assessment procedures which form part of your course.

Fully comprehensive answers to all questions, tasks and assessments are provided, with the exception of those which are designated as being specifically for classroom work.

You will find that completion of all the elements of this workbook will prepare you admirably for the assessments which you must carry out to pass Unit 17 and 18.

Class Activities

A feature of this workbook is the section at the end comprising Activities which are specially designed for classroom use. The answers to these are not included in the workbook but are reproduced in the **new College Kit** which is available to college lecturers who adopt our material.

New College Kits

In addition to the Textbooks and Workbooks, AT Foulks Lynch offers colleges adopting our material the new **'College Kits'**.

The College Kits for units assessed by Devolved Assessment contain:

- additional Devolved Assessment material in looseleaf form which can be photocopied to provide practice classwork for students; and
- the looseleaf answers to the class examples from the Workbooks.

These Kits are supplied at no extra cost and may be photocopied under the limited licence which is granted to adopting colleges.

RATES AND ALLOWANCES (up to and including Finance Act 1998)

(A) INCOME TAX

(1) **Rates**

	1997/98			*1998/99*	
Rate	*Band of income*	*Cumulative tax*	*Rate*	*Band of income*	*Cumulative tax*
%	£	£	%	£	£
20	1 - 4,100	820	20	1 - 4,300	860
23	4,101 - 26,100	5,060	23	4,301 - 27,100	5,244
		5,880			6,104
40	26,101 -		40	27,100 -	

(2) **Personal allowances and reliefs**

	1997/98	*1998/99*
	£	£
Personal allowance	4,045	4,195
Married couple's allowance	1,830*	1,900*
Age allowance (65 - 74)		
personal	5,220	5,410
married couple's	3,185*	3,305*
income limit	15,600	16,200
Age allowance (75 or over)		
personal	5,400	5,600
married couple's	3,225*	3,345*
income limit	15,600	16,200
Additional personal allowance	1,830*	1,900*
Widow's bereavement allowance	1,830*	1,900*
Blind person's allowance	1,280	1,330

* Relief restricted to 15%

(3) **Pension contribution limits**

Age at start of tax year	*Personal pension schemes (%)*
35 or less	17½
36 - 45	20
46 - 50	25
51 - 55	30
56 - 60	35
61 and over	40

(4) **First year allowance rates**

Date expenditure incurred on plant and machinery	*FYA rate*
2 July 1997 - 1 July 1998	50%
2 July 1998 - 1 July 1999	40%

(5) **Pension earnings cap**

1996/97	£82,000
1997/98	£84,000
1998/99	£87,600

(6) **Rent a room relief**

1998/99 and 1997/98	£4,250 p.a.

(B) CORPORATION TAX

	FY 1994	*FY 1995*	*FY 1996*	*FY 1997*	*FY 1998*	*FY*
	1999					
Rate	33%	33%	33%	31%	31%	30%
Small companies rate (up to £300,000)	25%	25%	24%	21%	21%	20%

Section 13(2) ICTA 1988 relief
(M-P) × $\frac{I}{P}$ × fraction

where M is £1,500,000

Fraction	$^1/_{50}$	$^1/_{50}$	$^9/_{400}$	$^1/_{40}$	$^1/_{40}$
	$^1/_{40}$				
Advance corporation tax	$^{20}/_{80}$	$^{20}/_{80}$	$^{20}/_{80}$	$^{20}/_{80}$	$^{20}/_{80}$
	N/A				

The amounts of dividends received or paid represent the actual amounts without any adjustment for tax credits or advance corporation tax.

(C) CAPITAL GAINS TAX

(1) **Annual exemption**

	£
1993/94	5,800
1994/95	5,800
1995/96	6,000
1996/97	6,300
1997/98	6,500
1998/99	6,800

(2) **Retail price index** (RPI)

	1982	*1983*	*1984*	*1985*
January	-	82.61	86.84	91.20
February	-	82.97	87.20	91.94
March	79.44	83.12	87.48	92.80
April	81.04	84.28	88.64	94.78
May	81.62	84.64	88.97	95.21
June	81.85	84.84	89.20	95.41
July	81.88	85.30	89.10	95.23
August	81.90	85.68	89.94	95.49
September	81.85	86.06	90.11	95.44
October	82.26	86.36	90.67	95.59
November	82.66	86.67	90.95	95.92
December	82.51	86.89	90.87	96.05

	1986	*1987*	*1988*	*1989*	*1990*	*1991*
January	96.25	100.0	103.3	111.0	119.5	130.2
February	96.60	100.4	103.7	111.8	120.2	130.9
March	96.73	100.6	104.1	112.3	121.4	131.4
April	97.67	101.8	105.8	114.3	125.1	133.1
May	97.85	101.9	106.2	115.0	126.2	133.5
June	97.79	101.9	106.6	115.4	126.7	134.1
July	97.52	101.8	106.7	115.5	126.8	133.8
August	97.82	102.1	107.9	115.8	128.1	134.1
September	98.30	102.4	108.4	116.6	129.3	134.6
October	98.45	102.9	109.5	117.5	130.3	135.1
November	99.29	103.4	110.0	118.5	130.0	135.6
December	99.62	103.3	110.3	118.8	129.9	135.7

	1992	*1993*	*1994*	*1995*	*1996*	*1997*	*1998*	*1999*
January	135.6	137.9	141.3	146.0	150.2	154.4	159.5	e164.8
February	136.3	138.8	142.1	146.9	150.9	155.0	160.3	e165.1
March	136.7	139.3	142.5	147.5	151.5	155.4	e160.7	e165.3
April	138.8	140.6	144.2	149.0	152.6	156.3	e161.2	e165.7
May	139.3	141.1	144.7	149.6	152.9	156.9	e161.3	
June	139.3	141.0	144.7	149.8	153.0	157.5	e161.8	
July	138.8	140.7	144.0	149.1	152.4	157.5	e162.6	
August	138.9	141.3	144.7	149.9	153.1	158.5	e162.2	
September	139.4	141.9	145.0	150.6	153.8	159.3	e163.3	
October	139.9	141.8	145.2	149.8	153.8	159.5	e163.8	
November	139.7	141.6	145.3	149.8	153.9	159.6	e163.9	
December	139.2	141.9	146.0	150.7	154.4	160.0	e164.1	

e - estimated

(3) **Lease percentages**

Years	*Percentage*	*Years*	*Percentage*	*Years*	*Percentage*
50 or more	100.000	33	90.280	16	64.116
49	99.657	32	89.354	15	61.617
48	99.289	31	88.371	14	58.971
47	98.902	30	87.330	13	56.167
46	98.490	29	86.226	12	53.191
45	98.059	28	85.053	11	50.038
44	97.595	27	83.816	10	46.695
43	97.107	26	82.496	9	43.154
42	96.593	25	81.100	8	39.399
41	96.041	24	79.622	7	35.414
40	95.457	23	78.055	6	31.195
39	94.842	22	76.399	5	26.722
38	94.189	21	74.635	4	21.983
37	93.497	20	72.770	3	16.959
36	92.761	19	70.791	2	11.629
35	91.981	18	68.697	1	5.983
34	91.156	17	66.470	0	0.000

(4) **Taper Relief**

Number of complete years after 5/4/98 for which asset held	*Percentage of Gain chargeable*	
	Business Assets	*Non-business Assets*
0	100	100
1	92.5	100
2	85	100
3	77.5	95
4	70	90
5	62.5	85
6	55	80
7	47.5	75
8	40	70
9	32.5	65
10 or more	25	60

(D) CAR AND FUEL BENEFITS

(1) **Car scale benefit**

35% of list price when new including accessories, delivery charges and VAT (subject to £80,000 maximum). Reductions in the charge are as follows:

Business mileage 2,500 to 17,999 pa	⅓
18,000 or more pa	⅔
Then, cars 4 years old and over at end of tax year	⅓
Second car 18,000 or more pa	⅓

Cars over 15 years old at tax year end with an open market value of more than £15,000 (which is also higher than the original list price) taxed by reference to the open market value.

(2) **Van scale benefit**

Vans (under 3.5 tonnes) including fuel	*Under 4 years*	*4 years and over*
	£	£
1998/99	500	350
1997/98	500	350
1996/97	500	350

(3) **Car fuel benefit (petrol)**

	1997/98	*1998/99*
	£	£
Cylinder capacity		
Up to 1400 cc	800	1,010
1401 - 2000 cc	1,010	1,280
over 2000 cc	1,490	1,890

(4) **Car fuel benefit (diesel)**

	1997/98	*1998/99*
	£	£
Cylinder capacity		
2000 cc or less	740	1,280
Over 2000 cc	940	1,890

(E) VALUE ADDED TAX

(1) Annual VAT inclusive scale value for output tax on private fuel

	1997/98	*1998/99*
	£	£
Cylinder capacity (petrol)		
1400 cc or less	800	850
Over 1400 cc up to 2000 cc	1,010	1,075
Over 2000 cc	1,490	1,585
Cylinder capacity (diesel)		
2000 cc or less	740	785
more than 2000 cc	940	995

TECHNICIAN STAGE

NVQ/SVQ LEVEL 4 IN ACCOUNTING

REVISED STANDARDS

AAT SPECIMEN SIMULATION

PREPARING BUSINESS TAXATION COMPUTATIONS

(UNIT 17)

Association of Accounting Technicians

DATA AND TASKS

INSTRUCTIONS

This simulation is designed to test your ability to prepare business taxation computations.

The situation is set out below.

The tasks to be completed are set out beyond.

You are allowed three hours to complete your work.

You should read the whole simulation before commencing work so as to gain an overall picture of what is required.

Any blank forms required will be found at the end of this simulation.

In completing this simulation the following details should be noted:

- **workings should be to the nearest month and to the nearest £;**
- **the effects of Value Added Taxation and National Insurance should be ignored throughout.**

THE SITUATION

You are a qualified accounting technician, working in the tax department of a firm of accountants, Badger and Co. You report to the tax department manager, Edwina Smith.

In the course of your work you are expected to prepare computations of tax liabilities for various businesses and to complete corporation tax returns.

Today, you have arrived at work to find that Edwina Smith has been called to a meeting at a client's premises. In her absence, she would like you to deal with some work on two of the tax department's clients:

- Unicorn Trading Limited
- Cordelia's Shoe Shop

Edwina has left you a memo which sets out the work that she would like you to do today.

MEMO

To: An Accounting Technician
From: Edwina Smith, Tax Department Manager

Subject: Tax work to be completed on:

- Unicorn Trading Limited
- Cordelia's Shoe Shop

As you know I shall be out of the office for some of today. I would like you to do some work on the above two clients in my absence. I have set out below the work that needs doing and a list of the documents I have put on your desk to help you to do the work.

UNICORN TRADING LIMITED

This company has been one of Badger and Co's clients for a number of years. It prepares accounts to 31 December each year, and the accounts are audited by Badger and Co's audit department.

Tasks to be completed on Unicorn Trading Limited:

I would like you to:

1. Prepare the corporation tax computation for Unicorn Trading Limited for the year ended 31 December 1998.

   To do this, I expect you to:
   (a) prepare a calculation of Schedule D Case I profits for the company for the year ended 31 December 1998;
   (b) prepare a computation of the company's capital allowances for the year ended 31 December 1998;
   (c) prepare a computation of the chargeable gain on the disposal of the land sold by Unicorn Trading Limited during the year ended 31 December 1998;
   (d) prepare the corporation tax computation of the company for the year ended 31 December 1998.

2. Complete the short form of the corporation tax return, Form CT200, for the company for the year ended 31 December 1998.

3. Write a covering letter, on my behalf, to John Jones, the Finance Director of Unicorn Trading Limited, enclosing the corporation tax computation and return, and advising him of the amount of corporation tax to be paid and of the due date by which payment should be made.

Information supplied concerning Unicorn Trading Limited

To help you to do this I have given you the following information

- Extracts from the audited accounts of Unicorn Trading Limited for the year ended 31 December 1998;

- Information (photocopies of various letters and schedules) from the audit files, which are relevant to the taxation computations;

- A copy of form CT6l, as submitted by the company.

CORDELIA TRAVERS—TRADING AS CORDELIA'S SHOE SHOP

Cordelia started to trade, selling shoes from a local shop, on 1 December 1998. She has approached Badger and Co. to act as her accountants and tax advisors. The accounts department have produced accounts for her first period of trading, which ended on 30 June 1999.

Tasks to be completed on Cordelia's Shoe Shop:

I would like you to:

4. Calculate the Schedule D Case I profits taxable on Cordelia for 1998/99, and 1999/00, based on the information available.

5. Calculate the overlap profits arising and explain how they will be relieved.

Information supplied concerning Cordelia' s Shoe Shop
To allow you to do this I have given you the following information:

- A copy of the adjusted Schedule D Case I computation of taxable profit as completed by you last week. I have reviewed and agreed this computation.
- Cordelia estimates that her adjusted trading profit for the year ended 30 June 2000 will be £18,000.

Extracts from accounts

Unicorn Trading Limited

Financial Statements

For the year ended 31 December 1998

UNICORN TRADING LIMITED
Profit and Loss Account
For the year ended 31 December 1998

	1998		1997	
	£	£	£	£
TURNOVER		43,446		98,710
Administration expenses	30,498		15,827	
Other Operating Charges	244		480	
		(30,742)		(16,307)
OPERATING PROFIT		12,704		82,403
Interest payable and similar Charges		(876)		(130)
Interest receivable and similar income		124,900		0
PROFIT ON ORDINARY ACTIVITIES		136,728		82,273
TAXATION ON PROFIT ON ORDINARY ACTIVITIES		(10,350)		(10,781)
PROFIT ON ORDINARY ACTIVITIES AFTER TAXATION		126,378		71,492
Dividends		(33,000)		(31,980)
RETAINED PROFIT FOR THE YEAR		93,378		39,512
RETAINED PROFIT BROUGHT FORWARD		139,346		99,834
RETAINED PROFIT CARRIED FORWARD		£232,724		£139,346

UNICORN TRADING LIMITED

Balance sheet as at 31 December 1998

	Note	1998 £	1998 £	1997 £	1997 £
FIXED ASSETS					
Tangible assets	7		28,917		134,650
CURRENT ASSETS					
Debtors		6,467		8,481	
Cash at bank and in hand		201,474		2,904	
		207,941		11,385	
CREDITORS					
Amounts falling due within one year		(4,034)		(6,589)	
NET CURRENT ASSETS			203,907		4,796
NET ASSETS			£232,824		£139,446
CAPITAL AND RESERVES					
Equity share capital			100		100
Reserves			232,724		139,346
			£232,824		£139,446

UNICORN TRADING LIMITED

Extracts from the notes to the account.

(The full notes to the accounts have not been reproduced, only those required to answer the assessment).

Note 7

Tangible Fixed Assets

	Land and Buildings	*Plant and Machinery*	*Motor Vehicles*	*Total*
	£	£	£	£
Cost				
At 1 January 1998	100,000	20,000	36,600	156,600
Additions	0	5,000	6,000	11,000
Disposals	(100,000)	(10,000)	(5,000)	(115,000)
At 31 December 1998	0	15,000	37,600	52,600
Depreciation				
At 1 January 1998	0	12,800	9,150	21,950
Charge for the year	0	1,520	7,613	9,133
Disposals	0	(5,400)	(2,000)	(7,400)
At 31 December 1998	0	8,920	14,763	23,683
NBV at 31 December 1998	£0	£6,080	£22,837	£28,917
NBV at 1 January 1998	£100,000	£7,200	£27,450	£134,650

Information from Audit files

UNICORN TRADING LIMITED — Date prepared 31.3.99 Prepared by: ES
Reviewed by: PS
Year ended: 31 December 1998

Analysis of Fixed Assets:

Additions

Plant and Machinery— Total £5,000

Cardboard Box Making Machine	£5,000	Date of Purchase. 10 June 1998

Motor Vehicles— Total £6,000

Nissan Micra Car	£6,000	Date of Purchase: 1 March 1998

Disposals:

Land and Buildings— Sale of plot of land*

Sale proceeds	£200,000	
Original cost (1 April 1992)	£100,000	
Accumulated Depreciation	£NIL	Date of Sale: 10 July 1998

Note: *(Company had hoped to build new premises on this land, but planning permission was refused).

Plant and Machinery—Sale of various machines — Date of Sale: 1 May 1998

Sale Proceeds	£15,000
Original Cost	£10,000
Accumulated Depreciation	£5,400

Note: all sold for less than £6,000 each.

Motor Vehicles—Sale of Ford Fiesta Car — Date of Sale: 20 February 1998

Sale Proceeds	£2,500
Original Cost	£5,000
Accumulated Depreciation	£2,000

UNICORN TRADING LIMITED

Date prepared: 31.3.99 Prepared by: ES
Reviewed by: PS
Year ended. 31 December 1998

Analysis of Fixed Assets:

Profit/(loss) on disposal of Fixed Assets:

Land and Buildings	£	£
Sale proceeds		200,000
less: Net book value (100,000 – 0)		(100,000)
Profit on sale		100,000

Plant and Machinery - (Various items, all costing and sold for less than £6,000)

	£	£
Sale Proceeds		15,000
less: Net book value		
Cost	10,000	
less: Accumulated Depreciation	(5,400)	
		(4,600)
Profit on sale		10,400

Motor Vehicle	£	£
Sale proceeds		2,500
less: Net Book value:		
Cost	5,000	
less: Accumulated Depreciation	(2,000)	
		3,000
(Loss) on sale		500

Total Profit/(loss) on sale:	
Land and Buildings	100,000
Plant and Machinery	10,400
Motor Vehicles	(500)
Profit on sale of fixed assets	109,900

UNICORN TRADING LIMITED Date prepared 1 April 99 Prepared by: ES
Reviewed by: PS
Year ended: 31 December 1998

Analysis of Bank Interest Accrual:

Interest receivable and similar income	£124,900	
Is made up as follows:		
Patent Royalties received	10,000	(Gross of income tax)
Bank interest receivable	5,000	
Profit on sale of fixed assets	109,900	
	£124,900	Agreed to financial statements

The Bank interest accrual is made up as follows:

	£
Interest accrued at 1 January 1998	(525)
Received in year	5,171
Interest accrued at 31 December 1998	354
Bank interest receivable at 31 December 1998	£5,000

Conclusion: The accrual for bank interest is reasonable.

UNICORN TRADING LIMITED Date prepared 31.3.99 Prepared by: ES
Reviewed by: PS
Year ended: 31 December 1998

Bad Debt Provision:

The charge to the profit and loss account for bad and doubtful debts if £710. This is made up as follows:

General Provision (2% of total debtors) at 1 January 1998	(170)
Specific Trade Debt—Written off	500
Loan to employee—Written off	250
General Provision (2% of total debtors) at 31 December 1998	130
	£710

Conclusion: The above figures have been vouched to the client's calculations (which have been checked). They appear reasonable in the light of bad and doubtful debts in previous accounting periods.

UNICORN TRADING LIMITED — Date prepared 1 April 99 — Prepared by: ES
Year ended: 31 December 1998

At the tax department's request we have photocopied the following documents:

Entertaining Expenses—	£3,562	the two invoices making up this amount are attached. (See pages 13/14).
Legal and professional fees—	£699	the two invoices making up this amount are attached. (See pages 15/16).
Advance Corporation Tax and Income Tax Paid—		a copy of the one form CT61 completed by the company in respect of the year ended 31 December 1997, is enclosed. (See pages 17/20).

INVOICE NUMBER 2113

WEDDINGS, PARTIES AND COMPANY FUNCTIONS CATERED FOR

The Grange Hotel
Grange View
Grange Road
Barchester

Unicorn Trading Limited
Unit 12
Barchester Business Park
Barchester

2 DECEMBER 1998

UNICORN TRADING LIMITED

STAFF CHRISTMAS PARTY (1 DECEMBER 1998) **£250**

TERMS: **PAYMENT DUE WITHIN 30 DAYS OF INVOICE DATE SHOWN ABOVE.**

INVOICE NUMBER 5444454

Fine Wines and Food our speciality.

La Cavatina Restaurant
The Old Street
Barchester

Unicorn Trading Limited
Unit 12
Barchester Business park
Barchester

30th August 1998

Invoice re Customer banquet 31 July 1998

Cost of formal banquet and wines for Unicorn Trading Limited and their customers (50 guests).

Total due	£3,312

Terms payment due immediately.

INVOICE NUMBER 3400

**SMITH, COOPER AND
HARTLEY SOLICITORS**

12 The Drive
Barchester

Unicorn Trading Limited
Unit 12
Barchester Business Park
Barchester

12 August 1998

Unicorn Trading Limited

Fees re review and updating of contracts of service for the employees of Unicorn Trading Limited	£125

Badger and Co
Chartered accountants
24 High Street, Barchester

Unicorn Trading Limited,
Unit 12, Barchester Business Park,
Barchester

10 September 1998

Please find below our account for taxation work carried out on your behalf:

	£
Dealing with routine computations of corporation tax liability and completion of corporation tax returns	250
Dealing with an appeal against a decision by the Inspector of Taxes	324
Total fees due	**£574**

Inland Revenue

Return of Company Payments, Distributions and Interest

Collector of Taxes
Inland Revenue Accounts Office (Shipley)
BRADFORD
West Yorkshire BD98 8AA

Telephone: Bradford (01274) 530750

1	2 Company regn. no.	3 Accounting date	4 Accounts Office ref.
	223421		

IMPORTANT: Please enter in these 4 boxes the details from your CT61 Notice

Advance Corporation Tax on **Qualifying Distributions**
Income Tax deducted from **Company Payments** and **Interest**
Income Tax payable on **Gilt Interest** received without deduction of tax
Tax on manufactured payments received from abroad

- Please use this form when you need to make a Return of company payments, distributions and interest. **You must give all the information asked for on this page and sign the declaration below.** But you need only fill in the other parts of the Return which are relevant to your company. Only use the CT61 Supplement if you need to make a return of Foreign Income Dividends, 'deemed FIDs' or Gilt Interest.
- You are required to make your Return, and pay any tax, within 14 days after the end of the Return Period. Send the Return back to me in the envelope provided.
- *The enclosed CT61 Notes will help you.*
- If your Return shows that tax is payable use the payslip on the enclosed form CT61Notice.
- When you send back this Return **please also enclose the CT61 Notice**, even if no payment is enclosed.

Company details

Name of company: UNICORN TRADING LIMITED

Address:
Enter the address you would like future CT61 Returns sent to

UNIT 12
BARCHESTER BUSINESS PARK
BARCHESTER
Postcode ______

Please tick if this is a change of Registered Office '√' [ ]

Period covered by this Return

Return Periods are fixed by law. See CT61 Notes page 3 for guidance.

	Day	Month	Year		Day	Month	Year
Return period ►	01	10	1998	to	31	12	1998
being part of the **Accounting period** ►	01	01	1998	to	31	12	1998

Example: Distribution paid on 25 April 1997, and the accounting period is year to 31 December 1997. Enter:

Return period ►	01	04	1997	to	30	06	1997
being part of the Accounting period ►	01	01	1997	to	31	12	1997

For official use only: 901

Declaration

False statements can result in prosecution

To the best of my knowledge the information given in this Return (and the Supplement, if used) is correct and complete

Signature: J. Jones

Name *in CAPITALS*: J JONES

State in what capacity you make this Return: FINANCE DIRECTOR

It would assist if you can state your daytime telephone number and extension here: ______

Date: 31-12-98

Please tick if CT61 Supplement is attached '√' [ ]

21267 4.97 Niceday Stationery & Print Limited BMSD4/97 W0H7003

1 Advance Corporation Tax (ACT) on Qualifying Distributions

Use Part 1 to calculate the ACT payable on Distributions paid.
Use Part 2 below to record Franked Investment Income received.
Franked investment income in box 23 is set-off to reduce the ACT payable in Part 1.
For further information see Notes page 2.

List separately the payments made on different dates. If you need more room please attach a schedule.
Take care to use the correct ACT rate.

	Date		Amount of distribution £	+	ACT payable £	=		Amount of franked payment £
Dividends and other qualifying distributions paid *Exclude – payments at 03 – Foreign Income Dividends (FIDS) – 'deemed FIDS' (see notes page 4)*	31.12.98	01	33000 00		8250 00		02	41,250 00
Dividends paid for which you wish to account for ACT despite an election under Section 247(1) ICTA 1988 *See Notes page 2*		03					04	

Total **franked payments**	02 + 04	05	41,250 00
Deduct **franked investment income to be set-off** ...	From Part 2, box 23	06	
Total **franked payments** for which ACT is payable	05 – 06	10	41250 00
Calculate the **Advance Corporation Tax (ACT)** included in the figure at 10	*See both examples in Notes page 2*	11	8250 00
Add the **ACT payable on Foreign Income Dividends (FIDs)**	From CT61 Supplement, boxes 67 and 72	12	
Total ACT for this return period ...	11 + 12	13	8250 00
Deduct Additional amounts paid to **non-residents** *See Notes page 4*	Enter all the additional amounts paid, and attach form 251B Divs FD in duplicate	14	
ACT payable Carry to **Payslip** on CT61 Notice ...	13 – 14	15	8250 00

Do not enter a 'minus' figure in box 15. If 14 is greater than 13, claim repayment of the excess in Part 8

2 Franked investment income - running record for set-off or repayment

Amount brought forward from last Return ...		16	
Adjustment, if any, agreed with Inspector ... or a claim under Section 242 ICTA 1988 not yet agreed	*Enter 'MINUS' if appropriate*	17	
	16 + or – 17	18	

	Date	Description	Amount
Franked investment income received since last return			
		Total 19	
Adjustment, if any, agreed with Inspector		*Enter 'MINUS' if appropriate* 20	

You can include income received in earlier return periods if you did not need to submit a form for those periods. See Notes page 1.
Do not enter Foreign Income Dividends here.
If you need more room please attach a schedule.

Total after adjustment ...	19 + or – 20	21	
Total franked investment income now available for set-off or repayment	18 + 21	22	
Deduct **Amount set-off against franked payments in Part 1**	From 22 or 05, whichever is smaller	23	

Carry this figure to Part 1, box 06

Franked investment income after above set-off ...	22 – 23	24	

Repayment of ACT previously paid. Franked investment income at 24 can be set-off against franked payments of earlier return periods for this accounting period only.

	ACT repayment now claimed		Amount of franked investment income set-off
25		26	

Carry this figure to Part 8, line b

Amount to be carried forward to next Return	24 – 26	27	

3 Income Tax on Annual Payments and Interest

Use Part 3 to calculate the Income Tax payable on payments made.
Use Part 4 to record Income Tax you have suffered on payments received. This can be set-off to reduce the tax due in Part 3. *For further information see Notes page 3.*

In boxes 28 and 29, group separately payments taxed at basic rate and payments taxed at lower rate.
If you need more room please attach a schedule.

	Date	Description	Box	Gross amount £	Box	Income Tax £
Annual payments etc made under deduction of Income Tax at basic rate or lower rate *See Notes page 3* *Include all manufactured interest, unless entered at 30 below.*			28		29	
Annual payments etc to non-residents made under deduction of reduced rate tax under a Double Taxation Agreement *See Notes page 4.* *Ref. no. of the authority* ▶			30		31	
Income Tax on annual payments etc above ... 29 + 31					32	

Interest paid by deposit-takers including distributions paid by **building societies**
Enter the Gross amount paid from which you deducted tax, and the lower rate Income Tax you deducted
See Notes page 3
Do not enter interest paid gross, eg TESSA interest

	Box	Gross amount	Box	Income Tax
Before 6 April	33		34	
From 6 April	35		36	

When the return period does not include 6 April use boxes 35 and 36

		Box	
Total Income Tax	32 + 34 + 36	37	
Less Income Tax deducted from income **received** now claimed as a **set-off**	From Part 4, box 53	38	
	37 – 38	39	
Less Income Tax on Gilt Interest received now claimed as a set-off	From CT61 Supplement, box 83	40	
Income Tax now payable Carry to **Payslip** on CT61 Notice	39 – 40	46	

4 Income Tax deducted - running record in this Accounting Period for set-off or repayment

		Box	
Amount of Income Tax **brought forward** from last Return for **this accounting period**		47	
Adjustment, if any, agreed with Inspector ...	*Enter 'MINUS' if appropriate*	48	
	47 + or – 48	49	

Income received under deduction of tax since last Return for **this accounting period**

You can include income received in earlier return periods in this accounting period if you did not need to submit a form for those periods. See Notes page 1.
If you need more room please attach a schedule.

Date	Description	Box	Gross amount	Box	Income Tax
10.12.95	Patent Royalty		10000.00		2300.00
	Totals	50	10000.00	51	2300.00

		Box	
Running total now available for set-off or repayment below	49 + 51	52	2300.00
Amount set-off against Income Tax in Part 3	From 52 or 37, whichever is smaller	53	◀ *Carry this figure to Part 3, box 38*
Repayment now claimed of tax paid on annual payments etc in Part 3 of an earlier Return **for this accounting period only**		54	◀ *Carry this figure to Part 8*
Total Income Tax now used for set-off or repayment ...	53 + 54	55	
Amount to be carried **forward** to next Return for **this accounting period**	52 – 55	56	2300.00

5 Certain other distributions

If you need more room please attach a schedule

	Date	Description	Amount £
a Qualifying distributions which are not money payments			
b Payments about which there is a doubt as to whether they are qualifying distributions			
c Distributions (excluding money payments) which, exceptionally, do not fall within an accounting period			

Do not account for ACT on the above payments. The Inspector will make any necessary assessment.

6 Tax on manufactured payments from abroad

See Notes page 4

a **Manufactured dividends received from abroad** *by UK resident companies*	(AMOUNTS RECEIVED)	Tax payable - *at ACT rate*	*Carry to Payslip on CT61 Notice*
b **Manufactured interest received from abroad** *by UK resident companies and by UK branches of overseas companies*	(GROSS INTEREST)	Income Tax payable at lower rate	*Carry to Payslip on CT61 Notice*

7 Income Tax on Gilt Interest received: totals from CT61 Supplement

a Income Tax **payable** on Gilt Interest received	From box 79		
b **Repayment** of excessive payment on account	78 – 77 if positive		
c **Repayment** of 'Gilts' Income Tax	From box 88		
d **Repayment** of 'other' Income Tax	From box 85		
e Total 'Gilts related' repayments	b + c + d		
f Net Income Tax **payable** · *Do not enter a minus figure here. If e is greater than a claim repayment of the excess in Part 8 below*	a – e		*Carry to Payslip on CT61 Notice*

8 Claim for repayment or reimbursement

Use this section to summarise any claims arising in other sections of your Return:

a *From Part 1*	Reimbursement of amounts paid to **non-residents**	14 – 13 if positive	
b *From Parts 2 and 9*	Repayment of **ACT previously paid**	From boxes 25 and 69	
c *From Part 4*	Repayment of **Income Tax previously paid**	From box 54	
d *From Part 7*	Net 'Gilts related' Income Tax repayments	7e – 7a if positive	
e	Total claimed	a + b + c + d	

Other forms

Please tick if you require a form to declare the following items:

	'✓'		'✓'
Non-qualifying distributions Form CT2 *See Notes page 2*	☐	**Stock dividends** Section 249 ICTA 1988 *Form CT101*	☐

When sending back this Return, please

- check you have filled in the blue boxes at the top of page 1
- check you have signed the declaration on page 1
- send the CT61 Notice with this Return, even if no payment is enclosed.

When we receive this Return we will send you another form for your company's next Return.

Please note If the Inspector considers that any distributions, payments, etc have been omitted from this Return, or is in any way dissatisfied with it, the Inland Revenue can issue an appropriate assessment.

Cordelia's Shoe Shop

Schedule D Case I Computation for the period from 1 December 1998 to 30 June 1999

Net profit per the accounts		6,789
ADD:		
Depreciation	2,739	
Work clothes	115	
Private telephone (£291 × 70%)	204	
Private car expenses (£495 + £274) × 40%	308	
Non trade magazine subscription	25	
		3,391
LESS:		
Capital allowances	2,130	
		(2,130)
		£8,050

Cordelia Travers
Trading as Cordelia's Shoe Shop
12 High Street
Barchester

Computations prepared by:
Badger and Co.
Chartered Accountants
24 High Street
Barchester

PREPARING BUSINESS TAXATION COMPUTATIONS

BLANK FORMS

ANSWERS (Task 1b)

UNICORN TRADING LIMITED

Capital Allowance Computation

	General Pool	*FA80 Pool*	*Expensive Car Land Rover Discovery*	*Total Allowances*
	£	£	£	£
TWDV at 1 January 1998	11,250	2,500	23,600	
Additions not qualifying for FYA				
Disposals				
WDA @ 25%				
WDA Restricted				
Balancing allowance/charge				
Additions qualifying for FYA				
FYA @ ……%				
TWDV at 31 December 1998				

Notes:

The above tax written down values have come from the tax files for last year's computations

ANSWERS (Task 2)

Inland Revenue

Page 1

Corporation Tax Return
Version 3

This form, or an approved substitute version of it, must be used whenever a company is required to do so, by a *Notice to deliver a Corporation Tax Return (form CT203)*. This return sets out the information we need and provides a standard format for calculations.

You should read this return form along with your *Notice to deliver a Corporation Tax Return (form CT203)* and *Filling in your Corporation Tax Return (leaflet CT200 Notes)* which you should have received with this form. The notes referred to throughout can be found in the leaflet *CT200 Notes*. You should contact your Tax Office if you need more help.

'Company' means any body chargeable to corporation tax, whether incorporated or not. This definition includes clubs, associations and voluntary organisations.

Sections to be completed

Members' clubs, associations and voluntary organisations - it is likely that you will only have to complete Sections 1 and 2. For further guidance see note 1 in the *Notes*.

All companies - including clubs, etc - You will not need to complete every Section, but you **must** complete the Declaration and Section 1 on this page. The *Notes* will help you decide whether you should complete the mutually exclusive *Short return* at Section 2 or the *Detailed return* at Section 3. Sections 9 and 10 are optional but you are asked to complete them if they are relevant to the company.

It is important that you read the *Notes* before completing any part of this form.

What to do when you have completed the return

- Make sure you have completed and signed the Declaration, then
- staple together the pages you have completed and attach any supporting calculations
- send these together with the relevant company accounts and, where prepared, directors' and auditors' reports, to your Tax Office using the envelope provided (see Note 3 for the date by which you should do this)
- pay any outstanding corporation tax (as you have shown at box box 65), as advised on the payslip attached to your *Notice to deliver a Corporation Tax Return (form CT203)*. Interest is charged on tax paid later than nine months and one day after the end of an accounting period. Tax is due without the making of an assessment.

Remember - ***Your tax return is not complete unless you send relevant accounts and documentation with this form. Penalties may be charged if your return, or any part of it, is late or incorrect.***

As soon as your figures are agreed

- we will send you an assessment setting out the tax position for the accounting period - unless there are no figures to assess
- we will issue an amended assessment if you have already received an estimated assessment and you have appealed against it.

Section 1: Summary

The company name

[ ]

The company address - only if changed since last return made.
Enter the UK registered office address, or the UK address if the company does not have a registered office. If the company does not have premises in the UK show the address of the person making the return.

[ ]

Company registration number *(if registered)*

[ ]

Reference
Enter the reference number shown on the *Notice to deliver a Corporation Tax Return (form CT203)*

XYZ ABCD123 4567

Corporation tax accounting period covered by this return
Cannot exceed 12 months. Enter start and end dates.

From [ ] To [ ]

If this period is not an accounting period of the company for corporation tax purposes (see note 2) put an 'X' in the box below, complete the Declaration to the right and return this form to your Tax Office. You do not need to complete the rest of this Section or other Sections of this form in these circumstances. [ ]

Profits chargeable *(Enter the firgure from box 30). If there are none enter '0'.*

£ [ ]

Corporation tax due *(Enter the figure from box 61 minus any entry in box 64). If none is due enter 0.00*

£ [ ] . p [ ]

Put an X in the appropriate box

Have you completed Section 8 (Repayments)? Yes [ ] No [ ]

Is the company name different from that shown in the *Notice (form CT203)*? Yes [ ] No [ ]

Declaration

Enter here the page numbers you are attaching

[ ]

Put an 'X' in the appropriate boxes to show the documents you are enclosing

- a copy of the accounts for the period to which this return relates [ ]
- a copy of the company accounts for a different period [ ]
- no accounts [ ]
- say why not [ ]
- calculations showing how the entries in the return form have been arrived at. [ ]

I declare that to the best of my knowledge and belief the return on this page and the pages attached is correct and complete.

Signature

[ ]

Except where a liquidator has been appointed, the company secretary, treasurer, or any other person who is authorised to do so may sign this declaration on behalf of the company. A photocopy of a signature is not acceptable.

Date [ ]

Name *(in capital letters)* [ ]

Status *(company secretary, treasurer, liquidator etc.)* [ ]

Page 2

Section 2: Short return

You may complete this section if

- it covers all the entries you need to make and
- each entry, including the company's total income and deductions, is less than £10 million.

In all other cases, or if you prefer, complete Section 3 instead. You should enclose an explanation and calculations of any figures which you have estimated or which are not immediately recognisable from the company's accounts.

The figures to be entered are those adjusted for tax purposes, after deducting capital allowances and adding balancing charges where appropriate. Section 4 should also be completed if capital allowances are claimed.

Please do not enter '0's where the company did not have the source specified in the return form.

		£		£
Trading profits *See note 5*	1			
Trading losses brought forward *Only include losses made in the same trade. Include charges treated as losses. Do not enter an amount larger than is needed to cover the profits in box 1. See note 6*	2			
Net trading profit *(box 1 minus box 2). If box 2 equals box 1, enter '0'. Leave this box blank if there are no trading profits in box 1*			3	
Trading losses of this accounting period *Where there is more than one trade give total for all trades. Do not set box 4 losses against box 1 profits, claim at box 22 against total profits.*	4			
Profits and gains from non-trading loan relationships and other Schedule D Case III income *Include interest and other profits and gains from non-trading loan relationships even if tax has been deducted. Complete box 57 to claim credit for income tax deducted. You will need to complete the Detailed return at Section 3 if you have deficits on non-trading loan relationships from this, earlier or later accounting periods to include. See note 8*			6	
Income within Schedule D Case VI - for example furnished lettings *Enter the figure net of allowable losses brought forward. Exclude income you enter in box 12. See note 7*			9	
Income from which income tax has been deducted - for example building society interest *Enter the gross amount before tax. Exclude any amount included in box 6 above. Complete box 57 to claim credit for income tax deducted. See note 9*			10	
Income from UK land and buildings *Enter the amount net of allowable expenses brought forward. Exclude income in box 9 above. See note 10*			12	
Chargeable gains *See note 11*				
Gross gains	13			
Allowable losses *Include any losses brought forward but do not enter an amount larger than the amount of gross gains in box 13 above.*	14			
Net chargeable gains *(box 13 minus box 14) If box 14 equals box 13, enter '0'*			15	
Profits *(total of boxes 3, 6, 9, 10, 12 and 15)*			17	
Relief for trading losses of this or of a later period *Put an 'X' in box 21 if amounts carried back from later accounting periods are included in box 22. See note 12*		21 ☐	22	
Profits before charges *(box 17 minus box 22)*			26	
Charges paid *Do not enter an amount larger than is needed to cover profits in box 26. See note 13*			27	
Profits chargeable to corporation tax *(box 26 minus box 27)* **Copy this figure into the box provided in Section 1 on page 1, and also into the box at the top of page 3**			30	

The short return is continued on page 3

Page 3

Profits chargeable to corporation tax

Enter the figure brought forward from page 2, box 30 ... ... £

If you claim tax is chargeable at the small companies' rate, or if you are claiming marginal small companies' relief, complete boxes 31 - 35. If there are no associated companies please enter '0' against the relevant financial year. *See note 15*

Franked investment income and foreign income dividends arising in the period covered by the return. *See note 15* ... 31 £

Number of companies associated with this company in the/each financial year covered by this return
Exclude this company. See note 15 ...

	Financial year		Number of associated companies
32	19	33	
34	19	35	

Corporation tax chargeable *See note 16*

	Financial years beginning 1 April		Amounts of profit £		Rates of tax *See note 16*		Tax £ p
36	19	37		38	•	39	•
43	19	44		45	•	46	•

Total corporation tax chargeable *(box 39 plus box 46)* 50

Marginal small companies' relief
Attach your computation (see notes 15, 16 and 29) ... 51 £ • p

Advance corporation tax restricted if necessary under Section 239(2) ICTA 1988
Put an 'X' in box 53 if amounts carried back from later accounting periods are included. See note 17. 53 54

Total of boxes 51 and 54
Total must not be larger than entry in box 50. Restrict if necessary 55

Net corporation tax chargeable *(box 50 minus box 55)* 56

Calculation of tax outstanding or overpaid

Income tax deducted from gross income included in return
Do not include deductions used to cover income tax for which the company was liable to account to the Inland Revenue on payments it has made. See note 18 57

Corporation tax due

Box 56 minus box 57. If box 57 equals or is greater than box 56, enter '0.00' and go to box 59. Copy the figure in box 61 to the box provided in Section 1 on page 1. See note 20 61

Income tax repayable to the company *(box 57 minus box 56). Complete Section 8 on page 8. Do not complete unless you are making a claim. See note 28*... ... 59

Corporation tax already paid (and not repaid). *See note 21* 63

Corporation tax outstanding *(box 61 minus box 63). This amount is payable to the Accounts Office. If box 63 equals or is greater than box 61, enter '0.00' and go to box 66. See note 23* 65

Corporation tax overpaid *(box 63 minus box 61). Complete Section 8 on page 8 also. See note 28* 66

This is the last page of the short return

Section 4: Claims for capital allowances and details of balancing charges arising

You must complete this section if you want to claim capital allowances, whether or not those allowances are reflected elsewhere in the return. You should also show balancing charges taken into account in the short or detailed return. Show details of qualifying expenditure on which writing-down allowances may be claimed, even if you do not want to claim any allowances for this period. *See note 25*

Notice of expenditure on machinery and plant *See note 25*

Expenditure on which first year allowance is claimed £	Qualifying expenditure on long life assets on which writing down allowances may be claimed £	Qualifying expenditure on other assets on which writing down allowances may be claimed £
68	91	69

Charges and allowances included in calculation of trading profit or losses

	Balancing charges £	Capital allowances £
Cars *Including leased out and "expensive" cars*	70	71
Machinery and plant *- long life assets*	92	93
- other	72	73
Industrial buildings and structures *Including qualifying hotels, and commercial buildings and hotels in enterprise zones*	74	75
Other charges and allowances *For example agricultural buildings, mineral extraction, scientific research, patents*	76	77
Charges and allowances not included in calculation of trading profit or losses	78	79

Section 5: Particulars of advance corporation tax and surplus advance corporation tax

Complete this section if you have surplus advance corporation tax brought forward or have paid advance corporation tax (and it has not been repaid) in respect of qualifying distributions made in the period covered by this return.

	£	p
Particulars of advance corporation tax paid		
Particulars of any surplus advance corporation tax brought forward		

Section 6: Amounts claimed as group relief

Complete this section if you have claimed group relief at box 29 (see note 26). Attach a separate sheet of paper if you need more space. Attach a copy of each surrendering company's notice of consent to the claim unless a special arrangement is in force. Include claims made under the consortium provisions.

Name of surrendering company	Accounting period Show the start and end dates of any accounting period which is different from the one to which this return relates.	Tax reference Show the Tax Office number and the tax inspector's file reference. If you do not know these, supply whatever information you have that will help us to identify the company, for example the company registration number.	Amount claimed from each company
			£
			£
			£
			£
			£
			£
			£
			£
			£
			£
			£
			£
			£
		Total *This figure should be the same as the one in box 29.*	£

ANSWERS (Task 3)

Covering letter, enclosing corporation tax computation

ANSWERS (Task 4)

Cordelia's Shoe Shop

Calculation of Schedule D Case I Profits Taxable for 1998/99 and 1999/00

ANSWERS (Task 5)

Cordelia's Shoe Shop

Calculation of Overlap Profits and Explanation of Method of Relief

ANSWERS (Tasks 4 and 5)

Cordelia's Shoe Shop

Working Paper

PREPARING BUSINESS TAXATION COMPUTATIONS

SUGGESTED ANSWERS

ANSWERS (Task 1(a))

UNICORN TRADING LIMITED

Adjustment of Profit for the purposes of Schedule D Case I

	£	£
Net Profit per accounts		136,728
Add:		
Depreciation	9,133	
Entertaining customers	3,312	
Non trade loan written off	250	
Legal fees re tax appeal	324	
		13,019
		149,747
Less:		
Profit on sale of fixed assets	109,900	
Capital Allowances (see task 1 (b))	7,313	
Reduction in general bad debt provision	40	
Bank interest receivable	5,000	
Patent royalties received	10,000	
		(132,253)
Schedule D Case I profit		£17,494

ANSWERS (Task 1b)

UNICORN TRADING LIMITED

Capital Allowance Computation

	General Pool	*FA80 Pool*	*Expensive Car Land Rover Discovery*	*Total Allowances*
	£	£	£	£
TWDV at 1 January 1998	11,250	2,500	23,600	
Additions not qualifying for FYA		6,000		
Disposals	(10,000)	(2,500)		
	1,250	6,000	23,600	
WDA @ 25%	(313)	(1,500)		1,813
WDA Restricted			(3,000)	3,000
Balancing allowance / charge				
Additions qualifying for FYA	5,000			
FYA @ 50%	(2,500)			2,500
TWDV at 31 December 1998	£3,437	£4,500	£20,600	£7,313

ANSWERS (Task 1c)

UNICORN TRADING LIMITED

Calculation of chargeable gain on the disposal of land

	£
Sale Proceeds	200,000
Less: Original cost	(100,000)
Unindexed Gain	100,000
Less: Indexation Allowance	
$100{,}000 \times \left(\frac{162.6 - 138.8}{138.8}\right)^*$	(17,100)
Chargeable gain	£82,900

* = 0.171

ANSWERS (Task 1d)

UNICORN TRADING LIMITED

Corporation tax Computation for the year ended 31 December 1998

	£	£
Schedule D Case I (W1, see task 1(a))	17,494	
Schedule D Case III	5,000	
Patent Royalties received	10,000	
Chargeable gain (see task 1(c))	82,900	
		115,394
Less: Charges on income		
PCTCT		£115,394

Corporation Tax Payable:
Profits are less than £300,000 therefore the company is a small company
Corporation tax payable:

Financial Year 1997 (£115,394 @ 21%) × 3/12	6,058
Financial Year 1998 (£115,394 @ 21%) × 9/12	18,175
	24,233
Less: ACT set off (W2)	(8,250)
	15,983
Less: Income tax suffered (W3)	(2,300)
MCT Liability	£13,683

ANSWERS (Task 1d, continued)

WORKINGS

(W2) Advance Corporation Tax

Per form CT61 Paid £8,250

Note: Maximum set off £115,394 (PCTCT) @ 20% = £23,079

(W3) Income Tax

per form CT61 Income Tax available for offset £2,300.

Inland Revenue

Page 1

Corporation Tax Return
Version 3

This form, or an approved substitute version of it, must be used whenever a company is required to do so, by a *Notice to deliver a Corporation Tax Return (form CT203)*. This return sets out the information we need and provides a standard format for calculations.

You should read this return form along with your *Notice to deliver a Corporation Tax Return (form CT203)* and *Filling in your Corporation Tax Return (leaflet CT200 Notes)* which you should have received with this form. The notes referred to throughout can be found in the leaflet *CT200 Notes*. You should contact your Tax Office if you need more help.

'Company' means any body chargeable to corporation tax, whether incorporated or not. This definition includes clubs, associations and voluntary organisations.

Sections to be completed
Members' clubs, associations and voluntary organisations - It is likely that you will only have to complete Sections 1 and 2. For further guidance see note 1 in the *Notes*.

All companies - including clubs, etc. - You will not need to complete every Section, but you **must** complete the Declaration and Section 1 on this page. The *Notes* will help you decide whether you should complete the mutually exclusive *Short return* at Section 2 or the *Detailed return* at Section 3. Sections 9 and 10 are optional but you are asked to complete them if they are relevant to the company.

It is important that you read the *Notes* before completing any part of this form.

What to do when you have completed the return
- Make sure you have completed and signed the Declaration, then
- staple together the pages you have completed and attach any supporting calculations
- send these together with the relevant company accounts and, where prepared, directors' and auditors' reports, to your Tax Office using the envelope provided (see Note 3 for the date by which you should do this)
- pay any outstanding corporation tax (as you have shown at box box 65), as advised on the payslip attached to your *Notice to deliver a Corporation Tax Return (form CT203)*. Interest is charged on tax paid later than nine months and one day after the end of an accounting period. Tax is due without the making of an assessment.

Remember - ***Your tax return is not complete unless you send relevant accounts and documentation with this form. Penalties may be charged if your return, or any part of it, is late or incorrect.***

As soon as your figures are agreed
- we will send you an assessment setting out the tax position for the accounting period - unless there are no figures to assess
- we will issue an amended assessment if you have already received an estimated assessment and you have appealed against it.

Section 1: Summary

The company name

UNICORN TRADING LTD

The company address - only if changed since last return made.
Enter the UK registered office address, or the UK address if the company does not have a registered office. If the company does not have premises in the UK show the address of the person making the return.

Company registration number *(if registered)*

223421

Reference
Enter the reference number shown on the *Notice to deliver a Corporation Tax Return (form CT203)*

XYZ/ABCD123/4567

Corporation tax accounting period covered by this return
Cannot exceed 12 months. Enter start and end dates.

From 01/01/98 To 31/12/98

If this period is not an accounting period of the company for corporation tax purposes (see note 2) put an 'X' in the box below, complete the Declaration to the right and return this form to your Tax Office. You do not need to complete the rest of this Section or other Sections of this form in these circumstances. ☐

Profits chargeable *(Enter the figure from box 30). If there are none enter '0'.*

£ 115,394

Corporation tax due *(Enter the figure from box 61 minus any entry in box 64). If none is due enter '0.00'.*

£ 13,683 . p –

Put an X in the appropriate box

Have you completed Section 8 (Repayments)? Yes ☐ No ☑

Is the company name different from that shown in the *Notice (form CT203)*? Yes ☐ No ☑

Declaration

Enter here the page numbers you are attaching

2, 3, 6

Put an 'X' in the appropriate boxes to show the documents you are enclosing
- a copy of the accounts for the period to which this return relates ☒
- a copy of the company accounts for a different period ☐
- no accounts ☐
- say why not
- calculations showing how the entries in the return form have been arrived at. ☒

I declare that to the best of my knowledge and belief the return on this page and the pages attached is correct and complete.

Signature

Except where a liquidator has been appointed, the company secretary, treasurer, or any other person who is authorised to do so may sign this declaration on behalf of the company. A photocopy of a signature is not acceptable.

Date / /

Name *(in capital letters)*

Status *(company secretary, treasurer, liquidator etc.)*

Page 2

Section 2: Short return

You may complete this section if

- it covers all the entries you need to make and
- each entry, including the company's total income and deductions, is less than £10 million.

In all other cases, or if you prefer, complete Section 3 instead. You should enclose an explanation and calculations of any figures which you have estimated or which are not immediately recognisable from the company's accounts.

The figures to be entered are those adjusted for tax purposes, after deducting capital allowances and adding balancing charges where appropriate. Section 4 should also be completed if capital allowances are claimed.
Please do not enter '0's where the company did not have the source specified in the return form.

	Box	£	Box	£
Trading profits *See note 5*	1	17,494		
Trading losses brought forward *Only include losses made in the same trade. Include charges treated as losses. Do not enter an amount larger than is needed to cover the profits in box 1. See note 6*	2			
Net trading profit *(box 1 minus box 2). If box 2 equals box 1, enter '0'. Leave this box blank if there are no trading profits in box 1*			3	17,494
Trading losses of this accounting period *Where there is more than one trade give total for all trades. Do not set box 4 losses against box 1 profits, claim at box 22 against total profits.*	4			
Profits and gains from non-trading loan relationships and other Schedule D Case III income *Include interest and other profits and gains from non-trading loan relationships even if tax has been deducted. Complete box 57 to claim credit for income tax deducted. You will need to complete the* **Detailed return** *at Section 3 if you have deficits on non-trading loan relationships from this, earlier or later accounting periods to include. See note 8*			6	5,000
Income within Schedule D Case VI - for example furnished lettings *Enter the figure net of allowable losses brought forward. Exclude income you enter in box 12. See note 7*			9	
Income from which income tax has been deducted - for example building society interest *Enter the gross amount before tax. Exclude any amount included in box 6 above. Complete box 57 to claim credit for income tax deducted. See note 9*			10	10,000
Income from UK land and buildings *Enter the amount net of allowable expenses brought forward. Exclude income in box 9 above. See note 10*			12	
Chargeable gains *See note 11*				
Gross gains	13	82900		
Allowable losses *Include any losses brought forward but do not enter an amount larger than the amount of gross gains in box 13 above.*	14			
Net chargeable gains *(box 13 minus box 14) If box 14 equals box 13, enter '0'*			15	82,900
Profits *(total of boxes 3, 6, 9, 10, 12 and 15)*			17	115,394
Relief for trading losses of this or of a later period *Put an 'X' in box 21 if amounts carried back from later accounting periods are included in box 22. See note 12*	21	☐	22	
Profits before charges *(box 17 minus box 22)*			26	
Charges paid *Do not enter an amount larger than is needed to cover profits in box 26. See note13*			27	
Profits chargeable to corporation tax *(box 26 minus box 27) Copy this figure into the box provided in Section 1 on page 1, and also into the box at the top of page 3*			30	115,394

The short return is continued on page 3

CT200(1997)

Page 3

Profits chargeable to corporation tax

Enter the figure brought forward from page 2, box 30 ... £ 115 394

If you claim tax is chargeable at the small companies' rate, or if you are claiming marginal small companies' relief, complete boxes 31 - 35. If there are no associated companies please enter '0' against the relevant financial year. *See note 15*

Franked investment income and foreign income dividends arising in the period covered by the return. *See note 15* ... 31 £ [ ]

Number of companies associated with this company in the/each financial year covered by this return *Exclude this company. See note 15*		Financial year		Number of associated companies
	32	1997	33	0
	34	1998	35	0

Corporation tax chargeable *See note 16*

	Financial years beginning 1 April		Amounts of profit £		Rates of tax *See note 16*		Tax £	p
36	1997	37	28,848	38	21 • 00	39	6058	00
43	1998	44	86,546	45	21 • 00	46	18,175	00

Total corporation tax chargeable *(box 39 plus box 46)* ... 50 24,233 • 00

Marginal small companies' relief
Attach your computation (see notes 15, 16 and 29) ... 51 £ [ ] • p [ ]

Advance corporation tax restricted if necessary under Section 239(2) ICTA 1988
Put an 'X' in box 53 if amounts carried back from later accounting periods are included. See note 17. 53 [ ] 54 8250 • 00

Total of boxes 51 and 54
Total must not be larger than entry in box 50. Restrict if necessary ... 55 8250 • 00

Net corporation tax chargeable *(box 50 minus box 55)* ... 56 15983 • 00

Calculation of tax outstanding or overpaid

Income tax deducted from gross income included in return
Do not include deductions used to cover income tax for which the company was liable to account to the Inland Revenue on payments it has made. See note 18 ... 57 2300 • 00

Corporation tax due

Box 56 minus box 57. If box 57 equals or is greater than box 56, enter '0.00' and go to box 59.
Copy the figure in box 61 to the box provided in Section 1 on page 1. *See note 20* ... 61 13683 • 00

Income tax repayable to the company *(box 57 minus box 56).*
Complete Section 8 on page 8. Do not complete unless you are making a claim. *See note 28*... 59 [ ] • [ ]

Corporation tax already paid (and not repaid). *See note 21* ... 63 [ ] • [ ]

Corporation tax outstanding *(box 61 minus box 63). This amount is payable to the Accounts Office. If box 63 equals or is greater than box 61, enter '0.00' and go to box 66. See note 23* ... 65 13683 • 00

Corporation tax overpaid *(box 63 minus box 61).*
Complete Section 8 on page 8 also. *See note 28* ... 66 [ ] • [ ]

This is the last page of the short return

Page 6

Section 4: Claims for capital allowances and details of balancing charges arising

You must complete this section if you want to claim capital allowances, whether or not those allowances are reflected elsewhere in the return. You should also show balancing charges taken into account in the short or detailed return. Show details of qualifying expenditure on which writing-down allowances may be claimed, even if you do not want to claim any allowances for this period. *See note 25*

Notice of expenditure on machinery and plant *See note 25*

Expenditure on which first year allowance is claimed £		Qualifying expenditure on long life assets on which writing down allowances may be claimed £		Qualifying expenditure on other assets on which writing down allowances may be claimed £	
68	5,000	91		69	6,000

Charges and allowances included in calculation of trading profit or losses

		Balancing charges £		Capital allowances £
Cars *Including leased out and "expensive" cars*	70		71	4,500
Machinery and plant *- long life assets*	92		93	
- other	72		73	2,813
Industrial buildings and structures *Including qualifying hotels, and commercial buildings and hotels in enterprise zones*	74		75	
Other charges and allowances *For example agricultural buildings, mineral extraction, scientific research, patents*	76		77	
Charges and allowances not included in calculation of trading profit or losses	78		79	

Section 5: Particulars of advance corporation tax and surplus advance corporation tax

Complete this section if you have surplus advance corporation tax brought forward or have paid advance corporation tax (and it has not been repaid) in respect of qualifying distributions made in the period covered by this return.

	£	p
Particulars of advance corporation tax paid	8,250	00
Particulars of any surplus advance corporation tax brought forward		

Section 6: Amounts claimed as group relief

Complete this section if you have claimed group relief at box 29 (see note 26). Attach a separate sheet of paper if you need more space. Attach a copy of each surrendering company's notice of consent to the claim unless a special arrangement is in force. Include claims made under the consortium provisions.

Name of surrendering company	Accounting period Show the start and end dates of any accounting period which is different from the one to which this return relates.	Tax reference Show the Tax Office number and the tax inspector's file reference. If you do not know these, supply whatever information you have that will help us to identify the company, for example the company registration number.	Amount claimed from each company
			£
			£
			£
			£
			£
			£
			£
			£
			£
			£
			£
			£
			£
		Total *This figure should be the same as the one in box 29.*	£

ANSWERS (Task 3)

Badger and Co
Chartered accountants

24 High Street, Barchester
Telephone: (0117) 420 5345 Fax: (0117) 420 5346

Mr John Jones,
Finance Director,
Unicorn Trading Limited,
Unit 12, Barchester Business Park,
Barchester

Today's Date

Dear Mr Jones

UNICORN TRADING LIMITED
CORPORATION TAX COMPUTATION AND CORPORATION TAX RETURN
YEAR ENDED 31 DECEMBER 1998

Please find enclosed three copies of the corporation tax computation for Unicorn Trading Limited for the year ended 31 December 1998, together with a completed Form CT200 Corporation Tax Return and a copy of this return. You may keep one copy of the computation and a copy of the corporation tax return for your own records.

I would be grateful if you would look through both the corporation tax computation and the corporation tax return, and if you are happy with them, please sign and date the corporation tax return and two copies of the corporation tax computation, where indicated, and return them to me for submission to the Inspector of Taxes.

The Corporation Tax Return and computation show that corporation tax of £13,683 is due for the accounting period ended 31 December 1998. This should be paid to the Collector of Taxes on or before 1 October 1999. The payment should accompany the Corporation Tax Return. If you wish to enclose a cheque with the signed return, please do so, making the cheque payable to HM Collector of Taxes.

If you have any questions please telephone me or write to me at the number / address shown above.

Yours sincerely

Edwina Smith
Tax Department Manager,
Badger and Co.

ANSWERS (Task 4)

Cordelia's Shoe Shop

Calculation of Schedule D Case I Profits for 1998/99 and 1999/00

Profits for the period from commencement of trade (1 December 1998) to the following 5 April (5 April 1999) will be taxed as Schedule D Case I profits for Cordelia for 1998/99.

1998/99 Schedule D Case I profit

$£8,050 \times \frac{4}{7} = \underline{£4,600}$

Profits for the first twelve months of trade (1.12.98–30.11.99) will be taxed as Schedule D Case I profit for Cordelia for 1999/00.

1999/00 Schedule D Case I profit:

	£
1.12.98–30.6.99	8,050
1.7.99–30.11.99	
$18,000 \times \frac{5}{12}$	7,500
	£15,550

ANSWERS (Task 5)

Calculation of overlap Profits

The period from 1.12.98–5.4.99 is taxed twice
The overlap profits are therefore £4,600.

Explanation of the use of Overlap Profits

Overlap profits are carried forward and deduced from the final Schedule D Case I taxable profit of the business on cessation of trade.

TECHNICIAN STAGE

NVQ/SVQ LEVEL 4 IN ACCOUNTING

REVISED STANDARDS

AAT SPECIMEN SIMULATION

PREPARING PERSONAL TAXATION COMPUTATIONS

(UNIT 18)

Association of Accounting Technicians

DATA AND TASKS

INSTRUCTIONS

This simulation is designed to test your ability to prepare personal taxation computations.

The situation is set out below.

The tasks to be completed are set out beyond.

You are allowed three hours to complete your work.

You should read the whole simulation before commencing work so as to gain an overall picture of what is required.

Any blank forms required will be found at the end of this simulation.

In completing this simulation the following details should be noted:

- **workings should be to the nearest month and to the nearest £;**
- **the effects of Value Added Taxation and National Insurance should be ignored throughout.**

THE SITUATION

You are a qualified accounting technician, working in the tax department of a firm of accountants, Mole and Co. You report to the tax department manager, Margaret Jones.

In the course of your work you are expected to prepare computations of income tax and capital gains tax liabilities for individuals.

Today, you have arrived at work to find that Margaret Jones has been called to a meeting at a client's premises. In her absence, she would like you to deal with some work for Mrs Jane Austen, one of the tax department's clients.

The attached memo sets out the work that Margaret would like you to do.

MEMO

To: An Accounting Technician

From: Margaret Jones—Tax Department Manager

Subject: Tax work outstanding on:

- Mrs Jane Austen

As you know I shall be out of the office for some of today. I would like you to do some work on the above client in my absence. I have set out below the work that needs doing and a list of the documents that I have put on your desk to help you to do the work.

MRS JANE AUSTEN
Mrs Austen has been one of Mole and Co's clients for a number of years. She is employed as a director of a local company and also has rental income.

Mrs Austen has both income tax and capital gains tax liabilities for 1998/99.

Tasks to be completed on Mrs Jane Austen's income tax liability

1. INCOME TAX

I would like you to:

1. Prepare an income tax computation for Mrs Austen for 1998/99.
   To do this, I expect you to:
   (a) prepare a calculation of Schedule E earnings for 1998/99;
   (b) prepare a computation of Schedule A rental income for 1998/99;
   (c) complete the employment and land and property supplementary pages for Mrs Austen's self assessment income tax return for 1998/99;
   (d) prepare her income tax computation for 1998/99 *either* by filling in the proforma income tax computation *or* by using the Inland Revenue income tax calculation working sheet supplied, and calculate the payments on account due for 1999/00 (if any).

Information supplied—Mrs Jane Austen—Income Tax

To help you to do this I have given you the following information

- Mrs Austen's Form P60.
- Mrs Austen's draft Form P11D.
- Mrs Austen's rental income statement, provided by the agents managing her rental properties and a letter concerning the repairs expense on the statement.
- Permanent file notes concerning Mrs Austen.

2. CAPITAL GAINS TAX

Mrs Austen sold two of her rental properties during the tax year 1998/99.

Tasks to be completed—Mrs Jane Austen's capital gains tax liability

I would like you to:

2. Calculate the capital gains on the two disposals in 1998/99.
3. Calculate the capital gains tax payable in 1998/99.
4. Complete the capital gains tax supplementary pages of the self assessment income tax return for 1998/99 in respect of capital gains.
5. Write a covering letter to Mrs Austen, enclosing the income tax computation, capital gains tax computation and self assessment return, and advising her of the amount of tax to be paid and of the due date by which payment should be made. You should also advise her of any payment on account which may be due for 1999/00.

Information supplied—Mrs Jane Austen—capital gains tax

To allow you to do this I have given you the following information:

- A copy of the solicitors' statement concerning the disposals;
- a file note concerning Mrs Austen's capital gains tax position.

Do not destroy

P60 Certificate of Pay, Income Tax and National Insurance contributions

Employer's name and address
BOOK SUPPLIES LTD
121 HIGH STREET
ANYTOWN

Tax Office name: ANYTOWN

Tax Office number and Reference: 039/ B452

For employer's use

Tax Year to 5 April 99

To the employee:
Please keep this certificate in a safe place as you will not be able to get a duplicate. **You will need it if you have to fill in a Tax Return.**
You can also use it to check that your employer is deducting the right type of National Insurance contributions for you and using your correct National Insurance number. If this is not the case, please tell your employer.
By law you are required to tell the Tax Office of any income that is not fully taxed, even if you are not sent a Tax Return. *INLAND REVENUE*

Employee's details

National Insurance number: NC 402030 E [redacted]

Sex: F ("M" if Male, "F" if Female)

Surname: AUSTEN

First two forenames: JANE

Works/payroll no. etc

Employee's private address
12 THE AVENUE
ANYTOWN

If you change your address, please let your Tax Office and the Contributions Agency know

National Insurance contributions in this employment

NI contribution table letter	Earnings on which employee's contributions payable (whole £s only) 1a £	Total of employee's and employer's contributions payable 1b £ p	Employee's contributions payable 1c £ p	Earnings on which employee's conts. at Contracted-out rate payable incl. in 1a (whole £s only) 1d £	Employee's contributions at Contracted-out rate included in 1c 1e £ p	Scheme Contracted-out number (For Contracted-out Money Purchase Schemes only)
		.	.		.	S
		.	.		.	S
		.	.		.	S
		.	.		.	S

Pay and Income Tax details

Employee's Widows & Orphans/ Life Assurance contributions in this employment £ p: .

Figures shown here should be used for your tax return, if you get one

	Pay £ p	Tax deducted £ p
In previous employment(s)	.	.
In this employment	41,000 ·00	12000·00
Total for year	41,000 ·00	12000·00

If net refund enter "R" in this box

Final tax code

From Employer/Paying Office:
This certificate shows the total amount of pay for Income Tax [redacted] purposes that I/we have paid to you in the year. Any overtime, bonus, commission etc, statutory sick pay or statutory maternity pay is included. It also gives details of the total Income Tax and National Insurance contributions deducted by me/us (less any refunds).

Week 53 payment indicator

P60

Inland Revenue

P11D EXPENSES AND BENEFITS 1998-99

Note to employer
Complete this return for a director, or an employee who earned at a rate of £8,500 a year or more during the year 6 April 1998 to 5 April 1999. Do not include expenses and benefits covered by a dispensation or PAYE settlement agreement. Read the P11D Guide and booklet 480, Chapter 24, before you complete the form. Send the completed P11D and form P11D(b) to the Tax Office by 6 July 1999. You must give a copy of this information to the director or employee by the same date. The term employee is used to cover both directors and employees throughout the rest of this form.

Note to employee
Your employer has filled in this form. Keep it in a safe place as you may not be able to get a duplicate. You will need it for your tax records and to complete your 1998-99 Tax Return if you get one. Your tax code may need to be adjusted to take account of the information given on this P11D. The box numbers on this P11D have the same numbering as the Employment Pages of the Tax Return, for example, 1.12. Include the total figures in the corresponding box on the Tax Return, unless you think some other figure is more appropriate.

Employer's details
Employer's name: BOOK SUPPLIES LTD
PAYE tax reference: 039 / B452

Employee's details
Employee's name: JANE AUSTEN
Tick here if a director: ✓
Works number or department:
National Insurance number: NC 40 20 30 E

A • **Assets transferred (cars, property, goods or other assets)**

Description of asset: | Cost/ Market value £ | – Amount made good or from which tax deducted £ | = 1.12 Cash equivalent £

B • **Payments made on behalf of employee**

Description of payment: | 1.12 £

Tax on notional payments not borne by employee within 30 days of receipt of each notional payment | 1.12 £

C • **Vouchers or credit cards**

Value of vouchers and payments made using credit cards or tokens: Gross amount £ | – Amount made good or from which tax deducted £ | = 1.13 Cash equivalent £

D • **Living accommmodation**

Cash equivalent of accommodation provided for employee, or his/ her family or household: 1.14 Cash equivalent £

E • **Mileage allowance**

Car and mileage allowances paid for employee's car: Gross amount £ | – Amount made good or from which tax deducted £ | = 1.15 Taxable payment £

F • **Cars and car fuel**
If more than two cars were made available, either at the same time or in succession, please give details on a separate sheet

	Car 1	Car 2
Make and Model	VAUXHALL VECTRA	
Dates first registered	10/01/95	/ /
Dates car was available	From 06/04/98 To 05/04/99	From / / To / /
Business mileage used in calculation for this car. *Tick only one box for each car.* (2,499 or less / 2,500 to 17,999 / 18,000 or more) *If the car was not available for part of the year, the business mileage limits are reduced proportionately.*	2,500 to 17,999 ✓	
Enter engine size and tick type of fuel *only if there is a car fuel scale charge* (Engine size in cc / Petrol / Diesel)	1,800 cc, Petrol ✓	cc
List price of car *If there is no list price, or if it is a classic car, employers see booklet 480; employees see leaflet IR133*	£19,000	£
Price of optional accessories fitted when car was first made available to the employee	£	£
Price of accessories added after the car was first made available to the employee	£	£
Capital contributions (maximum £5,000) the employee made towards the cost of car or accessories	£	£
Amount paid by employee for private use of the car	£ 600	£
Cash equivalent of each car	£	£
Total cash equivalent of all cars available in 1998-99		1.16 £
Cash equivalent of fuel for each car	£	£
Total cash equivalent of fuel for all cars available in 1998-99		1.17 £

TO BE CALCULATED

P11D(1999) BMSD 11/98

G • **Vans**

Cash equivalent of all vans made available for private use — **1.18** £

H • **Interest-free and low interest loans**

If the total amount outstanding on all loans does not exceed £5,000 at any time in the year, there is no need for details in this section.

	Loan 1	Loan 2
Purpose of loan(s) – *please use the code shown in P11D Guide for employers*		
Number of joint borrowers *(if applicable)*		
Tick the box if the loan is within MIRAS		
Amount outstanding at 5 April 1998 or at date loan was made if later	£	£
Amount outstanding at 5 April 1999 or at date loan was discharged if earlier	£	£
Maximum amount outstanding at any time in the year	£	£
Total amount of interest paid by the borrower in 1998 - 99 – *enter "NIL" if none was paid*	£	£
Date loan was made or discharged in 1998 - 99 if applicable	/ /	/ /
Cash equivalent of loans after deducting any interest paid by the borrower	**1.19** £	**1.19** £

I • **Mobile telephones**

Cash equivalent of mobile telephones provided — ONE TELEPHONE — **1.20** £ 400

J • **Private medical treatment or insurance**

	Cost to you		Amount made good or from which tax deducted		Cash equivalent
Private medical treatment or insurance	£ 965	–	£	=	**1.21** £ 965

K • **Qualifying relocation expenses payments and benefits (non-qualifying expenses go in P below)**

Excess over £8,000 of all qualifying relocation expenses payments and benefits for each move — **1.22** £

L • **Services supplied**

	Cost to you		Amount made good or from which tax deducted		Cash equivalent
Services supplied to the employee	£	–	£	=	**1.22** £

M • **Assets placed at the employee's disposal**

		Annual value plus expenses incurred		Amount made good or from which tax deducted		Cash equivalent
Description of asset	VIDEO RECORDER MADE AVAILABLE ON 1.7.98	£ 1500 COST ON 1.7.98	–	£	=	**1.22** £ 1,500

N • **Shares**

Tick the box if during the year there have been share-related benefits for the employee ☐

O • **Other items**

		Cost to you		Amount made good or from which tax deducted		Cash equivalent
Subscriptions and professional fees		£	–	£	=	**1.22** £
Description of other items		£	–	£	=	**1.22** £

Income tax paid but not deducted from director's remuneration — Tax paid **1.22** £

P • **Expenses payments made to, or on behalf of, the employee**

		Cost to you		Amount made good or from which tax deducted		Taxable payment
Travelling and subsistence payments		£	–	£	=	**1.23** £
Entertainment *(trading organisations read P11D Guide and then enter a tick or a cross as appropriate here)*	✓	£ 3,500	–	£	=	**1.23** £ 3,500
General expenses allowance for business travel		£	–	£	=	**1.23** £
Payments for use of home telephone		£	–	£	=	**1.23** £
Non-qualifying relocation expenses *(those not shown in section K)*		£	–	£	=	**1.23** £
Description of other expenses		£	–	£	=	**1.23** £

Property Rental Agencies Limited

Rental income and expenditure statement

Client: Mrs Jane Austen

Dates: 6 April 1998 to 5 April 1999

		1	2	3	4	
Furnished Property Let:						
Rental Income		4,000	3,000	2,000	6,500	
Less	Expenses					
	Management fees	400	300	200	650	
	Buildings insurance	100	100	100	100	
	Contents insurance	50	50	50	50	
	Cleaning	260	260	260	260	
	Repairs	100	250	3,000	50	
	Council Tax	450	350	200	350	
	Total remitted to client in year	2,640	1,690	(1,810)	5,040	**Total £7,560**

Please note: all properties were fully let all year and are fully furnished.

Property Rental Agencies Limited
12 Another Street
Anytown

MARGARET JONES
TAX MANAGER
MOLE AND CO
CHARTERED ACCOUNTANTS
24 MAIN STREET
ANYTOWN

Dear Ms Jones

MRS JANE AUSTEN—PROPERTY RENTAL STATEMENT FOR 1998/99

Further to your recent letter concerning the repairs expenditure shown on the above statement, we are able to provide the following additional information:

Property	Amount £	Description
1.	100	Repainting the doors and windows
2.	250	Repairing a chimney damaged by bad weather
3.	3,000	Building a kitchen extension
4.	50	Repainting the front door

I hope this is enough information, but should you require any more details please contact us.

Yours Sincerely

John Smith

Property Letting Consultant

Mrs Jane Austen
Notes from permanent file

Date of Birth: 31 March 1966

Marital Status: Single

Dependents: None

Employment: Director of Book Supplies limited
In receipt of salary (see Form P60)
and benefits in kind (see Form P11 D)
Entertaining expenditure is generally all deductible under Section 198.

Toad & Co
Solicitors
25 High Street
Anytown

Completion Statement:

Client: Mrs Jane Austen

Sale of two rental properties:

1. Sale of property 5 on 6 April 1998

Sale Proceeds	£301,375
Costs of sale (Toad & Co's fees)	£1,500
Original cost of building on 21 March 1980	£100,000
(The property was valued at £125,000 on 31 March 1982)	

2. Sale of property 6 on 6 April 1998

Sale proceeds	£100,350
Costs of sale (Toad & Co's fees)	£2,000
Original cost on 25 June 1994	£25,000

Mrs Jane Austen

File Note
Capital Gains Tax

In 1996/97 Mrs Austen had capital losses of £10,000, unused and available to carry forward against future capital gains.

Margaret Jones

Tax Manager

PREPARING PERSONAL TAXATION COMPUTATIONS BLANK FORMS

Task 1(c)

Inland Revenue

Income for the year ended 5 April 1999

LAND AND PROPERTY

Fill in these boxes first

Name	Tax reference
JANE AUSTEN	54 180 62344

Are you claiming Rent a Room relief for gross rents of £4,250 or less? No Yes

(Or £2,125 if the claim is shared?)

Read the Notes on page LN2 to find out

- whether you can claim Rent a Room relief; and
- how to claim relief for gross rents over £4,250

If 'Yes', and this is your only income from UK property, you have finished these Pages

Is your income from furnished holiday lettings? No Yes

If 'No', turn over and fill in Page L2 to give details of your property income

If 'Yes', fill in boxes 5.1 to 5.18 before completing Page L2

Furnished holiday lettings

- Income from furnished holiday lettings — 5.1 £
- *Expenses* (furnished holiday lettings only)
- Rent, rates, insurance, ground rents etc. — 5.2 £
- Repairs, maintenance and renewals — 5.3 £
- Finance charges, including interest — 5.4 £
- Legal and professional costs — 5.5 £
- Cost of services provided, including wages — 5.6 £
- Other expenses — 5.7 £ — total of boxes 5.2 to 5.7 — 5.8 £

Net profit (put figures in brackets if a loss) — box 5.1 *minus* box 5.8 — 5.9 £

- *Tax adjustments*
- Private use — 5.10 £
- Balancing charges — 5.11 £ — box 5.10 + box 5.11 — 5.12 £
- Capital allowances — 5.13 £

Profit for the year (copy to box 5.19). If loss, enter '0' in box 5.14 and put the loss in box 5.15 — boxes 59 + 5.12 *minus* box 5.13 — 5.14 £

Loss for the year (if you have entered '0' in box 5.14) — boxes 59 + 5.12 *minus* box 5.13 — 5.15 £

- Loss offset against 1998-99 total income — 5.16 £
- Loss carried back — see Notes, page LN4 — 5.17 £
- Loss offset against other income from property (copy to box 5.38) — see Notes, page LN4 — 5.18 £

SA105

BMSD 12/98 NET

Please turn over

Other property income

■ *Income*

• Furnished holiday lettings profits	copy from box 5.14 5.19 £		
• Rents and other income from land and property	5.20 £	Tax deducted 5.21 £	boxes 5.19 + 5.20 + 5.22 5.23 £
• Chargeable premiums	5.22 £		

■ *Expenses* (do not include figures you have already put in boxes 5.2 to 5.7 on Page L1)

• Rent, rates, insurance, ground rents etc.	5.24 £		
• Repairs, maintenance and renewals	5.25 £		
• Finance charges, including interest	5.26 £		
• Legal and professional costs	5.27 £		
• Costs of services provided, including wages	5.28 £		total of boxes 5.24 to 5.29 5.30 £
• Other expenses	5.29 £		
Net profit (put figures in brackets if a loss)			box 5.23 *minus* box 5.30 5.31 £

■ *Tax adjustments*

• Private use	5.32 £		box 5.32 + box 5.33 5.34 £
• Balancing charges	5.33 £		
• Rent a Room exempt amount	5.35 £		
• Capital allowances	5.36 £		
• 10% wear and tear	5.37 £		total of boxes 5.35 to 5.38 5.39 £
• Furnished holiday lettings losses (from box 5.18)	5.38 £		
Adjusted profit (if loss enter '0' in box 5.40 and put the loss in box 5.41)			boxes 5.31 + 5.34 *minus* box 5.39 5.40 £
Adjusted loss (if you have entered '0' in box 5.40)		boxes 5.31 + 5.34 *minus* box 5.39 5.41 £	
• Loss brought forward from previous year			5.42 £
Profit for the year			box 5.40 *minus* box 5.42 5.43 £
• Loss offset against total income		5.44 £	
• Loss to carry forward to following year		5.45 £	
• Pooled expenses from 'one estate election' carried forward		5.46 £	

Tick box 5.47 if these Pages include details of property let jointly — 5.47 ☐

Now fill in any other supplementary Pages that apply to you.
Otherwise, go back to page 2 of your Tax Return and finish filling it in.

Income for the year ended 5 April 1999

Inland Revenue

EMPLOYMENT

Name: JANE AUSTEN

Tax reference: 54150 62344

Fill in these boxes first

If you want help, look up the box numbers in the Notes

Details of employer

Employer's PAYE reference
1.1

Employer's name
1.2

Date employment started
(only if between 6 April 1998 and 5 April 1999)
1.3 / /

Employer's address
1.5

Postcode

Date finished (only if between 6 April 1998 and 5 April 1999)
1.4 / /

Tick box 1.6 if you were a director of the company
1.6

and, if so, tick box 1.7 if it was a close company
1.7

Income from employment

■ *Money* - see Notes, page EN3

- Payments from P60 (or P45 or pay slips) — Before tax 1.8 £
- Payments not on P60 etc.
  - tips — 1.9 £
  - other payments (excluding expenses shown below and lump sums and compensation payments or benefits shown overleaf) — 1.10 £
- UK tax deducted from payments in boxes 1.8 to 1.10 — Tax deducted 1.11 £

■ *Benefits and expenses* - *see Notes, pages EN3 to EN6. If any benefits connected with termination of employment were received, or enjoyed, after that termination and were from a* ***former*** *employer you need to complete Help Sheet IR204, available from the Orderline. Do not enter such benefits here.*

• Assets transferred/ payments made for you	Amount 1.12 £	• Vans	Amount 1.18 £
• Vouchers/credit cards	Amount 1.13 £	• Interest-free and low-interest loans	Amount 1.19 £
• Living accommodation	Amount 1.14 £	• Mobile telephones	Amount 1.20 £
• Mileage allowance	Amount 1.15 £	• Private medical or dental insurance	Amount 1.21 £
• Company cars	Amount 1.16 £	• Other benefits	Amount 1.22 £
• Fuel for company cars	Amount 1.17 £	• Expenses payments received and balancing charges	Amount 1.23 £

Income from employment continued

■ ***Lump sums and compensation payments or benefits including such payments and benefits from a former employer***
Note that 'lump sums' here includes any contributions which your employer made to an unapproved retirement benefits scheme

*You must read page EN6 of the Notes **before** filling in boxes 1.24 to 1.30*

Reliefs

- £30,000 exemption — **1.24** £
- Foreign service and disability — **1.25** £
- Retirement and death lump sums — **1.26** £

Taxable lump sums

- From box H of *Help Sheet IR204* — **1.27** £
- From box Q of *Help Sheet IR204* — **1.28** £
- From box R of *Help Sheet IR204* — **1.29** £
- Tax deducted from payments in boxes 1.27 to 1.29 — Tax deducted **1.30** £

■ ***Foreign earnings not taxable in the UK in year ended 5 April 1999** - see Notes, page EN6* — **1.31** £

■ ***Expenses you incurred in doing your job** - see Notes, starting on page EN6*

- Travel and subsistence costs — **1.32** £
- Fixed deductions for expenses — **1.33** £
- Professional fees and subscriptions — **1.34** £
- Other expenses and capital allowances — **1.35** £
- Tick box 1.36 if the figure in box 1.32 includes travel between your home and a permanent workplace — **1.36**

■ ***Foreign Earnings Deduction*** — **1.37** £

■ ***Foreign tax for which tax credit relief not claimed*** — **1.38** £

Additional information

Now fill in any other supplementary Pages that apply to you.
Otherwise, go back to page 2 in your Tax Return and finish filling it in.

ANSWERS (Task 1(d))

Mrs Jane Austen

Income Tax Computation for 1998/99

NOTE:

EITHER: complete the computation on this page

OR: complete the Inland Revenue income tax calculation working sheets which follow

Mrs Jane Austen

Income Tax Computation for 1998/99

	£	£	*Tax deducted at source* £
Earned Income			
Investment Income:			
1 Savings income			
2 Non Savings income			
Less: Charges on income			
Statutory Total income			
Less: Personal allowance			
Taxable income			
Tax Thereon:			

Calculating your tax bill - continued

If any of the sums on this page result in a negative amount, enter a zero in the appropriate box

Total income from: **(copy figures from your Tax Return)**

- *Employment* including benefits and *minus* expenses for **each** employment

Add income in:
- boxes 1.8 to 1.10, **and**
- boxes 1.12 to 1.23, **and**
- boxes 1.27 and 1.28

	First employment		Other employments	
Add income in (boxes above)	£		£	
Deduct any figures in boxes 1.31 to 1.38	£		£	
Total taxable income	£	+	£	W1 £

- *Share schemes* (from box 2.31) — W2 £
- *Self-employment* (from box 3.88) — W3 £
- *Partnerships* (from boxes 4.35, 4.70 and 4.73) — W4 £
- *UK land and property* (from box 5.43) — W5 £
- *Foreign income* (from boxes 6.2, 6.4 and 6.5) — W6 £
- *Trusts, settlements or estates of deceased persons* (add together any figures in the 'right hand' column of the Trusts etc. Pages and deduct any figure in box 7.19) — W7 £
- *UK savings and investments* (total any figures in the 'right hand' column on page 3 of your Tax Return) — W8 £
- *UK pensions, retirement annuities and benefits* (add together any figures in the 'right hand' column of Question 11 on page 4 of your Tax Return *minus* any deduction in box 11.13) — W9 £
- *Maintenance or alimony received* (from box 12.3) — W10 £
- *Other income* (copy the figure in box 13.3 *minus* any figure in box 13.5) — W11 £

Total income
total boxes W1 to W11
W12 £

Deductions for

- *Personal pension* (add together any figures in boxes 14.5, 14.10, 14.15, 14.16 and 14.17) — W13 £
- *Vocational training* (multiply any figure in box 15.1 by $^{100}/_{77}$) — W14 £
- *Interest on qualifying loans* (from box 15.3) — W15 £
- *Maintenance or alimony paid* (see the notes on page 2 of this Guide) — W16 £
- *Charitable covenants, annuities, Gift Aid and Millennium Gift Aid payments* (multiply any figures in boxes 15.9 and 15.10 by $^{100}/_{77}$) — W17 £
- *Losses and post-cessation expenses* (from boxes 3.81, 4.15, 4.61, 5.16, 5.44, 8.13A and 15.11) — W18 £
- *Trade union and friendly society death benefit payments* (from box 15.12) — W19 £

Total deductions
total boxes W13 to W19
W20 £

Total income minus deductions
box W12 *minus* box W20
W21 £

now copy the figure in box W21 to box W22 on page 6

Calculating your tax bill - continued

If any of the sums on this page result in a negative amount, enter a zero in the appropriate box

Reliefs
- you get basic rate relief automatically - further relief will be due if you are liable to higher rate tax.

from box W21 — W22 £

- *Pension payments* (from boxes 14.15 and 14.17) — W23.1 £
- *Vocational training* (from box W14) — W23.2 £

box W23.1 + box W23.2 — W23 £

box W22 + box W23 — W24 £

Allowances given as a deduction from your income
- you may need to check your entitlement - see notes starting on page 3 of this Guide.

- *Personal allowance* - normally £4,195 unless you are non-resident and not claiming allowances — W25.1 £ +
- *Age-related personal allowance* - see notes page 3 — W25.2 £ +
- *Blind person's allowance* - enter £1,330 — W25.3 £ +
- *Transitional allowance* (from box 16.4) — W25.4 £ +
- *Blind person's surplus allowance from your spouse* (from box 16.27) — W25.5 £

total boxes W25.1 to W25.5 — W25 £

If the figure in box W26 is £4,300 or less, do not fill in boxes W28 to W38

box W24 *minus* box W25 — W26 £

box W26 x 20% — W27 £

Savings income taxable at the lower (20%) rate

- *Partnership savings* (from boxes 4.35 and 4.70) — W28.1 £ +
- *UK savings* (from box W8) — W28.2 £ +
- *Foreign savings* (from box 6.2) — W28.3 £
- *Trusts, settlements and estate income* (from boxes 7.6, 7.12 and 7.15) — W28.4 £

total boxes W28.1 to W28.4 — W28 £

box W26 *minus* box W28 — W29 £

W30 £ 4,300

box W29 *minus* box W30 — W31 £

box W31 x 3% — W32 £

If the figure in box W33 is £27,100 or less, do not fill in boxes W35 to W38

box W26 *minus* box W23 *minus* box 12.9 — W33 £

W34 £ 27,100

box W33 *minus* box W34 — W35 £

box W35 x 17% — W36 £

lower of box W28 *or* box W35 — W37 £

box W37 x 3% — W38 £

boxes W27 + W32 + W36 + W38

Income Tax due — W39 £

Copy box W39 to top of page 7

Calculating your tax bill - continued

If any of the sums on this page result in a negative amount, enter a zero in the appropriate box

from page 6

W39 £

- *Venture Capital Trust and Enterprise Investment Scheme subscriptions*

box 15.7 + box 15.8 — W40 £ → box W40 x 20% — W41 £

box 15.2 x 10% — W42 £

Allowances and reliefs given in terms of tax
- these reduce your tax bill - you may need to use the Question 16 notes on pages 23 to 26 of the Tax Return Guide and starting on page 4 of this Guide.

- *Married couple's allowance* - see notes on pages 4 and 9 of this Guide — W43.1 £
  +
- *Married couple's surplus allowance* (from box 16.28) — W43.2 £
  +
- *Additional personal allowance* - usually £1,900, may be split with another person - see the notes — W43.3 £
  +
- *Widow's bereavement allowance - £1,900* (if your husband died in 1997-98 or 1998-99 and you have not remarried) — W43.4 £
- *Maintenance and alimony* (boxes 15.4 and 15.5 - see the notes for box W16 on page 2 of this Guide) — W43.5 £

total boxes W43.1 to W43.5 — W43.6 £ → box W43.6 x 15% — W43 £

Notional tax is not repayable and so has to be calculated as an allowance given in terms of tax rather than being regarded as tax deducted at source.

- *Partnership notional tax* (from box 4.78) — W44.1 £
  +
- *Notional tax on UK scrip dividends and FIDs* (from boxes 10.22, 10.25, 10.28 and 10.31) — W44.2 £
- *Notional tax on estate income* (from box 7.14) — W44.3 £

total boxes W44.1 to W44.3 — W44 £

- *Tax credit relief on foreign income and treaty relief on UK income* (and see the notes on page 9 of this Guide) — from boxes 6.9 and 9.35 — W45 £

boxes W41 to W45 — W46 £

Income Tax due, after allowances and reliefs — box W39 *minus* box W46 — W47 £
If the figure in box W46 is more than the figure in box W39, enter a zero

- *Recoverable tax on charitable covenants, annuities, Gift Aid and Millennium Gift Aid payments* (box W17 x 23%) — W48 £
- *Class 4 National Insurance Contributions* (from box 3.91 or box 4.25) — W49 £

Income Tax and Class 4 National Insurance Contributions — boxes W47 + W48 + W49 — W50 £

Copy the figure in box W50 to box W50 on page 8

Calculating your tax bill - continued

(copy figure from box W50 on page 7) **Income Tax and Class 4 NIC due** — W50 £

- *Unpaid tax for earlier years included in PAYE code for 1998-99* — W51 £ → box W50 + box W51 — W52 £

Copy the figure in box W51 to box 18.1 in your Tax Return

Tax paid at source

- *Employment* (from boxes 1.11 and 1.30) — W53.1 £
- *Self-employment* (from boxes 3.92 and 3.120) — W53.2 £
- *Partnerships* (from box 4.77) — W53.3 £
- *UK land and property* (from box 5.21) — W53.4 £
- *Foreign income* (from boxes 6.1 and 6.3) — W53.5 £
- *Trusts, settlements or estate income* (from boxes 7.2, 7.5, 7.8 and 7.11) — W53.6 £
- *UK savings* (from boxes 10.3, 10.6, 10.10, 10.13, 10.16 and 10.19) — W53.7 £
- *UK pensions, retirement annuities and benefits* (from boxes 11.8 and 11.11) — W53.8 £
- *Other income* (from box 13.2) — W53.9 £ → total boxes W53.1 to W53.9 — W53 £
- *Tax due for 1998-99 included in 1999-2000 PAYE tax code* — W54 £ → box W53 + box W54 — W55 £

Copy the figure in box W54 to box 18.2 in your Tax Return

Total tax and Class 4 NIC due for 1998-99 (overpayment in brackets) — box W52 *minus* box W55 — W56 £

Copy the figure in box W56 to box 18.3 in your Tax Return

Tax owed or overpaid in 1998-99

- *1998-99 tax already refunded* (from box 17.1) — W57A £
- *Tax due for earlier years* — W57 £ → boxes W56 + W57A + W57 — W58 £

Copy the figure in box W57 to box 18.4 in your Tax Return

- *Tax overpaid for earlier years* — W59 £

Tick box 18.5 and copy the figure in box W59 to the 'Additional information' box on page 8 of your Tax Return

- *Payments already made* (from your Statements of Account) — W60 £ → box W59 + box W60 — W61 £

Tax you owe for 1998-99 — box W58 *minus* box W61 — W62 £

OR

Tax you have overpaid for 1998-99 — box W61 *minus* box W58 — W63 £

Payments on account for 1999-2000

If there is a figure in box W62, add it to any figure in box W59. If the total is less than £1,000 and you would like the amount you owe collected through your 2000-2001 tax code, copy W62 to W64. Otherwise enter zero — W64 £

If W65 is **less than £500**, you do not need to make payments on account. Leave box 18.6 blank and tick box 18.8. **If W65 is equal to or more than £500,** carry on — box W56 *minus* box W64 — W65 £

- *Income Tax due, after allowances and reliefs* — from boxes W44 + W47 + W48 — W66 £
- *Class 4 National Insurance Contributions* — from box W49 — W67 £ → box W66 + box W67 — W68 £ → box W68 x 20% — W69 £

If W65 is **less** than W69, you do not need to make payments on account. Leave box 18.6 blank and tick box 18.8

If W65 is **equal to or more** than W69, **you do have to make payments on account. Fill in box W70**

This is the amount of each payment on account for 1999-2000 — box W65 x 50% — W70 £

Copy the figure in box W70 **(including pence)** to box 18.6 in your Tax Return

ANSWERS (Task 2)

Mrs Jane Austen
Calculation of Capital Gains for 1998/99

ANSWERS (Task 3)

This page is intentionally blank so that the 2nd and 3rd pages of the Capital gains supplement are set out facing each other as would apply in practice.

ANSWERS (Task 4)

Inland Revenue

For the year ended 5 April 1999

CAPITAL GAINS

Fill in these boxes first

Name	Tax reference
JANE AUSTEN	54180 62344

If you want help, look up the box numbers in the Notes.

Please complete Pages CG2 and CG before filling in the rest of this Page. If you think you will need more than one copy of Pages CG2 and CG3 make photocopies before you begin filling them in.

Your 1998-99 Capital Gains Tax liability

- Total taxable gains from Page CG3 overleaf — 8.7 £
- Your taxable gains *minus* the annual exempt amount — box 8.7 *minus* £6,800 — 8.8 £
- Additional liability in respect of non-resident or dual resident trusts — 8.9 £

Capital losses

(Remember if your loss arose on a transaction with a connected person, see Notes page CGN11, you can only set that loss agains gains you make on disposals to that same connected person)

■ ***This year's losses***

- Total from Page CG2 — 8.10 £
- Used against gains — 8.11 £
- Used against earlier years' gains (see Notes, page CGN8) — 8.12 £
- Used against income (see Notes, page CGN7) — 8.13A £ amount claimed against income of 1998-99; 8.13B £ amount claimed against income of 1997-98; box 8.13A + box 8.13B — 8.13 £
- This year's unused losses — box 8.10 *minus* (boxes 8.11 + 8.12 + 8.13) — 8.14 £

■ ***Earlier years' losses***

- Unused losses of 1996-97 and 1997-98 — 8.15 £
- Used this year (losses from box 8.15 are used in priority to losses from box 8.18) — 8.16 £
- Remaining unused losses of 1996-97 and 1997-98 — box 8.15 *minus* box 8.16 — 8.17 £
- Unused losses of 1995-96 and earlier years — 8.18 £
- Used this year (losses from box 8.15 are used in priority to losses from box 8.18) — box 8.6 *minus* box 8.16 — 8.19 £

■ ***Total of unused losses to carry forward***

- Carried forward losses of 1996-97 and later years — box 8.14 + box 8.17 — 8.20 £
- Carried forward losses of 1995-96 and earlier years — box 8.18 *minus* box 8.19 — 8.21 £

SA108

Your 1998-99 Capital Gains Tax liability

Gains (on assets without mixed use)

	A Description of asset [illegible]	B Tick box [illegible]	C Tick [illegible] valuation used	D Tick box [illegible] 1982	E Insert the [illegible] acquisition and 16 March 1998	F Insert the [illegible]	G Disposal proceeds	H Tick box if relief claimed or due	I Chargeable gains after reliefs but before losses and taper
1					/ /	/ /	£		£
2					/ /	/ /	£		£
3					/ /	/ /	£		£
4					/ /	/ /	£		£
5					/ /	/ /	£		£
6					/ /	/ /	£		£
7					/ /	/ /	£		£
8					/ /	/ /	£		£

Gains on mixed business and non-business use assets (see the notes on pages CGN2 and CGN15)

9					/ /	/ /	£		£
									£
10					/ /	/ /	£		£
									£

Total 8.1 £

Total column

Losses

	Description of asset	Tick box if unquoted shares	Tick box if estimate or valuation used	Tick box if asset held at 31 March 1982	Disposal proceeds	Tick box if relief claimed or due	Net losses
13					£		£
14					£		£
15					£		£
16					£		£

Total net losses of year 8.2 £

J nter ɛ' if, usiness sset	K Taper rate	L Losses deducted			M Gains after losses	N Tapered gains (gains from column M x % in column K)	O Further information
		L1 Allowable losses of the year	L2 Income losses set against gains	L3 Unused losses b/f from earlier years			
	%	£	£	£	£	£	
	%	£	£	£	£	£	
	%	£	£	£	£	£	
	%	£	£	£	£	£	
	%	£	£	£	£	£	
	%	£	£	£	£	£	
	%	£	£	£	£	£	
	%	£	£	£	£	£	
B	%	£	£	£	£	£	
	100%	£	£	£	£	£	
B	%	£	£	£	£	£	
	100%	£	£	£	£	£	
			8.5 £	**8.6** £		**8.3** £	
			Total column L2	*Total column L3*		*Total column N*	

1 **Attributed gains** *(enter source in right hand column)* £

2 **Attributed gains** *(enter source in right hand column)* £

Total of attributed gains **8.4** £

box 8.3 + box 8.4

Total Taxable Gains £

copy to box 8.7 on Page CG1

Answers (Task 5)

PREPARING PERSONAL TAXATION COMPUTATIONS

SUGGESTED ANSWERS

ANSWERS (Task 1(a))

Mrs Jane Austen
Calculation of Schedule E Earnings for 1998/99

	£	£
Salary		41,000
Car Benefit		
Vauxhall Vectra		
£19,000 × 35% = 6,650 × 2/3	4,433	
Contribution towards private use of the car	(600)	
		3,833
Fuel Benefit		
Vauxhall Vectra Petrol 1,401cc–2,000cc = 1,280		1,280
Private medical insurance		965
Entertainment		3,500
Mobile Telephone		200
Asset made available for private use (video recorder)		
£1,500 × 20% = £300 × 9/12 =		225
		51,003
Less S 198 claim for expenses incurred wholly, exclusively and necessarily in the course of employment		
Entertaining costs		(3,500)
Schedule E Earnings		£47,503

ANSWERS (Task 1(b))

Mrs Jane Austen
Computation of Schedule A Rental Income for 1998/99

Property	1	2	3	4	Total
	£	£	£	£	£
Rental Income	4,000	3,000	2,000	6,500	15,500
Less Allowable expenses:					
Management fees	400	300	200	650	1,550
Buildings Insurance	100	100	100	100	400
Contents Insurance	50	50	50	50	200
Cleaning	1,260	260	260	260	1,040
Repairs	100	250	nil	50	400
Council Tax	450	350	200	350	1,350
Wear and Tear Allowance (10% Rent-Council Tax)	355	265	180	615	1,415
	£2,285	£1,425	£1,010	£4,425	£9,145

Total Schedule A Income £9,145

ANSWERS (Task 1(c))

Inland Revenue

Income for the year ended 5 April 1999

LAND AND PROPERTY

Fill in these boxes first

Name: JANE AUSTEN

Tax reference: 541S0 62344

Are you claiming Rent a Room relief for gross rents of £4,250 or less?
(Or £2,125 if the claim is shared?)
Read the Notes on page LN2 to find out
- **whether you can claim Rent a Room relief; and**
- **how to claim relief for gross rents over £4,250**

No ✓ Yes

If 'Yes', and this is your only income from UK property, you have finished these Pages

Is your income from furnished holiday lettings?
If 'No', turn over and fill in Page L2 to give details of your property income

No ✓ Yes

If 'Yes', fill in boxes 5.1 to 5.18 before completing Page L2

Furnished holiday lettings

- Income from furnished holiday lettings — 5.1 £

■ *Expenses* (furnished holiday lettings only)

- Rent, rates, insurance, ground rents etc. — 5.2 £
- Repairs, maintenance and renewals — 5.3 £
- Finance charges, including interest — 5.4 £
- Legal and professional costs — 5.5 £
- Cost of services provided, including wages — 5.6 £
- Other expenses — 5.7 £

total of boxes 5.2 to 5.7 — 5.8 £

Net profit (put figures in brackets if a loss) — box 5.1 *minus* box 5.8 — 5.9 £

■ *Tax adjustments*

- Private use — 5.10 £
- Balancing charges — 5.11 £
- Capital allowances — 5.13 £

box 5.10 + box 5.11 — 5.12 £

Profit for the year (copy to box 5.19). If loss, enter '0' in box 5.14 and put the loss in box 5.15 — boxes 5.9 + 5.12 *minus* box 5.13 — 5.14 £

Loss for the year (if you have entered '0' in box 5.14) — boxes 5.9 + 5.12 *minus* box 5.13 — 5.15 £

- Loss offset against 1998-99 total income — 5.16 £
- Loss carried back — see Notes, page LN4 — 5.17 £
- Loss offset against other income from property (copy to box 5.38) — see Notes, page LN4 — 5.18 £

SA105

Other property income

■ **Income**

	Box	£	Box	Tax deducted £	Box	£
• Furnished holiday lettings profits	5.19 (copy from box 5.14)					
• Rents and other income from land and property	5.20	15,500	5.21			
• Chargeable premiums	5.22				5.23 (boxes 5.19 + 5.20 + 5.22)	15,500

■ ***Expenses*** (do not include figures you have already put in boxes 5.2 to 5.7 on Page L1)

	Box	£	Box	£
• Rent, rates, insurance, ground rents etc.	5.24	1,950		
• Repairs, maintenance and renewals	5.25	400		
• Finance charges, including interest	5.26			
• Legal and professional costs	5.27	1,550		
• Costs of services provided, including wages	5.28	1,040		
• Other expenses	5.29		5.30 (total of boxes 5.24 to 5.29)	4,940
Net profit (put figures in brackets if a loss)			5.31 (box 5.23 *minus* box 5.30)	10,560

■ ***Tax adjustments***

	Box	£	Box	£
• Private use	5.32			
• Balancing charges	5.33		5.34 (box 5.32 + box 5.33)	
• Rent a Room exempt amount	5.35			
• Capital allowances	5.36			
• 10% wear and tear	5.37	1415		
• Furnished holiday lettings losses (from box 5.18)	5.38		5.39 (total of boxes 5.35 to 5.38)	1415

	Box	£	Box	£
Adjusted profit (if loss enter '0' in box 5.40 and put the loss in box 5.41)			5.40 (boxes 5.31 + 5.34 *minus* box 5.39)	9,145
Adjusted loss (if you have entered '0' in box 5.40)	5.41 (boxes 5.31 + 5.34 *minus* box 5.39)			
• Loss brought forward from previous year			5.42	
Profit for the year			5.43 (box 5.40 *minus* box 5.42)	9,145
• Loss offset against total income	5.44			
• Loss to carry forward to following year	5.45			
• Pooled expenses from 'one estate election' carried forward	5.46			

Tick box 5.47 if these Pages include details of property let jointly **5.47** ☐

Now fill in any other supplementary Pages that apply to you.
Otherwise, go back to page 2 of your Tax Return and finish filling it in.

Inland Revenue

Income for the year ended 5 April 1999

EMPLOYMENT

Fill in these boxes first

Name	Tax reference
JANE AUSTEN	54180 62344

If you want help, look up the box numbers in the Notes

Details of employer

Employer's PAYE reference **1.1** 039 B452	Employer's name **1.2** BOOK SUPPLIES LTD
Date employment started (only if between 6 April 1998 and 5 April 1999) **1.3** / /	Employer's address **1.5** 121 HIGH STREET, ANY TOWN; Postcode
Date finished (only if between 6 April 1998 and 5 April 1999) **1.4** / /	
Tick box 1.6 if you were a director of the company **1.6** ✓	and, if so, tick box 1.7 if it was a close company **1.7**

Income from employment

■ ***Money*** - see Notes, page EN3

• Payments from P60 (or P45 or pay slips)		Before tax **1.8** £ 41,000
• Payments not on P60 etc. - tips		**1.9** £
- other payments (excluding expenses shown below and lump sums and compensation payments or benefits shown overleaf)		**1.10** £
• UK tax deducted from payments in boxes 1.8 to 1.10	Tax deducted **1.11** £ 12,000	

■ ***Benefits and expenses*** - see Notes, pages EN3 to EN6. *If any benefits connected with termination of employment were received, or enjoyed, after that termination and were from a **former** employer you need to complete Help Sheet IR204, available from the Orderline. Do not enter such benefits here.*

	Amount		Amount
• Assets transferred/ payments made for you	**1.12** £	• Vans	**1.18** £
• Vouchers/credit cards	**1.13** £	• Interest-free and low-interest loans	**1.19** £
• Living accommodation	**1.14** £	• Mobile telephones	**1.20** £ 200
• Mileage allowance	**1.15** £	• Private medical or dental insurance	**1.21** £ 965
• Company cars	**1.16** £ 3,833	• Other benefits	**1.22** £ 225
• Fuel for company cars	**1.17** £ 1,280	• Expenses payments received and balancing charges	**1.23** £ 3500

Income from employment continued

■ *Lump sums and compensation payments or benefits including such payments and benefits from a former employer*
Note that 'lump sums' here includes any contributions which your employer made to an unapproved retirement benefits scheme

*You must read page EN6 of the Notes **before** filling in boxes 1.24 to 1.30*

Reliefs

- £30,000 exemption — **1.24** £
- Foreign service and disability — **1.25** £
- Retirement and death lump sums — **1.26** £

Taxable lump sums

- From box H of *Help Sheet IR204* — **1.27** £
- From box Q of *Help Sheet IR204* — **1.28** £
- From box R of *Help Sheet IR204* — **1.29** £
- Tax deducted from payments in boxes 1.27 to 1.29 — Tax deducted **1.30** £

■ *Foreign earnings not taxable in the UK in year ended 5 April 1999* - see Notes, page EN6 — **1.31** £

■ *Expenses you incurred in doing your job* - see Notes, starting on page EN6

- Travel and subsistence costs — **1.32** £
- Fixed deductions for expenses — **1.33** £
- Professional fees and subscriptions — **1.34** £
- Other expenses and capital allowances — **1.35** £ 3,500
- Tick box 1.36 if the figure in box 1.32 includes travel between your home and a permanent workplace — **1.36**

■ *Foreign Earnings Deduction* — **1.37** £

■ *Foreign tax for which tax credit relief not claimed* — **1.38** £

Additional information

Now fill in any other supplementary Pages that apply to you.
Otherwise, go back to page 2 in your Tax Return and finish filling it in.

ANSWERS (Task 1(d))

Mrs Jane Austen

Income Tax Computation for 1998/99

			Tax deducted at source
	£	£	£
Earned Income			
Schedule E Earnings (from above)	47,503		12,000
		47,503	
Investment Income:			
1. Savings Income			
2. Non Savings Income			
Schedule A profits (from above)	9,145		
Less Charges on income	-		
		9,145	
Statutory Total income		56,648	
Less Personal allowance		(4,195)	
Taxable income		£52,453	
Tax Thereon:			
£4,300 × 20%		860	
£22,800 × 23%		5,244	
£25,353 × 40%		10,141	
£52,453		16,245	
Less PAYE deducted at source		(12,000)	
		£4,245	

Note: payment on account for 1999/00 = 50% × £4,245 = £2,123

Calculating your tax bill - continued

If any of the sums on this page result in a negative amount, enter a zero in the appropriate box

Total income from: (copy figures from your Tax Return)

- *Employment* including benefits and *minus* expenses for **each** employment

Add income in:
- boxes 1.8 to 1.10, **and**
- boxes 1.12 to 1.23, **and**
- boxes 1.27 and 1.28

	First employment	Other employments	
Add income in boxes	£ 51,003	£	
Deduct any figures in boxes 1.31 to 1.38	£ 3,500	£	
Total taxable income	£	+ £	= W1 £ 47,503

- *Share schemes* (from box 2.31) — W2 £
- *Self-employment* (from box 3.88) — W3 £
- *Partnerships* (from boxes 4.35, 4.70 and 4.73) — W4 £
- *UK land and property* (from box 5.43) — W5 £ 9,145
- *Foreign income* (from boxes 6.2, 6.4 and 6.5) — W6 £
- *Trusts, settlements or estates of deceased persons* (add together any figures in the 'right hand' column of the Trusts etc. Pages and deduct any figure in box 7.19) — W7 £
- *UK savings and investments* (total any figures in the 'right hand' column on page 3 of your Tax Return) — W8 £
- *UK pensions, retirement annuities and benefits* (add together any figures in the 'right hand' column of Question 11 on page 4 of your Tax Return *minus* any deduction in box 11.13) — W9 £
- *Maintenance or alimony received* (from box 12.3) — W10 £
- *Other income* (copy the figure in box 13.3 *minus* any figure in box 13.5) — W11 £

Total income (total boxes W1 to W11) — W12 £ 56,648

Deductions for

- *Personal pension* (add together any figures in boxes 14.5, 14.10, 14.15, 14.16 and 14.17) — W13 £
- *Vocational training* (multiply any figure in box 15.1 by $^{100}/_{77}$) — W14 £
- *Interest on qualifying loans* (from box 15.3) — W15 £
- *Maintenance or alimony paid* (see the notes on page 2 of this Guide) — W16 £
- *Charitable covenants, annuities, Gift Aid and Millennium Gift Aid payments* (multiply any figures in boxes 15.9 and 15.10 by $^{100}/_{77}$) — W17 £
- *Losses and post-cessation expenses* (from boxes 3.81, 4.15, 4.61, 5.16, 5.44, 8.13A and 15.11) — W18 £
- *Trade union and friendly society death benefit payments* (from box 15.12) — W19 £

Total deductions (total boxes W13 to W19) — W20 £

Total income minus deductions (box W12 *minus* box W20) — W21 £ 56,648

now copy the figure in box W21 to box W22 on page 6

Calculating your tax bill - continued

Reliefs
- you get basic rate relief automatically - further relief will be due if you are liable to higher rate tax.

	from box W21 — W22	£ 56,648
• *Pension payments* (from boxes 14.15 and 14.17)	W23.1	£
• *Vocational training* (from box W14)	W23.2	£
box W23.1 + box W23.2	W23	£
box W22 + box W23	W24	£ 56,648

If any of the sums on this page result in a negative amount, enter a zero in the appropriate box

Allowances given as a deduction from your income
- you may need to check your entitlement - see notes starting on page 3 of this Guide.

• *Personal allowance* - normally £4,195 unless you are non-resident and not claiming allowances	W25.1	£ 4195
• *Age-related personal allowance* - see notes page 3	W25.2	£
• *Blind person's allowance* - enter £1,330	W25.3	£
• *Transitional allowance* (from box 16.4)	W25.4	£
• *Blind person's surplus allowance from your spouse* (from box 16.27)	W25.5	£
total boxes W25.1 to W25.5	W25	£ 4195
box W24 *minus* box W25 (If the figure in box W26 is £4,300 or less, do not fill in boxes W28 to W38)	W26	£ 52,453
box W26 x 20%	W27	£ 10491

Savings income taxable at the lower (20%) rate

• *Partnership savings* (from boxes 4.35 and 4.70)	W28.1	£
• *UK savings* (from box W8)	W28.2	£
• *Foreign savings* (from box 6.2)	W28.3	£
• *Trusts, settlements and estate income* (from boxes 7.6, 7.12 and 7.15)	W28.4	£
total boxes W28.1 to W28.4	W28	£
box W26 *minus* box W28	W29	£ 52,453
	W30	£ 4,300
box W29 *minus* box W30	W31	£ 48,153
box W31 x 3%	W32	£ 1444
box W26 *minus* box W23 *minus* box 12.9 (If the figure in box W33 is £27,100 or less, do not fill in boxes W35 to W38)	W33	£ 52,453
	W34	£ 27,100
box W33 *minus* box W34	W35	£ 25,353
box W35 x 17%	W36	£ 4310
lower of box W28 *or* box W35	W37	£
box W37 x 3%	W38	£
Income Tax due — boxes W27 + W32 + W36 + W38	W39	£ 16,245

Copy box W39 to top of page 7

Calculating your tax bill - continued

If any of the sums on this page result in a negative amount, enter a zero in the appropriate box

from page 6

W39 £ 16,245

- *Venture Capital Trust and Enterprise Investment Scheme subscriptions* — box 15.7 + box 15.8: W40 £ — box W40 x 20%: W41 £

box 15.2 x 10%: W42 £

Allowances and reliefs given in terms of tax
- these reduce your tax bill - you may need to use the Question 16 notes on pages 23 to 26 of the Tax Return Guide and starting on page 4 of this Guide.

- *Married couple's allowance* - see notes on pages 4 and 9 of this Guide — W43.1 £
  +
- *Married couple's surplus allowance* (from box 16.28) — W43.2 £
  +
- *Additional personal allowance* - usually £1,900, may be split with another person - see the notes — W43.3 £
  +
- *Widow's bereavement allowance - £1,900* (if your husband died in 1997-98 or 1998-99 and you have not remarried) — W43.4 £
- *Maintenance and alimony* (boxes 15.4 and 15.5 - see the notes for box W16 on page 2 of this Guide) — W43.5 £

total boxes W43.1 to W43.5: W43.6 £ — box W43.6 x 15%: W43 £

Notional tax is not repayable and so has to be calculated as an allowance given in terms of tax rather than being regarded as tax deducted at source.

- *Partnership notional tax* (from box 4.78) — W44.1 £
  +
- *Notional tax on UK scrip dividends and FIDs* (from boxes 10.22, 10.25,10.28 and 10.31) — W44.2 £
- *Notional tax on estate income* (from box 7.14) — W44.3 £

total boxes W44.1 to W44.3: W44 £

- *Tax credit relief on foreign income and treaty relief on UK income* (and see the notes on page 9 of this Guide) — from boxes 6.9 and 9.35: W45 £

boxes W41 to W45: W46 £

Income Tax due, after allowances and reliefs — box W39 *minus* box W46: W47 £ 16,245

If the figure in box W46 is more than the figure in box W39, enter a zero

- *Recoverable tax on charitable covenants, annuities, Gift Aid and Millennium Gift Aid payments* (box W17 x 23%) — W48 £
- *Class 4 National Insurance Contributions* (from box 3.91 or box 4.25) — W49 £

Income Tax and Class 4 National Insurance Contributions — boxes W47 + W48 + W49: W50 £ 16,245

Copy the figure in box W50 to box W50 on page 8

Calculating your tax bill - continued

(copy figure from box W50 on page 7) **Income Tax and Class 4 NIC due** — W50 £ 16,245

- *Unpaid tax for earlier years included in PAYE code for 1998-99* — W51 £

box W50 + box W51 — W52 £ 16,245

Copy the figure in box W51 to box 18.1 in your Tax Return

Tax paid at source

- *Employment* (from boxes 1.11 and 1.30) — W53.1 £ 12000
- *Self-employment* (from boxes 3.92 and 3.120) — W53.2 £
- *Partnerships* (from box 4.77) — W53.3 £
- *UK land and property* (from box 5.21) — W53.4 £
- *Foreign income* (from boxes 6.1 and 6.3) — W53.5 £
- *Trusts, settlements or estate income* (from boxes 7.2, 7.5, 7.8 and 7.11) — W53.6 £
- *UK savings* (from boxes 10.3, 10.6, 10.10, 10.13, 10.16 and 10.19) — W53.7 £
- *UK pensions, retirement annuities and benefits* (from boxes 11.8 and 11.11) — W53.8 £
- *Other income* (from box 13.2) — W53.9 £

total boxes W53.1 to W53.9 — W53 £ 12000

- *Tax due for 1998-99 included in 1999-2000 PAYE tax code* — W54 £

Copy the figure in box W54 to box 18.2 in your Tax Return

box W53 + box W54 — W55 £ 12000

Total tax and Class 4 NIC due for 1998-99 (overpayment in brackets) — box W52 *minus* box W55 — W56 £ 4245

Copy the figure in box W56 to box 18.3 in your Tax Return

Tax owed or overpaid in 1998-99

- *1998-99 tax already refunded* (from box 17.1) — W57A £
- *Tax due for earlier years* — W57 £
  Copy the figure in box W57 to box 18.4 in your Tax Return

boxes W56 + W57A + W57 — W58 £ 4 245

- *Tax overpaid for earlier years* — W59 £
  Tick box 18.5 and copy the figure in box W59 to the 'Additional information' box on page 8 of your Tax Return
- *Payments already made* (from your Statements of Account) — W60 £

box W59 + box W60 — W61 £

Tax you owe for 1998-99 — box W58 *minus* box W61 — W62 £ 4245

OR

Tax you have overpaid for 1998-99 — box W61 *minus* box W58 — W63 £

Payments on account for 1999-2000

If there is a figure in box W62, add it to any figure in box W59. If the total is less than £1,000 and you would like the amount you owe collected through your 2000-2001 tax code, copy W62 to W64. Otherwise enter zero — W64 £

If W65 is ***less than £500****, you do not need to make payments on account. Leave box 18.6 blank and tick box 18.8.* ***If W65 is equal to or more than £500****, carry on* — box W56 *minus* box W64 — W65 £ 4245

- *Income Tax due, after allowances and reliefs* — from boxes W44 + W47 + W48 — W66 £ 16,245
- *Class 4 National Insurance Contributions* — from box W49 — W67 £

box W66 + box W67 — W68 £ 16,245

box W68 x 20% — W69 £ 3,249

If W65 is ***less than*** *W69, you do not need to make payments on account. Leave box 18.6 blank and tick box 18.8.*
If W65 is ***equal to or more than*** *W69,* ***you do have to make payments on account. Fill in box W70***

This is the amount of each payment on account for 1999-2000 — box W65 x 50% — W70 £ 2123

Copy the figure in box W70 ***(including pence)*** *to box 18.6 in your Tax Return*

ANSWERS (Task 2)

Mrs Jane Austen
Calculation of Capital Gains for 1998/99

1. Sale of property 5

		Cost		*MV '82*
		£		£
Sale Proceeds (April 1998)		301,375		301,375
Less costs of sale		(1,500)		(1,500)
Less original cost		(100,000)		(125,000)
Unindexed gain		199,875		174,875
Less: Indexation allowance				
$£125{,}000 \times \dfrac{161.2 - 79.44}{79.44}$	(1.029)	(128,625)		(128,625)
		71,250		46,250
Lower gain taken			£46,250	

2. Sale of Property 6

		£
Sale Proceeds (April 1998)		100,350
Less costs of sale		(2,000)
Less original cost		(25,000)
Unindexed gain		73,350
Less Indexation allowance		
$£25{,}000 \times \dfrac{161.2 - 144.7}{144.7}$	(0.114)	(2,850)
Gain		£70,500

ANSWERS (Task 3)

Mrs Jane Austen
Calculation of Capital Gains Tax payable for 1998/99

Total Gains chargeable to tax:	£
Sale of Property 5	46,250
Sale of Property 6	70,500
	116,750
Less Annual Exemption 1998/99	(6,800)
Less Capital losses brought forward	(10,000)
Taxable gains	99,950
Tax payable £99,950 × 40%	39,980

This page is intentionally blank so that the 2nd and 3rd pages of the Capital gains supplement are set out facing each other as would apply in practice.

ANSWERS (Task 4)

Inland Revenue

For the year ended 5 April 1999

CAPITAL GAINS

Fill in these boxes first

Name	Tax reference
JANE AUSTEN	54180 62344

If you want help, look up the box numbers in the Notes.

Please complete Pages CG2 and CG ***before*** *filling in the rest of this Page. If you think you will need more than one copy of Pages CG2 and CG3 make photocopies before you begin filling them in.*

Your 1998-99 Capital Gains Tax liability

• Total taxable gains from Page CG3 overleaf	8.7	£ 106,750
• Your taxable gains *minus* the annual exempt amount	8.8 (box 8.7 *minu* £6,800)	£ 99,950
• Additional liability in respect of non-resident or dual resident trusts	8.9	£

Capital losses

(Remember if your loss arose on a transaction with a connected person, see Notes page CGN11, you can only set that loss agains gains you make on disposals to that same connected person)

■ ***This year's losses***

• Total from Page CG2	8.10	£
• Used against gains	8.11	£
• Used against earlier years' gains (see Notes, page CGN8)	8.12	£
8.13A £ — amount claimed against income of 1998-99		
• Used against income (see Notes, page CGN7) — 8.13B £ — amount claimed against income of 1997-98	8.13 (box 8.13A + box 8.13B)	£
• This year's unused losses	8.14 (box 8.10 *minus* (boxes 8.11 + 8.12 + 8.13))	£

■ ***Earlier years' losses***

• Unused losses of 1996-97 and 1997-98	8.15	£ 10,000
• Used this year (losses from box 8.15 are used in priority to losses from box 8.18)	8.16	£ 10,000
• Remaining unused losses of 1996-97 and 1997-98	8.17 (box 8.15 *minu* box 8.16)	£
• Unused losses of 1995-96 and earlier years	8.18	£
• Used this year (losses from box 8.15 are used in priority to losses from box 8.18)	8.19 (box 8.6 *minu* box 8.16)	£

■ ***Total of unused losses to carry forward***

• Carried forward losses of 1996-97 and later years	8.20 (box 8.14 + box 8.17)	£
• Carried forward losses of 1995-96 and earlier years	8.21 (box 8.18 *minu* box 8.19)	£

SA108

Your 1998-99 Capital Gains Tax liability

Gains (on assets without mixed use)

	A Description of asset	B Tick box if unquoted shares	C Tick box if estimate or valuation used	D Tick box if asset held at 31 March 1982	E Insert the later of date of acquisition and 16 March 1998	F Insert the date of disposal	G Disposal proceeds	H Tick box if relief claimed or due	I Chargeable Gains after reliefs but before losses and taper
1	Property 5		✓	✓	16/3/98	6/4/98	£ 301,375		£ 46,25
2	Property 6				16/3/98	6/4/98	£ 100,350		£ 70,50
3					/ /	/ /	£		£
4					/ /	/ /	£		£
5					/ /	/ /	£		£
6					/ /	/ /	£		£
7					/ /	/ /	£		£
8					/ /	/ /	£		£

Gains on mixed business and non-business use assets (see the notes on pages CGN2 and CGN15)

9		/ /	/ /	£		£
						£
10		/ /	/ /	£		£
						£

Total **8.1** £ 116,75

Total column

Losses

	Description of asset	Tick box if unquoted shares	Tick box if estimate of valuation used	Tick box if asset held at 31 March 1982	Disposal proceeds	Tick box if relief claimed or due	Net losses
13					£		£
14					£		£
15					£		£
16					£		£

Total net losses of year **8.2** £

J ...ated 'I' if ...business ...sset	K Taper rate	L Losses deducted: L1 Allowable losses of the year	L2 Income losses set against gains	L3 Unused losses b/f from earlier years	M Gains after losses	N Tapered gains (gains from column M x % in column K)	O Further information
	100 %	£	£	£ 10000	£ 36,250	£ 36,250	
	100 %	£	£	£	£ 70500	£ 70,500	
	%	£	£	£	£	£	
	%	£	£	£	£	£	
	%	£	£	£	£	£	
	%	£	£	£	£	£	
	%	£	£	£	£	£	
	%	£	£	£	£	£	
B	%	£	£	£	£	£	
	100%	£	£	£	£	£	
B	%	£	£	£	£	£	
	100%	£	£	£	£	£	

8.5 £ — Total column L2

8.6 £10000 — Total column L3

8.3 £106,750 — Total column N

1 Attributed gains *(enter source in right hand column)* £

2 Attributed gains *(enter source in right hand column)* £

Total of attributed gains 8.4 £

box 8.3 + box 8.4

Total Taxable Gains £106750

copy to box 8.7 on Page CG1

ANSWERS (Task 5)

MOLE AND CO
CHARTERED ACCOUNTANTS
94 MAIN STREET
ANYTOWN
TELEPHONE (0116) 520 9345
FAX (0116) 520 9346

Jane Austen
Book Supplies Limited
121 High Street
Anytown

Today's date

Dear Mrs Austen

Self Assessment Income Tax Return and Tax Payable

Please find enclosed copies of your income tax computation and capital gains tax computation for 1998/99, together with your completed Self Assessment Income Tax Return.

I would be grateful if you would look through both the income tax computation and the self assessment income tax return, and if you are happy with them, please sign and date the self assessment income tax return and return it to me for submission to the Inland Revenue.

The Income Tax Return and computation show that income tax of £16,245 and capital gains tax of £39,980 are due for 1998/99. The total due of £56,225 less the £12,000 paid under PAYE leaves £44,225 payable. This should be paid to the Collector of Taxes on or before 31 January 2000. The first payment on account of tax due for 1999/00 of £2,123 is also due by 31 January 2000, increasing the total tax due to £46,348. You should receive a statement of account, including a payslip and prepaid envelope, to enable you to make the payment If you need any assistance in making the payment, please contact us.

If you require any further help or information please telephone me on the number shown above.

Yours sincerely

Margaret Jones
Tax Department Manager
Mole and Co

QUESTIONS

1-5 INTRODUCTION TO PERSONAL TAXATION

1 Activity

Arthur owned a furnished house in a holiday resort which was available for commercial letting when not occupied by Arthur and his family.

In the tax year 1998/99 it was let for the following periods, no letting to the same person exceeding 30 days:

Month	*Days*
April	7
May	14
June	7
July	31
August	30 - occupied by Arthur
September	14

Apart from the above periods and two weeks in April when it was being decorated the house was available for letting throughout the tax year. The total rent received was £1,900 and the following expenditure was incurred:

	£
Insurance	250
Repairs and decorating	308
Water rates	160
Accountancy	60
Cleaning	480
Advertising	200
Interest on loan to purchase property	608
Replacement furniture	140

The annual allowance of 10% of rent (less water rates) has been agreed for wear and tear of furniture.

Arthur has also purchased two shops in the resort.

Shop 1. The annual rent was £3,000 on a tenant's repairing lease which expired on 30 June 1998. Arthur took advantage of the shop being empty to carry out repairs and decorating. The shop was let to another tenant on a five-year tenant's repairing lease at £4,000 per annum from 1 October 1998.

Shop 2. The shop was purchased on 10 April 1998 and required treatment for dry-rot. Arthur also undertook some normal re-decorating work before the shop was let on 1 October 1998 on a seven-year tenant's repairing lease at an annual rental of £6,000. A premium of £2,000 was received from the incoming tenant upon signing the lease on 1 October 1998.

The rent for both shops was due in advance on the usual calendar quarter days.

The following expenditure was incurred for 1998/99:

	Shop 1	*Shop 2*
	£	£
Insurance	190	300
Ground rent	10	40
Repairs and decorating	3,900 *(Note 1)*	5,000 *(Note 2)*
Accountancy	50	50
Advertising for tenant	100	100

Notes:

(1) Includes £2,500 for re-roofing the shop following gale damage in February 1998. Because the roof had been badly maintained the insurance company refused to pay for the repair work.

(2) Includes £3,000 for dry-rot remedial treatment which was present when the shop was bought in April 1998.

Task

Calculate the income assessable on Arthur for 1998/99 from the house and both shops and to show how any losses would be dealt with.

2 Activity

For many years Tom Jones has owned six houses in Upland Avenue which are available for letting unfurnished. He is responsible for the repairs to numbers 21, 23, 25 and 67. The tenants are responsible for the repairs to numbers 38 and 40.

Tom's mother lives at number 67. The rent she pays is about 25% of a commercial rate and the Revenue's practice is to disallow expenses in excess of the rent.

The following details have been provided by the client.

	Property number					
	21	*23*	*25*	*38*	*40*	*67*
	£	£	£	£	£	£
Rent due for y/e 5.4.99	2,080	1,820	2,340	1,300	1,300	520
Insurance due for y/e 5.4.99	280	220	340	150	150	140

(1) Tom employs a gardener to look after all the properties and pays him £1,200 a year. There are also accountancy charges of £480 a year; both of these costs are allocated equally to each property.

(2) Numbers 23 and 40 had new tenancies in the year. The cost of advertising for tenants was £50 in respect of number 23 and £100 for number 40. The new tenant at number 23 took over immediately the old tenant moved out. Unfortunately, the old tenant at No 40 defaulted on rent of £350 due before the new tenant moved in.

(3) During the year Tom had to replace the boiler in number 40 at a cost of £800. During the year he also had to replace the water tank at number 21 at a cost of £100 and a new roof for number 25 cost him £5,000.

(4) Tom has loans outstanding on each of the six properties and pays interest of £500 per year on each loan.

Task 1

Compute the amount assessable under Schedule A for 1998/99.

Task 2

Explain how relief can be obtained for any losses.

3 **Activity**

Long Life, a single man aged 35 on 6 April 1997, has been trading for many years as a barrel manufacturer. His adjusted trading results net of capital allowances for 1997/98 and 1998/99 were £14,400 and £23,000 respectively.

During 1998/99 he received building society interest of £1,984. His only other income assessable in 1998/99 was £3,300 interest which arose on his holding of 3½% War Loan. He also took out a £25,000 mortgage on 1 July 1998 for the purchase of his new residence. The net interest paid during 1998/99 under MIRAS was £1,725.

He also entered into two deeds of covenant payable annually from August 1998 as follows:

Save the Children (a charity)	£3,500 (gross)
His mother	£600 (gross)

He paid a personal pension contribution of £2,000 on 3 April 1998. He also paid personal pension plan contributions totalling £6,000 in 1998/99. There was no unused relief as at 6 April 1997.

Payments on account totalling £2,700 had been made on 31 January and 31 July 1999.

Task

Calculate Long Life's further tax payable for 1998/99 (taking advantage of any unused pension relief brought forward).

6-7 EMOLUMENTS AND BENEFITS

1 Activity

Mr F Darcy, managing director of the Pemberley Trading Co Ltd, is paid an annual salary of £36,000 and also bonuses based on the company's performance. Pemberley's accounting year ends on 31 December each year and the bonuses are normally determined and paid on 31 May thereafter. In recent years bonuses have been

Year to 31 December 1996	£4,000
Year to 31 December 1997	£8,000
Year to 31 December 1998	£4,000

Mr Darcy pays 7% of his basic salary to an approved occupational pension scheme. He uses a company car (3,500cc) purchased in 1996 for £20,000, for 25,000 miles during 1998/99, of which 25% is for non-business use. Running expenses including car fuel paid by the company were £2,600 in the year.

On 2 April 1997 the company set up a scholarship fund for its employees and their relatives. Mr Darcy's son, who is 23 years old and has no income of his own, was awarded a scholarship of £2,940 per year for three years from 1 October 1998 to continue to study for a doctorate at the University of London while continuing to live with his father. It is paid each year on 1 December.

Under the terms of the company's approved profit-sharing scheme Mr Darcy was allotted 1,000 ordinary £1 shares of the company, the market value of which is £4.25 per share, on 21 January 1999.

Mr Darcy pays charitable deeds of covenant totalling £4,235 (net).

Mr Darcy's wife died in 1990. He is a UK resident.

Task

Compute Mr Darcy's income tax payable for 1998/99. Briefly give reasons for your treatment of items included or excluded in arriving at his taxable income.

2 Activity

Mr K is chairman and chief executive of AD Ltd.

He receives a salary of £45,000 per annum and during the income tax year 1998/99 he is provided with the following benefits:

The company has provided him with the use of a *Jaguar* motor car costing £26,000 from 6 April 1998. The distributor's list price was £26,700 at that time.

On 31 July 1998 he was involved in a serious road accident and the car was written off. At that date he had covered 7,000 miles on company business. He was charged with dangerous driving and the company met his legal costs of £2,000.

When he resumed work on 1 October 1998, he was provided with a *Mercedes* car costing £30,000 (list price 30,450) and the use of a chauffeur. This car is used solely for business purposes, and, up to 5 April 1999, covered 8,000 miles.

While he had use of the *Jaguar*, he contributed £120 being 50% of the cost of his private fuel.

Throughout the year, his wife, who is not employed by the company, has been provided with the use of a *BMW* car costing £15,000, the list price, four years ago; the company meets all running costs and fuel bills.

He occupies a house which had cost the company £80,000 when purchased in 1983 and on which expenditure of £40,000 on improvements had been incurred prior to being first occupied by Mr K in 1993 when its market value was £140,000. Its annual value is agreed at £3,600. Mr K pays no rent but does meet all running costs.

He is provided with the use of two suits which had been purchased by the company at a cost of £800 in total.

Task

Compute the total amount of benefits in kind assessable on Mr K for the income tax year 1998/99.

Fuel scale benefits appropriate to the above motor cars:

	£
Jaguar	1,890
Mercedes	1,890
BMW	1,280

Assume an official rate of interest of 8%.

3 **Activity**

Mr B, the chairman of your company, is a married man aged 57 and has a salary of £80,000 for the income tax year 1998/99.

He is provided with the following benefits during the year:

(i) A Mercedes car which is one year old and which cost £35,000. It has an engine capacity of 3,000 cc. His business mileage for the tax year was 12,000. All private fuel was paid for by the company.

(ii) A BMW car with an engine capacity of 1,900 cc which is five years old and had originally cost £14,000. This is used exclusively by his wife who is not employed by the company. Again, all fuel was paid for by the company.

(iii) The use of a house, which the company had bought new last year for £180,000. Mr B pays a sum equal to the agreed annual value. The costs of heating and lighting, amounting to £2,600, were paid by the company.

(iv) The use of three suits, each costing £400.

During the tax year 1994/95, Mr B was provided with the use of a video system costing £3,000. During 1998/99 he took over the system, and paid the company £300, which was the agreed market value of the system at the date of transfer.

Task 1

Compute the additional income tax which Mr B will pay as a result of receiving the above benefits.

Task 2

Describe how the information regarding the benefits will be conveyed to the Inland Revenue and explain the method of collecting any tax due.

You may assume an official rate of interest of 8.0%.

8-11 INTRODUCTION TO CGT

1 **Activity**

Y Ltd, a manufacturing and processing business, made the following disposals during its accounting year to 31 March 1999. The company had failed to make an election within the permitted time limit for using the market value at 31 March 1982 in calculating the gains arising on the disposal of all assets held at that date.

31 October 1998

Sold the following holdings in shares which had all been acquired in single batches:

Company	*Date of purchase*	*Cost*	*Market value at 31.3.82*	*Proceeds*
		£	£	£
F Ltd	January 1978	6,000	10,000	8,000
Q Ltd	July 1981	13,000	18,000	21,000
R Ltd	August 1981	12,000	4,000	38,000
S Ltd	January 1982	6,000	5,000	1,000

28 February 1999

Sold a lease of a factory for £600,000.

This lease had been acquired in February 1991 for a thirty-year term at a cost of £400,000 and in March 1993 £40,000 was spent on improvements which were immediately reflected in the value of the lease and continued to influence its value at February 1999.

The directors are considering using the proceeds of this disposal to purchase outright either an investment property or an additional factory which it currently occupies on a short lease and uses for processing of materials.

Task 1

Compute the amount which will be included in the company's corporation tax computation for the year ended 31 March 1999 as a result of the above disposals.

Task 2

Advise the directors of any opportunities available to them to delay the payment of corporation tax on the above gains.

Indexation factors:	March 1982 - October 1998	1.062
	February 1991 - February 1999	0.261
	March 1993 - February 1999	0.185
Table percentages for leases	22 years	76.399
	27 years 11 months	84.950

30 years	87.330

2 **Activity**

XY Ltd made the following disposals in relation to its interests in land and property during its accounting year ended 31 March 1999.

March 1999

Sold a lease of business premises for £880,000.

This lease had been acquired in March 1989 for a thirty-five year term at a cost of £500,000, and in March 1990 £60,000 was expended on improvements which were immediately reflected in the value of the lease and continued to influence that value until the date of disposal.

The following is an extract from the table of percentages relating to leases: 35 years 91.98; 34 years 91.15; 25 years 81.10.

November 1998

Sold an investment property, not used for the purposes of the trade, for £260,000.

This had been acquired in April 1985 at a cost of £120,000 and in June 1986, £20,000 of expenditure had been incurred in respect of capital improvements.

Indexation factors are as follows:

March 1989	-	March 1999	0.472
March 1990	-	March 1999	0.362
April 1985	-	November 1998	0.729
June 1986	-	November 1998	0.676

Task 1

Compute the amount which will be included in the corporation tax computation of XY Ltd for the year ended 31 March 1999 in respect of capital gains.

Task 2

Advise the directors of the opportunities available to them to delay the payment of corporation tax on the above gains.

3 **Activity**

In January 1981 Philip acquired 1,000 ordinary shares in Leisure Products plc, a quoted company, for £1,500. In January 1988, when the price of the shares was £3 each, the company made a rights issue of 1 for 5 at a price of £2.00. Philip sold all his rights for 70p per share. Philip sold his original 1,000 shares in August 1998 for £7,500.

The share price on 31 March 1982 was £1.60 per share.

No election has been, or will be made, under S35(5), TCGA 1992, to have all pre-31 March 1982 acquisitions re-based to 31 March 1982.

Task

Calculate, before annual exemption, the capital gain assessable on Philip for 1998/99. The shares do not qualify as business assets for taper relief.

12-14 RETIREMENT AND REPLACEMENT

1 **Activity**

The directors of P Ltd have taken a view that the economy is on the way to recovery and have decided to make an investment in manufacturing machinery of approximately £1 million.

In order to raise most of the required funds they decided to make a number of asset disposals during its accounting period of twelve months to 31 March 1999.

The assets sold were as follows:

(a) 31 October 1998

An office block was sold for £520,000. Its cost was made up of:

		£
November 1979	Original cost	120,000
December 1980	Extension built	25,000
October 1986	Lift installed	80,000
August 1990	New roof fitted	30,000

This building had been acquired as an investment property for renting. It has never been used for the purpose of P Ltd's trade. Its market value at 31 March 1982 was £160,000.

(b) 30 November 1998

A plot of land was sold for £140,000. This had been acquired in February 1982 at a cost of £40,000. This purchase had been partly funded from the sale of a plot of land sold in February 1982 for £38,000. This latter plot had cost £30,000 in July 1980 and the gain arising on it had been rolled over against the replacement land. The plot now being sold had a market value at 31 March 1982 of £41,000.

(c) 30 December 1998

An office building, which had been used for business purposes, but which was now surplus to requirements, was sold for £210,000 (net of costs). This had been bought in April 1989 for £120,000, using all of the proceeds of the sale, during April 1989, of a previously-owned building. This latter building had been purchased in August 1983 for £50,000 and, on its sale, full roll-over relief had been claimed against the new building for the gain arising in April 1989.

Task 1

Compute the capital gains arising from each of the above disposals.

Task 2

Advise the directors on the extent to which they may claim to have the above gains rolled over against their proposed investment in the new machinery.

You are **NOT** required to compute any corporation tax payable.

The following indexation factors may be used:

August 1983	-	April 1989	0.334
April 1989	-	December 1998	0.436
March 1982	-	November 1998	1.063
March 1982	-	October 1998	1.062
October 1986	-	October 1998	0.664
August 1990	-	October 1998	0.279

2 Activity

(a) In April 1975 Ian bought some freehold land costing £50,000. In August 1986 part of the land was sold for £150,000 when the value of the remainder was £200,000. In June 1998 the remainder of the land was sold for £250,000. The value of all the land originally purchased was £175,000 on 31 March 1982.

No election has been, or will be made, under S35(5), TCGA 1992, to have all pre-31 March 1982 acquisitions re-based to 31 March 1982. The land was not a business asset for taper relief.

Task 1

Calculate, before annual exemption, the capital gain assessable on Ian for 1998/99.

(b) In September 1998 Roy who was then 60 years old gave all his shares in his 'personal' company, Magic Motors Ltd, to his son Colin. At that time the shares had a market value of £500,000 and had been purchased by Roy in September 1979 for £100,000. The total value of the shares on 31 March 1982 was £80,000. Roy had been a full-time working officer of the company since September 1991. Roy and Colin made a joint claim for any capital gain to be held over. All chargeable assets of the company are chargeable business assets.

No election has been, or will be made under S35(5), TCGA 1992, to have all pre-31 March 1982 acquisitions re-based to 31 March 1982.

Task 2

Calculate, before annual exemption, the capital gain assessable on Roy for 1998/99 and the cost which will be available to Colin to set against future disposals.

3 Activity

(a) On 31 March 1999, her 58th birthday, Angela sold all her shares in Scott Stockings Ltd, a manufacturing company.

(1) Holdings of ordinary shares in the company were held as follows:

Angela	15
Michael, Angela's husband	15
Martin, Angela's brother	15
Raquel, Michael's sister	10
Yvonne, Angela's cousin	15
Charles, Angela's uncle	15
David, Angela's uncle	15
	100%

(2) Angela had been a full-time working officer of the company for the last six years and had owned 15% of the shares for the last eight years.

(3) The capital gain, after indexation, was £290,000.

(4) The market values of the company's assets on 31 March 1999 were:

	£'000
Land and buildings	2,000
Plant and machinery*	1,000
Goodwill	500
Investments in gilt-edged securities	250
Net current assets	1,500
	5,250

* All items of plant and machinery have a market value of more than £6,000.

Task 1

Calculate Angela's assessable capital gain for 1998/99, assuming no other disposals of chargeable assets in the year.

(b) Victor had the following transactions in the ordinary shares of Victorious Vulcanising plc, a quoted company.

	No of shares	*Total amount* £
1.8.78 Bought	600	7,200
1.4.87 Bought	1,000	11,000
1.9.89 (1 for 2 rights) Bought	800	4,800
1.8.98 Sold	2,100	36,400

The value per share on 31 March 1982 was £8.

Task 2

Calculate Victor's capital gain for 1998/99 before the annual exemption. The shares do not qualify as business assets for taper relief.

15 PRINCIPAL PRIVATE RESIDENCE RELIEF

1 **Activity**

Adrienne bought 1,000 ordinary £1 shares in Pokhara Ltd for £100,000 in March 1982. She sold her entire holding in December 1998 for £320,000. The shares are not business assets for taper relief.

She bought an investment on 1 June 1999 for £250,000.

You may assume that Adrienne's investment qualifies for EIS deferral relief.

Adrienne made no other disposals in 1998/99.

Task

Calculate how much EIS deferral relief Adrienne will claim.

2 **Activity**

Lucas sold his only residence for £135,475 on 31 March 1999. He bought it on 1 April 1979 for £14,000. He used the whole property exclusively for himself and his wife for the first ten years, and then for the last ten years let the basement, comprising one-third of the house. No structural alterations were made and the basement was not a self-contained flat. The market value of the house on 31 March 1982 was £35,000.

Lucas elects for market value at 31 March 1982 basis to be used for all assets owned on that date.

Task

Compute the amount of the chargeable gain, assuming any necessary elections are made.

3 **Activity**

On 6 April 1967 Butler purchased a freehold house for £6,215. The house was empty until 6 October 1968, when Butler commenced occupation. On 6 October 1970 he moved to France, and was employed there as a saleman until 6 October 1973, when he returned to work in England in an employment which required him to live away from home in rented accommodation.

On 6 October 1978 he resumed occupation until 6 October 1988 when again his employment required that he live some distance from his home. On 6 October 1995, having been told he was going to work permanently in the distant location, Butler returned to his house for a month's holiday during which he redecorated the house and put it on the market. It was sold on 6 July 1998 for £86,175 (net). Market value at 31 March 1982 was agreed to be £35,000.

Task

Compute any chargeable gain arising.

16-17 PERSONAL TAX COMPUTATIONS & RETURNS

1 Activity

Kevin Winterburn started trading as a builder in May 1995. His agreed Case I profit for the year ended 31 December 1998 was £15,000. In the year ended 31 December 1999 Kevin expects to incur a trading loss which is likely to be agreed at £20,000 for income tax purposes. On 17 July 1998 he sold some land which resulted in an assessable capital gain after indexation of £9,100.

His wife, Susan, to whom Kevin has been married for five years, is headmistress at a girls' boarding school. The following information is provided:

(1) Susan's remuneration for the year ended 5 April 1999 was £25,000.

(2) She is also provided with a house where she is required to live by her employers for the better performance of her duties. The gross annual value of the house, which is owned by the school was £1,000. The house cost £70,000 in 1996.

(3) In the tax year ended 5 April 1999, the school paid £1,500 for gas, electricity and decorating in respect of the house.

(4) The school also provided Susan with a new 1300cc company car costing £7,000 on 6 October 1998. No car had been provided previously. The running costs of the car, including all petrol, were £800 to 5 April 1999. The total mileage in the period was 4,000, of which 1,000 was on school business.

(5) Susan sold some shares on 12 April 1998 resulting in an assessable capital gain after indexation of £3,000.

Kevin and Susan had a joint account with a UK bank. The interest credited on 31 December 1998 was £1,000.

Task 1

Calculate the tax liabilities of

(a) Kevin, and
(b) Susan,

for 1998/99. You should assume that any elections which may reduce the overall tax liability are made but you should state the nature of the elections.

Task 2

State how advantage might have been taken of any unused allowances, exemptions or reliefs.

2 Activity

Dawn Warr, who is unmarried, has been in business since 1 May 1996 running a small private educational centre, specialising in modern language teaching. Her adjusted tax profits, before capital allowances, have been:

	£
Year ended 30 April 1997	15,000
Year ended 30 April 1998	12,000
Period to 30 September 1998	9,000

The following purchases were made during the year ended 30 April 1997

	£
Plant and machinery	3,200
Car (used by Dawn and private use agreed at 75%)	5,600
Car (used by Dawn's assistant and private use agreed at 50%)	4,000

On 1 June 1997 new recording equipment was purchased for £1,000.

On 1 January 1998 Dawn traded in her car for a new one. She paid £4,800 and was allowed a £3,000 cash allowance on the existing car. Private use remained at 75%.

On 6 May 1998 new furniture costing £500 was purchased.

On 30 September 1998 all the business assets were sold for the following amounts

	£
Plant and machinery (all less than cost)	2,500
Dawn's car	6,000
Dawn's assistant's car	2,000

On 30 September 1998 Dawn closed the business and on 1 October 1998, her thirtieth birthday, took up a job as regional manager with a firm of travel agents specialising in European holidays. Her salary was £24,000 per annum payable monthly in arrears. She was provided with a new 1,600 cc car, on commencement of her new job, which cost £9,750. In 1998/99 she did 12,000 miles in her company car, of which 1,000 were private. All running costs, including private petrol, were paid for by Dawn's employers. Details of other income and outgoings are

(1) Dawn's employers did not have a pension scheme and she decided to pay the maximum amount permissible under the personal pension plan rules, relative to her employment.

(2) Interest on a deposit account with Barlloyd Bank. The account had been opened in 1994 and interest was credited as follows:

31 December 1997	£300
31 December 1998	£491

(3) Interest on a NSB ordinary account, which was opened in May 1996 and closed in May 1999. Interest had been credited as follows:

31 December 1996	£189
31 December 1997	£190
31 December 1998	£199
31 May 1999	£120

(4) Dawn had a mortgage on her house for £20,000. Interest of £1,400 (gross) was paid in 1998/99 under the MIRAS arrangements.

(5) Dawn had entered into a charitable deed of covenant with the local church of £77 per annum (net) on 8 April 1998 for ten years.

(6) Dawn realised capital gains of £22,000 in 1998/99 (after indexation but before annual exemption).

Task 1

Calculate the assessable amounts, for the tax years 1996/97, 1997/98 and 1998/99 of Dawn's business profits.

Task 2

Calculate the income tax and tax on chargeable gains payable for the tax year 1998/99.

3 **Activity**

Joshua Wrekin retired from his job as technical director with Wenlock Engineers Ltd on 30 April 1998, his 65th birthday. He received an ex-gratia payment from his employers of £25,250 plus his company car which was valued at £6,500. The Revenue accept that this is a termination payment (assessable under S148) and not a payment under an unapproved retirement benefit arrangement.

His monthly salary, payable on the last day of the month was £2,775. The car was a 2500cc, BMW costing £18,500 when first provided for Joshua in January 1995. The business mileage in April 1998 was 120. The running costs of the car were £400 including approximately half of the petrol used for Joshua's private motoring. Wenlock Engineers Ltd paid Joshua's subscription to BUPA, a private health insurance company, of £42 for the month of April 1998.

Joshua decided to use his engineering skills and business contacts as a self-employed consultant. He commenced on 1 May 1998 and made up his first accounts to 30 April 1999. He did not qualify for enterprise allowance. His summarised accounts for the first period of trading were:

	£	£	£
Consultancy fees			29,510
Reference books - *Note 1*		300	
Wife's wages as secretary - *Note 2*		4,200	
Car expenses - *Note 3*			
Depreciation	1,600		
Petrol and oil	1,500		
Servicing	200		
AA subscription	60		
Replacement tyres	150		
Insurance	1,000		
		4,510	
Depreciation of furniture and equipment		250	
Rent of office		7,000	
Premium payment for lease - *Note 4*		2,500	
Office running costs		1,500	
			(20,260)
Net profit			9,250

Notes:

(1) The reference books were purchased in May 1998.

(2) Wife's wages of £350 were paid on the last day of the month and accepted by the Revenue as being at a commercial rate.

(3) The BMW was used in the business. Joshua's business mileage in the period covered by the first set of accounts was 20,000 and his private mileage was 2,000. This proportion is expected to apply for future periods.

(4) The lease was for 10 years from 1 May 1998.

(5) Capital purchases were made as follows:

		£
May 1998	Office furniture	1,000
May 1998	Computer/word processor	1,500
June 1998	Photocopier	920
June 1999	New telephone and fax system	1,088

No election was to be made to treat any of the assets purchased as 'short-life' assets.

Joshua estimates that the profits adjusted for tax purposes but before deducting capital allowances, for the years ending 30 April 2000 and 2001 will be £10,000 and £15,000 respectively.

Joshua's wife, Brenda, had purchased a life annuity from an insurance company on her 65th birthday during 1997 which paid her £100 a month. The income element has been agreed with the Revenue at £50. She received £1,752 interest from the Northern Shires Building Society on 31 December 1998 and paid £924 (net) to a national charity under a four-year deed of covenant on 1 January each year.

Joshua and Brenda received National Insurance Retirement Pensions of £4,082 and £2,449 respectively for the year 1998/99.

Task 1

Calculate the Schedule D Case II assessable amounts for the first three tax years in respect of Joshua's business.

Task 2

Calculate the income tax liability of Joshua for 1998/99.

Task 3

Calculate the income tax liability of Brenda for 1998/99.

18-20 INTRODUCTION TO BUSINESS TAXATION

1 Activity

John Openshaw imports kitchen appliances from Europe which he sells to wholesale distributors in the United Kingdom. His trading and profit and loss account for his first year of trading to 30 June 1998 is:

	£	£
Sales		167,400
Purchases	89,200	
Closing stock	(27,700)	
		(61,500)
Gross profit		105,900
Wages and salaries	43,900	
Rent and rates	2,100	
Lighting and heating	1,690	
Depreciation of furniture	500	
Insurance	1,280	
Travelling and entertaining *(Note 1)*	6,450	
Bad debts *(Note 2)*	6,750	
Depreciation of vehicles	5,000	
Car expenses *(Note 3)*	3,050	
Sundry expenses *(note 4)*	230	
Legal and professional charges *(note 5)*	1,040	
Interest on bank overdraft	1,400	
Van expenses	2,100	
		75,490
Net profit		30,410

Notes:

(1) Travelling and entertaining expenses

	£
John Openshaw's business travelling expenses	3,500
Christmas presents for staff	200
Entertaining overseas suppliers	750
Entertaining UK customers	2,000
	6,450

(2) Bad debts

	£
Trading debts written off	3,250
Provisions against specific debtors	1,800
General provision in view of uncertain trading conditions	1,700
	6,750

(3) Car expenses
All these related to John Openshaw.
One quarter of his mileage was private.

(4) Sundry expenses are all allowable for income tax purposes.

(5) Legal and professional charges

	£
Obtaining 21-year lease of business premises	100
Accountancy	270
Legal fees in connection with action by employee for unfair dismissal	220
Debt collection	450
	1,040

The following capital purchases were made:

	£
1 July 1997 office furniture and equipment	5,000
7 July 1997 car for use by John Openshaw	9,500
10 July 1997 van	7,000
18 May 1998 office furniture	1,000

Task

Calculate the adjusted Schedule D Case I profits for the year to 30 June 1998.

2 Activity

Roger Riviere is a self-employed wholesale clothing distributor who commenced trading on 1 July 1996. His summarised accounts for the year ended 30 June 1998 are:

	£	£
Sales (1)		400,000
Opening stock (2)	40,000	
Purchases	224,000	
	264,000	
Closing stock (2)	(32,000)	232,000
Gross profit		168,000
Wages and national insurance (3)		52,605
Rent and business rates		31,060
Repairs and renewals (4)		3,490
Miscellaneous expenses (5)		665
Taxation (Roger's income tax)		15,590
Bad debts (6)		820
Legal expenses (7)		1,060
Depreciation		570
Lease rental on car (Roger's car) (8)		8,400
Loss on sale of office furniture		60
Deeds of covenant (9)		80
Transport costs		4,250
Interest (10)		990
Motor car running expenses (Roger's car) (11)		2,000
Premium on lease (12)		6,000
Lighting and heating		1,250
Sundry expenses (all allowable)		710
Re-location expenditure (13)		2,400
Net profit		36,000
		168,000

Figures in brackets refer to notes to the accounts.

Notes to accounts:

(1) Sales include £500 reimbursed by Roger's family for clothing taken from stock. This reimbursement represented cost price.

(2) Stock. The basis of both opening and closing stock valuations was 'lower of cost or market value' less a contingency reserve of 50% in view of the recession.

(3) Wages. Included in wages are Roger's drawings of £50 per week, his national insurance contributions of £320 for the year and wages and national insurance contributions in respect of his wife totalling £11,750. His wife worked full-time in the business as a secretary.

(4) Repairs and renewals. The charge includes £3,000 for fitting protective covers over the factory windows and doors to prevent burglary.

(5) Miscellaneous expenses

	£
Theft of money by employee	65
Political donation to Green Party	100
Gifts of 100 'Riviere' calendars	500
	665

(6) Bad debts:

	£	
Trade debt written off		720
Loan to former employee written off		250
Provision for bad debts (2% of debtors)	450	
Less: Opening provision	(600)	
		(150)
		820

(7) Legal expenses:

	£
Defending action in respect of alleged faulty goods	330
Costs in connection with lease of new larger premises	250
Successful appeal against previous year's income tax assessment	200
Defending Roger in connection with speeding offence	190
Debt collection	90
	1,060

(8) Lease rental on car. Roger's car was a BMW costing £30,000. The lease was entered into on 1 July 1996.

(9) Deeds of covenant (payable for next 4 years) (gross amounts)

	£
Local children's hospital	50
Oxfam	30
	80

(10) Interest

	£
Bank overdraft interest (business account)	1,020
Interest on overdue tax	130
Interest credited on National Savings Bank ordinary account	(160)
	990

(11) Motor car running expenses. One-third of Roger's mileage is private. Included in the charge is £65 for a speeding fine incurred by Roger whilst delivering goods to a customer.

(12) Premium on lease. The premium was for a lease of six years.

(13) Re-location expenditure. The expenditure was incurred in transferring the business to new and larger premises.

(14) Capital allowances for the year to 30 June 1998 are £480.

Task

Prepare a profit adjustment statement in respect of the accounting period to 30 June 1998 showing the Schedule D Case I adjusted profit.

3 **Activity**

Eastwood, a manufacturer of mobile phones, prepares accounts annually to 31 December. Accounts for the year to 31 December 1998 showed an adjusted profit of £85,000 before taking account of capital allowances.

As at 1 January 1998 there was the following unrelieved expenditure for capital allowance purposes:

Pool of plant - £42,000
Car costing £7,200 in January 1997 with 30% private use - £5,400

In the year to 31 December 1998 the following purchases and sales of plant were made:

Purchases		
	10 February 1998	Plastic moulding machine cost £27,500
	1 March 1998	Car, cost £10,000 (no private use)
	1 September 1998	Car, cost £15,000 (no private use)
Sales		
	21 August 1998	Plasting moulding machine for £5,500 (original cost £14,000)

Task 1

Prepare a capital allowance computation based on the above information

Task 2

State the amount of Schedule D Case I profit for the year to 31 December 1998.

21-22 BASIS PERIODS AND TRADING LOSSES

1 **Activity**

Michael started in business as a hairdresser on 1 March 1996 and finished on 31 October 2002.

His profits, adjusted for taxation, were as follows:

	£
Period ended 30.4.97	15,000
Year ended 30.4.98	17,000
Year ended 30.4.99	12,000
Year ended 30.4.00	14,000
Year ended 30.4.01	18,000
Year ended 30.4.02	13,000
Period ended 31.10.02	3,000

Task

Calculate the assessable amounts for all relevant years, taking into account any relief which Michael is entitled to.

2 **Activity**

Caren Montaine, the wife of a successful derivatives dealer, has been a fashion consultant for five years. Caren had always made taxable profits and her adjusted trading results over the next three years are expected to be:

Year ended 31 August 1998	£4,000 profit
Year ended 31 August 1999	£(11,000) loss
Year ended 31 August 2000	£13,000 profit

Her only other income is likely to be in the tax year 1999/00 when she expects to receive building society interest of £1,600 net of tax. The adjusted results in each year are after deducting £2,400 of capital allowances arising from an expensive car with some private use.

Task 1

State the possible ways in which Caren could obtain relief for the trading loss sustained in the year ended 31 August 1999.

Task 2

Calculate the effect of the method of loss utilisation which you would recommend to her.

(You may assume that the income tax rates and personal allowances figures provided for 1998/99 apply to all years affected).

3 **Activity**

Mr J commenced trading on 1 January 1998 and decided to make up accounts to 30 June each year. His profits, for tax purposes are:

	£
Period to 30 June 1998	18,000
Year ending 30 June 1999	40,000 (estimated)
Year ending 30 June 2000	30,000 (estimated)

Task

(a) Compute the amounts assessable under Schedule D Case I for the tax years 1997/98 to 1999/00.

(b) Identify any 'overlap relief' arising AND explain how this will be relieved.

4 **Activity**

Mr D commenced trading as a sole trader on 1 June 1997. Just prior to commencing, he purchased a motor van for £16,000 and machinery for £12,000.

He decided that May would not be the best month to prepare accounts and that August would be a better date. His first set of accounts was prepared for the period to 31 August 1998 and showed an agreed profit of £36,000 before deducting capital allowances.

The business did not perform well and his profits for the year to 31 August 1999 fell to £15,000.

He has advised you that he will cease trading on 31 March 2000 and has estimated that his profit for each month from 1 September 1999 till he ceases will be £800. He also estimates that he will sell the van and machinery for a total of £12,000 on 31 March 2000.

Task

Show the Schedule D Case I assessment for **each** of the income tax years involved, showing clearly your calculation of overlap relief and the way in which it is finally relieved.

23 TAXATION OF PARTNERSHIPS

1 **Activity**

Dominic and Justin commenced in partnership on 1 July 1996 and decided to produce their accounts to 30 June annually. On 1 January 1998, Simon joined the partnership.

The partnership's accounts show the following adjusted profits:

	£
Year ended 30 June 1997	10,000
Year ended 30 June 1998	13,500
Year ended 30 June 1999	18,000

Task

Show the amounts assessable on the individual partners for all the years affected by the above information, assuming that profits are shared equally.

2 **Activity**

Bert and Harold commenced trading on 1 October 1994. Their accounts for the year ended 30 September 1998 show an adjusted trading profit of £16,500.

Bert and Harold changed their profit-sharing ratio on 1 July 1998. The old profit-sharing ratio applies until 30 June 1998, and the new ratio applies from 1 July 1998.

	Bert	*Harold*
Old ratio:		
Salaries pa	£3,000	£2,000
Share of balance	3/5	2/5
New ratio:		
Salaries pa	£6,000	£4,000
Share of balance	2/3	1/3

The partnership made a loan of £10,000 to Harold's nephew who pays interest of 9% annually. This interest is received on 1 June and 1 December.

Task 1

Show the time apportionment of the 1998/99 Schedule DI income.

Task 2

Show the allocation of the Schedule DI income.

Task 3

Show the allocation of the partnership loan interest.

24-25 INTRODUCTION TO CORPORATION TAX

1 Activity

Unsurpassable Umbrellas Ltd is a United Kingdom resident trading company which began to trade in 1964 and has no associated companies. Accounts have always been prepared to 31 December and the summarised results for the year ended 31 December 1998 are as follows:

	£
Schedule D Case I adjusted profit	290,000
Income from property (after expenses)	4,000
Bank interest received (30.9.98)	1,900
Chargeable gain (17.3.98)	8,200
Patent royalties received (net) (31.12.98)	924
Debenture interest received (gross) (31.12.98)	27,000
Dividend from UK company (17.2.98)	14,000
Dividend from UK company (17.7.98)	18,000
Final dividend for 1997 (paid 31.3.98)	29,000
Interim dividend for 1998 (paid 19.9.98)	35,000

The Schedule D Case I adjusted profit includes a deduction for loan interest of £20,000 on an accruals basis. The gross equivalent of the amount actually paid on 30.6.98 is £22,000.

The accrued gross amounts of interest received and paid for the year are as follows:

	£
Bank interest receivable	2,000
Debenture interest receivable	27,000
Loan interest payable	20,000

Notes:

(1) Trading losses of £60,000 were brought forward from 1997.
(2) Income tax had been deducted from the debenture interest received.
(3) Dates in brackets are dates upon which the transactions occurred.

Task 1

Calculate the advance corporation tax payable in respect of the dividends paid during the chargeable accounting period ended 31 December 1998, showing the dates when the tax is due.

Task 2

Calculate the income tax payable to the Inland Revenue in respect of charges or interest paid during the chargeable accounting period ended 31 December 1998, showing the dates when the tax is due.

Task 3

Calculate the mainstream corporation tax payable for the year ended 31 December 1998.

2 Activity

(a) Elliptical Extensions Ltd is a UK resident company which manufactures industrial springs. It has no associated companies. It commenced trading in 1987, in a factory which it purchased that year for £40,000. The cost of administration offices included in the original purchase price of £40,000 was £5,000.

The company's results for the year ended 31 March 1999 are summarised below:

	£
Adjusted trading profit before capital allowances	335,000
Dividends received from UK companies	15,000
Bank interest receivable	3,000
Loan interest receivable from UK companies (gross amount)	10,000
Chargeable gains	50,000
Patent royalties paid (gross amount)	2,000
Dividends paid in year ended 31.3.99	263,420

The amount of bank interest actually received was £2,875 and loan interest received was £9,800 (gross).

An extension to the original factory was built in 1990 and cost £70,000 of which £25,000 was for administration offices.

In 1991 a premium of £22,500 was paid to the local authority for the long lease of a new factory costing £50,000, erected on a nearby industrial estate. The local authority had made the appropriate joint election with Elliptical Extensions Ltd. Neither factory was situated in an Enterprise Zone but both were in use for qualifying purposes at 31 March 1999.

On 1 April 1998 the tax written-down values of plant and machinery were:

	£
Pool	75,000
Expensive car	7,000
Car pool	31,000
Short-life asset (spring end grinding machine)	17,500

The short-life asset was purchased on 7 August 1993 and sold on 19 November 1998 for £5,000.

On 1 January 1999 the expensive car was traded in for £6,000 against a new car costing £14,000.

There were no other purchases or sales during the year.

Notes:

(1) The company has claimed maximum set-off of advance corporation tax in all periods to 31 March 1998.

(2) The company had no surplus franked investment income, advance corporation tax or trading losses to carry forward on 1 April 1998.

(3) There were capital losses brought forward at 1 April 1998 of £60,000.

(4) The company had always made up accounts to the end of March.

Task 1

You are required to calculate the mainstream corporation tax payable for the year ended 31 March 1999, showing any balances carried forward at that date.

(b) Manchester Models Ltd makes up annual accounts to 31 March 1999:

30 April 1998	Received ordinary dividend from Midway Ltd - £48,000
31 May 1998	Received loan interest from Pearl Lingerie Ltd - £8,000 (net).
31 July 1998	Paid debenture interest - £3,200 (net)
31 August 1998	Paid final dividend for year ended 31 March 1998 - £192,000
30 September 1998	Received loan interest from Roselea Ltd - £4,800 (net)
30 November 1998	Paid debenture interest £11,200 (net)
31 December 1998	Received preference dividend from Coral Clothing Ltd - £160,000
31 January 1999	Received ordinary dividend from Cedartree Ltd - £32,000
28 February 1999	Received loan interest from Abbey Fashions Ltd - £6,400 (net)
31 March 1999	Paid interim dividend for year ended 31 March 1999 - £96,000

Task 2

You are required to prepare entries relating to advance corporation tax and income tax as they would appear on forms CT 61 submitted to the Collector of Taxes for the year ended 31 March 1999.

3 **Activity**

Unbelievable Upshots Ltd is a UK resident company which manufactures industrial springs. It has no associated companies. It commenced trading in 1990 in a factory which it purchased that year for £40,000. The cost of administration offices included in the original purchase price of £40,000 was £5,000.

The company's results for the year ended 28 February 1999 are summarised below:

	£
Adjusted trading profit before capital allowances	283,000
Dividends received from UK companies (June 1998)	33,000
Bank interest receivable	3,000
Loan interest receivable from UK companies (gross amount)	10,000
Chargeable gains	50,000
Dividends paid (March 1998)	186,000

Included in the adjusted trading profit is a deduction for debenture interest of £2,000 (gross amount). The debentures were for trading purposes.

An extension to the original factory was built in 1991 and cost £70,000 of which £25,000 was for administration offices.

In 1992 a premium of £22,500 was paid to the local authority for the long lease of a new factory costing £50,000, erected on a nearby industrial estate. The local authority had made the appropriate joint election with Unbelievable Upshots Ltd. Neither factory was situated in an Enterprise Zone but both were in use for qualifying purposes at 28 February 1999.

In the year ended 28 February 1999 the amounts of interest paid and received are the same as the amounts accrued.

On 1 March 1998 the tax written-down values of plant and machinery were:

	£
Pool	75,000
Expensive car	7,000
Car pool	27,000
Short life asset (spring end grinding machine)	17,500

The short-life asset was purchased in August 1993 and sold on 19 November 1998 for £5,000.

On 1 January 1999 the expensive car was traded in for £6,000 against a new car costing £14,000.

There were no other purchases or sales during the year.

Notes:

(1) The company has claimed maximum set-off of advance corporation tax in all periods to 28 February 1998.

(2) The company had no surplus franked investment income, advance corporation tax or trading losses to carry forward on 1 March 1998.

(3) There were capital losses brought forward at 1 March 1998 of £60,000.

(4) The company had always made up accounts to the end of February.

Task

Calculate the mainstream corporation tax payable for the year ended 28 February 1999.

4 Activity

P Ltd is a company with various shareholdings in other UK companies. As a means of avoiding National Insurance Contributions, it pays regular dividends to its directors, who are the only shareholders. It is in receipt of periodic payments in respect of patent royalties and it pays debenture interest twice in each accounting period.

The following is a list, in date order, of the various transaction of the above type during the year ended 31 March 1999 showing the actual net amount paid or received.

		£
10 April 1998	Dividends received from UK companies	12,000
8 May 1998	Dividends paid to directors	9,600
10 May 1998	Patent royalties received	28,122
12 July 1998	Debenture interest paid	36,000
15 August 1998	Dividends paid	40,000
30 August 1998	Patent royalties received	16,070
12 October 1998	Dividends received from UK companies	4,800
16 November 1998	Dividends received from UK companies	14,400
24 November 1998	Debenture interest paid	34,080
30 November 1998	Charitable covenant paid	9,642
15 January 1999	Patent royalties received	24,104
30 January 1999	Dividends paid	19,200

The directors wish to have information on the cash inflows and outflows arising from the taxation associated with each transactions.

Task

Calculate, by means of quarterly settlement statements for both ACT/FII and Income Tax, the amounts which became payable and/or recoverable in each case, stating the date, or approximate date, concerned.

5 **Activity**

CD Ltd is a UK resident company with no associated companies. It provides the following information in respect of its accounting period of sixteen months ended 31 July 1998:

		£
Income		
Adjusted trading profit (before deducting capital allowances and debenture interest payable)		1,381,968
Rent receivable - due monthly in advance		24,000
Patent royalties received (gross figure)	30 June 1997	24,000
	30 June 1998	5,666
Dividends from UK companies (including tax credit)		
	31 May 1997	7,750
	31 May 1998	30,000

		£
Charges and interest paid		
Debenture interest (gross figures)	30 April 1997	10,000
	30 April 1998	10,000
Charitable covenant (gross figure)	30 June 1998	4,000

	£
Dividends paid	
31 May 1997	320,000
30 April 1998	304,000

The balances brought forward at 1 April 1997 for capital allowances purposes were:

General pool	*Motor cars (under £12,000)*	*Expensive car (Jaguar)*	*Computer (short life)*
£48,000	£16,000	£16,000	£18,000

The Jaguar was purchased after 9 March 1992.
Asset transactions during the period:

Purchases		£	*Sales*		£
30 September 1997	Motor car	7,200			
30 January 1998	Plant	12,000	31 May 1997	Plant	6,000
30 April 1998			15 April 1998	Computer	8,500
Mercedes car:					
Cost	24,000				
Less: Jaguar traded in	10,000	14,000			

Task 1

Compute the maximum capital allowances which the company may claim for **each** of the **two** accounting periods.

Task 2

Compute the mainstream corporation tax payable by the company for **each** of the **two** accounting periods showing clearly your treatment of both advance corporation tax (ACT) and income tax.

Task 3

State the dates on which the above mainstream corporation tax (MCT) is due for payment.

Note: you are NOT required to show the quarterly settlements for ACT and income tax.

26-28 CT LOSSES, CLOSE COMPANIES & CT RETURNS

1 **Activity**

Unique Unicycles Ltd is a United Kingdom resident trading company which manufactures mountain bike components. It has been trading since 1960 and has no associated companies.

The recent results of the company are summarised below:

	12 months to 31 July 1997 £	*12 months to 31 July 1998* £
Adjusted trading profit/(loss) before capital allowances	80,000	(294,800)
Bank interest receivable	4,000	–
Profit on sale of factory	–	75,000
Dividends received from UK companies	–	12,000
Loan interest received (gross)	8,000	6,000
Charitable deed of covenant payments (gross)	10,000	8,000
Dividend paid	40,000	–
Capital allowances on plant and machinery	20,000	24,600

The loan interest was received on 31 January and 31 July each year. No interest was accrued at the year ends.

The company's original factory was purchased new and unused on 1 June 1983 for £60,000 and sold on 6 May 1988 for £85,000. Rollover relief on the chargeable gain was claimed against the cost of the new and unused replacement factory purchased on 1 June 1987 for £120,000. The second factory was sold in December 1997 for £207,000 following a decision to move into smaller rented accommodation. Neither factory was situated in an Enterprise Zone and there has not been any non-qualifying use of either factory. The first factory had been brought into use immediately it was acquired. The second factory was not brought into use until 1 August 1987.

Notes

(1) The company has claimed maximum set-off of advance corporation tax in all periods to 31 July 1996.

(2) The company had no surplus franked investment income, advance corporation tax or losses to carry forward on 1 August 1996.

(3) Income tax has been deducted from the loan interest received.

(4) The company has claimed maximum writing down allowances on the second factory.

(5) The dividends from UK companies were received in August 1997.

(6) The dividend was paid in March 1997.

Task 1

Calculate the loss relief available for the year ended 31 July 1998 and show the utilisation of the loss, assuming all available claims are made against the earliest available profits.

Task 2

Calculate the total profits chargeable to corporation tax for both years before utilisation of any loss relief in respect of the loss sustained in the year ended 31 July 1998.

Task 3

Calculate the mainstream corporation tax payable for both years (if any) after utilisation of any loss relief in respect of the loss sustained in the year ended 31 July 1998, and state the amount of any unrelieved charges.

Task 4

Calculate

(a) the unrelieved loss to carry forward at 31 July 1998;
(b) the unrelieved advance corporation tax carried forward at 31 July 1998; and
(c) the surplus franked investment income carried forward at 31 July 1998

2 **Activity**

Underground Upheavals Limited is a United Kingdom resident trading company which commenced trading in 1961 and has no associated companies. Accounts have always been prepared to 31 December but in 1998 the accounting date was changed to 30 September. The company's results for the year ended 31 December 1997 and the nine month period to 30 September 1998 are summarised as follows

	Year ended 31 December 1997	*Period 1 January 1998 to 30 September 1998*
	£	£
Trading profits/(losses) as adjusted for taxation but before capital allowances	750,000	(362,500)
Bank interest receivable	1,700	1,250
Dividends received from UK companies	95,000	105,000
Debenture interest receivable (gross)	18,000	13,500
Profit on sale of property	–	121,000
Payment to charity under deed of covenant (gross)	10,000	10,000
Capital allowances	217,000	156,000

Notes:

(1) The bank interest is the amount receivable on an accruals basis in the respective accounting periods.

(2) The dividends received from UK companies were

£20,000 on 1 March 1997
£75,000 on 1 September 1997
£35,000 on 10 March 1998
£70,000 on 20 August 1998

(3) The debenture interest was received on the following dates

£9,000 on 30 June 1997
£9,000 on 31 December 1997
£9,000 on 30 June 1998
£4,500 was accrued at 30 September 1998

Although these are gross amounts the debenture interest has been received net of lower rate tax.

(4) Loan interest of £12,500 (gross) was paid on 30 September 1998. Deductions have been made on an accruals basis in arriving at the adjusted trading results.

(5) The covenanted payments were paid on 30 April each year.

(6) The book profit on the sale of property of £121,000 on 28 February 1998 resulted in a chargeable gain of £55,500 (after indexation).

(7) Capital allowances for both periods were writing-down allowances on plant and machinery.

(8) The company paid dividends on each of its 600,000 issued ordinary shares as follows

8 April 1997	18p final for the year ended 31 December 1996
3 September 1997	10p interim for the year ended 31 December 1997
31 March 1998	22p final for the year ended 31 December 1997
28 August 1998	5p interim for the period ended 30 September 1998

(9) The company had no surplus franked investment income, advance corporation tax or losses to carry forward on 1 January 1997, nor did it have any corporation tax profits in either 1995 or 1996.

(10) The company has claimed maximum set-off of advance corporation tax in the periods to 31 December 1996.

Task 1

Prepare entries relating to advance corporation tax and income tax as they would appear on the CT61 returns submitted to the Collector of Taxes in respect of the appropriate transactions in the year ended 31 December 1997 and the period ended 30 September 1998.

Task 2

Calculate the loss relief available in respect of the trading loss for the period to 30 September 1998, and show how this loss can be utilised assuming that all available claims are made against the earliest available profits.

Task 3

Calculate the mainstream corporation tax payable (if any) for the year ended 31 December 1997 after utilisation of any loss relief in respect of the loss sustained in the accounting period to 30 September 1998.

3 Activity

Task 1

Describe the main features of Pay and File.

Task 2

Describe the procedure for appealing against an assessment and how that appeal may be determined.

PRACTICE ASSESSMENT ACTIVITIES

QUESTIONS

ASSESSMENT ACTIVITIES - CONTENTS

AAT Assessments

The workbook contains four Assessments set by the AAT between June 1996 and December 1997. These were set for Unit 19 which predates the Revised Standards of Units 17 and 18.

We set out below the contents of this section and the Revised Unit to which the various tasks relate.

Note that Unit 19 assessed both Personal and Business Taxation as one subject. However the tasks in the assessments do divide neatly into those now assessed in Unit 17 and those now assessed in Unit 18.

Clearly you should only attempt the tasks of the units you are studying for.

In one case (Task 2 June 1996), the task requires knowledge of both units 17 and 18, and you should only attempt this task if you are studying for both units.

AAT June 1996

Task	1	Unit	17
	2		17 & 18
	3		18
	4		17
	5		17

AAT December 1996

Section 1			
Task	1.1	Unit	17
	1.2		17
Section 2			
Task	2.1	Unit	18
Section 3			
Task	3.1	Unit	18
	3.2		18

AAT June 1997

Section 1			
Task	1.1	Unit	17
	1.2		17
	1.3		17
Section 2			
Task	2.1	Unit	18
	2.2		18
Section 3			
Task	3.1	Unit	17

AAT December 1997

Section 1			
Task	1.1	Unit	18
	1.2		18
	1.3		18
Section 2			
Task	2.1	Unit	17
	2.2		17
Section 3			
Task	3.1	Unit	18
	3.2		18

TECHNICIAN STAGE
NVQ/SVQ LEVEL 4 IN ACCOUNTING
CENTRAL ASSESSMENT (TAX)
PREPARING TAXATION
COMPUTATIONS

AAT
ASSOCIATION
OF ACCOUNTING
TECHNICIANS

FRIDAY 21 JUNE 1996

Time allowed—**3 hours plus 15 minutes' reading time**

ANSWER ALL QUESTIONS

DURING THE 15 MINUTES' READING TIME YOU MAY READ AND WRITE NOTES ON THE ASSESSMENT PAPER ITSELF BUT YOU MUST NOT WRITE IN THE ANSWER BOOKLET UNTIL THE SUPERVISOR GIVES PERMISSION TO DO SO.

PLEASE DO NOT OPEN THIS BOOKLET UNTIL INSTRUCTED TO DO SO BY THE SUPERVISOR

Notes

1. Calculations should be made to the nearest month and the nearest £.
2. Ignore the effects of National Insurance in all questions.

This central assessment consists of five assessment tasks, all of which relate to the data given in the following memorandum. You should answer all five tasks.

Marks will be awarded for presentation.

The times next to each task are suggested maximum times to be spent on each task and are for guidance only. You may spend more or less than these times on each task, depending upon your skills and experience.

Any blank forms required will be found at the end of this assessment.

Task 1 Calculation of Schedule D Case 1 assessment (30 minutes)

Task 2 Income tax computation and completion of income tax return (45 minutes)

Task 3 Draft letter in answer to client's query (35 minutes)

Task 4 Calculation of capital gains (40 minutes)

Task 5 Corporation tax computation (30 minutes)

Introduction

You are an accounting technician working for a firm of accountants, Lucas and Collins. The manager of the tax department has asked you to help him with some of the tax department's work.

MEMORANDUM

Lucas and Collins

To: A Technician
From: Tax Department Manager

Subject: Tax Computations

As you know, I would like you to help me complete some of the tax department's work. I have two clients I would like you to work on:

1. Miss Bennet, who owns her own business: 'Longbourn Gift Shop'.
2. Plantagenet Limited, a company that has made certain capital asset disposals and paid a recent dividend.

The work I would like you to complete on each client is as follows:

MISS KITTY BENNET

Task 1 Calculate Miss Bennet's Schedule D Case I assessment for the 1998/99 year of assessment.

Task 2 Prepare an income tax computation for Miss Bennet for 1998/99 and complete the self employment and land and property pages for Miss Bennet's 1999 income tax return. You also need to include her savings income and claim for allowances and complete the tax calculation.

Task 3 Draft a reply to the query in Miss Bennet's letter of 10 June 1999, concerning the employment offer she has received, including computations of the figures you have used in your letter.

PLANTAGENET LIMITED

Task 4 Calculate the capital gains on the disposal of assets by Plantagenet Limited during the year ended 31 December 1998.

Task 5 Complete the corporation tax computation of Plantagenet Limited for the year ended 31 December 1998:

- add in the value of chargeable gains calculated in Task 4;
- compute the corporation tax payable;
- compute the advance corporation tax paid in the accounting period;
- show the deduction of advance corporation tax paid from the year ended 31 December 1998 and earlier years.

Tasks 1, 2 and 3

Longbourn House
Meryton
Hertfordshire

Lucas and Collins
Accountants
Barrack Road
Meryton
Hertfordshire

10 June 1999

Dear Sirs

Income tax return 1999

Further to your recent letter, I enclose all the paperwork needed to complete my tax return for the year ended 5 April 1999 as follows:

1. A statement showing the income I receive and expenses I incur from letting my flat at Pemberley Court.

2. Statements from various banks and building societies concerning interest received.

3. Dividend vouchers for my shares.

4. As you prepare the accounts for my business I presume you will already have the information concerning my business profits.

I hope this is all you need to complete the return, but if you need any further information, please do not hesitate to contact me.

Offer of employment

I've just received an offer of employment with a large giftware supplier (Darcy's Derbyshire Delights). The details of the offer are on the photocopied letter enclosed with this one.

If I accept this offer, I would keep my shop but use shop staff to run it on a day-to-day basis.

Assuming I start the employment on 1 August 1999, and that I receive the minimum commission of £100 per month, please would you write to me and let me know the following:

1. As I pay tax at 40% already, how much pay would I be left with every month, after tax, for the rest of the 1999/00 tax year? I would also like you to show me how you calculated this figure.

(NOTE: For the purposes of this calculation, assume tax rates and allowances for 1998/99 will apply during the 1999/00 tax year).

2. I understand that I will be taxed on the company car and fuel, as 'benefits-in-kind'. Please explain how you have valued the car and its fuel for tax purposes in the above calculation.

3. At the moment, I pay tax on my gift shop profits twice a year. As an employee, I understand that I would pay tax on my salary as I went along, under something called the PAYE system. Could you explain what this means, please?

I look forward to receiving your reply to these queries.

Yours faithfully

K. Bennet

Kitty Bennet

Darcy's Derbyshire Delights

Pemberley Industrial Estate
Pemberley Village
Derbyshire
SK17 5XD

Miss Kitty Bennet
Longbourn House
Meryton
Hertfordshire

Dear Miss Bennet

JOB OFFER

I am pleased to inform you that your application to become a sales executive with Darcy's Derbyshire Delights has been successful. You are already aware of the terms and conditions of the position, but I set out below details of the salary and benefit package we would offer you, for clarification.

Position:	Sales Executive (Hertfordshire)
Basic Salary:	£29,250 per annum
Commission:	Typically £100 per month
Benefits:	**Company car** New Audi A4 (2,500cc) Diesel, cost £26,000
	Diesel All fuel provided both for business and private use.

We would expect your business mileage to be approximately 12,000 miles per annum.

We look forward to hearing from you once you have had time to consider our offer.

Yours Sincerely

James Fitzwilliam

J. Fitzwilliam

Darcy's Derbyshire Delights

Pemberley Court flat
Statement of income and expenditure
Rental income

Rented from 1 January 1997 to 30 September 1998 at an annual rental of £4,000.
Rented from 1 October 1998 to date at an annual rental of £5,000.

Expenses 1998/99	£
Property management fees	800
Interest on £35,000 loan to purchase the flat	2,450
Repairs to flat roof	400

Dividend Vouchers—shares held
Wickham plc

Final dividend for the year ended 31 December 1997
Paid 31 October 1998

Tax credit	Net dividend received
£800	£3,200

Wickham plc
Interim dividend for the year ended 31 December 1998
Paid 31 March 1999

Tax credit	Net dividend received
£400	£1,600

DERBYSHIRE BUILDING SOCIETY

Interest statement 1998/99

Extra Interest Account

Miss Kitty Bennet

Account Number ABC123456

Date	Gross interest £	Tax deducted at source £	Net interest £
30.06.98	2,500.00	500.00	2,000.00
31.12.98	2,100.00	420.00	1,680.00

BANK OF DERBY

Interest statement 1998/99

Miss K Bennet

Date	Gross interest £	Tax deducted at source £	Net interest £
Deposit account no: 44332211C			
30.09.98	752.50	150.50	602.00
31.03.99	1,000.00	200.00	800.00
Business account no: 73298100B			
30.4.98	237.50	47.50	190.00

Permanent file note
Name: Kitty Bennet
Date of birth: 31 March 1965
National Insurance Number NB 61 72 21 F
Marital status: Single: one child George (born 18.2.96) living with and maintained by Miss Bennet.
Occupation: Gift shop proprietor. ('Longbourn Gift Shop')
Accounting year end: 30 April
Property owned: Main residence—Longbourn House, Meryton.
Rented property—Pemberley Court (flat). Purchased August 1989 for £40,000.

Kitty Bennet
Trading as 'Longbourn Gift Shop'
Accounts for the year ended 30 April 1998

LUCAS AND COLLINS

ACCOUNTANTS

BARRACK ROAD

MERYTON

HERTFORDSHIRE

Kitty Bennet
Trading as 'Longbourn Gift Shop'
Profit and loss account for the year ended 30 April 1998

	£	£
Sales		137,450
Less: cost of sales		
Opening stock	5,350	
Purchases	60,859	
	66,209	
Closing stock	(7,550)	
		(58,659)
Gross profit		78,791
Less: Expenses		
Wages and PAYE	25,394	
Heat and light	4,746	
Rates and insurance	4,440	
Telephone	305	
Postage and stationery	1,650	
Paper and carrier bags	617	
Motor expenses Peugeot Cars	1,229	
Motor expenses Maestro Van	725	
Professional fees	3,980	
Bank charges and interest	1,481	
Repairs and renewals	1,886	
Cleaning	925	
Profit on disposal of fixed assets	(1,158)	
Depreciation	3,715	
Sundry expenses	204	
Bank interest received	(190)	
		(49,949)
Net profit for the year		28,842

Kitty Bennet
Trading as 'Longbourn Gift Shop'
Balance sheet as at 30 April 1998

	£	£	£
Fixed assets—see schedule 1			99,454
Current assets			
Stock	7,550		
Debtors	276		
Cash at bank	3,458		
Cash in hand	4,321		
		15,605	
Current liabilities			
Trade creditors	2,626		
Sundry creditors and accruals	5,523		
Bank overdraft	5,332		
		(13,481)	
Net current assets			2,124
			101,578
Represented by			
Capital brought forward			99,516
Net profit for the year			28,842
			128,358
Drawings			(26,780)
			101,578

Kitty Bennet
Trading as 'Longbourn Gift Shop'
Fixed assets schedule 1

	Land and buildings	*Fixtures and fittings*	*Motor vehicles*	*Total*
	£	£	£	£
COST				
As at 1 May 1997	75,625	27,785	10,985	114,395
Additions	-	1,060	7,431	8,491
Disposals	-	-	(7,209)	(7,209)
As at 30 April 1998	75,625	28,845	11,207	115,677
DEPRECIATION				
As at 1 May 1997	Nil	11,246	3,410	14,656
Charge for the year	Nil	2,640	1,075	3,715
Disposals	Nil	—	(2,148)	(2,148)
As at 30 April 1998	Nil	13,886	2,337	16,223
NET BOOK VALUE				
As at 1 May 1997	£75,625	£16,539	£7,575	£99,739
As at 30 April 1998	£75,625	£14,959	£8,870	£99,454

Notes to the Tax Department from the Accounts Department concerning Kitty Bennet's accounts for the year ended 30 April 1998

Wages includes a salary of £15,000 paid to Kitty Bennet's sister, Lydia Bennet, who works full-time in the business.

Analysis of sundry expenses £204	£
Parking Fines—Kitty Bennet	30
Donation to local Playgroup	50
Donation to Oxfam	100
Chamber of Commerce subscription	24
	£204

Bank interest received net, received 30 April 1998	190

Analysis of additions to fixed assets

1 August 1997	Cash register	567
10 August 1997	Peugeot 205	7,431
1 January 1998	Sales counter	493

Disposals of fixed assets—sale proceeds

10 August 1997	Peugeot 405	2,107
2 February 1998	Maestro Van	4,113

Neither vehicle was sold for more than original cost

Telephone and motor expenses
The telephone bills are 10% private and 90% business, and the Peugeot cars are used 40% privately and 60% for business.

NOTE: The tax written down values brought forward, for capital allowance purposes are as follows:

General pool: £6,500
Peugeot 405: £7,985

Tasks 4 and 5

MEMORANDUM

Lucas and Collins

To: A Technician

From: Tax Manager

Subject: Plantagenet Limited

Date: 17 June 1999

The main director and sole shareholder of this company, Mr Palliser, is considering retirement in the next few weeks.

To this end, the company paid him a very large dividend. The dividend cheque paid from the company to Mr Palliser was £800,000. The dividend was paid on 30 December 1998.

The company received a dividend cheque of £20,000 from its 100% U.K. subsidiary, Silverbridge Limited, on the same date. Silverbridge Limited had paid the advance corporation tax of £5,000 to the Inland Revenue.

I have given you the corporation tax computations of the company for the last four years (shown on the next page).

I should be grateful if you would revise the corporation tax computations for the five years to 31 December 1998 as appropriate:

(a) by calculating the capital gains on the sale of assets (year ended 31 December 1998)—details on next page;

(b) by calculating ACT paid on the dividend paid to Mr Palliser (year ended 31 December 1998) and showing how it will be offset against corporation tax in the accounting periods shown (years ended 31 December 1994 to 31 December 1998).

I enclose a brief note on the uses of surplus ACT, which was on Plantagenet Limited's file from last year, and which you may find helpful:

Surplus ACT
Surplus ACT is ACT paid in excess of the maximum permissible offset of ACT in a particular accounting period.

Uses of surplus ACT:
Surplus ACT can be used as follows:

- Carried back and deducted from corporation tax liabilities of the accounting periods beginning in the six years preceding the accounting period of surplus, claiming against later periods before earlier periods; and

- Carried forward against the corporation tax liabilities of future accounting periods, indefinitely.

Note: the amount of ACT deducted from the corporation tax liability of an accounting period can never exceed the maximum for that period calculated as:

Profits Chargeable to Corporation Tax × ACT rate for the accounting period.

Plantagenet Limited
Abbreviated corporation tax computations

	Year ended 31/12/94	*Year ended 31/12/95*	*Year ended 31/12/96*	*Year ended 31/12/97*	*Year ended 31/12/98*
	£	£	£	£	£
Sch D Case 1 per computations	1,111,337	1,113,059	504,325	159,095	663,143
Capital gains	372,836	142,517	136,477	0	*
Capital allowances	(97,493)	(82,435)	(85,059)	(96,566)	(99,614)
Charges on income	(148,537)	(10,132)	(241,619)	(199,570)	(217,497)
Profits chargeable to tax	£1,238,143	£1,163,009	£314,124	NIL	*
Corporation tax	408,587	383,793	94,127	0	*
Less ACT	0	(100,000)	(10,000)	0	*
	£408,587	£283,793	£84,127	0	*

* = figure not yet entered.

Plantagenet Limited
Capital asset disposals
Year ended 31 December 1998

Cars

Rolls Royce	
Purchased	31 July 1954
Cost	£550
Sold	30 December 1998
Proceeds	£13,000

Property

Purchased	17 January 1970	
Cost	£2,000	
Enhancements		
13 April 1976	£9,500	
2 August 1982	£17,500	(The enhancement of £17,500 was in respect of a temporary warehouse which was demolished in May 1992)
31 October 1992	£85,000	
Sold	1 July 1998	
Proceeds	£419,539	
Cost of disposal	£4,000	
Market Value March 1982	£125,000	

Shares in Phineas Finn Limited (unconnected third party)
Listed on London Stock Exchange

Purchased

No of shares		Cost (£)
100	13 August 1982	100
20,000	7 November 1987	25,000
20,100	12 December 1989	Bonus
160,300	13 February 1993	275,000

Sold

No of shares		Disposal Proceeds (£)
85,000	21 July 1998	325,000

Income for the year ended 5April 1999

Inland Revenue **SELF-EMPLOYMENT**

Fill in these boxes first

Name	Tax reference
Kitty Bennett	

If you want help, look up the box numbers in the Notes

Business details

Name of business	Description of business
3.1 Longbourn Gift Shop	3.2 Gift Shop

Address of business

3.3

Postcode

Accounting period - *read the Notes, page SEN2 before filling in these boxes*

Start	End
3.4 01/05/97	3.5 30/04/98

- Tick box 3.5A if you entered details for all relevant accounting periods on last year's Tax Return and boxes 3.11 to 3.70 will be blank — 3.5A
- Tick box 3.6 if details in boxes 3.1 or 3.3 have changed since your last Tax Return — 3.6
- Tick box 3.7 if your accounts do not cover the period from the last accounting date (explain why in the 'Additional information' box below) — 3.7
- Tick box 3.8A if your accounting date has changed (only if this is a permanent change and you want it to count for tax) — 3.8A
- Tick box 3.8B if this is the second or further change (explain why you have not used the same date as last year in the 'Additional information' box) — 3.8B
- Date of commencement if after 5 April 1996 — 3.9 / /
- Date of cessation if before 6 April 1999 — 3.10 / /

Additional information

Income and expenses - annual turnover below £15,000

*If your annual turnover is £15,000 or more, **ignore** boxes 3.11 to 3.13.* *Now fill in Page SE2*

*If your annual turnover is below £15,000, **fill in boxes 3.11 to 3.13 instead of Page SE2**. Read the Notes, page SEN2.*

- Turnover, other business receipts and goods etc. taken for personal use (and balancing charges) — 3.11 £
- Expenses allowable for tax (including capital allowances) — 3.12 £

box 3.11 *minus* box 3.12

Net profit (put figure in brackets if a loss) — 3.13 £

Now fill in Page SE3

SA103

Income and expenses - annual turnover £15,000 or more

You must fill in this Page if your annual turnover is £15,000 or more - read the Notes, page SEN2

If you were registered for VAT, do the figures in boxes 3.16 to 3.51, include VAT? **3.14** [ ] or exclude VAT? **3.15** ✓

	Disallowable expenses included in boxes 3.33 to 3.50	Total expenses	Sales/business income (turnover)
			3.16 £137,450.00
• Cost of sales	**3.17** £	**3.33** £58,659.00	
• Construction industry subcontractor costs	**3.18** £	**3.34** £	
• Other direct costs	**3.19** £	**3.35** £617-00	box 3.16 *minus* (box 3.33 + box 3.34 + box 3.35)
		Gross profit/(loss)	**3.36** £78174-00
		Other income/profits	**3.37** £190
• Employee costs	**3.20** £	**3.38** £25,394	
• Premises costs	**3.21** £	**3.39** £10111	
• Repairs	**3.22** £	**3.40** £1886	
• General administrative expenses	**3.23** £ 31	**3.41** £1955	
• Motor expenses	**3.24** £ 492	**3.42** £1954	
• Travel and subsistence	**3.25** £	**3.43** £	
• Advertising, promotion and entertainment	**3.26** £	**3.44** £	
• Legal and professional costs	**3.27** £	**3.45** £3,980	
• Bad debts	**3.28** £	**3.46** £	
• Interest	**3.29** £	**3.47** £1,481	
• Other finance charges	**3.30** £	**3.48** £	
• Depreciation and loss/(profit) on sale	**3.31** £2557	**3.49** £2,557	
• Other expenses	**3.32** £130	**3.50** £204	total of boxes 3.38 to 3.50
	Put the total of boxes 3.17 to 3.32 in **box 3.53 below**	Total expenses	**3.51** £
			boxes 3.36 + 3.37 *minus* box 3.51
		Net profit/(loss)	**3.52** £28,842.00

Tax adjustments to net profit or loss

	total of boxes 3.17 to 3.32	
• Disallowable expenses	**3.53** £3210	
• Goods etc. taken for personal use and other adjustments (apart from disallowable expenses) that increase profits	**3.54** £	
• Balancing charges	**3.55** £	boxes 3.53 + 3.54 + 3.55
Total additions to net profit (deduct from net loss)		**3.56** £3210
• Capital allowances	**3.57** £5769	boxes 3.57 + 3.58
• Deductions from net profit (add to net loss)	**3.58** £190	**3.59** £5959
		boxes 3.52 + 3.56 *minus* box 3.59
Net business profit for tax purposes (put figure in brackets if a loss)		**3.60** £26093

Now fill in Page SE3

You must fill in this Page (leave blank any boxes that do not apply to you)

Capital allowances - summary

	Capital allowances	Balancing charge
• Motor cars (Separate calculations must be made for each motor car costing more than £12,000 and for cars used partly for private motoring.)	3.61 £ 4642	3.62 £
• Other business plant and machinery	3.63 £ 1127	3.64 £
• Agricultural or Industrial Buildings Allowance (A separate calculation must be made for each block of expenditure.)	3.65 £	3.66 £
• Other capital allowances claimed (Separate calculations must be made.)	3.67 £	3.68 £
	total of column above	total of column above
Total capital allowances/balancing charges	3.69 £ 5769	3.70 £

Adjustments to arrive at taxable profit or loss

Basis period begins 3.71 01 / 05 / 97 and ends 3.72 30 / 04 / 98

- Tick box 3.72A if the figure in box 3.88 is provisional 3.72A
- Tick box 3.72B if the special arrangements for certain trades detailed in the guidance notes apply 3.72B

Profit or loss of this account for tax purposes (box 3.13 or 3.60) 3.73 £ 26,093

Adjustment to arrive at profit or loss for this basis period 3.74 £

- Overlap profit brought forward 3.75 £
- Deduct overlap relief used this year 3.76 £
- Overlap profit carried forward 3.77 £

Adjustment for farmers' averaging (see Notes, page SEN8 if you made a loss for 1998-99) 3.78 £

Net profit for 1998-99 (if loss, enter '0') 3.79 £ 26,093

Allowable loss for 1998-99 (if you make a profit, enter '0') 3.80 £

- Loss offset against other income for 1998-99 3.81 £
- Loss to carry back 3.82 £
- Loss to carry forward (that is allowable loss not claimed in any other way) 3.83 £
- Losses brought forward from last year 3.84 £
- Losses brought forward from last year used this year 3.85 £

Taxable profit after losses brought forward (box 3.79 *minus* box 3.85) 3.86 £ 26,093

- Any other business income (for example, Business Start-up Allowance received in 1998-99) 3.87 £

Total taxable profits from this business (box 3.86 + box 3.87) 3.88 £ 26,093

Class 4 National Insurance Contributions

- Tick this box if exception or deferment applies — **3.89** [ ]
- Adjustments to profit chargeable to Class 4 National Insurance Contributions — **3.90** £

Class 4 National Insurance Contributions due — **3.91** £

Subcontractors in the construction industry

- Deductions made by contractors on account of tax (you must send your SC60s to us) — **3.92** £

Summary of balance sheet

Leave these boxes blank if you do not have a balance sheet

■ ***Assets***

• Plant, machinery and motor vehicles	3.93	£ 23829		
• Other fixed assets (premises, goodwill, investments etc.)	3.94	£ 75625		
• Stock and work in progress	3.95	£ 7550		
• Debtors/prepayments/other current assets	3.96	£ 276		
• Bank/building society balances	3.97	£ 3458		total of boxes 3.93 to 3.98
• Cash in hand	3.98	£ 4,321	3.99	£ 115059

■ ***Liabilities***

• Trade creditors/accruals	3.100	£ 8149		
• Loans and overdrawn bank accounts	3.101	£ 5332		total of boxes 3.100 to 3.102
• Other liabilities	3.102	£	3.103	£ 13481

■ ***Net business assets*** (put the figure in brackets if you had net business liabilities) — box 3.99 *minus* box 3.103 — **3.104** £ 101,578

■ ***Represented by***

Capital Account

• Balance at start of period*	3.105	£ 99 516		
• Net profit/(loss)*	3.106	£ 28842		
• Capital introduced	3.107	£		
• Drawings	3.108	£ 26 780		total of boxes 3.105 to 3.107 *minus* box 3.108
• Balance at end of period*			3.109	£ 101 578

* If the Capital Account is overdrawn, or the business made a net loss, show the figure in brackets.

Tax deducted from trading income

- Any tax deducted (excluding deductions made by contractors on account of tax) from trading income. — **3.120** £

Note: box numbers 3.110 to 3.119 are not used

Additional information

Now fill in any other supplementary Pages that apply to you.
Otherwise, go back to Page 2 of your Tax Return and finish filling it in.

Inland Revenue

Income for the year ended 5 April 1999

LAND AND PROPERTY

Fill in these boxes first

Name

Tax reference

Are you claiming Rent a Room relief for gross rents of £4,250 or less? No Yes

(Or £2,125 if the claim is shared?)

Read the Notes on page LN2 to find out

- **whether you can claim Rent a Room relief; and**
- **how to claim relief for gross rents over £4,250**

If 'Yes', and this is your only income from UK property, you have finished these Pages

Is your income from furnished holiday lettings? No Yes

If 'No', turn over and fill in Page L2 to give details of your property income

If 'Yes', fill in boxes 5.1 to 5.18 before completing Page L2

Furnished holiday lettings

- Income from furnished holiday lettings — **5.1** £

■ *Expenses* (furnished holiday lettings only)

- Rent, rates, insurance, ground rents etc. — **5.2** £
- Repairs, maintenance and renewals — **5.3** £
- Finance charges, including interest — **5.4** £
- Legal and professional costs — **5.5** £
- Cost of services provided, including wages — **5.6** £
- Other expenses — **5.7** £

total of boxes 5.2 to 5.7 — **5.8** £

box 5.1 *minus* box 5.8

Net profi (put figures in brackets if a loss) — **5.9** £

■ *Tax adjustments*

- Private use — **5.10** £
- Balancing charges — **5.11** £

box 5.10 + box 5.11 — **5.12** £

- Capital allowances — **5.13** £

boxes 59 + 5.12 *minus* box 5.13

Profit for the year (copy to box 5.19). If loss, enter '0' in box 5.14 and put the loss in box 5.15 — **5.14** £

boxes 59 + 5.12 *minus* box 5.13

Loss for the yea (if you have entered '0' in box 5.14) — **5.15** £

- Loss offset against 1998-99 total income — **5.16** £

see Notes, page LN4

- Loss carried back — **5.17** £

see Notes, page LN4

- Loss offset against other income from property (copy to box 5.38) — **5.18** £

SA105

Other property income

■ ***Income***

• Furnished holiday lettings profits	copy from box 5.14 **5.19** £		
• Rents and other income from land and property	**5.20** £	Tax deducted **5.21** £	
• Chargeable premiums	**5.22** £		boxes 5.19 + 5.20 + 5.22 **5.23** £

■ ***Expenses*** (do not include figures you have already put in boxes 5.2 to 5.7 on Page L1)

• Rent, rates, insurance, ground rents etc.	**5.24** £		
• Repairs, maintenance and renewals	**5.25** £		
• Finance charges, including interest	**5.26** £		
• Legal and professional costs	**5.27** £		
• Costs of services provided, including wages	**5.28** £		
• Other expenses	**5.29** £		total of boxes 5.24 to 5.29 **5.30** £
Net profit (put figures in brackets if a loss)			box 5.23 *minus* box 5.30 **5.31** £

■ ***Tax adjustments***

• Private use	**5.32** £		
• Balancing charges	**5.33** £		box 5.32 + box 5.33 **5.34** £
• Rent a Room exempt amount	**5.35** £		
• Capital allowances	**5.36** £		
• 10% wear and tear	**5.37** £		
• Furnished holiday lettings losses (from box 5.18)	**5.38** £		total of boxes 5.35 to 5.38 **5.39** £
Adjusted profit (if loss enter '0' in box 5.40 and put the loss in box 5.41)			boxes 5.31 + 5.34 *minus* box 5.39 **5.40** £
Adjusted loss (if you have entered '0' in box 5.40)		boxes 5.31 + 5.34 *minus* box 5.39 **5.41** £	
• Loss brought forward from previous year			**5.42** £
Profit for the year			box 5.40 *minus* box 5.42 **5.43** £
• Loss offset against total income		**5.44** £	
• Loss to carry forward to following year		**5.45** £	
• Pooled expenses from 'one estate election' carried forward		**5.46** £	

Tick box 5.47 if these Pages include details of property let jointly	**5.47**

Now fill in any other supplementary Pages that apply to you.
Otherwise, go back to page 2 of your Tax Return and finish filling it in.

INCOME *for the year ended 5 April 1999*

Q10 Did you receive any income from UK savings and investments? NO [ ] YES [ ]

If yes, fill in boxes 10.1 to 10.32 as appropriate. Include only your share from any joint savings and investments.

■ *Interest*

	Amount after tax deducted	Tax deducted	Gross amount before tax
• Interest from UK banks, building societies and deposit takers			
- where **no tax** has been deducted			Taxable amount 10.1 £
- where **tax has** been deducted	10.2 £	10.3 £	10.4 £
• Interest distributions from UK authorised unit trusts and open-ended investment companies (dividend distributions go below)	10.5 £	10.6 £	10.7 £
• National Savings (other than FIRST Option Bonds and the first £70 of interest from a National Savings Ordinary Account)			Taxable amount 10.8 £
• National Savings FIRST Option Bonds	10.9 £	10.10 £	10.11 £
• Other income from UK savings and investments (except dividends)	10.12 £	10.13 £	10.14 £

■ *Dividends*

• Dividends and other qualifying distributions from UK companies	Dividend/distribution 10.15 £	Tax credit 10.16 £	Dividend/distribution plus credit 10.17 £
• Dividend distributions from UK authorised unit trusts and open-ended investment companies	Dividend/distribution 10.18 £	Tax credit 10.19 £	Dividend/distribution plus credit 10.20 £
• Scrip dividends from UK companies	Dividend 10.21 £	Notional tax 10.22 £	Dividend plus notional tax 10.23 £
• Foreign income dividends from UK companies	Dividend 10.24 £	Notional tax 10.25 £	Dividend plus notional tax 10.26 £
• Foreign income dividend distributions from UK authorised unit trusts and open-ended investment companies	Dividend 10.27 £	Notional tax 10.28 £	Dividend plus notional tax 10.29 £
• Non-qualifying distributions and loans written off	10.30 £	Notional tax 10.31 £	Taxable amount 10.32 £

 Please turn over

ALLOWANCES for the year ended 5 April 1999

Q16 *You get your personal allowance of £4,195 automatically.* ***If you were born before 6 April 1934, enter your date of birth in box 21.4*** *- you may get higher age-related allowances.*

Do you want to claim any of the following allowances? NO ☐ YES ☐ If yes, please read pages 23 to 26 of your Tax Return Guide and then fill in boxes 16.1 to 16.28 as appropriate.

- ***Blind person's allowance*** — Date of registration (if first year of claim) 16.1 / / — Local authority (or other register) 16.2

- ***Transitional allowance*** (for some wives with husbands on low income if received in earlier years).
  - Tick to claim and give details in the 'Additional information' box on page 8 *(please see page 23 of your Tax Return Guide for what is needed)* 16.3
  - If you want to calculate your tax, enter the amount of transitional allowance you can have in box 16.4 16.4 £

- ***Married couple's allowance for a married man** - see page 24 of your Tax Return Guide.*
  - Wife's full name 16.5
  - Date of marriage (if after 5 April 1998) 16.6 / /
  - Wife's date of birth (if before 6 April 1934) 16.7 / /
  - Tick box 16.8 if you or your wife have allocated **half** the allowance to her 16.8
  - *box number 16.9 is not used*
  - Tick box 16.10 if you and your wife have allocated **all** the allowance to her 16.10

- ***Married couple's allowance for a married woman** - see page 24 of your Tax Return Guide.*
  - Date of marriage (if after 5 April 1998) 16.11 / /
  - Husband's full name 16.12
  - Tick box 16.13 if you or your husband have allocated **half** the allowance to you 16.13
  - *box number 16.14 is not used*
  - Tick box 16.15 if you and your husband have allocated **all** the allowance to you 16.15

- ***Additional personal allowance** (available in some circumstances if you have a child living with you - see page 25 of your Tax Return Guide).*
  - Tick box 16.16A if you are claiming the married couple's allowance **and** additional personal allowance because your spouse was unable to work, because of illness or disablement, throughout the year ended 5 April 1999 16.16A
  - Name of the child claimed for 16.16
  - Child's date of birth 16.17 / /
  - Tick if child lives with you 16.18
  - Name of university etc/type of training if the child is 16 or over on 6 April 1998 and in full time education or training 16.19

Sharing a claim

Name and address of other person claiming 16.20

Postcode

- Enter your share as a percentage 16.21 %
- If share not agreed, enter the number of days in the year ended 5 April 1999 that the child lived with
  - you 16.22 days
  - other person 16.23 days

- ***Widow's bereavement allowance*** — Date of your husband's death 16.24 / /

- ***Transfer of surplus allowances** - see page 26 of your Tax Return Guide before you fill in boxes 16.25 to 16.28.*
  - Tick if you want your spouse to have your unused allowances 16.25
  - Tick if you want to have your spouse's unused allowances 16.26

***Please give details in the 'Additional information' box on page 8** - see page 26 of your Tax Return Guide for what is needed.*

If you want to calculate your tax, enter the amount of the surplus allowance you can have.

- Blind person's **surplus** allowance 16.27 £
- Married couple's **surplus** allowance 16.28 £

OTHER INFORMATION *for the year ended 5 April 1999*

Q17 **Have you already had any 1998-99 tax refunded or set off by your Tax Office or the DSS Benefits Agency?** *Read the notes for box 17.1 on page 26 of your Tax Return Guide* — NO / YES — If yes, enter the amount of the refund in box 17.1.

17.1 £

Q18 **Do you want to calculate your tax?** — NO / YES — If yes, do it now and then fill in boxes 18.1 to 18.9. Your Tax Calculation Guide will help.

- Unpaid tax for earlier years included in your tax code for 1998-99 — 18.1 £
- Tax due for 1998-99 included in your tax code for a later year — 18.2 £
- Total tax and Class 4 NIC due for 1998-99 **before** you made any payments on account *(put the amount in brackets if an overpayment)* — 18.3 £
- Tax due for earlier years — 18.4 £
- Tick box 18.5 if you have calculated tax overpaid for earlier years (and enter the amount in the 'Additional information' box on page 8) — 18.5
- Your first payment on account for 1999-2000 *(include the pence)* — 18.6 £

  Tick box 18.7 if you are making a claim to reduce your 1999-2000 payments on account and say why in the 'Additional information' box — 18.7

  Tick box 18.8 if you do **not** need to make 1999-2000 payments on account — 18.8
- 1999-2000 tax you are reclaiming now — 18.9 £

Q19 **Do you want to claim a repayment if you have paid too much tax?** *(If you tick 'No' or the tax you have overpaid is below £10, I will use the amount you are owed to reduce your next tax bill.)* — NO / YES — If yes, fill in boxes 19.1 to 19.12 as appropriate.

Should the repayment (or payment) be sent:

- to you? *Tick box 19.1* — 19.1

or

- to your bank or building society account or other nominee? *Tick box 19.2* — 19.2

If you ticked either box 19.2 or 19.9, fill in boxes 19.3 to 19.8, 19.11 and 19.12 as appropriate.

Your (or your nominee's) bank or building society — 19.3

Branch sort code — 19.4 – –

Account number — 19.5

Name of account — 19.6

Building society ref. — 19.7

If your nominee is your agent, *tick box 19.9 and complete boxes 19.10 to 19.12* — 19.9

Agent's ref. for you — 19.10

I authorise — 19.8 Name of your nominee/agent

Nominee's address — 19.11 Postcode

to receive on my behalf the amount due

This authority must be signed by you. A photocopy of your signature will not do. — 19.12 Signature

Q20 **Are your details on the front of the Tax Return wrong?** — NO / YES — If yes, please make any corrections on the front of the form.

Q21 **Please give other personal details in boxes 21.1 to 21.6** *This information helps us to be more efficient and effective and may support claims you have made elsewhere in your Tax Return*

Please give a daytime telephone number if convenient. It is often simpler to phone if we need to ask you about your Tax Return.

Your telephone number — 21.1

or, if you prefer, your agent's telephone number — 21.2

(also give your agent's name and reference in the 'Additional information' box on page 8)

Enter your first two forenames — 21.5

Say if you are single, married, widowed, divorced or separated — 21.3

Date of birth — 21.4 / /

Enter your date of birth if you are self-employed, or you were born before 6 April 1934, or you have ticked the 'Yes' box in Question 14, or you are claiming relief for Venture Capital Trust subscriptions

Enter your National Insurance number (if known) — 21.6

TECHNICIAN STAGE
NVQ/SVQ LEVEL 4 IN ACCOUNTING
CENTRAL ASSESSMENT (TAX)
PREPARING TAXATION
COMPUTATIONS

AAT
ASSOCIATION
OF ACCOUNTING
TECHNICIANS

FRIDAY 6 DECEMBER 1996

Time allowed—**3 hours plus 15 minutes' reading time**

ANSWER ALL QUESTIONS

DURING THE 15 MINUTES' READING TIME YOU MAY READ AND WRITE NOTES ON THE ASSESSMENT PAPER ITSELF BUT YOU MUST NOT WRITE IN THE ANSWER BOOKLET UNTIL THE SUPERVISOR GIVES PERMISSION TO DO SO.

PLEASE DO NOT OPEN THIS BOOKLET UNTIL INSTRUCTED TO DO SO BY THE SUPERVISOR

Notes:

1. All calculations should be made to the nearest month and the nearest £.

2. Ignore the effects of national insurance in all questions.

This central assessment consists of three sections, all of which are to be answered using the information given in this assessment paper. You are reminded that competence must be achieved in each section and you should answer ALL tasks within EACH section.

The times next to each task within a section are suggested maximum times to be spent on each task and are for guidance only. You may spend more or less than these times on each task, depending upon your skills and experience.

Any blank forms required will be found at the end of this assessment.

Marks will be awarded for presentation.

SECTION 1

Task 1.1 Corporation tax computation (40) minutes)
Task 1.2 Complete form CT200 (corporation tax return using the short version of the return) (25 minutes)

SECTION 2:

Task 2.1 Income tax computation and completion of income tax return (45 minutes)

SECTION 3

Task 3.1 Capital gains tax computation (30 minutes)
Task 3.2 Draft letter in answer to client's queries (40 minutes)

Introduction

You are Nick Prince, an accounting technician working for a firm of accountants, Garrett, Turner and Co. The firm has a specialist tax department, and you have been asked to help out with some of the tax department's work. The work required is set out in the attached memorandum from the partner in charge of the tax department.

MEMORANDUM

Garrett, Turner and Co

To:	Nick Prince, Accounting Technician	**Date:**	6 December 1999
From:	Alison Handel, Tax Partner		

Subject: **Tax Department Work**

I am pleased that you are going to have some time to help us out. We have a lot of work outstanding at the moment and I would like you to prepare some computations and returns for one of our clients, Cole Limited.

The company is a local engineering firm and our responsibility is for the corporate tax affairs of the company itself and the income tax affairs of its main shareholder, Mr Nathaniel King, and his wife Peggy.

Our audit department has just finalised the company's accounts for the accounting year ended 31 March 1999.

I would like you to do the following work:

Cole Limited

Section 1

Task 1.1 Prepare a corporation tax computation for Cole Limited for the year ended 31 March 1999. (Using the extracts from the accounts, accounts file schedules and completed form CT61 provided.)

Task 1.2 Complete form CT200 for Cole Limited for the year ended 31 March 1999. Please note that, as usual, we will use the short version of the return. This means that we will complete Section 2 of the return instead of Section 3; Sections 4, 5, 8 and 9 of the return may require completion if there is relevant information.

Mr Nathaniel King and Mrs Peggy King

Section 2

Task 2.1 Prepare an income tax computation for 1998/99 for Mr Nathaniel King (showing the balance of tax due under self-assessment, after offset of tax already deducted at source) and complete pages 3, 5, 6 and 7, and the employment pages of his 1999 income tax return (the return for the 1998/99 tax year), using the information provided.

Section 3

Task 3.1 Prepare a computation of capital gains tax payable by Mrs Peggy King for 1998/99.

Task 3.2 Draft a reply to Mrs Peggy King's letter of 25 November 1999, concerning the tax implications of her investment plans.

Information for Section 1, Tasks 1.1 and 1.2

Extracts from accounts

Cole Limited
Financial Statements
For the year ended 31 March 1999

Garret, Turner & Co
Accountants
Debit Street
Barchester

Cole Limited

Extract From The Report of the Directors

The directors present their annual report and the accounts for the year ended 31 March 1999.

Principal Activity

The company's principal activity during the year was the supply of engineering services.

Directors and their interests

The directors in office at the date of this report, both of whom served throughout the year, were Mr Nathaniel King and Mrs Peggy King.

The interest of the directors in the share capital of the company was as follows:

	Interest in £1 ordinary shares	
	At 31/3/99	At 31/3/98
Mr N King	98	98
Mrs P King	2	2

Cole Limited - Profit and Loss Account
For the year ended 31 March 1999

	1999		*1998*	
	£	£	£	£
TURNOVER		53,346		98,710
Administration expenses	30,498		15,827	
Other operating charges	244		480	
		(30,742)		(16,307)
OPERATING PROFIT		22,604		82,403
Interest payable and similar charges		(876)		(130)
Interest receivable and similar income		15,000		0
PROFIT ON ORDINARY ACTIVITIES		36,728		82,273
TAXATION ON PROFIT ON ORDINARY ACTIVITIES		(10,350)		(10,781)
PROFIT ON ORDINARY ACTIVITIES AFTER TAXATION		26,378		71,492
Dividends		(33,000)		(31,980)
RETAINED (LOSS)/PROFIT FOR THE YEAR		(6,622)		39,512
RETAINED PROFIT/ (LOSS) BROUGHT FORWARD		39,346		(166)
RETAINED PROFIT CARRIED FORWARD		32,724		39,346

Cole Limited
Balance sheet as at 31 March 1999

	Note	1999 £	1999 £	1998 £	1998 £
FIXED ASSETS					
Tangible assets	7		28,917		34,650
CURRENT ASSETS					
Debtors		6,467		8,481	
Cash at bank and in hand		1,474		2,904	
		7,941		11,385	
CREDITORS					
Amounts falling due within one year		(4,034)		(6,589)	
NET CURRENT ASSETS			3,907		4,796
NET ASSETS			£32,824		£39,446
CAPITAL AND RESERVES					
Equity share capital			100		100
Reserves			32,724		39,346
			£32,824		£39,446

Cole Limited
Extracts from the notes to the accounts
(The full notes to the accounts have not been reproduced, only those required to answer the assessment.)

Note 7
Tangible Fixed Assets

	Motor vehicles £	Plant and Machinery £	Total £
Cost			
At 1 April 1998	36,600	20,000	56,600
Additions	6,000	5,000	11,000
Disposals	(5,000)	(10,000)	(15,000)
At 31 March 1999	37,600	15,000	52,600
Depreciation			
At 1 April 1998	9,150	12,800	21,950
Charge for the year	7,613	1,520	9,133
Disposals	(2,000)	(5,400)	(7,400)
At 31 March 1999	14,763	8,920	23,683
NBV at 31 March 1999	*£22,837*	*£6,080*	*£28,917*
NBV at 1 April 1998	*£27,450*	*£7,200*	*£34,650*

Cole Limited
Accounts file information
Note from the Accounts Department to the Tax Department
Concerning information collected during the preparation of Cole Limited's accounts for the year ended 31 March 1999
Please find attached the information you requested concerning Cole Limited's accounts:

1. Fixed assets:

Additions:
Motor Vehicles
21.12.98 Purchase of Vauxhall Corsa car for £6,000
Plant and Machinery
30.6.98 Purchase of new grinding machine for £5,000

Disposals
Motor Vehicles
21.12.98 Sold Vauxhall Nova car for £2,500 (original cost £5,000)
Plant and machinery
10.9.98 Sold old grinding machine for £15,000 (original cost £10,000)
Note: Please ignore any capital gains consequences on the sale of the old grinding machine

Profit on sale of fixed assets
The profit on sale of fixed assets credited to the profit and loss account of the company was £9,900.

Note: The tax written down values of the assets at 1 April 1998 are as follows:

General pool:	£11,250
FA 80 pool:	£2,500
Expensive car	
Land Rover Discovery:	£23,600

2. Profit and loss account income and expenditure:

Details of the profit and loss account expenditure (incurred in arriving at profit on ordinary activities before taxation) you asked for are as follows:

Entertaining:	£
Costs of entertaining customers	3,483
Cost of a staff party at Christmas	250
	£3,733

Bad debts:	£
The bad and doubtful debts account was made up as follows:	
General provision brought forward (2% of debtors)	(170)
Specific trade debt written off	500
Loan to employee written off	250
General provision carried forward at 31 March 1999 (2% of debtors)	130
Charge to the profit and loss account	£710

Motor expenses:
Motor expenses included £2,000 incurred in the running costs of
Mr King's (the managing director of Cole Limited) Land Rover Discovery.

Cole Limited
Extracts from the accounts file (continued)

Legal and professional fees:	£
Costs of recovering trade debts	250
Legal fees re employee contracts of service	125
Legal fees re costs of successful tax appeal	324
	£699

Other payments:

Gift aid payment to the St Johns Ambulance Association (a charity): £5,000 (grossed up for basic rate for inclusion in the accounts).

Details of profit and loss account income are as follows:

Interest receivable and similar income:	£	
Patent royalties received	10,000	(gross)
Bank interest receivable (analysis of this figure is shown below)	5,000	
	15,000	

Bank interest receivable is made up as follows:	£
Accrued income at 1 April 1998	(525)
Received in year	5,171
Accrued income at 31 March 1999	354
Bank interest receivable per the profit and loss account	5,000

3. Tax payments:

In error, the company paid £1,000 of corporation tax on account on 1 December 1999 in respect of its year ended 31 March 1999. Corporation tax was not due until 1 January 2000. Please take this payment into account when completing Form CT200.

4. Payments of ACT and Income Tax

The company completed Inland Revenue form CT61 for the return period ended 31 December 1998 during its accounting period. A copy of this form is reproduced for your information.

Note: Form CT61 is the return used to show advance corporation tax (ACT) payments on dividends paid and received, and income tax payments and tax credits.

Inland Revenue

Return of Company Payments, Distributions and Interest

Collector of Taxes
Inland Revenue Accounts Office (Shipley)
BRADFORD
West Yorkshire BD98 8AA
Telephone: Bradford (01274) 530750

1	2	3	4
	223421	31.12.98	313 42679 00013
	Company regn. no.	Accounting date	Accounts Office ref.

IMPORTANT: Please enter in these 4 boxes the details from your CT61 Notice

Advance Corporation Tax on **Qualifying Distributions**
Income Tax deducted from **Company Payments** and **Interest**
Income Tax payable on **Gilt Interest** received without deduction of tax
Tax on manufactured payments received from abroad

- Please use this form when you need to make a Return of company payments, distributions and interest. **You must give all the information asked for on this page and sign the declaration below.** But you need only fill in the other parts of the Return which are relevant to your company. Only use the CT61 Supplement if you need to make a return of Foreign Income Dividends, 'deemed FIDs' or Gilt Interest.
- You are required to make your Return, and pay any tax, within 14 days after the end of the Return Period. Send the Return back to me in the envelope provided.
- *The enclosed CT61 Notes will help you.*
- If your Return shows that tax is payable use the payslip on the enclosed form CT61Notice.
- When you send back this Return **please also enclose the CT61 Notice**, even if no payment is enclosed.

Company details

Name of company: COLE LIMITED

Address:
Enter the address you would like future CT61 Returns sent to

UNIT 1
BARCHESTER TRADING ESTATE
BARCHESTER
Postcode

Please tick if this is a change of Registered Office '✓' [ ]

Period covered by this Return

Return Periods are fixed by law. See CT61 Notes page 3 for guidance.

	Day	Month	19	Year	to	Day	Month	19	Year
Return period ►	01	10	19	98	to	31	12	19	98
being part of the Accounting period ►	01	04	19	98	to	31	03	19	98

Example: Distribution paid on 25 April 1997, and the accounting period is year to 31 December 1997. Enter:

Return period ►	01	04	19	97	to	30	06	19	97
being part of the Accounting period ►	01	01	19	97	to	31	12	19	97

For official use only
901

Declaration

False statements can result in prosecution

To the best of my knowledge the information given in this Return (and the Supplement, if used) is correct and complete

Signature: N King

Name *in CAPITALS*: NATHANIEL KING

State in what capacity you make this Return: MANAGING DIRECTOR

It would assist if you can state your daytime telephone number and extension here

Date: 31.12.98

Please tick if CT61 Supplement is attached '✓' [ ]

21267 4.97 Niceday Stationery & Print Limited BMSD4/97 W0H7003

1 Advance Corporation Tax (ACT) on Qualifying Distributions

Use Part 1 to calculate the ACT payable on Distributions paid.
Use Part 2 below to record Franked Investment Income received.
Franked investment income in box 23 is set-off to reduce the ACT payable in Part 1.
For further information see Notes page 2.

List separately the payments made on different dates. If you need more room please attach a schedule.

Take care to use the correct ACT rate.

	Date		Amount of distribution £	+	ACT payable £	=		Amount of franked payment £
Dividends and other qualifying distributions paid *Exclude – payments at 03 – Foreign Income Dividends (FIDS) – 'deemed FIDS' (see notes page 4)*	31.12.95	01	33000.00		8250.00		02	41,250.00
Dividends paid for which you wish to account for ACT despite an election under Section 247(1) ICTA 1988 *See Notes page 2*		03					04	

Total **franked payments**	02 + 04	05	41,250.00
Deduct **franked investment income to be set-off** ...	From Part 2, box 23	06	
Total **franked payments** for which ACT is payable	05 – 06	10	41,250.00
Calculate the **Advance Corporation Tax (ACT)** included in the figure at **10**	*See both examples in Notes page 2*	11	8250.00
Add the **ACT payable on Foreign Income Dividends (FIDs)**	From CT61 Supplement, boxes 67 and 72	12	
Total ACT for this return period ...	11 + 12	13	8,250.00
Deduct Additional amounts paid to **non-residents** *See Notes page 4*	**Enter all the additional amounts paid, and attach form 251B Divs FD in duplicate**	14	
ACT payable Carry to Payslip on CT61 Notice ...	13 – 14	15	8250.00

Do not enter a 'minus' figure in box 15. If 14 is greater than 13, claim repayment of the excess in Part 8

2 Franked investment income - running record for set-off or repayment

Amount brought forward from last Return ...		16	
Adjustment, if any, agreed with Inspector or a claim under Section 242 ICTA 1988 not yet agreed ...	*Enter 'MINUS' if appropriate*	17	
	16 + or – 17	18	

	Date	Description	Amount
Franked investment income received since last return			

You can include income received in earlier return periods if you did not need to submit a form for those periods. See Notes page 1.
Do not enter Foreign Income Dividends here.
If you need more room please attach a schedule.

	Total	19	
Adjustment, if any, agreed with Inspector	*Enter 'MINUS' if appropriate*	20	
Total after adjustment ...	19 + or – 20	21	
Total franked investment income now available for set-off or repayment	18 + 21	22	
Deduct **Amount set-off against franked payments in Part 1**	From 22 or 05, whichever is smaller	23	*Carry this figure to Part 1, box 06*
Franked investment income after above set-off ...	22 – 23	24	

Repayment of ACT previously paid. Franked investment income at 24 can be set-off against franked payments of earlier return periods for this accounting period only.

ACT repayment now claimed		Amount of franked investment income set-off	
25	*Carry this figure to Part 8, line b*	26	

Amount to be carried forward to next Return	24 – 26	27	

2

3 Income Tax on Annual Payments and Interest

In boxes 28 and 29, group separately payments taxed at basic rate and payments taxed at lower rate.

If you need more room please attach a schedule.

Use Part 3 to calculate the Income Tax payable on payments made.
Use Part 4 to record Income Tax you have suffered on payments received. This can be set-off to reduce the tax due in Part 3. *For further information see Notes page 3.*

	Date	Description		Gross amount £		Income Tax £
Annual payments etc made under deduction of Income Tax at basic rate or lower rate *See Notes page 3*	10.12.95	GIFT AID	28	5000.00	29	1150.00
Include all manufactured interest, unless entered at 30 below.						

		Gross amount		Income Tax
Annual payments etc to **non-residents** made under deduction of **reduced rate** tax under a Double Taxation Agreement *See Notes page 4.* *Ref. no. of the authority* ▶	30		31	
Income Tax on annual payments etc above ... 29 + 31			32	1150.00

Interest paid by deposit-takers including distributions paid by **building societies**
Enter the Gross amount paid from which you deducted tax, and the lower rate Income Tax you deducted
See Notes page 3
Do not enter interest paid gross, eg TESSA interest

		Gross amount		Income Tax
Before 6 April	33		34	
From 6 April	35		36	

When the return period does not include 6 April use boxes 35 and 36

Total Income Tax	32 + 34 + 36	37	1150.00
Less Income Tax deducted from income **received** now claimed as a **set-off**	From Part 4, box 53	38	1150.00
	37 – 38	39	
Less Income Tax on **Gilt Interest received** now claimed as a set-off	From CT61 Supplement, box 83	40	
Income Tax now payable Carry to **Payslip** on CT61 Notice	39 – 40	46	

4 Income Tax deducted – running record in this Accounting Period for set-off or repayment

Amount of Income Tax **brought forward** from last Return for this **accounting period**		47	
Adjustment, if any, agreed with Inspector	*Enter 'MINUS' if appropriate*	48	
	47 + or – 48	49	

Income received under deduction of tax since last Return for **this accounting period**

	Date	Description	Gross amount		Income Tax
You can include income received in earlier return periods in this accounting period if you did not need to submit a form for those periods. See Notes page 1. If you need more room please attach a schedule.	10.12.95	PATENT ROYALTY	10000.00		2300.00
Totals			50 — 10000.00	51	2300.00

Running total now available for set-off or repayment below	49 + 51		52	2300.00
Amount set-off against Income Tax in Part 3	From 52 or 37, whichever is smaller	53	1150.00	◀ *Carry this figure to Part 3, box 38*
Repayment now claimed of tax paid on annual payments etc in Part 3 of an earlier Return **for this accounting period only**		54		◀ *Carry this figure to Part 8*
Total Income Tax now used for set-off or repayment	53 + 54		55	1150.00
Amount to be **carried forward** to next Return for **this accounting period**	52 – 55		56	1150.00

5 Certain other distributions

If you need more room please attach a schedule

	Date	Description	Amount £
a Qualifying distributions which are not money payments			
b Payments about which there is a doubt as to whether they are qualifying distributions			
c Distributions (excluding money payments) which, exceptionally, do not fall within an accounting period			

Do not account for ACT on the above payments. The Inspector will make any necessary assessment.

6 Tax on manufactured payments from abroad

See Notes page 4

a **Manufactured dividends received from abroad** *by UK resident companies*	(AMOUNTS RECEIVED)	Tax payable - *at ACT rate*	*Carry to Payslip on CT61 Notice*
b **Manufactured interest received from abroad** *by UK resident companies and by UK branches of overseas companies*	(GROSS INTEREST)	Income Tax payable at lower rate	*Carry to Payslip on CT61 Notice*

7 Income Tax on Gilt Interest received: totals from CT61 Supplement

a Income Tax **payable** on Gilt Interest received	From box 79	
b **Repayment** of excessive payment on account	*78 – 77 if positive*	
c **Repayment** of 'Gilts' Income Tax	From box 88	
d **Repayment** of 'other' Income Tax	From box 85	
e Total 'Gilts related' repayments	b + c + d	
f Net Income Tax **payable** - *Do not enter a minus figure here. If e is greater than a claim repayment of the excess in Part 8 below*	a – e	*Carry to Payslip on CT61 Notice*

8 Claim for repayment or reimbursement

Use this section to summarise any claims arising in other sections of your Return:

a *From Part 1*	Reimbursement of amounts paid to non-residents	14 – 13 if positive	
b *From Parts 2 and 9*	Repayment of ACT previously paid	From boxes 25 and 69	
c *From Part 4*	Repayment of Income Tax previously paid	From box 54	
d *From Part 7*	Net 'Gilts related' Income Tax repayments	7e – 7a if positive	
e	Total claimed	a + b + c + d	

Other forms

Please tick if you require a form to declare the following items:

Non-qualifying distributions *Form CT2* *See Notes page 2* '✓' ☐

Stock dividends Section 249 ICTA 1988 *Form CT101* '✓' ☐

When sending back this Return, please

- check you have filled in the blue boxes at the top of page 1
- check you have signed the declaration on page 1
- send the CT61 Notice with this Return, even if no payment is enclosed.

When we receive this Return we will send you another form for your company's next Return.

Please note If the Inspector considers that any distributions, payments, etc have been omitted from this Return, or is in any way dissatisfied with it, the Inland Revenue can issue an appropriate assessment.

Information for Section 2, Task 2.1

King House
Queen Street
Barchester

Garrett, Turner & Co
Accountants
Debit Street
Barchester

Dear Ms Handel,

INCOME TAX RETURN

Further to your requests for information to complete my income tax return for the 1998/99 tax year I enclose the following:

1. A copy of the draft Form P11D completed by Cole Limited. I have mislaid my copy of the final version as would have been filed, but there were no benefits other than those noted.
   Please note that I have kept a record of the telephone calls made from home and 10% of the calls were for business purposes.
   All of the entertaining costs were for business purposes.
   The value of any benefits relating to my car has not been calculated, and I presume that you will be calculating the value of these benefits for me.

2. Dividend vouchers for my share holdings.

3. Interest statement for my building society accounts.

4. My P60 showed pay of £12,530 for 1998/99, with deductions under PAYE of £2,973.

In addition to this information, you asked for details of any deeds of covenant or gift aid payments during the year. I paid £154 to the charity Oxfam under a six year deed of covenant arrangement and £500 under the gift aid scheme to the RSPCA, a charity.

I pay pension contributions to the 'Irish Widows Pension Company' of £50 per month (Policy number 1234567B). Cole Limited also pays pension contributions of £50 per month on my behalf. These contributions will continue at the same level for 1999/00.

My wife and I have a mortgage with The Irish Bank for £150,000 (account number 33445566U). Interest on the mortgage, under the MIRAS arrangements, amounts to £9,000 for the tax year.

Finally, I am not sure if it is relevant, but I have gambling winnings of £295, won at the three horse racing meetings I attended this year.

If you need any further information please do not hesitate to contact me.

Yours sincerely

Nathaniel King

Inland Revenue

P11D EXPENSES AND BENEFITS 1998-99

Note to employer
Complete this return for a director, or an employee who earned at a rate of £8,500 a year or more during the year 6 April 1998 to 5 April 1999. Do not include expenses and benefits covered by a dispensation or PAYE settlement agreement. Read the P11D Guide and booklet 480, Chapter 24, before you complete the form. Send the completed P11D and form P11D(b) to the Tax Office by 6 July 1999. You must give a copy of this information to the director or employee by the same date. The term employee is used to cover both directors and employees throughout the rest of this form.

Note to employee
Your employer has filled in this form. Keep it in a safe place as you may not be able to get a duplicate. You will need it for your tax records and to complete your 1998-99 Tax Return if you get one. Your tax code may need to be adjusted to take account of the information given on this P11D. The box numbers on this P11D have the same numbering as the Employment Pages of the Tax Return, for example, 1.12. Include the total figures in the corresponding box on the Tax Return, unless you think some other figure is more appropriate.

Employer's details
Employer's name: COLE LIMITED
PAYE tax reference: 299/C21

Employee's details
Employee's name: NATHANIEL KING
Tick here if a director: ✓
Works number or department:
National Insurance number: NB 52 26 79C

A • **Assets transferred (cars, property, goods or other assets)**

Description of asset	Cost/ Market value		Amount made good or from which tax deducted		Cash equivalent
	£	–	£	= 1.12	£

B • **Payments made on behalf of employee**

Description of payment ______ 1.12 £

Tax on notional payments not borne by employee within 30 days of receipt of each notional payment 1.12 £

C • **Vouchers or credit cards**

	Gross amount		Amount made good or from which tax deducted		Cash equivalent
Value of vouchers and payments made using credit cards or tokens	£	–	£	= 1.13	£

D • **Living accommodation**

Cash equivalent of accommodation provided for employee, or his/ her family or household — Cash equivalent 1.14 £

E • **Mileage allowance**

	Gross amount		Amount made good or from which tax deducted		Taxable payment
Car and mileage allowances paid for employee's car	£	–	£	= 1.15	£

F • **Cars and car fuel**
If more than two cars were made available, either at the same time or in succession, please give details on a separate sheet

	Car 1	Car 2
Make and Model	LAND ROVER DISCOVERY	
Dates first registered	01/08/97	/ /
Dates car was available	From 06/04/98 To 05/04/99	From / / To / /
Business mileage used in calculation for this car. *Tick only one box for each car.* *If the car was not available for part of the year, the business mileage limits are reduced proportionately.*	2,499 or less ☐ 2,500 to 17,999 ✓ 18,000 or more ☐	2,499 or less ☐ 2,500 to 17,999 ☐ 18,000 or more ☐
Enter engine size and tick type of fuel *only if there is a car fuel scale charge*	Engine size in cc 2200 cc; Petrol ☐ Diesel ✓	Engine size in cc ___ cc; Petrol ☐ Diesel ☐

	Car 1	Car 2
List price of car *If there is no list price, or if it is a classic car, employers see booklet 480; employees see leaflet IR133*	£ 25900	£
Price of optional accessories fitted when car was first made available to the employee	£ 700	£
Price of accessories added after the car was first made available to the employee	£	£
Capital contributions (maximum £5,000) the employee made towards the cost of car or accessories	£	£
Amount paid by employee for private use of the car	£	£
Cash equivalent of each car	£ 26600	£
Total cash equivalent of all cars available in 1998-99		1.16 £ 26600
Cash equivalent of fuel for each car	£	£ 1890
Total cash equivalent of fuel for all cars available in 1998-99		1.17 £ ~~28~~ 490

P11D(1999) BMSD 11/98

G • **Vans**

Cash equivalent of all vans made available for private use — **1.18** £

H • **Interest-free and low interest loans**

If the total amount outstanding on all loans does not exceed £5,000 at any time in the year, there is no need for details in this section.

	Loan 1	Loan 2
Purpose of loan(s) – *please use the code shown in P11D Guide for employers*		
Number of joint borrowers *(if applicable)*		
Tick the box if the loan is within MIRAS		
Amount outstanding at 5 April 1998 or at date loan was made if later	£	£
Amount outstanding at 5 April 1999 or at date loan was discharged if earlier	£	£
Maximum amount outstanding at any time in the year	£	£
Total amount of interest paid by the borrower in 1998 - 99 – *enter "NIL" if none was paid*	£	£
Date loan was made or discharged in 1998 - 99 if applicable	/ /	/ /
Cash equivalent of loans after deducting any interest paid by the borrower	**1.19** £	**1.19** £

I • **Mobile telephones**

Cash equivalent of mobile telephones provided — **1.20** £

J • **Private medical treatment or insurance**

	Cost to you		Amount made good or from which tax deducted		Cash equivalent
Private medical treatment or insurance	£ 625	–	£	=	**1.21** £ 625

K • **Qualifying relocation expenses payments and benefits (non-qualifying expenses go in P below)**

Excess over £8,000 of all qualifying relocation expenses payments and benefits for each move — **1.22** £

L • **Services supplied**

	Cost to you		Amount made good or from which tax deducted		Cash equivalent
Services supplied to the employee	£	–	£	=	**1.22** £

M • **Assets placed at the employee's disposal**

MADE AVAILABLE 1-10-98

		Annual value plus expenses incurred		Amount made good or from which tax deducted		Cash equivalent
Description of asset	COMPUTER	£ 3650	–	£	=	**1.22** £ 3650

COST 1.10.98 £3650 – FOR PRIVATE USE AT HOME

N • **Shares**

Tick the box if during the year there have been share-related benefits for the employee ☐

O • **Other items**

		Cost to you		Amount made good or from which tax deducted		Cash equivalent
Subscriptions and professional fees	INSTITUTE OF DIRECTORS	£ 120	–	£	=	**1.22** £ 120
Description of other items		£	–	£	=	**1.22** £

Income tax paid but not deducted from director's remuneration — Tax paid **1.22** £

P • **Expenses payments made to, or on behalf of, the employee**

		Cost to you		Amount made good or from which tax deducted		Taxable payment
Travelling and subsistence payments		£	–	£	=	**1.23** £
Entertainment *(trading organisations read P11D Guide and then enter a tick or a cross as appropriate here)*	✓	£ 1550	–	£	=	**1.23** £ 1550
General expenses allowance for business travel		£	–	£	=	**1.23** £
Payments for use of home telephone	RENTAL CALLS	£ 100 500	–	£	=	**1.23** £ 600
Non-qualifying relocation expenses *(those not shown in section K)*		£	–	£	=	**1.23** £
Description of other expenses		£	–	£	=	**1.23** £

COLE LIMITED
Dividend Voucher
Interim dividend for the year ended 31 March 1998

Paid 31 December 1998

Date	***No of shares***	***Dividend***	***Tax credit***
		£	£
31.12.98	98	32,340	8,085

James Brown Limited
Dividend Voucher
Interim dividend for the year ended 31 December 1999

Paid 31 March 1999

Date	***No of shares***	***Dividend***	***Tax credit***
		£	£
31.3.99	1,000	500	125

Barchester Building Society
Interest Statement as at 31 December 1998

Account no	**Account Type**	**Gross Interest**	**Tax deducted**	**Net Interest**
		£	£	£
0011223344X	Ordinary Share	13,333	2,667	10,667
4433221100Z	Tax Exempt Special Savings Account (TESSA)	500	Nil	

Information for Section 3, Task 3.1

Details of assets sold by Mrs Peggy King
For the attention of Alison Handel (Tax Partner, Garrett, Turner & Co):

The following is a list of the assets I have sold between 6 April 1998 and 5 April 1999. I have given you the dates of purchase and sale, the sale proceeds and cost of each asset as requested.

Regards,
Peggy King

Assets sold:

1. Sale of my shares in Morse plc:
Transactions in these shares have been as follows:
Shares Purchased

Date	*No of Shares*	*Cost*
		£
10.1.72	100	200
15.9.90	1,000	5,000

There was also a bonus issue of shares on 21.6.94 (one bonus share was issued for every 4 shares held on that date).
Shares sold:
I sold all my shares in Morse plc for £8,250 on 10 January 1999.
Note: The value of these shares on 31 March 1982 was quoted at £3 per share.

2. Sale of my flat in London
Owned for my own personal use, when visiting London (never my principal private residence).
Sold for £120,000 on 21 April 1998.
Estate Agent's and legal fees for the sale amounted to £5,000.
Bought for £50,000 on 31 March 1982.

3. Sale of a painting by E. Costello (a popular artist of the 1980s)
Sold for £10,000 on 31 March 1999.
Bought for £12,000 on 20 December 1993.
Commission paid to gallery on purchase amounted to £120, in addition to the £12,000 paid for the painting.

4. Sale of antique writing desk
Sold for £4,000 on 17 September 1998.
Bought for £2,000 on 21 June 1985.

5. Sale of Sports Car
Sold for £5,000 on 12 June 1998
Bought for £1,000 on 30 May 1980
Value on 31 March 1982 £2,000.

Please note: You are not expected to enter any figures on Mrs King's income tax return.

Information for Section 3, Task 3.2

King House
Queen Street
Barchester
25 November 1999

Dear Alison,

Investment of sale proceeds

In addition to calculating the capital gains tax due on the sales of assets I have made in 1998/99, I would be grateful if you could give me some advice on the tax implications of investing the cash received from my recent sales.

I have been considering reinvesting the money in:

(a) local property which I would rent out to long-term tenants;

(b) local property which I would rent out for holidays (that is holidays of 1 or 2 weeks' duration);

(c) additional ordinary shares in our unquoted trading company, Cole Limited.

Please advise me on:

(1) the possibility of any of these reinvestments reducing the capital gains tax due on the investment sales made in 1998/99. No calculations are required at this stage, just a simple written explanation of the requirements to be fulfilled if a reduction in the capital gains tax due is to be achieved;

(2) the income tax implications of owning the assets listed (a) to (c) above (assuming that the rates of tax and allowances remain at the same levels as in 1998/99). You are aware that I have no income of my own other than the dividends I receive from my two shares in Cole Limited (dividend received of £660 in 1998/99) and currently I pay no income tax and do not use all my personal allowance;

(3) the capital gains tax implications of any future sale of the assets listed at (a) to (c) above.

I have also been considering using two of the spare rooms in our house for "bed and breakfast" accommodation (overnight holiday accommodation) for local visitors. I understand that I may not have to pay income tax on rental income from letting rooms in my own home. Can you outline the circumstances in which this may be the case?

I look forward to hearing from you with your reply in due course.

Best wishes

Peggy King

Inland Revenue

Page 1

Corporation Tax Return
Version 3

This form, or an approved substitute version of it, must be used whenever a company is required to do so, by a *Notice to deliver a Corporation Tax Return (form CT203)*. This return sets out the information we need and provides a standard format for calculations.

You should read this return form along with your *Notice to deliver a Corporation Tax Return (form CT203)* and *Filing in your Corporation Tax Return (leaflet CT200 Notes)* which you should have received with this form. The notes referred to throughout can be found in the leaflet *CT200 Notes*. You should contact your Tax Office if you need more help.

'Company' means any body chargeable to corporation tax, whether incorporated or not. This definition includes clubs, associations and voluntary organisations.

Sections to be completed

Members' clubs, associations and voluntary organisations - It is likely that you will only have to complete Sections 1 and 2. For further guidance see note 1 in the *Notes*.

All companies - including clubs, etc. - You will not need to complete every Section, but you **must** complete the Declaration and Section 1 on this page. The *Notes* will help you decide whether you should complete the mutually exclusive *Short return* at Section 2 or the *Detailed return* at Section 3. Sections 9 and 10 are optional but you are asked to complete them if they are relevant to the company.

It is important that you read the *Notes* before completing any part of this form.

What to do when you have completed the return

- Make sure you have completed and signed the Declaration, then
- staple together the pages you have completed and attach any supporting calculations
- send these together with the relevant company accounts and, where prepared, directors' and auditors' reports, to your Tax Office using the envelope provided (see Note 3 for the date by which you should do this)
- pay any outstanding corporation tax (as you have shown at box box 65), as advised on the payslip attached to your *Notice to deliver a Corporation Tax Return (form CT203)*. Interest is charged on tax paid later than nine months and one day after the end of an accounting period. Tax is due without the making of an assessment.

Remember - ***Your tax return is not complete unless you send relevant accounts and documentation with this form. Penalties may be charged if your return, or any part of it, is late or incorrect.***

As soon as your figures are agreed

- we will send you an assessment setting out the tax position for the accounting period - unless there are no figures to assess
- we will issue an amended assessment if you have already received an estimated assessment and you have appealed against it.

Section 1: Summary

The company name

The company address - only if changed since last return made.
Enter the UK registered office address, or the UK address if the company does not have a registered office. If the company does not have premises in the UK show the address of the person making the return.

Company registration number *(if registered)*

Reference
Enter the reference number shown on the *Notice to deliver a Corporation Tax Return (form CT203)*

/ /

Corporation tax accounting period covered by this return
Cannot exceed 12 months. Enter start and end dates.

From / / To / /

If this period is not an accounting period of the company for corporation tax purposes (see note 2) put an 'X' in the box below, complete the Declaration to the right and return this form to your Tax Office. You do not need to complete the rest of this Section or other Sections of this form in these circumstances. ☐

Profits chargeable *(Enter the firgure from box 30). If there are none enter '0'.*
£

Corporation tax due £ p
(Enter the figure from box 61 minus any entry in box 64). If none is due enter '0.00'.

Put an 'X' in the appropriate box

Have you completed Section 8 (Repayments)? Yes ☐ No ☐

Is the company name different from that shown in the *Notice (form CT203)*? Yes ☐ No ☐

Declaration

Enter here the page numbers you are attaching

Put an 'X' in the appropriate boxes to show the documents you are enclosing

- a copy of the accounts for the period to which this return relates ☐
- a copy of the company accounts for a different period ☐
- no accounts ☐
- say why not
- calculations showing how the entries in the return form have been arrived at. ☐

I declare that to the best of my knowledge and belief the return on this page and the pages attached is correct and complete.

Signature

Except where a liquidator has been appointed, the company secretary, treasurer, or any other person who is authorised to do so may sign this declaration on behalf of the company. A photocopy of a signature is not acceptable.

Date
/ /

Name *(in capital letters)*

Status *(company secretary, treasurer, liquidator etc.)*

Section 2: Short return

You may complete this section if

- it covers all the entries you need to make and
- each entry, including the company's total income and deductions, is less than £10 million.

In all other cases, or if you prefer, complete Section 3 instead. You should enclose an explanation and calculations of any figures which you have estimated or which are not immediately recognisable from the company's accounts.

The figures to be entered are those adjusted for tax purposes, after deducting capital allowances and adding balancing charges where appropriate. Section 4 should also be completed if capital allowances are claimed.
Please do not enter '0's where the company did not have the source specified in the return form.

	Box	£	Box	£
Trading profits *See note 5* ...	1			
Trading losses brought forward *Only include losses made in the same trade. Include charges treated as losses. Do not enter an amount larger than is needed to cover the profits in box 1. See note 6* ...	2			
Net trading profit *(box 1 minus box 2). If box 2 equals box 1, enter '0'. Leave this box blank if there are no trading profits in box 1* ...			3	
Trading losses of this accounting period *Where there is more than one trade give total for all trades. Do not set box 4 losses against box 1 profits, claim at box 22 against total profits.* ...	4			
Profits and gains from non-trading loan relationships and other Schedule D Case III income *Include interest and other profits and gains from non-trading loan relationships even if tax has been deducted. Complete box 57 to claim credit for income tax deducted. You will need to complete the* **Detailed return** *at Section 3 if you have deficits on non-trading loan relationships from this, earlier or later accounting periods to include. See note 8* ...			6	
Income within Schedule D Case VI - for example furnished lettings *Enter the figure net of allowable losses brought forward. Exclude income you enter in box 12. See note 7* ...			9	
Income from which income tax has been deducted - for example building society interest *Enter the gross amount before tax. Exclude any amount included in box 6 above. Complete box 57 to claim credit for income tax deducted. See note 9* ...			10	
Income from UK land and buildings *Enter the amount net of allowable expenses brought forward. Exclude income in box 9 above. See note 10* ...			12	
Chargeable gains *See note 11*				
Gross gains ...	13			
Allowable losses *Include any losses brought forward but do not enter an amount larger than the amount of gross gains in box 13 above.* ...	14			
Net chargeable gains *(box 13 minus box 14) If box 14 equals box 13, enter '0'* ...			15	
Profits *(total of boxes 3, 6, 9, 10, 12 and 15)* ...			17	
Relief for trading losses of this or of a later period *Put an 'X' in box 21 if amounts carried back from later accounting periods are included in box 22. See note 12* ...	21		22	
Profits before charges *(box 17 minus box 22)* ...			26	
Charges paid *Do not enter an amount larger than is needed to cover profits in box 26. See note13* ...			27	
Profits chargeable to corporation tax *(box 26 minus box 27)* **Copy this figure into the box provided in Section 1 on page 1, and also into the box at the top of page 3** ...			30	

The short return is continued on page 3

Page 3

Profits chargeable to corporation tax

Enter the figure brought forward from page 2, box 30 ... £ [ ]

If you claim tax is chargeable at the small companies' rate, or if you are claiming marginal small companies' relief, complete boxes 31 - 35. If there are no associated companies please enter '0' against the relevant financial year. *See note 15*

Franked investment income and foreign income dividends arising in the period covered by the return. *See note 15* ... 31 £ [ ]

Number of companies associated with this company in the/each financial year covered by this return
Exclude this company. See note 15 ...

Financial year		Number of associated companies	
32	[ ]	33	[ ]
34	[ ]	35	[ ]

Corporation tax chargeable *See note 16*

	Financial years beginning 1 April		Amounts of profit £		Rates of tax *See note 16*		Tax £ p
36	[ ]	37	[ ]	38	[ ] • [ ]	39	[ ] • [ ]
43	[ ]	44	[ ]	45	[ ] • [ ]	46	[ ] • [ ]

Total corporation tax chargeable *(box 39 plus box 46)* ... 50 [ ] • [ ]

Marginal small companies' relief
Attach your computation (see notes 15, 16 and 29) ... 51 £ [ ] • p [ ]

Advance corporation tax restricted if necessary under Section 239(2) ICTA 1988
Put an 'X' in box 53 if amounts carried back from later accounting periods are included. See note 17. 53 [ ] 54 [ ] • [ ]

Total of boxes 51 and 54
Total must not be larger than entry in box 50. Restrict if necessary ... 55 [ ] • [ ]

Net corporation tax chargeable *(box 50 minus box 55)* ... 56 [ ] • [ ]

Calculation of tax outstanding or overpaid

Income tax deducted from gross income included in return
Do not include deductions used to cover income tax for which the company was liable to account to the Inland Revenue on payments it has made. See note 18 ... 57 [ ] • [ ]

Corporation tax due

Box 56 minus box 57. If box 57 equals or is greater than box 56, enter '0.00' and go to box 59.
Copy the figure in box 61 to the box provided in Section 1 on page 1. See note 20 ... 61 [ ] • [ ]

Income tax repayable to the company *(box 57 minus box 56).*
Complete Section 8 on page 8. Do not complete unless you are making a claim. See note 28... 59 [ ] • [ ]

Corporation tax already paid (and not repaid). *See note 21* ... 63 [ ] • [ ]

Corporation tax outstanding *(box 61 minus box 63). This amount is payable to the Accounts Office. If box 63 equals or is greater than box 61, enter '0.00' and go to box 66. See note 23* ... 65 [ ] • [ ]

Corporation tax overpaid *(box 63 minus box 61).*
Complete Section 8 on page 8 also. See note 28 ... 66 [ ] • [ ]

This is the last page of the short return

Page 6

Section 4: Claims for capital allowances and details of balancing charges arising

You must complete this section if you want to claim capital allowances, whether or not those allowances are reflected elsewhere in the return. You should also show balancing charges taken into account in the short or detailed return. Show details of qualifying expenditure on which writing-down allowances may be claimed, even if you do not want to claim any allowances for this period. *See note 25*

Notice of expenditure on machinery and plant *See note 25*

Expenditure on which first year allowance is claimed £	Qualifying expenditure on long life assets on which writing down allowances may be claimed £	Qualifying expenditure on other assets on which writing down allowances may be claimed £
68	91	69

Charges and allowances included in calculation of trading profit or losses

	Balancing charges £	Capital allowances £
Cars *Including leased out and "expensive" cars*	70	71
Machinery and plant *- long life assets*	92	93
- other	72	73
Industrial buildings and structures *Including qualifying hotels, and commercial buildings and hotels in enterprise zones*	74	75
Other charges and allowances *For example agricultural buildings, mineral extraction, scientific research, patents*	76	77
Charges and allowances not included in calculation of trading profit or losses	78	79

Section 5: Particulars of advance corporation tax and surplus advance corporation tax

Complete this section if you have surplus advance corporation tax brought forward or have paid advance corporation tax (and it has not been repaid) in respect of qualifying distributions made in the period covered by this return.

	£	p
Particulars of advance corporation tax paid		
Particulars of any surplus advance corporation tax brought forward		

Section 6: Amounts claimed as group relief

Complete this section if you have claimed group relief at box 29 (see note 26). Attach a separate sheet of paper if you need more space. Attach a copy of each surrendering company's notice of consent to the claim unless a special arrangement is in force. Include claims made under the consortium provisions.

Name of surrendering company	**Accounting period** Show the start and end dates of any accounting period which is different from the one to which this return relates.	**Tax reference** Show the Tax Office number and the tax inspector's file reference. If you do not know these, supply whatever information you have that will help us to identify the company, for example the company registration number.	Amount claimed from each company
			£
			£
			£
			£
			£
			£
			£
			£
			£
			£
			£
			£
			£
		Total *This figure should be the same as the one in box 29.*	£

Page 8

Section 8: Overpayments and repayment claims

Complete this section if you are claiming a repayment (including a payment of tax credits). *See note 28* Attach your calculations unless you have already done so in Section 2 or 3.

	£	p
Repayment of corporation tax *Include construction industry deductions repayable*		
Repayment of income tax *Enclose vouchers to cover the amount of repayment claimed*		
Payment of tax credits *Enclose vouchers to cover the amount of payment claimed*		
Repayment of advance corporation tax *See note 27*		
Total		

Bank details (for person to whom the repayment is to be made)

Repayments of corporation tax (but not income tax, tax credits, advance corporation tax or construction industry deductions) for accounting periods ending after 30 September 1993 are made by direct credit to a bank or building society account. You should provide the following details of the account to which the repayment is to be made.

Bank (or building society)

Branch sort code

Account number

Name of account

Building society reference

Other repayments will be made by payable order.

How total overpayment is to be dealt with

Please show how you want the overpayment to be dealt with.

To be repaid ... ...

- **to the company** '✓'
- **to the nominee shown in the following authority** '✓'

Surrendered under S102 Finance Act 1989 ... ...
Note that a repayment of advance corporation tax cannot be surrendered

The required joint notice

- **is attached**
- **will follow, where an amount is not final.** The Inspector is asked to stop repayment of until the Notice is received

Payments to a person other than the company

Complete the authority below if you want the repayment to be made to a person other than the company. The Revenue reserves the right not to make a repayment to a nominee and will not normally make a repayment to an overseas nominee.

I, as *(enter status - Company Secretary, Treasurer etc.)*

of

authorise

Name

Address

Postcode

Nominee reference

to receive on the company's behalf the amount due Signed

Name in capital letters

Except where a liquidator has been appointed, any person who is authorised to do so may sign this authority on behalf of the company. A photocopy of a signature is not acceptable.

This is the last section of the statutory return form, but it would be helpful if you would complete Sections 9 and 10 if they are applicable.

Page 9

Section 9: Figures brought forward and carried forward

Please complete this section if any of the following items are
- brought forward from the previous accounting period *or*
- available for carry forward from the period to which this return relates.

Please provide a reconciliation of any figures that are not explained elsewhere in your accounts and calculations. Attach a separate sheet of paper if you need more space.

	Total brought forward	Less amount used	Plus net amount available to carry forward from this accounting period	Total to carry forward
Trading losses *include trade charges treated as losses*	£	£	£	£
Schedule D case VI losses	£	£	£	£
Excess management expenses *Include business charges treated as management expenses*	£	£	£	£
Surplus ACT *Enter the figure net of amounts set off or repaid or surrendered to subsidiaries*	£ p	£ p	£ p	£ p
Surplus franked investment income	£ p	£ p	£ p	£ p
Losses allowable against chargeable gains	£	£	£	£
Net non-trade deficits and losses on loan relationships (including interest), exchange fluctuations, and certain financial instruments *See note 8.*	£	£	£	£
Others *Please specify*	£	£	£	£
	£	£	£	£
	£	£	£	£
	£	£	£	£

INCOME for the year ended 5 April 1999

Q10 Did you receive any income from UK savings and investments? NO ☐ YES ☐

If yes, fill in boxes 10.1 to 10.32 as appropriate. Include only your share from any joint savings and investments.

■ *Interest*

• Interest from UK banks, building societies and deposit takers			
- where **no tax** has been deducted			Taxable amount 10.1 £
- where **tax has** been deducted	Amount after tax deducted 10.2 £	Tax deducted 10.3 £	Gross amount before tax 10.4 £
• Interest distributions from UK authorised unit trusts and open-ended investment companies (dividend distributions go below)	Amount after tax deducted 10.5 £	Tax deducted 10.6 £	Gross amount before tax 10.7 £
• National Savings (other than FIRST Option Bonds and the first £70 of interest from a National Savings Ordinary Account)			Taxable amount 10.8 £
• National Savings FIRST Option Bonds	Amount after tax deducted 10.9 £	Tax deducted 10.10 £	Gross amount before tax 10.11 £
• Other income from UK savings and investments (except dividends)	Amount after tax deducted 10.12 £	Tax deducted 10.13 £	Gross amount before tax 10.14 £

■ *Dividends*

• Dividends and other qualifying distributions from UK companies	Dividend/distribution 10.15 £	Tax credit 10.16 £	Dividend/distribution plus credit 10.17 £
• Dividend distributions from UK authorised unit trusts and open-ended investment companies	Dividend/distribution 10.18 £	Tax credit 10.19 £	Dividend/distribution plus credit 10.20 £
• Scrip dividends from UK companies	Dividend 10.21 £	Notional tax 10.22 £	Dividend plus notional tax 10.23 £
• Foreign income dividends from UK companies	Dividend 10.24 £	Notional tax 10.25 £	Dividend plus notional tax 10.26 £
• Foreign income dividend distributions from UK authorised unit trusts and open-ended investment companies	Dividend 10.27 £	Notional tax 10.28 £	Dividend plus notional tax 10.29 £
• Non-qualifying distributions and loans written off	10.30 £	Notional tax 10.31 £	Taxable amount 10.32 £

Please turn over

RELIEFS for the year ended 5 April 1999

Q14 Do you want to claim relief for pension contributions? NO [ ] YES [ ] If yes, fill in boxes 14.1 to 14.17 as appropriate.

Do not include contributions deducted from your pay by your employer to their pension scheme, because tax relief is given automatically. But do include your contributions to personal pension schemes.

■ ***Retirement annuity contracts***

Qualifying payments made in 1998-99	14.1 £	1998-99 payments used in an earlier year	14.2 £	Relief claimed box 14.1 *minus* (boxes 14.2 and 14.3, but not 14.4)
1998-99 payments now to be carried back	14.3 £	Payments brought back from 1999-2000	14.4 £	14.5 £

■ ***Self-employed contributions to personal pension plans***

Qualifying payments made in 1998-99	14.6 £	1998-99 payments used in an earlier year	14.7 £	Relief claimed box 14.6 *minus* (boxes 14.7 and 14.8, but not 14.9)
1998-99 payments now to be carried back	14.8 £	Payments brought back from 1999-2000	14.9 £	14.10 £

■ ***Employee contributions to personal pension plans*** *(include your gross contribution - see the note on box 14.11 in your Tax Return Guide)*

Qualifying payments made in 1998-99	14.11 £	1998-99 payments used in an earlier year	14.12 £	Relief claimed box 14.11 *minus* (boxes 14.12 and 14.13, but not 14.14)
1998-99 payments now to be carried back	14.13 £	Payments brought back from 1999-2000	14.14 £	14.15 £

■ ***Contributions to other pension schemes***

- Amount of contributions to employer's schemes **not deducted** at source from pay — 14.16 £
- Gross amount of free-standing additional voluntary contributions paid in 1998-99 — 14.17 £

Q15 Do you want to claim any of the following reliefs? NO [ ] YES [ ] If yes, fill in boxes 15.1 to 15.12, as appropriate.

- Payments you made for vocational training — Amount of payment 15.1 £
- Interest eligible for relief on loans to buy your main home (other than MIRAS) — Amount of payment 15.2 £
- Interest eligible for relief on other qualifying loans — Amount of payment 15.3 £
- Maintenance or alimony payments you have made under a court order, Child Support Agency assessment or legally binding order or agreement — Amount claimed under 'new' rules 15.4 £; Amount claimed under 'old' rules up to £1,900 15.5 £; Amount claimed under 'old' rules over £1,900 15.6 £
- Subscriptions for Venture Capital Trust shares (up to £100,000) — Amount on which relief claimed 15.7 £
- Subscriptions under the Enterprise Investment Scheme (up to £150,000) — Amount on which relief claimed 15.8 £
- Charitable covenants or annuities — Amount of payment 15.9 £
- Gift Aid and Millennium Gift Aid — Amount of payment 15.10 £
- Post-cessation expenses and losses on relevant discounted securities etc. — Amount of payment 15.11 £
- Payments to a trade union or friendly society for death benefits — Half amount of payment 15.12 £

Please turn over

ALLOWANCES *for the year ended 5 April 1999*

Q16

You get your personal allowance of £4,195 automatically. If you were born before 6 April 1934, enter your date of birth in box 21.4 - you may get higher age-related allowances.

Do you want to claim any of the following allowances? NO ☐ YES ☐ If yes, please read pages 23 to 26 of your Tax Return Guide and then fill in boxes 16.1 to 16.28 as appropriate.

- ***Blind person's allowance*** — Date of registration (if first year of claim) **16.1** / / — Local authority (or other register) **16.2**
- ***Transitional allowance*** (for some wives with husbands on low income if received in earlier years).
  - Tick to claim and give details in the 'Additional information' box on page 8 *(please see page 23 of your Tax Return Guide for what is needed)* **16.3**
  - If you want to calculate your tax, enter the amount of transitional allowance you can have in box 16.4 **16.4** £
- ***Married couple's allowance for a married man*** *- see page 24 of your Tax Return Guide.*
  - Wife's full name **16.5**
  - Date of marriage (if after 5 April 1998) **16.6** / /
  - Wife's date of birth (if before 6 April 1934) **16.7** / /
  - Tick box 16.8 if you or your wife have allocated **half** the allowance to her **16.8**
  - *box number 16.9 is not used*
  - Tick box 16.10 if you and your wife have allocated **all** the allowance to her **16.10**
- ***Married couple's allowance for a married woman*** *- see page 24 of your Tax Return Guide.*
  - Date of marriage (if after 5 April 1998) **16.11** / /
  - Husband's full name **16.12**
  - Tick box 16.13 if you or your husband have allocated **half** the allowance to you **16.13**
  - *box number 16.14 is not used*
  - Tick box 16.15 if you and your husband have allocated **all** the allowance to you **16.15**
- ***Additional personal allowance*** *(available in some circumstances if you have a child living with you - see page 25 of your Tax Return Guide).*
  - Tick box 16.16A if you are claiming the married couple's allowance **and** additional personal allowance because your spouse was unable to work, because of illness or disablement, throughout the year ended 5 April 1999 **16.16A**
  - Name of the child claimed for **16.16**
  - Child's date of birth **16.17** / /
  - Tick if child lives with you **16.18**
  - Name of university etc/type of training if the child is 16 or over on 6 April 1998 and in full time education or training **16.19**

Sharing a claim

Name and address of other person claiming **16.20**

Postcode

- Enter your share as a percentage **16.21** %
- If share not agreed, enter the number of days in the year ended 5 April 1999 that the child lived with
  - you **16.22** days
  - other person **16.23** days

- ***Widow's bereavement allowance*** — Date of your husband's death **16.24** / /
- ***Transfer of surplus allowances*** *- see page 26 of your Tax Return Guide before you fill in boxes 16.25 to 16.28.*
  - Tick if you want your spouse to have your unused allowances **16.25**
  - Tick if you want to have your spouse's unused allowances **16.26**

Please give details in the 'Additional information' box on page 8 - see page 26 of your Tax Return Guide for what is needed.

If you want to calculate your tax, enter the amount of the surplus allowance you can have.

- Blind person's **surplus** allowance **16.27** £
- Married couple's **surplus** allowance **16.28** £

OTHER INFORMATION *for the year ended 5 April 1999*

Q17 **Have you already had any 1998-99 tax refunded or set off by your Tax Office or the DSS Benefits Agency?** *Read the notes for box 17.1 on page 26 of your Tax Return Guide*

NO ☐ YES ☐ If yes, enter the amount of the refund in box 17.1.

17.1 £

Q18 **Do you want to calculate your tax?**

NO ☐ YES ☐ If yes, do it now and then fill in boxes 18.1 to 18.9. Your Tax Calculation Guide will help.

- Unpaid tax for earlier years included in your tax code for 1998-99 — 18.1 £
- Tax due for 1998-99 included in your tax code for a later year — 18.2 £
- Total tax and Class 4 NIC due for 1998-99 **before** you made any payments on account *(put the amount in brackets if an overpayment)* — 18.3 £
- Tax due for earlier years — 18.4 £
- Tick box 18.5 if you have calculated tax overpaid for earlier years (and enter the amount in the 'Additional information' box on page 8) — 18.5 ☐
- Your first payment on account for 1999-2000 *(include the pence)* — 18.6 £

  Tick box 18.7 if you are making a claim to reduce your 1999-2000 payments on account and say why in the 'Additional information' box — 18.7 ☐

  Tick box 18.8 if you do **not** need to make 1999-2000 payments on account — 18.8 ☐
- 1999-2000 tax you are reclaiming now — 18.9 £

Q19 **Do you want to claim a repayment if you have paid too much tax?** *(If you tick 'No' or the tax you have overpaid is below £10, I will use the amount you are owed to reduce your next tax bill.)*

NO ☐ YES ☐ If yes, fill in boxes 19.1 to 19.12 as appropriate.

Should the repayment (or payment) be sent:

- to you? *Tick box 19.1* — 19.1 ☐

or

- to your bank or building society account or other nominee? *Tick box 19.2* — 19.2 ☐

If you ticked either box 19.2 or 19.9, fill in boxes 19.3 to 19.8, 19.11 and 19.12 as appropriate.

Your (or your nominee's) bank or building society — 19.3

Branch sort code — 19.4 – –

Account number — 19.5

Name of account — 19.6

Building society ref. — 19.7

If your nominee is your agent, *tick box 19.9 and complete boxes 19.10 to 19.12* — 19.9 ☐

Agent's ref. for you — 19.10

I authorise — 19.8 Name of your nominee/agent

Nominee's address — 19.11

Postcode

to receive on my behalf the amount due

This authority must be signed by you. A photocopy of your signature will not do. — 19.12 Signature

Q20 **Are your details on the front of the Tax Return wrong?**

NO ☐ YES ☐ If yes, please make any corrections on the front of the form.

Q21 **Please give other personal details in boxes 21.1 to 21.6** *This information helps us to be more efficient and effective and may support claims you have made elsewhere in your Tax Return*

Please give a daytime telephone number if convenient. It is often simpler to phone if we need to ask you about your Tax Return.

Your telephone number — 21.1

or, if you prefer, your agent's telephone number — 21.2

(also give your agent's name and reference in the 'Additional information' box on page 8)

Enter your first two forenames — 21.5

Say if you are single, married, widowed, divorced or separated — 21.3

Date of birth — 21.4 / /

Enter your date of birth if you are self-employed, or you were born before 6 April 1934, or you have ticked the 'Yes' box in Question 14, or you are claiming relief for Venture Capital Trust subscriptions

Enter your National Insurance number (if known) — 21.6

Income for the year ended 5 April 1999

Inland Revenue

EMPLOYMENT

Name

Tax reference

Fill in these boxes first

If you want help, look up the box numbers in the Notes

Details of employer

Employer's PAYE reference

1.1

Employer's name

1.2

Date employment started
(only if between 6 April 1998 and 5 April 1999)

1.3 / /

Employer's address

1.5

Postcode

Date finished (only if between 6 April 1998 and 5 April 1999)

1.4 / /

Tick box 1.6 if you were a director of the company

1.6

and, if so, tick box 1.7 if it was a close company

1.7

Income from employment

■ *Money* - see Notes, page EN3

		Before tax
• Payments from P60 (or P45 or pay slips)		1.8 £
• Payments not on P60 etc.	- tips	1.9 £
	- other payments (excluding expenses shown below and lump sums and compensation payments or benefits shown overleaf)	1.10 £

	Tax deducted
• UK tax deducted from payments in boxes 1.8 to 1.10	1.11 £

■ *Benefits and expenses* - *see Notes, pages EN3 to EN6. If any benefits connected with termination of employment were received, or enjoyed, after that termination and were from a **former** employer you need to complete Help Sheet IR204, available from the Orderline. Do not enter such benefits here.*

	Amount		Amount
• Assets transferred/ payments made for you	1.12 £	• Vans	1.18 £
• Vouchers/credit cards	1.13 £	• Interest-free and low-interest loans	1.19 £
• Living accommodation	1.14 £	• Mobile telephones	1.20 £
• Mileage allowance	1.15 £	• Private medical or dental insurance	1.21 £
• Company cars	1.16 £	• Other benefits	1.22 £
• Fuel for company cars	1.17 £	• Expenses payments received and balancing charges	1.23 £

Income from employment continued

■ ***Lump sums and compensation payments or benefits including such payments and benefits from a former employer***
Note that 'lump sums' here includes any contributions which your employer made to an unapproved retirement benefits scheme

*You must read page EN6 of the Notes **before** filling in boxes 1.24 to 1.30*

Reliefs

- £30,000 exemption — **1.24** £
- Foreign service and disability — **1.25** £
- Retirement and death lump sums — **1.26** £

Taxable lump sums

- From box H of *Help Sheet IR204* — **1.27** £
- From box Q of *Help Sheet IR204* — **1.28** £
- From box R of *Help Sheet IR204* — **1.29** £
- Tax deducted from payments in boxes 1.27 to 1.29 — Tax deducted **1.30** £

■ ***Foreign earnings not taxable in the UK in year ended 5 April 1999** - see Notes, page EN6* — **1.31** £

■ ***Expenses you incurred in doing your job** - see Notes, starting on page EN6*

- Travel and subsistence costs — **1.32** £
- Fixed deductions for expenses — **1.33** £
- Professional fees and subscriptions — **1.34** £
- Other expenses and capital allowances — **1.35** £
- Tick box 1.36 if the figure in box 1.32 includes travel between your home and a permanent workplace — **1.36**

■ ***Foreign Earnings Deduction*** — **1.37** £

■ ***Foreign tax for which tax credit relief not claimed*** — **1.38** £

Additional information

Now fill in any other supplementary Pages that apply to you.
Otherwise, go back to page 2 in your Tax Return and finish filling it in.

TECHNICIAN STAGE
NVQ/SVQ LEVEL 4 IN ACCOUNTING
CENTRAL ASSESSMENT (TAX)
PREPARING TAXATION
COMPUTATIONS

AAT
ASSOCIATION
OF ACCOUNTING
TECHNICIANS

FRIDAY 20 JUNE 1997

Time allowed—**3 hours plus 15 minutes' reading time**

ANSWER ALL SECTIONS

DURING THE 15 MINUTES' READING TIME YOU MAY READ AND WRITE NOTES ON THE ASSESSMENT PAPER ITSELF BUT YOU MUST NOT WRITE IN THE ANSWER BOOKLET UNTIL THE SUPERVISOR GIVES PERMISSION TO DO SO.

PLEASE DO NOT OPEN THIS BOOKLET UNTIL INSTRUCTED TO DO SO BY THE SUPERVISOR

Notes:

1. All calculations should be made to the nearest month and the nearest £

2. Ignore the effects of National Insurance in all questions.

This central assessment consists of THREE sections, all of which are to be answered using the information given in this assessment paper. You are reminded that competence must be achieved in each section and you should answer ALL tasks within EACH section.

The times next to each task within a section are suggested maximum times to be spent on each task and are for guidance only. You may spend more or less than these times on each task, depending upon your skills and experience.

Any blank forms required will be found at the end of this assessment.

You should show all workings.

Credit will be given for presentation.

SECTION 1:

Task 1.1 Capital gains tax computation (30 minutes)
Task 1.2 Corporation tax computation (45 minutes)
Task 1.3 Complete form CT200 (corporation tax return using the short version of the return) (20 minutes)

SECTION 2

Task 2.1 Draft letter in answer to client's queries on employment income (30 minutes)

Task 2.2 Income tax computation (35 minutes)

SECTION 3

Task 3.1 Completion of extract from the 1998/99 income tax return (20 minutes)

Introduction

You are Susan Spanner, an accounting technician working for a firm of accountants Hammer, Wrench and Co. The firm has a specialist tax department, and you have been asked to help out with some of the tax department's work. The work required is set out in the attached memo from the manager in charge of the tax department.

MEMO

Hammer, Wrench and Co

To:	Susan Spanner, Accounting Technician
From:	Diana Drill, Tax Manager
Subject:	Tax Department Work
Date:	20 June 1999

I would like you to do the following work for me on some of the tax department's clients:

SECTION 1

Nuts and Bolts Limited is a manufacturing company making nuts and bolts.

Task 1.1: Calculate the capital gains arising on the disposal of the two freehold properties sold by Nuts and Bolts Limited during the year ended 31 March 1999.

Task 1.2: Prepare a corporation tax computation for Nuts and Bolts Limited for the year ended 31 March 1999 (using the extracts from the accounts and accounts file schedules provided).

Task 1.3: Complete form CT200 for Nuts and Bolts Limited for the year ended 31 March 1999. Please note that, as usual, we will use the short version of the return. This means that we will complete Section 2 of the return instead of Section 3; Sections 4, 5, and 9 of the return may require completion if there is relevant information.

SECTION 2

Mr Frederick Fuse is the managing Director of Nuts and Bolts Limited.

Task 2.1: Draft a reply to Mr Fuse's letter of 31 May 1999, calculating the value of his benefits in kind and answering the questions he has raised about the taxation of his employment income.

Task 2.2 Prepare an income tax computation for 1998/99 for Mr Fuse (showing the balance of tax due by self-assessment, after offset of tax already deducted at source).

SECTION 3

Mrs Fiona Fuse is married to Mr Frederick Fuse. She has her own business making and selling children's toys.

Task 3.1: Complete the self-employment pages of the 1998/99 income tax return provided, in respect of Mrs Fuse's Schedule D Case I income.

Information for Section 1, Task 1.1

Nuts and Bolts Limited disposed of two freehold properties in the year ended 31 March 1999. The details of the disposals are as follows:

1. Sale of Manchester factory on 10 April 1998

Sale Proceeds (10 April 1998)	£500,000	(including £50,000 for the land)
Costs of sale (10 April 1998–legal fees)	£1,500	
Original cost of building	£90,000	
Original cost of land	£10,000	
Total cost on 1 January 1980	£100,000	
The land and buildings were valued on 31 March 1982 at	£125,000	

2. Sale of half a plot of land at Wigan on 10 December 1998

Sale proceeds of half the plot of land (10 December 1998)	£100,200
Value of the remaining half (on 10 December 1998)	£50,000
Original cost of the whole plot of land on 25 June 1996	£50,000

Information for Section 1, Tasks 1.2 and 1.3

Extracts from accounts

Nuts and Bolts Limited
Financial Statements
For the year ended 31 March 1999

Hammer, Wrench & Co
Accountants
Credit Street
Lanchester

Nuts and Bolts Limited

Extract From The Report of the Directors
The directors present their annual report and the accounts for the year ended 31 March 1999.

Principal Activity
The company's principal activity during the year was the manufacture and sale of nuts and bolts.

Directors and their interests
The directors in office at the date of this report, both of whom served throughout the year, were Mr Frederick Fuse and Mrs Patricia Plug.

The interest of the directors in the share capital of the company was as follows:

	Interest in £1 ordinary shares	
	At 31/3/99	At 31/3/98
Mr Frederick Fuse	50%	50%
Mrs Patricia Plug	50%	50%

Nuts and Bolts Limited
Profit and Loss Account
For the year ended 31 March 1999

	1999		*1998*	
	£	£	£	£
TURNOVER		745,444		450,153
Administration expenses	214,576		172,324	
Other operating charges	375,010		215,141	
		(589,586)		(387,465)
OPERATING PROFIT		155,858		62,688
Interest payable and similar charges		(2,325)		(1,383)
Other interest receivable and similar income		493,000		251,000
PROFIT ON ORDINARY ACTIVITIES		646,533		312,305
TAXATION ON PROFIT ON ORDINARY ACTIVITIES		(194,000)		(104,000)
PROFIT ON ORDINARY ACTIVITIES AFTER TAXATION		452,533		208,305
Dividends		(1,600)		(1,500)
RETAINED PROFIT FOR THE YEAR		450,933		206,805
RETAINED PROFIT BROUGHT FORWARD		381,805		175,000
RETAINED PROFIT CARRIED FORWARD		832,738		381,805

Information for Section 1, Tasks 1.2 and 1.3

Nuts and Bolts Limited
Balance sheet as at 31 March 1999

	Note	*1999* £	£	*1998* £	£
FIXED ASSETS					
Tangible assets	7		242,950		342,900
CURRENT ASSETS					
Stock		50,000		45,000	
Debtors		17,500		15,000	
Cash at bank and in hand		559,677		2,500	
		627,177		62,500	
CREDITORS					
Amounts falling due within one year		(36,389)		(22,595)	
NET CURRENT ASSETS			590,788		39,905
NET ASSETS			833,738		382,805
CAPITAL AND RESERVES					
Equity share capital			1,000		1,000
Reserves			832,738		381,805
			833,738		382,805

Nuts and Bolts Limited
Extracts from the notes to the accounts
(The full notes to the accounts have not been reproduced, only those required to answer the tasks.)

Note 7

Tangible Fixed Assets

	Land and Buildings £	*Motor vehicles* £	*Plant and Machinery* £	*Total* £
Cost				
At 1 April 1998	350,000	40,000	150,000	540,000
Additions	nil	37,000	25,000	62,000
Disposals	(125,000)	(21,000)	(30,000)	(176,000)
At 31 March 1999	225,000	56,000	145,000	426,000
Depreciation				
At 1 April 1998	60,600	24,000	112,500	197,100
Charge for the year	nil	11,200	36,250	47,450
Disposals	(30,600)	(8,400)	(22,500)	(61,500)
At 31 March 1999	30,000	26,800	126,250	183,050
NBV at 31 March 1999	£195,000	£29,200	£18,750	£242,950
NBV at 1 April 1998	£289,400	£16,000	£37,500	£342,900

Nuts and Bolts Limited

Accounts file information

Note from the Accounts Department to the Tax Department

Concerning information collected during the preparation of Nuts and Bolts Limited's accounts for the year ended 31 March 1999

Please find attached the information you requested concerning Nuts and Bolts Limited's accounts:

1. **Fixed assets:**
Additions:

Motor Vehicles		*Cost*
1 October 1998	Purchase of Ford Mondeo car for	£15,000
11 January 1999	Purchase of Ford Fiesta car for	£8,000
15 March 1999	Purchase of Ford Transit van for	£14,000
Total motor vehicle additions per accounts		£37,000

Plant and Machinery		
10 August 1998	Purchase of new bolt grinding machine for	£25,000
Total Plant and Machinery additions per accounts		£25,000

Disposals:

		Sale Proceeds	*Original cost*
Motor Vehicles		£	£
20 October 1998	Sold Vauxhall Cavalier car	5,000	13,000
10 January 1999	Sold Vauxhall Nova car	1,000	5,000
25 March 1999	Sold Vauxhall Bedford van	500	3,000
Plant and machinery			
1 August 1998	Sold old bolt grinding machine	1,000	30,000

Property disposals:
Details of the sale of the two freehold properties by the company during the year ended 31 March 1999 were given earlier (in the information for task 1.1).

Industrial buildings allowances had been claimed on the qualifying cost of the Manchester factory building (for details of the cost of the building see the information for task 1.1). The building had been in continuous use for industrial purposes throughout its period of ownership. The building was new on 1 January 1980, the date that Nuts and Bolts Limited bought the factory and brought it into industrial use. The tax written down value of the building on 1 April 1998, according to the industrial buildings allowance computations, was £25,200.

No other building qualified for industrial buildings allowances.

Profit on sale of fixed assets
The profit on sale of fixed assets credited to the profit and loss account of the company was £493,000.

Note: The tax written down values of the assets at 1 April 1998 were as follows

General pool	£3,400
FA80 pool	£6,000
Expensive car - Vauxhall Cavalier	£7,500

Nuts and Bolts Limited

Extracts from the accounts file (continued)

2. **Profit and loss account expenditure:**
Details of the profit and loss account expenditure (incurred in arriving at profit on ordinary activities before taxation) you asked for are as follows:

Entertaining	£
Costs of entertaining customers	15,500
Cost of a staff party at Christmas	2,900
Gifts to customers (800 bottles of wine with 'with the compliments of Nuts and Bolts Ltd' on the label)	7,200
	25,600

Bad debts:	£
The bad and doubtful debts account was made up as follows:	
General provision brought forward (a general percentage of debtors)	(2,400)
Specific trade debt written off	10,000
General provision carried forward at 31 March 1999 (a general percentage of debtors)	25,000
Charge to the profit and loss account	32,600

Legal and professional fees:	£
Costs of recovering trade debts	2,000
Legal fees re employee contracts of service	4,000
Legal fees re sale of Manchester factory	1,500
	7,500

Subscriptions and donations:	£	
Deed of covenant to The Red Cross (a charity)	10,000	(gross)
Subscription to a manufacturers' association	1,000	
	11,000	

Interest payable
Interest payable relates to interest payable on the company's current account during the year.

3. **Profit and loss account income:**

Turnover includes £12,000 of rental income receivable in the year ended 31 March 1999, on the rental of a warehouse owned by the company. (There are no expenses of rental to set against this income.)

Nuts and Bolts Limited
Other information

1. Tax payments:
   The company has not paid any corporation tax, on account, in respect of its year ended 31 March 1999.

2. Payments of ACT
   The company paid a dividend of £1,600 during the year ended 31 March 1999. The company did not receive any dividends in the year ended 31 March 1999.

3. Losses brought forward from previous accounting periods:
   On reviewing the tax files of the company you discover that the following tax losses have been brought forward at 1 April 1998:

Capital loss brought forward	£10,000
Trade losses brought forward	£5,000

4. Associated companies
   For the purposes of calculating corporation tax, Nuts and Bolts Limited has one associated company in the year ended 31 March 1999.

Information for Section 2, Tasks 2.1 and 2.2

25 Town Road
Lanchester

Hammer, Wrench and Co
Accountants
Credit Street
Lanchester

31 May 1999

Dear Ms Drill,

INCOME TAX YEAR ENDED 5 APRIL 1999

As usual, I enclose the information you require to calculate my income tax liability for 1998/99, as follows:

1. I receive a gross salary of £41,000 from my employment as Managing Director of Nuts and Bolts Limited. Income tax of £15,300 was deducted under the PAYE (Pay As You Earn) scheme, according to my form P60 for the tax year 1998/99.

2. A copy of the draft Form P11D from Nuts and Bolts Limited, showing the benefits in kind I received during the 1998/99 tax year.

   - Unfortunately, the new company accountant is confused by the style of forms, and although he has entered all of the details needed to calculate the benefits in kind, he has not calculated the car and car fuel benefits, or the benefit for private use of a company computer.
   - Please note that I have kept a record of the telephone calls made from home. Of the £700 of home telephone expenses paid for by my employer, £100 was for line rental and £600 was for reimbursement of call charges; 50% of the calls were for business purposes.
   - £2,900 of the entertaining costs were for business purposes.

3. Dividend vouchers for my share holdings in Nuts and Bolts Limited and S and S plc.

4. Interest statements for my bank and building society accounts.

5. I also received £165 of National Savings Bank Interest on my ordinary account on 31 December 1998.

A copy of the statement issued by my personal pension company recording payments made is also enclosed.

Income tax queries

In addition to enclosing the above information I have some requests to make. Please would you perform the following tasks and answer the following questions:

1. Please send me a schedule showing:

   (a) The value of my Schedule E earnings from employment (including benefits in kind) for 1998/99.

   (b) An explanation of the calculation of the tax value of the benefits in kind I have received.

2. The accountant at Nuts and Bolts Limited wants me to contribute towards some of the benefits I receive. He has suggested the followed payments for 1999/00:

Payment towards the private use of the car	£100 per month
Payment towards the cost of private fuel	£10 per month (a contribution only, the full cost of private fuel would be approximately £1,000 for the year).

Please tell me how these contributions would affect the benefits in kind I will be taxed on for 1999/00.

If you need further information please contact me.

Yours sincerely

Frederick Fuse

Note: You may assume that the rules for taxing benefits in kind in 1999/00 will be the same as they were in 1998/99.

Inland Revenue

P11D EXPENSES AND BENEFITS 1998-99

Note to employer
Complete this return for a director, or an employee who earned at a rate of £8,500 a year or more during the year 6 April 1998 to 5 April 1999. Do not include expenses and benefits covered by a dispensation or PAYE settlement agreement. Read the P11D Guide and booklet 480, Chapter 24, before you complete the form. Send the completed P11D and form P11D(b) to the Tax Office by 6 July 1999. You must give a copy of this information to the director or employee by the same date. The term employee is used to cover both directors and employees throughout the rest of this form.

Note to employee
Your employer has filled in this form. Keep it in a safe place as you may not be able to get a duplicate. You will need it for your tax records and to complete your 1998-99 Tax Return if you get one. Your tax code may need to be adjusted to take account of the information given on this P11D. The box numbers on this P11D have the same numbering as the Employment Pages of the Tax Return, for example, 1.12. Include the total figures in the corresponding box on the Tax Return, unless you think some other figure is more appropriate.

Employer's details
Employer's name: NUTS AND BOLTS LIMITED
PAYE tax reference: NB 100

Employee's details
Employee's name: FREDERICK FUSE
Tick here if a director: ✓
Works number or department:
National Insurance number: PD 50 60 70 D

A • **Assets transferred (cars, property, goods or other assets)**

Description of asset | Cost/ Market value £ – Amount made good or from which tax deducted £ = **1.12** Cash equivalent £

B • **Payments made on behalf of employee**

Description of payment | **1.12** £

Tax on notional payments not borne by employee within 30 days of receipt of each notional payment | **1.12** £

C • **Vouchers or credit cards**

Value of vouchers and payments made using credit cards or tokens | Gross amount £ – Amount made good or from which tax deducted £ = **1.13** Cash equivalent £

D • **Living accommmodation**

Cash equivalent of accommodation provided for employee, or his/ her family or household | **1.14** Cash equivalent £

E • **Mileage allowance**

Car and mileage allowances paid for employee's car | Gross amount £ – Amount made good or from which tax deducted £ = **1.15** Taxable payment £

F • **Cars and car fuel**
If more than two cars were made available, either at the same time or in succession, please give details on a separate sheet

	Car 1	Car 2
Make and Model	VAUXHALL CAVALIER	
Dates first registered	01/10/96	/ /
Dates car was available	From 06/04/98 To 05/04/99	From / / To / /
Business mileage used in calculation for this car. *Tick only one box for each car.* *If the car was not available for part of the year, the business mileage limits are reduced proportionately.* (2,499 or less / 2,500 to 17,999 / 18,000 or more)	2,500 to 17,999 ✓	
Enter engine size and tick type of fuel *only if there is a car fuel scale charge* (Engine size in cc / Petrol / Diesel)	1600 cc, Petrol ✓	cc

	Car 1	Car 2
List price of car *If there is no list price, or if it is a classic car, employers see booklet 480; employees see leaflet IR133*	£ 14003	£
Price of optional accessories fitted when car was first made available to the employee	£ NIL	£
Price of accessories added after the car was first made available to the employee	£ NIL	£
Capital contributions (maximum £5,000) the employee made towards the cost of car or accessories	£ NIL	£
Amount paid by employee for private use of the car	£ NIL	£
Cash equivalent of each car	£	£
Total cash equivalent of all cars available in 1998-99		**1.16** £
Cash equivalent of fuel for each car	£	£
Total cash equivalent of fuel for all cars available in 1998-99		**1.17** £

P11D(1999) BMSD 11/98

G • **Vans**

Cash equivalent of all vans made available for private use | **1.18** £

H • **Interest-free and low interest loans**

If the total amount outstanding on all loans does not exceed £5,000 at any time in the year, there is no need for details in this section.

	Loan 1	Loan 2
Purpose of loan(s) – *please use the code shown in P11D Guide for employers*		
Number of joint borrowers *(if applicable)*		
Tick the box if the loan is within MIRAS		
Amount outstanding at 5 April 1998 or at date loan was made if later	£	£
Amount outstanding at 5 April 1999 or at date loan was discharged if earlier	£	£
Maximum amount outstanding at any time in the year	£	£
Total amount of interest paid by the borrower in 1998 - 99 – *enter "NIL" if none was paid*	£	£
Date loan was made or discharged in 1998 - 99 if applicable	/ /	/ /
Cash equivalent of loans after deducting any interest paid by the borrower	**1.19** £	**1.19** £

I • **Mobile telephones**

Cash equivalent of mobile telephones provided ONE PHONE | **1.20** £ 600

J • **Private medical treatment or insurance**

	Cost to you		Amount made good or from which tax deducted		Cash equivalent
Private medical treatment or insurance	£ 865	–	£ NIL	=	**1.21** £ 865

K • **Qualifying relocation expenses payments and benefits (non-qualifying expenses go in P below)**

Excess over £8,000 of all qualifying relocation expenses payments and benefits for each move | **1.22** £

L • **Services supplied**

	Cost to you		Amount made good or from which tax deducted		Cash equivalent
Services supplied to the employee	£	–	£	=	**1.22** £

M • **Assets placed at the employee's disposal**

		Annual value plus expenses incurred		Amount made good or from which tax deducted		Cash equivalent
Description of asset	COMPUTER	£	–	£	=	**1.22** £

MADE AVAILABLE ON 6.12.98
£10,000 - COST ON 6.12.98

N • **Shares**

Tick the box if during the year there have been share-related benefits for the employee ☐

O • **Other items**

		Cost to you		Amount made good or from which tax deducted		Cash equivalent
Subscriptions and professional fees		£	–	£	=	**1.22** £
Description of other items		£	–	£	=	**1.22** £

Income tax paid but not deducted from director's remuneration | Tax paid **1.22** £

P • **Expenses payments made to, or on behalf of, the employee**

		Cost to you		Amount made good or from which tax deducted		Taxable payment
Travelling and subsistence payments		£	–	£	=	**1.23** £
Entertainment *(trading organisations read P11D Guide and then enter a tick or a cross as appropriate here)*	✓	£ 3000	–	£ NIL	=	**1.23** £ 3000
General expenses allowance for business travel		£	–	£	=	**1.23** £
Payments for use of home telephone		£ 700	–	£ NIL	=	**1.23** £ 700
Non-qualifying relocation expenses *(those not shown in section K)*		£	–	£	=	**1.23** £
Description of other expenses		£	–	£	=	**1.23** £

NUTS AND BOLTS LIMITED
Dividend Voucher

Paid 31 December 1998

Date	*No of shares*	*Dividend*	*Tax credit*
		£	£
31.12.98	500	800	200

S AND S PLC
Dividend Voucher

Paid 31 March 1999

Date	*No of shares*	*Dividend*	*Tax credit*
		£	*£*
31.3.99	*21,000*	*2,100*	*525*

Lanchester Building Society
Interest Statement as at 31 December 1998

Account no	Account type	Gross interest	Tax deducted	Net interest
		£	£	£
4142434445A	Bright Sparks Extra Interest	5,625	1,125	4,500
1112131415B	Tax Exempt Special Savings Account (TESSA)	630	Nil	

National Bank plc
Interest Statement for 1998/99

Account no	Payment Date	Gross Interest	Tax deducted	Net Interest
		£	£	£
21 22 23 24 25C	30 June 1998	625	125	500
	31 December 1998	750	150	600

Frederick Fuse

Pension Contributions
This statement is to certify that Mr Frederick Fuse paid pension contributions of £165 per month (net of basic rate tax) from 30 April 1998 to 31 March 1999.

Information for Section 3, Task 3.1

MEMO

To: Susan Spanner
From: Diana Drill
Subject: Mrs Fiona Fuse's self employed income.

Mrs Fuse runs a small business making soft toys for children. I have already calculated the figures on which Mrs Fuse will be taxed for 1998/99 in respect of her Schedule D Case I business and I would like you to put these figures on the self employment pages of Mrs Fuse's 1998/99 self assessment income tax return.

General information on Mrs Fuse's business

Fuse's Furry Animals
25 Town Road
Lanchester

Makers and distributors of soft toys.

Business started 10 April 1996 and makes up accounts to 31 December each year. Overlap profit brought forward at 1 January 1998 is £2,301.

Mrs Fuse is not registered for VAT.

FIONA FUSE
TRADING AS FUSE'S FURRY ANIMALS
PROFIT AND LOSS ACCOUNT FOR THE YEAR ENDED 31 DECEMBER 1998

	£	£	£
Sales			19,396
Less cost of sales			(577)
Gross Profit			18,819
Less Expenses			
Employee costs—staff wages		3,673	
Premises:			
Rent	1,870		
Light and heat	2,100		
		3,970	
Repairs		31	
General Administrative expenses:			
Telephone		366	
Motor Expenses:			
Petrol	495		
Car tax and insurance	275		
		770	
Advertising		36	
Depreciation		2,739	
Other Expenses:			
Magazine	55		
Work clothes	115		
Business insurance	255		
		425	
			(12,010)
Net Profit			6,809

Note: as the turnover is small no balance sheet has been produced.

MRS FIONA FUSE—TRADING AS FUSE'S FURRY ANIMALS
SCHEDULE D CASE I CALCULATION FOR YEAR ENDED 31 DECEMBER 1998

	£	£
Net profit per the accounts		6,809
Add:		
Depreciation	2,739	
Work clothes	115	
Private telephone	204	
Private car expenses (£495 + £275) x 40%	308	
Non trade magazine subscription	25	
		3,391
		10,200
Less: Capital allowances		
Cars	1,000	
Plant and machinery	1,500	
		(2,500)
		7,700

Inland Revenue

Page 1

Corporation Tax Return
Version 3

This form, or an approved substitute version of it, must be used whenever a company is required to do so, by a *Notice to deliver a Corporation Tax Return (form CT203)*. This return sets out the information we need and provides a standard format for calculations.

You should read this return form along with your *Notice to deliver a Corporation Tax Return (form CT203)* and *Filling in your Corporation Tax Return (leaflet CT200 Notes)* which you should have received with this form. The notes referred to throughout can be found in the leaflet *CT200 Notes*. You should contact your Tax Office if you need more help.

'Company' means any body chargeable to corporation tax, whether incorporated or not. This definition includes clubs, associations and voluntary organisations.

Sections to be completed

Members' clubs, associations and voluntary organisations - It is likely that you will only have to complete Sections 1 and 2. For further guidance see note 1 in the *Notes*.

All companies - including clubs, etc. - You will not need to complete every Section, but you **must** complete the Declaration and Section 1 on this page. The *Notes* will help you decide whether you should complete the mutually exclusive *Short return* at Section 2 or the *Detailed return* at Section 3. Sections 9 and 10 are optional but you are asked to complete them if they are relevant to the company.

It is important that you read the *Notes* before completing any part of this form.

What to do when you have completed the return

- Make sure you have completed and signed the Declaration, then
- staple together the pages you have completed and attach any supporting calculations
- send these together with the relevant company accounts and, where prepared, directors' and auditors' reports, to your Tax Office using the envelope provided (see Note 3 for the date by which you should do this)
- pay any outstanding corporation tax (as you have shown at box box 65), as advised on the payslip attached to your *Notice to deliver a Corporation Tax Return (form CT203)*. Interest is charged on tax paid later than nine months and one day after the end of an accounting period. Tax is due without the making of an assessment.

Remember - ***Your tax return is not complete unless you send relevant accounts and documentation with this form. Penalties may be charged if your return, or any part of it, is late or incorrect.***

As soon as your figures are agreed

- we will send you an assessment setting out the tax position for the accounting period - unless there are no figures to assess
- we will issue an amended assessment if you have already received an estimated assessment and you have appealed against it.

Section 1: Summary

The company name

[ ]

The company address - only if changed since last return made.
Enter the UK registered office address, or the UK address if the company does not have a registered office. If the company does not have premises in the UK show the address of the person making the return.

[ ]

Company registration number *(if registered)*

0987654

Reference
Enter the reference number shown on the *Notice to deliver a Corporation Tax Return (form CT203)*

XXX / 12345 / 91011

Corporation tax accounting period covered by this return
Cannot exceed 12 months. Enter start and end dates.

From [/ /] To [/ /]

If this period is not an accounting period of the company for corporation tax purposes (see note 2) put an 'X' in the box below, complete the Declaration to the right and return this form to your Tax Office. You do not need to complete the rest of this Section or other Sections of this form in these circumstances. [ ]

Profits chargeable *(Enter the firgure from box 30). If there are none enter 0'.*

£ [ ]

Corporation tax due *(Enter the figure from box 61 minus any entry in box 64). If none is due enter '0.00'.*

£ [ ] • p [ ]

Put an X in the appropriate box

Have you completed Section 8 (Repayments)? Yes [ ] No [ ]

Is the company name different from that shown in the *Notice* (form CT203)? Yes [ ] No [ ]

Declaration

Enter here the page numbers you are attaching

[ ]

Put an 'X' in the appropriate boxes to show the documents you are enclosing

- a copy of the accounts for the period to which this return relates [ ]
- a copy of the company accounts for a different period [ ]
- no accounts [ ]
- say why not [ ]
- calculations showing how the entries in the return form have been arrived at. [ ]

I declare that to the best of my knowledge and belief the return on this page and the pages attached is correct and complete.

Signature

[ ]

Except where a liquidator has been appointed, the company secretary, treasurer, or any other person who is authorised to do so may sign this declaration on behalf of the company. A photocopy of a signature is not acceptable.

Date

[/ /]

Name *(in capital letters)*

[ ]

Status *(company secretary, treasurer, liquidator etc.)*

[ ]

CT200(1997) Page 1 BMSD 8/97

Page 2

Section 2: Short return

You may complete this section if
- it covers all the entries you need to make and
- each entry, including the company's total income and deductions, is less than £10 million.

In all other cases, or if you prefer, complete Section 3 instead. You should enclose an explanation and calculations of any figures which you have estimated or which are not immediately recognisable from the company's accounts.

The figures to be entered are those adjusted for tax purposes, after deducting capital allowances and adding balancing charges where appropriate. Section 4 should also be completed if capital allowances are claimed.

Please do not enter '0's where the company did not have the source specified in the return form.

	£	£
Trading profits *See note 5* ... 1		
Trading losses brought forward *Only include losses made in the same trade. Include charges treated as losses.* ***Do not enter an amount larger than is needed to cover the profits in box 1.*** *See note 6* ... 2		
Net trading profit *(box 1 minus box 2). If box 2 equals box 1, enter '0'. Leave this box blank if there are no trading profits in box 1* ... 3		
Trading losses of this accounting period *Where there is more than one trade give total for all trades. Do not set box 4 losses against box 1 profits, claim at box 22 against total profits.* ... 4		
Profits and gains from non-trading loan relationships and other Schedule D Case III income *Include interest and other profits and gains from non-trading loan relationships even if tax has been deducted. Complete box 57 to claim credit for income tax deducted. You will need to complete the* **Detailed return** *at Section 3 if you have deficits on non-trading loan relationships from this, earlier or later accounting periods to include. See note 8* ... 6		
Income within Schedule D Case VI - for example furnished lettings *Enter the figure net of allowable losses brought forward. Exclude income you enter in box 12. See note 7* ... 9		
Income from which income tax has been deducted - for example building society interest *Enter the gross amount before tax. Exclude any amount included in box 6 above. Complete box 57 to claim credit for income tax deducted. See note 9* ... 10		
Income from UK land and buildings *Enter the amount net of allowable expenses brought forward. Exclude income in box 9 above. See note 10* ... 12		
Chargeable gains *See note 11*		
Gross gains ... 13		
Allowable losses *Include any losses brought forward but do not enter an amount larger than the amount of gross gains in box 13 above.* ... 14		
Net chargeable gains *(box 13 minus box 14) If box 14 equals box 13, enter '0'* ... 15		
Profits *(total of boxes 3, 6, 9, 10, 12 and 15)* ... 17		
Relief for trading losses of this or of a later period *Put an 'X' in box 21 if amounts carried back from later accounting periods are included in box 22. See note 12* ... 21 ☐ 22		
Profits before charges *(box 17 minus box 22)* ... 26		
Charges paid *Do not enter an amount larger than is needed to cover profits in box 26. See note 13* ... 27		
Profits chargeable to corporation tax *(box 26 minus box 27)* ***Copy this figure into the box provided in Section 1 on page 1, and also into the box at the top of page 3*** ... 30		

The short return is continued on page 3

Page 3

Profits chargeable to corporation tax

Enter the figure brought forward from page 2, box 30 ... £ [ ]

If you claim tax is chargeable at the small companies' rate, or if you are claiming marginal small companies' relief, complete boxes 31 - 35. If there are no associated companies please enter '0' against the relevant financial year. *See note 15*

Franked investment income and foreign income dividends arising in the period covered by the return. *See note 15* ... 31 £ [ ]

Number of companies associated with this company in the/each financial year covered by this return
Exclude this company. See note 15 ...

	Financial year		Number of associated companies
32	[ ]	33	[ ]
34	[ ]	35	[ ]

Corporation tax chargeable *See note 16*

	Financial years beginning 1 April		Amounts of profit £		Rates of tax *See note 16*		Tax £ p
36	[ ]	37	[ ]	38	[ ] • [ ]	39	[ ] • [ ]
43	[ ]	44	[ ]	45	[ ] • [ ]	46	[ ] • [ ]

Total corporation tax chargeable *(box 39 plus box 46)* ... 50 [ ] • [ ]

Marginal small companies' relief
Attach your computation (see notes 15, 16 and 29) ... 51 £ [ ] • p [ ]

Advance corporation tax restricted if necessary under Section 239(2) ICTA 1988
Put an 'X' in box 53 if amounts carried back from later accounting periods are included. See note 17. 53 [ ] 54 [ ] • [ ]

Total of boxes 51 and 54
Total must not be larger than entry in box 50. Restrict if necessary ... 55 [ ] • [ ]

Net corporation tax chargeable *(box 50 minus box 55)* ... 56 [ ] • [ ]

Calculation of tax outstanding or overpaid

Income tax deducted from gross income included in return
Do not include deductions used to cover income tax for which the company was liable to account to the Inland Revenue on payments it has made. See note 18 ... 57 [ ] • [ ]

Corporation tax due

Box 56 minus box 57. If box 57 equals or is greater than box 56, enter '0.00' and go to box 59.
Copy the figure in box 61 to the box provided in Section 1 on page 1. *See note 20* ... 61 [ ] • [ ]

Income tax repayable to the company *(box 57 minus box 56).*
Complete Section 8 on page 8. Do not complete unless you are making a claim. *See note 28*... 59 [ ] • [ ]

Corporation tax already paid (and not repaid). *See note 21* ... 63 [ ] • [ ]

Corporation tax outstanding *(box 61 minus box 63). This amount is payable to the Accounts Office.*
If box 63 equals or is greater than box 61, enter '0.00' and go to box 66. *See note 23* ... 65 [ ] • [ ]

Corporation tax overpaid *(box 63 minus box 61).*
Complete Section 8 on page 8 also. *See note 28* ... 66 [ ] • [ ]

This is the last page of the short return

Page 6

Section 4: Claims for capital allowances and details of balancing charges arising

You must complete this section if you want to claim capital allowances, whether or not those allowances are reflected elsewhere in the return. You should also show balancing charges taken into account in the short or detailed return. Show details of qualifying expenditure on which writing-down allowances may be claimed, even if you do not want to claim any allowances for this period. *See note 25*

Notice of expenditure on machinery and plant *See note 25*

Expenditure on which first year allowance is claimed £	Qualifying expenditure on long life assets on which writing down allowances may be claimed £	Qualifying expenditure on other assets on which writing down allowances may be claimed £
68	91	69

Charges and allowances included in calculation of trading profit or losses

	Balancing charges £	Capital allowances £
Cars *Including leased out and "expensive" cars*	70	71
Machinery and plant *- long life assets*	92	93
- other	72	73
Industrial buildings and structures *Including qualifying hotels, and commercial buildings and hotels in enterprise zones*	74	75
Other charges and allowances *For example agricultural buildings, mineral extraction, scientific research, patents*	76	77
Charges and allowances not included in calculation of trading profit or losses	78	79

Section 5: Particulars of advance corporation tax and surplus advance corporation tax

Complete this section if you have surplus advance corporation tax brought forward or have paid advance corporation tax (and it has not been repaid) in respect of qualifying distributions made in the period covered by this return.

	£	p
Particulars of advance corporation tax paid		
Particulars of any surplus advance corporation tax brought forward		

Section 6: Amounts claimed as group relief

Complete this section if you have claimed group relief at box 29 (see note 26). Attach a separate sheet of paper if you need more space. Attach a copy of each surrendering company's notice of consent to the claim unless a special arrangement is in force. Include claims made under the consortium provisions.

Name of surrendering company	Accounting period Show the start and end dates of any accounting period which is different from the one to which this return relates.	Tax reference Show the Tax Office number and the tax inspector's file reference. If you do not know these, supply whatever information you have that will help us to identify the company, for example the company registration number.	Amount claimed from each company
			£
			£
			£
			£
			£
			£
			£
			£
			£
			£
			£
			£
			£
		Total *This figure should be the same as the one in box 29.*	£

Page 9

Section 9: Figures brought forward and carried forward

Please complete this section if any of the following items are
- brought forward from the previous accounting period *or*
- available for carry forward from the period to which this return relates.

Please provide a reconciliation of any figures that are not explained elsewhere in your accounts and calculations. Attach a separate sheet of paper if you need more space.

	Total brought forward	Less amount used	Plus net amount available to carry forward from this accounting period	Total to carry forward
Trading losses *include trade charges treated as losses*	£	£	£	£
Schedule D case VI losses	£	£	£	£
Excess management expenses *Include business charges treated as management expenses*	£	£	£	£
Surplus ACT *Enter the figure net of amounts set off or repaid or surrendered to subsidiaries*	£ p	£ p	£ p	£ p
Surplus franked investment income	£ p	£ p	£ p	£ p
Losses allowable against chargeable gains	£	£	£	£
Net non-trade deficits and losses on loan relationships (including interest), exchange fluctuations, and certain financial instruments *See note 8.*	£	£	£	£
Others *Please specify*	£	£	£	£
	£	£	£	£
	£	£	£	£
	£	£	£	£

Income for the year ended 5April 1999

Inland Revenue

SELF-EMPLOYMENT

Fill in these boxes first

Name: MRS FIONA FUSE

Tax reference: FF205

If you want help, look up the box numbers in the Notes

Business details

Name of business **3.1**

Description of business **3.2**

Address of business **3.3**

Postcode

Accounting period - *read the Notes, page SEN2 before filling in these boxes*

Start **3.4** / /

End **3.5** / /

- Tick box 3.5A if you entered details for all relevant accounting periods on last year's Tax Return and boxes 3.11 to 3.70 will be blank **3.5A**
- Tick box 3.6 if details in boxes 3.1 or 3.3 have changed since your last Tax Return **3.6**
- Tick box 3.7 if your accounts do not cover the period from the last accounting date (explain why in the 'Additional information' box below) **3.7**
- Tick box 3.8A if your accounting date has changed (only if this is a permanent change and you want it to count for tax) **3.8A**
- Tick box 3.8B if this is the second or further change (explain why you have not used the same date as last year in the 'Additional information' box) **3.8B**
- Date of commencement if after 5 April 1996 **3.9** / /
- Date of cessation if before 6 April 1999 **3.10** / /

Additional information

Income and expenses - annual turnover below £15,000

*If your annual turnover is £15,000 or mor , **ignore** boxes 3.11 to 3.13.* *Now fill in Page SE2*

*If your annual turnover is below £15,00 , **fill in boxes 3.11 to 3.13 instead of Page SE2**. Read the Notes, page SEN2.*

- Turnover, other business receipts and goods etc. taken for personal use (and balancing charges) **3.11** £
- Expenses allowable for tax (including capital allowances) **3.12** £

Net profit (put figure in brackets if a loss) — box 3.11 *minus* box 3.12 **3.13** £

Now fill in Page SE3

SA103

Income and expenses - annual turnover £15,000 or more

You must fill in this Page if your annual turnover is £15,000 or more - read the Notes, page SEN2

If you were registered for VAT, do the figures in boxes 3.16 to 3.51, include VAT? **3.14** [ ] or exclude VAT? **3.15** [ ]

	Disallowable expenses included in boxes 3.33 to 3.50	Total expenses	Sales/business income (turnover)
			3.16 £
• Cost of sales	**3.17** £	**3.33** £	
• Construction industry subcontractor costs	**3.18** £	**3.34** £	
• Other direct costs	**3.19** £	**3.35** £	box 3.16 *minus* (box 3.33 + box 3.34 + box 3.35)
		Gross profit/(loss)	**3.36** £
		Other income/profits	**3.37** £
• Employee costs	**3.20** £	**3.38** £	
• Premises costs	**3.21** £	**3.39** £	
• Repairs	**3.22** £	**3.40** £	
• General administrative expenses	**3.23** £	**3.41** £	
• Motor expenses	**3.24** £	**3.42** £	
• Travel and subsistence	**3.25** £	**3.43** £	
• Advertising, promotion and entertainment	**3.26** £	**3.44** £	
• Legal and professional costs	**3.27** £	**3.45** £	
• Bad debts	**3.28** £	**3.46** £	
• Interest	**3.29** £	**3.47** £	
• Other finance charges	**3.30** £	**3.48** £	
• Depreciation and loss/(profit) on sale	**3.31** £	**3.49** £	
• Other expenses	**3.32** £	**3.50** £	total of boxes 3.38 to 3.50
	Put the total of boxes 3.17 to 3.32 in **box 3.53 below**	Total expenses	**3.51** £
			boxes 3.36 + 3.37 *minus* box 3.51
		Net profit/(loss)	**3.52** £

Tax adjustments to net profit or loss

	total of boxes 3.17 to 3.32	
• Disallowable expenses	**3.53** £	
• Goods etc. taken for personal use and other adjustments (apart from disallowable expenses) that increase profits	**3.54** £	
• Balancing charges	**3.55** £	boxes 3.53 + 3.54 + 3.55
Total additions to net profit (deduct from net loss)		**3.56** £
• Capital allowances	**3.57** £	boxes 3.57 + 3.58
• Deductions from net profit (add to net loss)	**3.58** £	**3.59** £
		boxes 3.52 + 3.56 *minus* box 3.59
Net business profit for tax purposes (put figure in brackets if a loss)		**3.60** £

Now fill in Page SE3

You must fill in this Page (leave blank any boxes that do not apply to you)

Capital allowances - summary

	Capital allowances	Balancing charge
• Motor cars (Separate calculations must be made for each motor car costing more than £12,000 and for cars used partly for private motoring.)	3.61 £	3.62 £
• Other business plant and machinery	3.63 £	3.64 £
• Agricultural or Industrial Buildings Allowance (A separate calculation must be made for each block of expenditure.)	3.65 £	3.66 £
• Other capital allowances claimed (Separate calculations must be made.)	3.67 £	3.68 £
	total of column above	total of column above
Total capital allowances/balancing charges	3.69 £	3.70 £

Adjustments to arrive at taxable profit or loss

Basis period begins **3.71** / / and ends **3.72** / /

- Tick box 3.72A if the figure in box 3.88 is provisional **3.72A**
- Tick box 3.72B if the special arrangements for certain trades detailed in the guidance notes apply **3.72B**

Profit or loss of this account for tax purposes (box 3.13 or 3.60) **3.73** £

Adjustment to arrive at profit or loss for this basis period **3.74** £

- Overlap profit brought forward **3.75** £
- Deduct overlap relief used this year **3.76** £
- Overlap profit carried forward **3.77** £

Adjustment for farmers' averaging (see Notes, page SEN8 if you made a loss for 1998-99) **3.78** £

Net profit for 1998-99 (if loss, enter '0') **3.79** £

Allowable loss for 1998-99 (if you make a profit, enter '0') **3.80** £

- Loss offset against other income for 1998-99 **3.81** £
- Loss to carry back **3.82** £
- Loss to carry forward (that is allowable loss not claimed in any other way) **3.83** £
- Losses brought forward from last year **3.84** £
- Losses brought forward from last year used this year **3.85** £

Taxable profit after losses brought forward (box 3.79 *minus* box 3.85) **3.86** £

- Any other business income (for example, Business Start-up Allowance received in 1998-99) **3.87** £

Total taxable profits from this business (box 3.86 + box 3.87) **3.88** £

Class 4 National Insurance Contributions

- Tick this box if exception or deferment applies — 3.89
- Adjustments to profit chargeable to Class 4 National Insurance Contributions — 3.90 £

Class 4 National Insurance Contributions due — 3.91 £

Subcontractors in the construction industry

- Deductions made by contractors on account of tax (you must send your SC60s to us) — 3.92 £

Summary of balance sheet

Leave these boxes blank if you do not have a balance sheet

- ***Assets***
  - Plant, machinery and motor vehicles — 3.93 £
  - Other fixed assets (premises, goodwill, investments etc.) — 3.94 £
  - Stock and work in progress — 3.95 £
  - Debtors/prepayments/other current assets — 3.96 £
  - Bank/building society balances — 3.97 £
  - Cash in hand — 3.98 £

  total of boxes 3.93 to 3.98 — 3.99 £

- ***Liabilities***
  - Trade creditors/accruals — 3.100 £
  - Loans and overdrawn bank accounts — 3.101 £
  - Other liabilities — 3.102 £

  total of boxes 3.100 to 3.102 — 3.103 £

- ***Net business assets*** (put the figure in brackets if you had net business liabilities) — box 3.99 *minus* box 3.103 — 3.104 £
- ***Represented by***

  Capital Account
  - Balance at start of period* — 3.105 £
  - Net profit/(loss)* — 3.106 £
  - Capital introduced — 3.107 £
  - Drawings — 3.108 £
  - Balance at end of period* — total of boxes 3.105 to 3.107 *minus* box 3.108 — 3.109 £

* If the Capital Account is overdrawn, or the business made a net loss, show the figure in brackets.

Tax deducted from trading income

- Any tax deducted (excluding deductions made by contractors on account of tax) from trading income. — 3.120 £

Note: box numbers 3.110 to 3.119 are not used

Additional information

Now fill in any other supplementary Pages that apply to you.
Otherwise, go back to Page 2 of your Tax Return and finish filling it in.

TECHNICIAN STAGE
NVQ/SVQ LEVEL 4 IN ACCOUNTING
CENTRAL ASSESSMENT (TAX)
PREPARING TAXATION
COMPUTATIONS

AAT
ASSOCIATION
OF ACCOUNTING
TECHNICIANS

FRIDAY 5 DECEMBER 1997 (MORNING)

Time allowed—**3 hours plus 15 minutes' reading time**

ANSWER ALL SECTIONS

DURING THE 15 MINUTES' READING TIME YOU MAY READ AND WRITE NOTES ON THE ASSESSMENT PAPER ITSELF BUT YOU MUST NOT WRITE IN THE ANSWER BOOKLET UNTIL THE SUPERVISOR GIVES PERMISSION TO DO SO.

PLEASE DO NOT OPEN THIS BOOKLET UNTIL INSTRUCTED TO DO SO BY THE SUPERVISOR

Notes:

1. All calculations should be made to the nearest month and the nearest £.
2. Ignore the effects of national insurance in all tasks.

This central assessment consists of THREE sections, all of which are to be answered using the information given in this assessment paper. You are reminded that competence must be achieved in each section. You should therefore attempt and aim to complete ALL tasks within EACH section.

The times next to each task within a section are suggested maximum times to be spent on each task and are for guidance only. You may spend more or less than these times on each task, depending upon your skills and experience.

Any blank forms required will be found at the end of this assessment.

You should show all workings.

Credit will be awarded for presentation.

SECTION 1

Task 1.1	Computation of Schedule A and Schedule E income	40 Minutes
Task 1.2	Completion of self-assessment income tax return	20 Minutes
Task 1.3	Calculation of income tax payable	20 Minutes

SECTION 2

Task 2.1	Use of Schedule D Case I Losses	30 Minutes
Task 2.2	Completion of form CT200	20 Minutes

SECTION 3

Task 3.1	Capital gains tax computation	30 Minutes
Task 3.2	Memo to tax manager explaining the computation in Task 3.1	20 Minutes

Introduction

You are an accounting technician seconded to the tax department of the firm you work for (Prescott and Co). Whilst working for the tax Department your manager, Harold Heath, has given you the task of bringing the tax affairs of a local family up to date. The Ashdown family, Harriet and Patrick (brother and sister), are directors of a local company, Ashdown Limited.

You have been asked to perform the following tasks:

Section 1 Harriet Ashdown's personal tax affairs:

Harriet Ashdown's personal tax affairs need to be brought up to date. You are asked to:

Task 1.1
(a) Calculate Harriet's Schedule A income for 1998/99 (income from rental of land and buildings in the United Kingdom).
(b) Calculate Harriet's Schedule E income for 1998/99 (income from her employment as a director of Ashdown Limited).

Task 1.2 Complete the relevant sections of Harriet's 1998/99 self assessment income tax return for 1998/99.

Task 1.3 Compute the income tax payable by Harriet for 1998/99, either using the tax computation working sheet supplied by the Inland Revenue, or using your own income tax computation. (You only need to complete ONE computation.).

Section 2 Ashdown Limited

The Schedule D Case I adjustment of profit/loss from trading activities, for the above company, for the year to 31 March 1999 has been completed and the company has recorded a Schedule D Case I loss for the accounting period.

Task 2.1 Show how the Schedule D Case I loss will be used (assuming that the company wishes to use the loss as early as possible). Your manager has given you a summary of the corporation tax computations of the accounting period to 31 March 1998, and an estimate for the year to 31 March 2000.

Note: For all years it is sufficient to show the figures of profits chargeable to corporation tax.

Task 2.2 Complete form CT200 for the year to 31 March 1999, showing all of the information provided in the corporation tax computations already prepared plus the details of corporation tax losses you have calculated. Use the short form of the return (Section 2).

Section 3 Patrick Ashdown's capital gains

Patrick has sold a house (this house has never been his principal private residence).

Task 3.1 Calculate the capital gains tax due on the sale and state the date on which it will be paid.

Task 3.2 Write a memo to Harold Heath explaining how the gain was computed and how the capital gains tax due is calculated.

Information for Section 1, Task 1.1 (a)

Harriet Ashdown

Income from land and buildings 1998/99

Harriet Ashdown inherited a property in Salford, from her aunt, in 1997. The property is split into four flats which are let unfurnished to tenants. The income and expenditure for these flats for 1998/99 are as follows:

	Flat 1	*Flat 2*	*Flat 3*	*Flat 4*
	£	*£*	*£*	*£*
Rental income (figures are stated per annum) (p.a.)				
Let from 1 January 1996 (5-year lease)	2,000 p.a.			
Let from 1 November 1997 to 31 October 1998		3,000 p.a.		
Let from 1 January 1997 (5-year lease)			4,000 p.a.	
Let up to 31 December 1998 (old lease)				5,000 p.a.
Let from 1 January 1999 (new lease)				6,000 p.a.
Expenses:				
Advertising for tenants		1,000		500
Management fees from letting agents	1,000	1,000	1,000	1,000
Buildings insurance	250	250	250	250
Repairs and building work (see below for details)	100	500	3,000	200

The repairs and building work expenses were made up as follows:

All repairs and building work expenses were small repairs to the fabric of the property except:

- The repair in Flat 2 - £500 - Repairs to damage caused by a storm, carried out whilst property was empty (a new tenant was found in May 1999).

- The building work to Flat 3 - £3,000 - was the cost of a kitchen extension built onto the flat.

Task 1.1 (a)

Using the above information calculate the amount of Schedule A rental income assessable on Harriet Ashdown for 1998/99.

Information for Section 1, Task 1.1(b)

MEMORANDUM

To:	An Accounting Technician
From:	Harold Heath
Subject:	Harriet Ashdown's Schedule E income from employment
Date:	5 December 1999

Harriet has sent us details of her employment for 1998/99 as follows.

Employer:	Ashdown Ltd
Employer's address:	Tin Lane St. Linton Devon
Employer's PAYE reference:	349/A53
Salary	£25,000
Tax deducted	£6,055

Harriet also receives various benefits in kind, and these are detailed on the enclosed draft form P11D. This has not been completed as far as the calculation of the value of the benefits in kind are concerned, but gives us enough information for our calculations.

We have asked for further clarification of these benefits and are assured that:

- the travelling and subsistence payments were 50% business and 50% private expenditure;
- the entertaining expenditure was all business expenditure, but included the cost of a subscription to the local golf club (cost £500), where Harriet entertains customers;
- the payments for the use of the home telephone were all reimbursement of business telephone calls.

Task 1.1 (b)

Using the above information and the enclosed Form P11D, calculate Harriet Ashdown's Schedule E income for 1998/99.

Inland Revenue

P11D EXPENSES AND BENEFITS 1998-99

Note to employer
Complete this return for a director, or an employee who earned at a rate of £8,500 a year or more during the year 6 April 1998 to 5 April 1999. Do not include expenses and benefits covered by a dispensation or PAYE settlement agreement. Read the P11D Guide and booklet 480, Chapter 24, before you complete the form. Send the completed P11D and form P11D(b) to the Tax Office by 6 July 1999. You must give a copy of this information to the director or employee by the same date. The term employee is used to cover both directors and employees throughout the rest of this form.

Note to employee
Your employer has filled in this form. Keep it in a safe place as you may not be able to get a duplicate. You will need it for your tax records and to complete your 1998-99 Tax Return if you get one. Your tax code may need to be adjusted to take account of the information given on this P11D.
The box numbers on this P11D have the same numbering as the Employment Pages of the Tax Return, for example, 1.12. Include the total figures in the corresponding box on the Tax Return, unless you think some other figure is more appropriate.

Employer's details
Employer's name: ASHDOWN LTD
PAYE tax reference: 349 / AS3

Employee's details
Employee's name: HARRIET ASHDOWN
Tick here if a director: ✓
Works number or department:
National Insurance number: MB431770C

A • **Assets transferred (cars, property, goods or other assets)**

Description of asset ____ Cost/ Market value £ ____ – Amount made good or from which tax deducted £ ____ = **1.12** Cash equivalent £ ____

B • **Payments made on behalf of employee**

Description of payment ____ **1.12** £ ____

Tax on notional payments not borne by employee within 30 days of receipt of each notional payment **1.12** £ ____

C • **Vouchers or credit cards**

Value of vouchers and payments made using credit cards or tokens: Gross amount £ ____ – Amount made good or from which tax deducted £ ____ = **1.13** Cash equivalent £ ____

D • **Living accommmodation**

Cash equivalent of accommodation provided for employee, or his/ her family or household **1.14** Cash equivalent £ ____

E • **Mileage allowance**

Car and mileage allowances paid for employee's car: Gross amount £ ____ – Amount made good or from which tax deducted £ ____ = **1.15** Taxable payment £ ____

F • **Cars and car fuel**
If more than two cars were made available, either at the same time or in succession, please give details on a separate sheet

	Car 1	Car 2
Make and Model	FORD PROBE	
Dates first registered	01/11/95	/ /
Dates car was available (From / To)	01/11/95 – 05/04/99	/ / – / /
Business mileage used in calculation for this car. *Tick only one box for each car.* (2,499 or less / 2,500 to 17,999 / 18,000 or more)	18,000 or more ✓	
Enter engine size and tick type of fuel *only if there is a car fuel scale charge* (Engine size in cc / Petrol / Diesel)	2500 cc, Petrol ✓	cc

If the car was not available for part of the year, the business mileage limits are reduced proportionately.

	Car 1	Car 2
List price of car *If there is no list price, or if it is a classic car, employers see booklet 480; employees see leaflet IR133*	£ 24600	£
Price of optional accessories fitted when car was first made available to the employee	£	£
Price of accessories added after the car was first made available to the employee	£	£
Capital contributions (maximum £5,000) the employee made towards the cost of car or accessories	£ 1000	£
Amount paid by employee for private use of the car	£ 500	£
Cash equivalent of each car	£	£
Total cash equivalent of all cars available in 1998-99		**1.16** £
Cash equivalent of fuel for each car	£	£
Total cash equivalent of fuel for all cars available in 1998-99		**1.17** £

TO BE CALCULATED

P11D(1999) BMSD 11/98

G • **Vans**

Cash equivalent of all vans made available for private use — **1.18** £

H • **Interest-free and low interest loans**

If the total amount outstanding on all loans does not exceed £5,000 at any time in the year, there is no need for details in this section.

	Loan 1	Loan 2
Purpose of loan(s) – *please use the code shown in P11D Guide for employers*		
Number of joint borrowers *(if applicable)*		
Tick the box if the loan is within MIRAS		
Amount outstanding at 5 April 1998 or at date loan was made if later	£	£
Amount outstanding at 5 April 1999 or at date loan was discharged if earlier	£	£
Maximum amount outstanding at any time in the year	£	£
Total amount of interest paid by the borrower in 1998 - 99 – *enter "NIL" if none was paid*	£	£
Date loan was made or discharged in 1998 - 99 if applicable	/ /	/ /
Cash equivalent of loans after deducting any interest paid by the borrower	**1.19** £	**1.19** £

I • **Mobile telephones**

Cash equivalent of mobile telephones provided — **1.20** £

J • **Private medical treatment or insurance**

	Cost to you		Amount made good or from which tax deducted		Cash equivalent
Private medical treatment or insurance	£ 550	–	£ 100	=	**1.21** £ 450

K • **Qualifying relocation expenses payments and benefits (non-qualifying expenses go in P below)**

Excess over £8,000 of all qualifying relocation expenses payments and benefits for each move — **1.22** £

L • **Services supplied**

	Cost to you		Amount made good or from which tax deducted		Cash equivalent
Services supplied to the employee	£	–	£	=	**1.22** £

M • **Assets placed at the employee's disposal**

		Annual value plus expenses incurred		Amount made good or from which tax deducted		Cash equivalent
Description of asset	COLOUR TELEVISION	COST ON 6.4.98 £ 1000	–	£ NIL	=	**1.22** £ 1000

N • **Shares**

Tick the box if during the year there have been share-related benefits for the employee ☐

O • **Other items**

		Cost to you		Amount made good or from which tax deducted		Cash equivalent
Subscriptions and professional fees		£	–	£	=	**1.22** £
Description of other items		£	–	£	=	**1.22** £

Income tax paid but not deducted from director's remuneration — Tax paid **1.22** £

P • **Expenses payments made to, or on behalf of, the employee**

		Cost to you		Amount made good or from which tax deducted		Taxable payment
Travelling and subsistence payments		£ 5000	–	£	=	**1.23** £ 5000
Entertainment *(trading organisations read P11D Guide and then enter a tick or a cross as appropriate here)*	☐	£ 3500	–	£	=	**1.23** £ 3500
General expenses allowance for business travel		£	–	£	=	**1.23** £
Payments for use of home telephone		£ 100	–	£	=	**1.23** £ 100
Non-qualifying relocation expenses *(those not shown in section K)*		£	–	£	=	**1.23** £
Description of other expenses		£	–	£	=	**1.23** £

Information for Section 1, Tasks 1.2 and 1.5

Harriet Ashdown has no income, other than the rental and employment income shown above, she is single (that is unmarried), with no children and makes no pension contributions.

Task 1.2

Harold Heath has asked you to complete the rental income and employment income pages for Harriet Ashdown's self assessment income tax return for 1998/99.

Task 1.3

Harold Heath has also asked you to calculate Harriet's income tax liability for 1998/99. You may do this in ONE of two ways:

(a) Complete the Inland Revenue tax computation working sheet; or
(b) Prepare your own income tax computation.

Information for Section 2, Task 2.1 and 2.2

Ashdown Limited

Summary Corporation Tax Computations for the three years ended 31 March 2000

	Year ended 31 March *1998*	*1999*	*2000 (estimated)*
	£	£	£
Adjusted trading profit	58,000	nil	32,000
Adjusted trading loss	nil	(170,000)	nil
Patent royalty income (gross)	15,000	6,000	11,000
Capital gains	2,000	20,000	nil
Charges on income paid:			
Patent royalty payments (gross)	4,000	8,000	6,000
Charitable deed of covenant	1,000	1,000	1,000

Using the above information:

Task 2.1 Prepare corporation tax computations for all three accounting periods, assuming the loss is set off as early as possible, and state whether there is any loss left to be carried forward.

Task 2.2 Enter the figures for the year ended 31 March 1999 onto the form CT200 Corporation Tax Return which follows (using the short form of the return, Section 2).

Information for Section 3, Task 3.1

The following statement has been received from Patrick Ashdown's solicitor, concerning the sale of a house Patrick owned for weekend use by him and his family:

STATEMENT OF INCOME AND EXPENSES ON THE SALE OF A HOUSE ON BEHALF OF PATRICK ASHDOWN:

DATE OF SALE 15 MARCH 1999

Income:		Expenses:	
Sale proceeds	150,000	Solicitors' Fees	2,500
		Estate Agents' fees	1,500
Totals	150,000		4,000

Cheque to client in full settlement of sale—£ 146,000

In addition you have discovered that the house was purchased on 10 June 1981 for £25,000 and that the following building work was performed on the house during Patrick's term of ownership:

Kitchen Extension August 1981 costing £15,000.
Bedroom Extension September 1991 costing £3,500.

The Valuations Office Agency has confirmed that the value of a similar house on 31 March 1982 would have been £35,000.

Patrick Ashdown has confirmed that the house has always been a second property and could never have been regarded as his principal private residence. He has made no other chargeable disposals in the 1998/99 tax year, but has capital losses brought forward of £10,000. Patrick's taxable income for 1998/99 amounted to £10,000.

Task 3.1

Harold Heath requires you to calculate the capital gains tax arising on the sale of the property and to state the date on which the capital gains tax will be paid.

Information for Section 3, Task 3.2

MEMO

From: Harold Heath

To: An Accounting Technician

Subject: Patrick Ashdown

Date: 4 December 1999

As part of your training in the tax department we have been teaching you how to calculate capital gains and losses and how to calculate the capital gains tax due on any gains made by our clients.

So that I can assess your progress, I would like you to prepare an explanation of how you have calculated the gain on the sale of the house, by Patrick Ashdown.

Task 3.2

Write a memo to Harold Heath, explaining how you have calculated the capital gain on the sale of Patrick Ashdown's house and how you have calculated the capital gains tax due on this disposal.

Income for the year ended 5 April 1999

Inland Revenue

LAND AND PROPERTY

Fill in these boxes first

Name

Tax reference

Are you claiming Rent a Room relief for gross rents of £4,250 or less?
(Or £2,125 if the claim is shared?)
Read the Notes on page LN2 to find out
- **whether you can claim Rent a Room relief; and**
- **how to claim relief for gross rents over £4,250**

No | Yes

If 'Yes', and this is your only income from UK property, you have finished these Pages

Is your income from furnished holiday lettings?
If 'No', turn over and fill in Page L2 to give details of your property income

No | Yes

If 'Yes', fill in boxes 5.1 to 5.18 before completing Page L2

Furnished holiday lettings

- Income from furnished holiday lettings — 5.1 £

■ *Expenses* (furnished holiday lettings only)

- Rent, rates, insurance, ground rents etc. — 5.2 £
- Repairs, maintenance and renewals — 5.3 £
- Finance charges, including interest — 5.4 £
- Legal and professional costs — 5.5 £
- Cost of services provided, including wages — 5.6 £
- Other expenses — 5.7 £

total of boxes 5.2 to 5.7 — 5.8 £

Net profit (put figures in brackets if a loss) — box 5.1 *minus* box 5.8 — 5.9 £

■ *Tax adjustments*

- Private use — 5.10 £
- Balancing charges — 5.11 £

box 5.10 + box 5.11 — 5.12 £

- Capital allowances — 5.13 £

Profit for the year (copy to box 5.19). If loss, enter '0' in box 5.14 and put the loss in box 5.15 — boxes 59 + 5.12 *minus* box 5.13 — 5.14 £

Loss for the yea (if you have entered '0' in box 5.14) — boxes 59 + 5.12 *minus* box 5.13 — 5.15 £

- Loss offset against 1998-99 total income — 5.16 £
- Loss carried back — see Notes, page LN4 — 5.17 £
- Loss offset against other income from property (copy to box 5.38) — see Notes, page LN4 — 5.18 £

SA105

Other property income

■ ***Income***

• Furnished holiday lettings profits	copy from box 5.14 5.19 £		
• Rents and other income from land and property	5.20 £	Tax deducted 5.21 £	
• Chargeable premiums	5.22 £		boxes 5.19 + 5.20 + 5.22 5.23 £

■ ***Expenses*** (do not include figures you have already put in boxes 5.2 to 5.7 on Page L1)

• Rent, rates, insurance, ground rents etc.	5.24 £		
• Repairs, maintenance and renewals	5.25 £		
• Finance charges, including interest	5.26 £		
• Legal and professional costs	5.27 £		
• Costs of services provided, including wages	5.28 £		
• Other expenses	5.29 £		total of boxes 5.24 to 5.29 5.30 £
Net profit (put figures in brackets if a loss)			box 5.23 *minus* box 5.30 5.31 £

■ ***Tax adjustments***

• Private use	5.32 £		
• Balancing charges	5.33 £		box 5.32 + box 5.33 5.34 £
• Rent a Room exempt amount	5.35 £		
• Capital allowances	5.36 £		
• 10% wear and tear	5.37 £		
• Furnished holiday lettings losses (from box 5.18)	5.38 £		total of boxes 5.35 to 5.38 5.39 £
Adjusted profit (if loss enter '0' in box 5.40 and put the loss in box 5.41)			boxes 5.31 + 5.34 *minus* box 5.39 5.40 £
Adjusted loss (if you have entered '0' in box 5.40)		boxes 5.31 + 5.34 *minus* box 5.39 5.41 £	
• Loss brought forward from previous year			5.42 £
Profit for the year			box 5.40 *minus* box 5.42 5.43 £
• Loss offset against total income		5.44 £	
• Loss to carry forward to following year		5.45 £	
• Pooled expenses from 'one estate election' carried forward		5.46 £	

Tick box 5.47 if these Pages include details of property let jointly **5.47** ☐

Now fill in any other supplementary Pages that apply to you.
Otherwise, go back to page 2 of your Tax Return and finish filling it in.

Income for the year ended 5 April 1999

Inland Revenue

EMPLOYMENT

Name

Tax reference

Fill in these boxes first

If you want help, look up the box numbers in the Notes

Details of employer

Employer's PAYE reference **1.1**

Employer's name **1.2**

Date employment started (only if between 6 April 1998 and 5 April 1999) **1.3** / /

Date finished (only if between 6 April 1998 and 5 April 1999) **1.4** / /

Employer's address **1.5**

Postcode

Tick box 1.6 if you were a director of the company **1.6**

and, if so, tick box 1.7 if it was a close company **1.7**

Income from employment

■ ***Money*** *- see Notes, page EN3*

		Before tax
• Payments from P60 (or P45 or pay slips)		**1.8** £
• Payments not on P60 etc.	- tips	**1.9** £
	- other payments (excluding expenses shown below and lump sums and compensation payments or benefits shown overleaf)	**1.10** £

• UK tax deducted from payments in boxes 1.8 to 1.10 — Tax deducted **1.11** £

■ ***Benefits and expenses*** *- see Notes, pages EN3 to EN6. If any benefits connected with termination of employment were received, or enjoyed, after that termination and were from a* ***former*** *employer you need to complete Help Sheet IR204, available from the Orderline. Do not enter such benefits here.*

	Amount		Amount
• Assets transferred/ payments made for you	**1.12** £	• Vans	**1.18** £
• Vouchers/credit cards	**1.13** £	• Interest-free and low-interest loans	**1.19** £
• Living accommodation	**1.14** £	• Mobile telephones	**1.20** £
• Mileage allowance	**1.15** £	• Private medical or dental insurance	**1.21** £
• Company cars	**1.16** £	• Other benefits	**1.22** £
• Fuel for company cars	**1.17** £	• Expenses payments received and balancing charges	**1.23** £

SA101

Income from employment continued

■ ***Lump sums and compensation payments or benefits including such payments and benefits from a former employer***
Note that 'lump sums' here includes any contributions which your employer made to an unapproved retirement benefits scheme

You must read page EN6 of the Notes ***before*** *filling in boxes 1.24 to 1.30*

Reliefs

- £30,000 exemption — **1.24** £
- Foreign service and disability — **1.25** £
- Retirement and death lump sums — **1.26** £

Taxable lump sums

- From box H of *Help Sheet IR204* — **1.27** £
- From box Q of *Help Sheet IR204* — **1.28** £
- From box R of *Help Sheet IR204* — **1.29** £
- Tax deducted from payments in boxes 1.27 to 1.29 — Tax deducted **1.30** £

■ ***Foreign earnings not taxable in the UK in year ended 5 April 1999** - see Notes, page EN6* — **1.31** £

■ ***Expenses you incurred in doing your job** - see Notes, starting on page EN6*

- Travel and subsistence costs — **1.32** £
- Fixed deductions for expenses — **1.33** £
- Professional fees and subscriptions — **1.34** £
- Other expenses and capital allowances — **1.35** £
- Tick box 1.36 if the figure in box 1.32 includes travel between your home and a permanent workplace — **1.36**

■ ***Foreign Earnings Deduction*** — **1.37** £

■ ***Foreign tax for which tax credit relief not claimed*** — **1.38** £

Additional information

Now fill in any other supplementary Pages that apply to you.
Otherwise, go back to page 2 in your Tax Return and finish filling it in.

Calculating your tax bill - continued

If any of the sums on this page result in a negative amount, enter a zero in the appropriate box

Total income from: **(copy figures from your Tax Return)**

- *Employment* including benefits and *minus* expenses for **each** employment

Add income in:
- boxes 1.8 to 1.10, **and**
- boxes 1.12 to 1.23, **and**
- boxes 1.27 and 1.28

	First employment		Other employments	
Add income in boxes above	£		£	
Deduct any figures in boxes 1.31 to 1.38	£		£	
Total taxable income	£	+	£	= W1 £

- *Share schemes* (from box 2.31) — W2 £
- *Self-employment* (from box 3.88) — W3 £
- *Partnerships* (from boxes 4.35, 4.70 and 4.73) — W4 £
- *UK land and property* (from box 5.43) — W5 £
- *Foreign income* (from boxes 6.2, 6.4 and 6.5) — W6 £
- *Trusts, settlements or estates of deceased persons* (add together any figures in the 'right hand' column of the Trusts etc. Pages and deduct any figure in box 7.19) — W7 £
- *UK savings and investments* (total any figures in the 'right hand' column on page 3 of your Tax Return) — W8 £
- *UK pensions, retirement annuities and benefits* (add together any figures in the 'right hand' column of Question 11 on page 4 of your Tax Return *minus* any deduction in box 11.13) — W9 £
- *Maintenance or alimony received* (from box 12.3) — W10 £
- *Other income* (copy the figure in box 13.3 *minus* any figure in box 13.5) — W11 £

Total income
total boxes W1 to W11 — W12 £

Deductions for

- *Personal pension* (add together any figures in boxes 14.5, 14.10, 14.15, 14.16 and 14.17) — W13 £
- *Vocational training* (multiply any figure in box 15.1 by $^{100}/_{77}$) — W14 £
- *Interest on qualifying loans* (from box 15.3) — W15 £
- *Maintenance or alimony paid* (see the notes on page 2 of this Guide) — W16 £
- *Charitable covenants, annuities, Gift Aid and Millennium Gift Aid payments* (multiply any figures in boxes 15.9 and 15.10 by $^{100}/_{77}$) — W17 £
- *Losses and post-cessation expenses* (from boxes 3.81, 4.15, 4.61, 5.16, 5.44, 8.13A and 15.11) — W18 £
- *Trade union and friendly society death benefit payments* (from box 15.12) — W19 £

Total deductions
total boxes W13 to W19 — W20 £

box W12 *minus* box W20
Total income minus deductions — W21 £

now copy the figure in box W21 to box W22 on page 6

Calculating your tax bill - continued

Reliefs
- you get basic rate relief automatically - further relief will be due if you are liable to higher rate tax.

If any of the sums on this page result in a negative amount, enter a zero in the appropriate box

from box W21
W22 £

- *Pension payments* (from boxes 14.15 and 14.17) W23.1 £
- *Vocational training* (from box W14) W23.2 £

box W23.1 + box W23.2
W23 £

box W22 + box W23
W24 £

Allowances given as a deduction from your income
- you may need to check your entitlement - see notes starting on page 3 of this Guide.

- ***Personal allowance*** - normally £4,195 unless you are non-resident and not claiming allowances W25.1 £ +
- ***Age-related personal allowance*** - see notes page 3 W25.2 £ +
- ***Blind person's allowance*** - enter £1,330 W25.3 £ +
- ***Transitional allowance*** (from box 16.4) W25.4 £ +
- ***Blind person's surplus allowance from your spouse*** (from box 16.27) W25.5 £

total boxes W25.1 to W25.5
W25 £

If the figure in box W26 is £4,300 or less, do not fill in boxes W28 to W38

box W24 *minus* box W25
W26 £

box W26 x 20%
W27 £

Savings income taxable at the lower (20%) rate

- ***Partnership savings*** (from boxes 4.35 and 4.70) W28.1 £ +
- ***UK savings*** (from box W8) W28.2 £ +
- ***Foreign savings*** (from box 6.2) W28.3 £
- ***Trusts, settlements and estate income*** (from boxes 7.6, 7.12 and 7.15) W28.4 £

total boxes W28.1 to W28.4
W28 £

box W26 *minus* box W28
W29 £

W30 £ 4,300

box W29 *minus* box W30
W31 £

box W31 x 3%
W32 £

If the figure in box W33 is £27,100 or less, do not fill in boxes W35 to W38

box W26 *minus* box W23 *minus* box 12.9
W33 £

W34 £ 27,100

box W33 *minus* box W34
W35 £

box W35 x 17%
W36 £

lower of box W28 *or* box W35
W37 £

box W37 x 3%
W38 £

boxes W27 + W32 + W36 + W38
Income Tax due W39 £

Copy box W39 to top of page 7

Calculating your tax bill - continued

If any of the sums on this page result in a negative amount, enter a zero in the appropriate box

from page 6

W39 £

- *Venture Capital Trust and Enterprise Investment Scheme subscriptions*

box 15.7 + box 15.8 — W40 £ → box W40 x 20% — W41 £

box 15.2 x 10% — W42 £

Allowances and reliefs given in terms of tax
- these reduce your tax bill - you may need to use the Question 16 notes on pages 23 to 26 of the Tax Return Guide and starting on page 4 of this Guide.

- ***Married couple's allowance*** - see notes on pages 4 and 9 of this Guide — W43.1 £
  +
- ***Married couple's surplus allowance*** (from box 16.28) — W43.2 £
  +
- ***Additional personal allowance*** - usually £1,900, may be split with another person - see the notes — W43.3 £
  +
- ***Widow's bereavement allowance - £1,900*** (if your husband died in 1997-98 or 1998-99 and you have not remarried) — W43.4 £
  +
- ***Maintenance and alimony*** (boxes 15.4 and 15.5 - see the notes for box W16 on page 2 of this Guide) — W43.5 £

total boxes W43.1 to W43.5 — W43.6 £ → box W43.6 x 15% — W43 £

Notional tax *is not repayable and so has to be calculated as an allowance given in terms of tax rather than being regarded as tax deducted at source.*

- ***Partnership notional tax*** (from box 4.78) — W44.1 £
  +
- ***Notional tax on UK scrip dividends and FIDs*** (from boxes 10.22, 10.25, 10.28 and 10.31) — W44.2 £
  +
- ***Notional tax on estate income*** (from box 7.14) — W44.3 £

total boxes W44.1 to W44.3 — W44 £

- ***Tax credit relief on foreign income and treaty relief on UK income*** (and see the notes on page 9 of this Guide) — from boxes 6.9 and 9.35 — W45 £

boxes W41 to W45 — W46 £

Income Tax due, after allowances and reliefs — box W39 *minus* box W46 — W47 £
If the figure in box W46 is more than the figure in box W39, enter a zero

- *Recoverable tax on charitable covenants, annuities, Gift Aid and Millennium Gift Aid payments* (box W17 x 23%) — W48 £

- *Class 4 National Insurance Contributions* (from box 3.91 or box 4.25) — W49 £

Income Tax and Class 4 National Insurance Contributions — boxes W47 + W48 + W49 — W50 £

Copy the figure in box W50 to box W50 on page 8

Calculating your tax bill - continued

(copy figure from box W50 on page 7) **Income Tax and Class 4 NIC due** — W50 £

- *Unpaid tax for earlier years included in PAYE code for 1998-99* — W51 £

Copy the figure in box W51 to box 18.1 in your Tax Return

box W50 + box W51 — W52 £

Tax paid at source

- *Employment* (from boxes 1.11 and 1.30) — W53.1 £
- *Self-employment* (from boxes 3.92 and 3.120) — W53.2 £
- *Partnerships* (from box 4.77) — W53.3 £
- *UK land and property* (from box 5.21) — W53.4 £
- *Foreign income* (from boxes 6.1 and 6.3) — W53.5 £
- *Trusts, settlements or estate income* (from boxes 7.2, 7.5, 7.8 and 7.11) — W53.6 £
- *UK savings* (from boxes 10.3, 10.6, 10.10, 10.13, 10.16 and 10.19) — W53.7 £
- *UK pensions, retirement annuities and benefits* (from boxes 11.8 and 11.11) — W53.8 £
- *Other income* (from box 13.2) — W53.9 £

total boxes W53.1 to W53.9 — W53 £

- *Tax due for 1998-99 included in 1999-2000 PAYE tax code* — W54 £

Copy the figure in box W54 to box 18.2 in your Tax Return

box W53 + box W54 — W55 £

box W52 *minus* box W55

Total tax and Class 4 NIC due for 1998-99 (overpayment in brackets) — W56 £

Copy the figure in box W56 to box 18.3 in your Tax Return

Tax owed or overpaid in 1998-99

- *1998-99 tax already refunded* (from box 17.1) — W57A £
- *Tax due for earlier years* — W57 £

Copy the figure in box W57 to box 18.4 in your Tax Return

boxes W56 + W57A + W57 — W58 £

- *Tax overpaid for earlier years* — W59 £

Tick box 18.5 and copy the figure in box W59 to the 'Additional information' box on page 8 of your Tax Return

- *Payments already made* (from your Statements of Account) — W60 £

box W59 + box W60 — W61 £

box W58 *minus* box W61

Tax you owe for 1998-99 — W62 £

OR

box W61 *minus* box W58

Tax you have overpaid for 1998-99 — W63 £

Payments on account for 1999-2000

If there is a figure in box W62, add it to any figure in box W59. If the total is less than £1,000 and you would like the amount you owe collected through your 2000-2001 tax code, copy W62 to W64. Otherwise enter zero — W64 £

box W56 *minus* box W64

If W65 is less than **£500**, you do not need to make payments on account. Leave box 18.6 blank and tick box 18.8. **If W65 is equal to or more than £500**, carry on — W65 £

- *Income Tax due, after allowances and reliefs* — from boxes W44 + W47 + W48 — W66 £
- *Class 4 National Insurance Contributions* — from box W49 — W67 £

box W66 + box W67 — W68 £

box W68 x 20% — W69 £

If W65 is **less** than W69, you do not need to make payments on account. Leave box 18.6 blank and tick box 18.8.
If W65 is equal to or more than W69, **you do have to make payments on account. Fill in box W70**

box W65 x 50%

This is the amount of each payment on account for 1999-2000 — W70 £

*Copy the figure in box W70 **(including pence)** to box 18.6 in your Tax Return*

Inland **Revenue**

Page 1

Corporation Tax Return
Version 3

This form, or an approved substitute version of it, must be used whenever a company is required to do so, by a *Notice to deliver a Corporation Tax Return (form CT203)*. This return sets out the information we need and provides a standard format for calculations.

You should read this return form along with your *Notice to deliver a Corporation Tax Return (form CT203)* and *Filling in your Corporation Tax Return (leaflet CT200 Notes)* which you should have received with this form. The notes referred to throughout can be found in the leaflet *CT200 Notes*. You should contact your Tax Office if you need more help.

'Company' means any body chargeable to corporation tax, whether incorporated or not. This definition includes clubs, associations and voluntary organisations.

Sections to be completed
Members clubs, associations and voluntary organisations - It is likely that you will only have to complete Sections 1 and 2. For further guidance see note 1 in the *Notes*.

All companies - including clubs, etc. - You will not need to complete every Section, but you **must** complete the Declaration and Section 1 on this page. The *Notes* will help you decide whether you should complete the mutually exclusive *Short return* at Section 2 or the *Detailed return* at Section 3. Sections 9 and 10 are optional but you are asked to complete them if they are relevant to the company.
It is important that you read the *Notes* before completing any part of this form.

What to do when you have completed the return
- Make sure you have completed and signed the Declaration, then
- staple together the pages you have completed and attach any supporting calculations
- send these together with the relevant company accounts and, where prepared, directors' and auditors' reports, to your Tax Office using the envelope provided (see Note 3 for the date by which you should do this)
- pay any outstanding corporation tax (as you have shown at box box 65), as advised on the payslip attached to your *Notice to deliver a Corporation Tax Return (form CT203)*. Interest is charged on tax paid later than nine months and one day after the end of an accounting period. Tax is due without the making of an assessment.

Remember - ***Your tax return is not complete unless you send relevant accounts and documentation with this form.***
Penalties may be charged if your return, or any part of it, is late or incorrect.

As soon as your figures are agreed
- we will send you an assessment setting out the tax position for the accounting period - unless there are no figures to assess
- we will issue an amended assessment if you have already received an estimated assessment and you have appealed against it.

Section 1: Summary

The company name

[ ]

The company address - only if changed since last return made.
Enter the UK registered office address, or the UK address if the company does not have a registered office. If the company does not have premises in the UK show the address of the person making the return.

[ ]

Company registration number *(if registered)*

[ ]

Reference
Enter the reference number shown on the *Notice to deliver a Corporation Tax Return (form CT203)*

[/ /]

Corporation tax accounting period covered by this return
Cannot exceed 12 months. Enter start and end dates.

From [/ /] To [/ /]

If this period is not an accounting period of the company for corporation tax purposes (see note 2) put an 'X' in the box below, complete the Declaration to the right and return this form to your Tax Office. You do not need to complete the rest of this Section or other Sections of this form in these circumstances. [ ]

Profits chargeable *(Enter the figure from box 30). If there are none enter '0'.*
£ [ ]

Corporation tax due *(Enter the figure from box 61 minus any entry in box 64). If none is due enter '0.00'.*
£ [ ] p [ ]

Put an X in the appropriate box

Have you completed Section 8 (Repayments)? Yes [ ] No [ ]

Is the company name different from that shown in the *Notice (form CT203)*? Yes [ ] No [ ]

Declaration

Enter here the page numbers you are attaching

[ ]

Put an 'X' in the appropriate boxes to show the documents you are enclosing

- **a copy of the accounts for the period to which this return relates** [ ]
- **a copy of the company accounts for a different period** [ ]
- **no accounts** [ ]
- **say why not** [ ]
- **calculations showing how the entries in the return form have been arrived at.** [ ]

I declare that to the best of my knowledge and belief the return on this page and the pages attached is correct and complete.

Signature

[ ]

Except where a liquidator has been appointed, the company secretary, treasurer, or any other person who is authorised to do so may sign this declaration on behalf of the company. A photocopy of a signature is not acceptable.

Date

[/ /]

Name *(in capital letters)*

[ ]

Status *(company secretary, treasurer, liquidator etc.)*

[ ]

Page 2

Section 2: Short return

You may complete this section if

- it covers all the entries you need to make and
- each entry, including the company's total income and deductions, is less than £10 million.

In all other cases, or if you prefer, complete Section 3 instead. You should enclose an explanation and calculations of any figures which you have estimated or which are not immediately recognisable from the company's accounts.

The figures to be entered are those adjusted for tax purposes, after deducting capital allowances and adding balancing charges where appropriate. Section 4 should also be completed if capital allowances are claimed.

Please do not enter '0's where the company did not have the source specified in the return form.

£

Trading profits *See note 5* ... 1 [ ]

Trading losses brought forward *Only include losses made in the same trade. Include charges treated as losses. Do not enter an amount larger than is needed to cover the profits in box 1. See note 6* ... 2 [ ]

£

Net trading profit *(box 1 minus box 2). If box 2 equals box 1, enter '0'. Leave this box blank if there are no trading profits in box 1* ... 3 [ ]

Trading losses of this accounting period *Where there is more than one trade give total for all trades. Do not set box 4 losses against box 1 profits, claim at box 22 against total profits.* ... 4 [ ]

Profits and gains from non-trading loan relationships and other Schedule D Case III income *Include interest and other profits and gains from non-trading loan relationships even if tax has been deducted. Complete box 57 to claim credit for income tax deducted. You will need to complete the* **Detailed return** *at Section 3 if you have deficits on non-trading loan relationships from this, earlier or later accounting periods to include. See note 8* ... 6 [ ]

Income within Schedule D Case VI - for example furnished lettings *Enter the figure net of allowable losses brought forward. Exclude income you enter in box 12. See note 7* ... 9 [ ]

Income from which income tax has been deducted - for example building society interest *Enter the gross amount before tax. Exclude any amount included in box 6 above. Complete box 57 to claim credit for income tax deducted. See note 9* ... 10 [ ]

Income from UK land and buildings *Enter the amount net of allowable expenses brought forward. Exclude income in box 9 above. See note 10* ... 12 [ ]

Chargeable gains *See note 11*

Gross gains ... 13 [ ]

Allowable losses
Include any losses brought forward but do not enter an amount larger than the amount of gross gains in box 13 above. ... 14 [ ]

Net chargeable gains *(box 13 minus box 14) If box 14 equals box 13, enter '0'* ... 15 [ ]

Profits *(total of boxes 3, 6, 9, 10, 12 and 15)* ... 17 [ ]

Relief for trading losses of this or of a later period
Put an 'X' in box 21 if amounts carried back from later accounting periods are included in box 22. See note 12 ... 21 [ ] 22 [ ]

Profits before charges *(box 17 minus box 22)* ... 26 [ ]

Charges paid *Do not enter an amount larger than is needed to cover profits in box 26. See note13* ... 27 [ ]

Profits chargeable to corporation tax *(box 26 minus box 27)*
Copy this figure into the box provided in Section 1 on page 1, and also into the box at the top of page 3 ... 30 [ ]

The short return is continued on page 3

Page 3

Profits chargeable to corporation tax

Enter the figure brought forward from page 2, box 30 ... £ [ ]

If you claim tax is chargeable at the small companies' rate, or if you are claiming marginal small companies' relief, complete boxes 31 - 35. If there are no associated companies please enter '0' against the relevant financial year. *See note 15*

Franked investment income and foreign income dividends arising in the period covered by the return. *See note 15* ... 31 £ [ ]

Number of companies associated with this company in the/each financial year covered by this return
Exclude this company. See note 15 ...

	Financial year		Number of associated companies
32	19	33	
34	19	35	

Corporation tax chargeable *See note 16*

	Financial years beginning 1 April		Amounts of profit £		Rates of tax *See note 16*		Tax £ p
36	19	37		38	•	39	•
43	19	44		45	•	46	•

Total corporation tax chargeable *(box 39 plus box 46)* ... 50 [ ] • [ ]

Marginal small companies' relief
Attach your computation (see notes 15, 16 and 29) ... 51 £ [ ] • p [ ]

Advance corporation tax restricted if necessary under Section 239(2) ICTA 1988
Put an 'X' in box 53 if amounts carried back from later accounting periods are included. See note 17. 53 [ ] 54 [ ] • [ ]

Total of boxes 51 and 54
Total must not be larger than entry in box 50. Restrict if necessary ... 55 [ ] • [ ]

Net corporation tax chargeable *(box 50 minus box 55)* ... 56 [ ] • [ ]

Calculation of tax outstanding or overpaid

Income tax deducted from gross income included in return
Do not include deductions used to cover income tax for which the company was liable to account to the Inland Revenue on payments it has made. See note 18 ... 57 [ ] • [ ]

Corporation tax due

Box 56 minus box 57. If box 57 equals or is greater than box 56, enter '0.00' and go to box 59. Copy the figure in box 61 to the box provided in Section 1 on page 1. See note 20 ... 61 [ ] • [ ]

Income tax repayable to the company *(box 57 minus box 56).*
Complete Section 8 on page 8. Do not complete unless you are making a claim. See note 28... 59 [ ] • [ ]

Corporation tax already paid (and not repaid). *See note 21* ... 63 [ ] • [ ]

Corporation tax outstanding *(box 61 minus box 63). This amount is payable to the Accounts Office. If box 63 equals or is greater than box 61, enter '0.00' and go to box 66. See note 23* ... 65 [ ] • [ ]

Corporation tax overpaid *(box 63 minus box 61).*
Complete Section 8 on page 8 also. See note 28 ... 66 [ ] • [ ]

This is the last page of the short return

CT200(1997) Page 3

PRACTICE DEVOLVED

ASSESSMENTS

PRACTICE DEVOLVED ASSESSMENT

UNIT 17 - PREPARING BUSINESS TAXATION COMPUTATIONS

NOTES:

In completing this assessment:

(1) workings should be made to the nearest month and to the nearest £;
(2) ignore National Insurance

Any blank forms required will be found at the end of this assessment.

THE SITUATION

You are a qualified accounting technician and you work in the business tax department of a firm of accountants, Templar and Co. 23 Back Lane, Casterbridge, Wessex CA11 2RT. You report to the tax department manager, Jane Simons.

As part of your duties you are required to prepare tax computations for various businesses and to prepare corporation tax returns.

When you arrive in the office you discover that Jane will be out all day visiting clients and she has left you a memo asking you to work on two clients:

(1) Jack's Novelties
(2) Wooden Toys (UK) Ltd.

MEMO

To: Accounting Technician
From: Jane Simons, Tax Department Manager

Re: (1) Jack's Novelties
(2) Wooden Toys (UK) Ltd

Whilst I am out of the office today, I would like you to work on the above two clients. I set out below the work to be done, and a list of the documents attached to this memo which contain the information you will need.

(1) Jack's Novelties

Jack (who is now 55) started trading as a vendor of novelties on 1 December 1997 and prepares accounts to 30 June. The adjusted Schedule D Case I computation for the period ended on 30 June 1998 showed taxable profits of £14,000. I have reviewed and agreed your computation for the year ended 30 June 1999 which you completed last week, and am attaching a copy.

Jack is thinking of selling the business on 31 March 2000. He estimates that taxable profits for the nine months to 31 March 2000 will be £30,000.

Jack estimates that he will realise a capital gain on the sale of goodwill of £100,000.

I would like you to:

(a) Calculate the Schedule D Case I profits taxable on Jack for 1997/98, 1998/99 and 1999/00, showing clearly the overlap profits arising and how they will be relieved.

(b) Prepare a note of any steps Jack can take to mitigate the capital gain.

(2) Wooden Toys (UK) Ltd

I attach extracts from the audited accounts for the year to 31 December 1998, copies of various schedules from the audit file, a copy of the single form CT61 submitted during the year and a summary of relevant information from last year's tax file.

I would like you to:

(a) prepare the capital allowances computation for the year to 31 December 1998.

(b) prepare the adjusted Schedule D Case I computation for the year to 31 December 1998.

(c) prepare the corporation tax computation for the year to 31 December 1998.

(d) complete the short form (section 2) of the corporation tax return CT200 for the year to 31 December 1998, together with sections 4, 5 and 9.

(e) complete the form CT61 for the quarter to 30 June 1999. The company has advised me that patent royalties of £7,700 (net) were received on 1 April 1999 and a payment of £10,000 (net) was made to charity under the Gift Aid Scheme on 2 June 1999. (Note: The basic rate of income tax is unchanged from 1998/99).

(f) draft a letter sending the forms CT200 and CT61 to Mr R. Wood for approval and signature and advising him of the tax due and the dates the payments should be made.

Jack Potts, Trading as

Jack's Novelties
11 Market Street
Casterbridge

Schedule D Case I Computation for the year to 30 June 1999

	£	£
Net profit per accounts		24,500
Add:		
Depreciation	2,054	
Entertaining suppliers	179	
Private car expenses 30% × (£500 + £400)	270	
Private telephone 40% × £350	140	
		2,643
Less:		
Capital allowances		(1,163)
Schedule D Case I profits		25,980

Templar and Co
23 Back Lane
Casterbridge

Extracts from accounts

WOODEN TOYS (UK) LIMITED
FINANCIAL STATEMENTS
FOR THE YEAR ENDED 31 DECEMBER 1998

Wooden Toys (UK) Limited
Profit and Loss Account
For the year ended 31 December 1998

		1998		1997
	£	£	£	£
TURNOVER		50,721		35,043
Administration expenses	31,254		37,472	
Other operating charges	2,017		3,094	
		(33,271)		40,566
OPERATING PROFIT/(LOSS)		17,450		(5,523)
Interest payable and similar charges		(1,010)		(7,217)
Interest receivable and similar income		12,460		10,050
PROFIT/(LOSS) ON ORDINARY ACTIVITIES		28,900		(2,690)
TAXATION ON PROFIT ON ORDINARY ACTIVITIES		(6,070)		570
PROFIT/(LOSS) ON ORDINARY ACTIVITIES AFTER TAXATION		22,830		(2,120)
Dividends		(15,000)		(5,000)
RETAINED PROFIT/(LOSS) FOR THE YEAR		7,830		(7,120)
RETAINED PROFIT BROUGHT FORWARD		25,015		32,135
RETAINED PROFIT CARRIED FORWARD		32,845		25,015

Wooden Toys (UK) Limited
Balance sheet as at 31 December 1998

	£	£	£	£
FIXED ASSETS				
Tangible assets (note 1)		124,500		60,000
CURRENT ASSETS				
Debtors	15,725		35,014	
Cash at bank and in hand	4,013		40,027	
	19,738		75,041	
CREDITORS				
Amounts falling due within one year	(11,393)		(10,026)	
NET CURRENT ASSETS		8,345		65,015
NET ASSETS		132,845		125,015
CAPITAL AND RESERVES				
Ordinary share capital		100,000		100,000
Reserves		32,845		25,015
		132,845		125,015

Wooden Toys (UK) Limited
Notes to the accounts for the year to 31 December 1998

Note 1 Tangible Fixed Assets

	Land and Buildings	*Plant and Machinery*	*Motor Vehicles*	*Total*
	£	£	£	£
COST				
At 1 January 1998	20,000	30,000	25,000	75,000
Additions	75,000	12,000	10,000	97,000
Disposals	-	(15,000)	(5,000)	(20,000)
At 31 December 1998	95,000	27,000	30,000	152,000
DEPRECIATION				
At 1 January 1998	-	7,000	8,000	15,000
Charge for the year	7,500	5,500	7,500	20,500
Disposals	-	(5,000)	(3,000)	(8,000)
At 31 December 1998	7,500	7,500	12,500	27,500
NBV at 31 December 1998	87,500	19,500	17,500	124,500
NBV at 1 January 1998	20,000	23,000	17,000	60,000

Extracts from Audit Files

Wooden Toys (UK) Limited	Prepared by	RT
Year ended 31 December 1998	Reviewed by	LV
	Date	13.6.99

Analysis of Fixed Assets

Additions

Land & Buildings		
Factory (built on land acquired 2 years ago for £20,000)	£75,000	Completed 1/5/98 and used immediately
Plant and Machinery		
Electric sawing and drilling machine	£12,000	Purchased 11.2.98
Motor Vehicles		
Ford Ka	£10,000	Purchased 19.8.98

Disposals

Plant and machinery			
Various machines	- proceeds	£8,000	Sold 13.3.98
	- cost	£15,000	
	- depreciation 1.1.98	£5,000	
(Note: all items sold for less than cost)			
Motor vehicles			
Ford Escort	- proceeds	£2,500	Sold 19.8.98
	- cost	£5,000	
	- depreciation 1.1.98	£3,000	

Profit/(Loss) on sale		
Plant and machinery	15,000 – 5,000 – 8,000	(2,000)
Motor vehicle	5,000 – 2,500 – 3,000	500
Net loss on sale		(1,500)

Note: included as part of administration costs

Wooden Toys (UK) Limited
Year ended 31 December 1998

Prepared by	RT
Reviewed by	LV
Date	14.6.99

Analysis of interest

Bank Interest payable	£
Accrued at 1.1.98	(250)
Paid during year	1,075
Accrued at 31.12.98	185
	1,010

Interest receivable and similar income

	Patent Royalties (gross) £	*Bank Interest* £	*Total* £
Accrued at 1.1.98	(4,000)	(400)	(4,400)
Received during year	8,000	3,600	11,600
Accrued at 31.12.98	5,000	260	5,260
	9,000	3,460	12,460

Wooden Toys (UK) Limited	Prepared by	RT
Year ended 31 December 1998	Reviewed by	LV
	Date	15.6.99

Analysis of Profit and loss expenses

Bad debt provision	£	
General provision 1.1.98 (2% of trade debtors)	(475)	
Specific debts written off	527	
Bad debt recovered	(40)	
General provision 31.12.98 (2% of trade debtors)	250	
	£262	P&L

Sundry expenses	£	
Entertaining UK customers	1,724	
UK suppliers	462	
Staff Xmas party	297	
Other expenses (all allowable)	941	
	£3,424	P&L

Legal and Professional fees	£	
Architects' fees for new factory	2,000	
Debt collection	470	
Staff employment contracts	135	
	£2,605	P&L

Wooden Toys (UK) Limited
Relevant information from tax file for the year to 31 December 1997

(1) Capital allowances

The tax written down values carried forward at 1 January 1998 were:

General Pool	£14,500
FA1980 Pool	£5,625
Expensive Car (BMW)	£9,000

(2) Trading loss carried forward at 1 January 1998 £3,726.

Inland Revenue

Return of Company Payments, Distributions and Interest

Collector of Taxes
Inland Revenue Accounts Office (Shipley)
BRADFORD
West Yorkshire BD98 8AA
Telephone: Bradford (01274) 530750

1	2 Company regn. no.	3 Accounting date	4 Accounts Office ref.

IMPORTANT: Please enter in these 4 boxes the details from your CT61 Notice

Advance Corporation Tax on **Qualifying Distributions**
Income Tax deducted from **Company Payments** and **Interest**
Income Tax payable on **Gilt Interest** received without deduction of tax
Tax on manufactured payments received from abroad

- Please use this form when you need to make a Return of company payments, distributions and interest. **You must give all the information asked for on this page and sign the declaration below.** But you need only fill in the other parts of the Return which are relevant to your company. Only use the CT61 Supplement if you need to make a return of Foreign Income Dividends, 'deemed FIDs' or Gilt Interest.
- You are required to make your Return, and pay any tax, within 14 days after the end of the Return Period. Send the Return back to me in the envelope provided.
- *The enclosed CT61 Notes will help you.*
- If your Return shows that tax is payable use the payslip on the enclosed form CT61 Notice.
- When you send back this Return **please also enclose the CT61 Notice**, even if no payment is enclosed.

Company details

Name of company
WOODEN TOYS (UK) LIMITED

Address:
Enter the address you would like future CT61 Returns sent to

UNIT 3
THE INDUSTRIAL ESTATE
CASTER BRIDGE
WESSEX Postcode CA11 2RQ

Please tick if this is a change of Registered Office '✓' [ ]

Period covered by this Return

Return Periods are fixed by law. See CT61 Notes page 3 for guidance.

	Day	Month	Year		Day	Month	Year
Return period ▶	01	04	19 98	to	30	06	19 98
being part of the **Accounting period** ▶	01	01	19 98	to	31	12	19 98

Example: Distribution paid on 25 April 1997, and the accounting period is year to 31 December 1997. Enter:

Return period ▶	01	04	19 97	to	30	06	19 97
being part of the Accounting period ▶	01	01	19 97	to	31	12	19 97

For official use only
901

Declaration

False statements can result in prosecution

To the best of my knowledge the information given in this Return (and the Supplement, if used) is correct and complete

Signature: R Wood

Name *in CAPITALS*: R WOOD

State in what capacity you make this Return: DIRECTOR

It would assist if you can state your daytime telephone number and extension here: 0111 473190

Date: 02/07/98

Please tick if CT61 Supplement is attached '✓' [ ]

21267 4.97 Niceday Stationery & Print Limited BMSD4/97 W0H7003

1 Advance Corporation Tax (ACT) on Qualifying Distributions

Use Part 1 to calculate the ACT payable on Distributions paid.
Use Part 2 below to record Franked Investment Income received.
Franked investment income in box 23 is set-off to reduce the ACT payable in Part 1.
For further information see Notes page 2.

List separately the payments made on different dates. If you need more room please attach a schedule.

Take care to use the correct ACT rate.

	Date		Amount of distribution £	+ ACT payable £	=	Amount of franked payment £
Dividends and other qualifying distributions paid *Exclude – payments at 03 – Foreign Income Dividends (FIDS) – 'deemed FIDS' (see notes page 4)*	01.06.95	01	15000 00	3750 00	02	18750 00
Dividends paid for which you wish to account for ACT despite an election under Section 247(1) ICTA 1988 *See Notes page 2*		03			04	

Total franked payments	02 + 04	05	18750 00
Deduct **franked investment income to be set-off**	From Part 2, box 23	06	
Total franked payments for which ACT is payable	05 – 06	10	18750 00
Calculate the **Advance Corporation Tax (ACT)** included in the figure at **10**	*See both examples in Notes page 2*	11	3750 00
Add the **ACT payable on Foreign Income Dividends (FIDs)**	From CT61 Supplement, boxes 67 and 72	12	
Total ACT for this return period	11 + 12	13	3750 00
Deduct Additional amounts paid to **non-residents** *See Notes page 4*	**Enter all the additional amounts paid, and attach form 251B Divs FD in duplicate**	14	
ACT payable Carry to **Payslip** on CT61 Notice	13 – 14	15	3750 00

Do not enter a 'minus' figure in box 15. If 14 is greater than 13, claim repayment of the excess in Part 8

2 Franked investment income - running record for set-off or repayment

Amount brought forward from last Return		16	
Adjustment, if any, agreed with Inspector or a claim under Section 242 ICTA 1988 not yet agreed	*Enter 'MINUS' if appropriate*	17	
	16 + or – 17	18	

	Date	Description	Amount
Franked investment income received since last return			
		Total 19	
Adjustment, if any, agreed with Inspector		*Enter 'MINUS' if appropriate* **20**	

You can include income received in earlier return periods if you did not need to submit a form for those periods. See Notes page 1.

Do not enter Foreign Income Dividends here.

If you need more room please attach a schedule.

Total after adjustment	19 + or – 20	21	
Total franked investment income now available for set-off or repayment	18 + 21	22	
Deduct **Amount set-off against franked payments in Part 1**	From 22 or 05, whichever is smaller	23	*Carry this figure to Part 1, box 06*
Franked investment income after above set-off	22 – 23	24	

Repayment of ACT previously paid. Franked investment income at 24 can be set-off against franked payments of earlier return periods **for this accounting period only.**

ACT repayment now claimed	25		*Carry this figure to Part 8, line b*
Amount of franked investment income set-off	26		

Amount to be carried forward to next Return	24 – 26	27	

3 Income Tax on Annual Payments and Interest

Use Part 3 to calculate the Income Tax payable on payments made.
Use Part 4 to record Income Tax you have suffered on payments received. This can be set-off to reduce the tax due in Part 3. *For further information see Notes page 3.*

In boxes 28 and 29, group separately payments taxed at basic rate and payments taxed at lower rate.
If you need more room please attach a schedule.

	Date	Description		Gross amount £		Income Tax £
Annual payments etc made under deduction of Income Tax at basic rate or lower rate *See Notes page 3* *Include all manufactured interest, unless entered at 30 below.*			28		29	
Annual payments etc to non-residents made under deduction of reduced rate tax under a Double Taxation Agreement *See Notes page 4.* *Ref. no. of the authority* ▶			30		31	

Income Tax on annual payments etc above	29 + 31	32	

Interest paid by deposit-takers including distributions paid by **building societies**
Enter the Gross amount paid from which you deducted tax, and the lower rate Income Tax you deducted
See Notes page 3
Do not enter interest paid gross, eg TESSA interest

		Gross amount		Income Tax
Before 6 April	33		34	
From 6 April	35		36	

When the return period does not include 6 April use boxes 35 and 36

Total Income Tax	32 + 34 + 36	37	
Less Income Tax deducted from income **received** now claimed as a **set-off**	From Part 4, box 53	38	
	37 – 38	39	
Less Income Tax on **Gilt Interest received** now claimed as a set-off	From CT61 Supplement, box 83	40	
Income Tax now payable Carry to **Payslip** on CT61 Notice	39 – 40	46	

4 Income Tax deducted - running record in this Accounting Period for set-off or repayment

Amount of Income Tax **brought forward** from last Return for **this accounting period**		47	
Adjustment, if any, agreed with Inspector	*Enter 'MINUS' if appropriate*	48	
	47 + or – 48	49	

Income received under deduction of tax since last Return for **this accounting period**

You can include income received in earlier return periods in this accounting period if you did not need to submit a form for those periods. See Notes page 1.
If you need more room please attach a schedule.

Date	Description		Gross amount		Income Tax
01.04.98	PATENT ROYALTY		8000 00		1840 00
	Totals	50	8000 00	51	1840 00

Running total now available for set-off or repayment below	49 + 51	52	1840 00
Amount set-off against Income Tax in Part 3	From 52 or 37, whichever is smaller	53	◀ *Carry this figure to Part 3, box 38*
Repayment now claimed of tax paid on annual payments etc in Part 3 of an earlier Return **for this accounting period only**		54	◀ *Carry this figure to Part 8*
Total Income Tax now used for set-off or repayment	53 + 54	55	
Amount to be **carried forward** to next Return for **this accounting period**	52 – 55	56	1840 00

5 Certain other distributions

If you need more room please attach a schedule

	Date	Description	Amount £
a Qualifying distributions which are not money payments			
b Payments about which there is a doubt as to whether they are qualifying distributions			
c Distributions (excluding money payments) which, exceptionally, do not fall within an accounting period			

Do not account for ACT on the above payments. The Inspector will make any necessary assessment.

6 Tax on manufactured payments from abroad

See Notes page 4

a **Manufactured dividends received from abroad** *by UK resident companies* (AMOUNTS RECEIVED) — Tax payable - *at ACT rate* — *Carry to Payslip on CT61 Notice*

b **Manufactured interest received from abroad** *by UK resident companies and by UK branches of overseas companies* (GROSS INTEREST) — Income Tax payable at lower rate — *Carry to Payslip on CT61 Notice*

7 Income Tax on Gilt Interest received: totals from CT61 Supplement

a Income Tax **payable** on Gilt Interest received — From box 79

b **Repayment** of excessive payment on account — 78 – 77 if positive

c **Repayment** of 'Gilts' Income Tax — From box 88

d **Repayment** of 'other' Income Tax — From box 85

e Total 'Gilts related' repayments ... b + c + d

f Net Income Tax **payable** - *Do not enter a minus figure here. If e is greater than a claim repayment of the excess in Part 8 below* — a – e — *Carry to Payslip on CT61 Notice*

8 Claim for repayment or reimbursement

Use this section to summarise any claims arising in other sections of your Return:

a *From Part 1*	Reimbursement of amounts paid to non-residents	14 – 13 if positive	
b *From Parts 2 and 9*	Repayment of ACT previously paid	From boxes 25 and 69	
c *From Part 4*	Repayment of Income Tax previously paid	From box 54	
d *From Part 7*	Net 'Gilts related' Income Tax repayments	7e – 7a if positive	
e	Total claimed ...	a + b + c + d	

Other forms

Please tick if you require a form to declare the following items:

Non-qualifying distributions *Form CT2* *See Notes page 2* '✓' ☐

Stock dividends Section 249 ICTA 1988 *Form CT101* '✓' ☐

When sending back this Return, please

- check you have filled in the blue boxes at the top of page 1
- check you have signed the declaration on page 1
- send the CT61 Notice with this Return, even if no payment is enclosed.

When we receive this Return we will send you another form for your company's next Return.

Please note If the Inspector considers that any distributions, payments, etc have been omitted from this Return, or is in any way dissatisfied with it, the Inland Revenue can issue an appropriate assessment.

ANSWERS

Task 2

(a) Wooden Toys (UK) Limited
Capital allowances computation
Year ended 31 December 1998

	General Pool £	*FA1980 Pool* £	*Expensive Car (BMW)* £	*Allowances* £
1.1.98 Tax WDV b/f				
Additions not qualifying for FYA				
Disposals				
WDA @ 25%				
Additions qualifying for FYA				
FYA @ %				
31/12/98 Tax WDV c/f				
Industrial building				
Cost				
WDA @ 4%				
Tax WDV c/f				
Total capital allowances				

(b) Wooden Toys (UK) Limited
Schedule D Case I computation
Year ended 31 December 1998

	£	£
Profit on ordinary activities		
Add		
Less		
Schedule D Case I Profit		

2(d)

Inland Revenue

Page 1

Corporation Tax Return
Version 3

This form, or an approved substitute version of it, must be used whenever a company is required to do so, by a *Notice to deliver a Corporation Tax Return (form CT203)*. This return sets out the information we need and provides a standard format for calculations.

You should read this return form along with your *Notice to deliver a Corporation Tax Return (form CT203)* and *Filling in your Corporation Tax Return (leaflet CT200 Notes)* which you should have received with this form. The notes referred to throughout can be found in the leaflet *CT200 Notes*. You should contact your Tax Office if you need more help.

'Company' means any body chargeable to corporation tax, whether incorporated or not. This definition includes clubs, associations and voluntary organisations.

Sections to be completed
Members' clubs, associations and voluntary organisations - It is likely that you will only have to complete Sections 1 and 2. For further guidance see note 1 in the *Notes*.

All companies - including clubs, etc. - You will not need to complete every Section, but you must complete the Declaration and Section 1 on this page. The *Notes* will help you decide whether you should complete the mutually exclusive *Short return* at Section 2 or the *Detailed return* at Section 3. Sections 9 and 10 are optional but you are asked to complete them if they are relevant to the company.

It is important that you read the *Notes* before completing any part of this form.

What to do when you have completed the return

- Make sure you have completed and signed the Declaration, then
- staple together the pages you have completed and attach any supporting calculations
- send these together with the relevant company accounts and, where prepared, directors' and auditors' reports, to your Tax Office using the envelope provided (see Note 3 for the date by which you should do this)
- pay any outstanding corporation tax (as you have shown at box box 65), as advised on the payslip attached to your *Notice to deliver a Corporation Tax Return (form CT203)*. Interest is charged on tax paid later than nine months and one day after the end of an accounting period. Tax is due without the making of an assessment.

Remember - ***Your tax return is not complete unless you send relevant accounts and documentation with this form. Penalties may be charged if your return, or any part of it, is late or incorrect.***

As soon as your figures are agreed

- we will send you an assessment setting out the tax position for the accounting period - unless there are no figures to assess
- we will issue an amended assessment if you have already received an estimated assessment and you have appealed against it.

Section 1: Summary

The company name

WOODEN TOYS (UK) LIMITED

The company address - only if changed since last return made.
Enter the UK registered office address, or the UK address if the company does not have a registered office. If the company does not have premises in the UK show the address of the person making the return.

Company registration number *(if registered)*

100000

Reference
Enter the reference number shown on the *Notice to deliver a Corporation Tax Return (form CT203)*

721 / 14973 / SC

Corporation tax accounting period covered by this return
Cannot exceed 12 months. Enter start and end dates.

From / / To / /

If this period is not an accounting period of the company for corporation tax purposes (see note 2) put an 'X' in the box below, complete the Declaration to the right and return this form to your Tax Office. You do not need to complete the rest of this Section or other Sections of this form in these circumstances. ☐

Profits chargeable *(Enter the firgure from box 30). If there are none enter '0'.*
£

Corporation tax due £ p
(Enter the figure from box 61 minus any entry in box 64). If none is due enter '0.00'.

Put an X in the appropriate box

Have you completed Section 8 (Repayments)? Yes ☐ No ☐

Is the company name different from that shown in the *Notice (form CT203)*? Yes ☐ No ☐

Declaration

Enter here the page numbers you are attaching

Put an 'X' in the appropriate boxes to show the documents you are enclosing

- a copy of the accounts for the period to which this return relates ☐
- a copy of the company accounts for a different period ☐
- no accounts ☐
- say why not
- calculations showing how the entries in the return form have been arrived at. ☐

I declare that to the best of my knowledge and belief the return on this page and the pages attached is correct and complete.

Signature

Except where a liquidator has been appointed, the company secretary, treasurer, or any other person who is authorised to do so may sign this declaration on behalf of the company. A photocopy of a signature is not acceptable.

Date / /

Name *(in capital letters)*

Status *(company secretary, treasurer, liquidator etc.)*

Page 2

Section 2: Short return

You may complete this section if
- it covers all the entries you need to make and
- each entry, including the company's total income and deductions, is less than £10 million.

In all other cases, or if you prefer, complete Section 3 instead. You should enclose an explanation and calculations of any figures which you have estimated or which are not immediately recognisable from the company's accounts.

The figures to be entered are those adjusted for tax purposes, after deducting capital allowances and adding balancing charges where appropriate. Section 4 should also be completed if capital allowances are claimed.
Please do not enter '0's where the company did not have the source specified in the return form.

		£	£
Trading profits *See note 5*	1		
Trading losses brought forward *Only include losses made in the same trade. Include charges treated as losses.* ***Do not enter an amount larger than is needed to cover the profits in box 1.*** *See note 6*	2		
Net trading profit *(box 1 minus box 2). If box 2 equals box 1, enter '0'. Leave this box blank if there are no trading profits in box 1*	3		
Trading losses of this accounting period *Where there is more than one trade give total for all trades. Do not set box 4 losses against box 1 profits, claim at box 22 against total profits.*	4		
Profits and gains from non-trading loan relationships and other Schedule D Case III income *Include interest and other profits and gains from non-trading loan relationships even if tax has been deducted. Complete box 57 to claim credit for income tax deducted. You will need to complete the* **Detailed return** *at Section 3 if you have deficits on non-trading loan relationships from this, earlier or later accounting periods to include. See note 8*	6		
Income within Schedule D Case VI - for example furnished lettings *Enter the figure net of allowable losses brought forward. Exclude income you enter in box 12. See note 7*	9		
Income from which income tax has been deducted - for example building society interest *Enter the gross amount before tax. Exclude any amount included in box 6 above. Complete box 57 to claim credit for income tax deducted. See note 9*	10		
Income from UK land and buildings *Enter the amount net of allowable expenses brought forward. Exclude income in box 9 above. See note 10*	12		
Chargeable gains *See note 11*			
Gross gains	13		
Allowable losses *Include any losses brought forward but do not enter an amount larger than the amount of gross gains in box 13 above.*	14		
Net chargeable gains *(box 13 minus box 14) If box 14 equals box 13, enter '0'*	15		
Profits *(total of boxes 3, 6, 9, 10, 12 and 15)*	17		
Relief for trading losses of this or of a later period *Put an 'X' in box 21 if amounts carried back from later accounting periods are included in box 22. See note 12*	21 ☐ 22		
Profits before charges *(box 17 minus box 22)*	26		
Charges paid *Do not enter an amount larger than is needed to cover profits in box 26. See note13*	27		
Profits chargeable to corporation tax *(box 26 minus box 27)* ***Copy this figure into the box provided in Section 1 on page 1, and also into the box at the top of page 3***	30		

The short return is continued on page 3

Page 3

Profits chargeable to corporation tax

Enter the figure brought forward from page 2, box 30 ... £

If you claim tax is chargeable at the small companies' rate, or if you are claiming marginal small companies' relief, complete boxes 31 - 35. If there are no associated companies please enter '0' against the relevant financial year. *See note 15*

Franked investment income and foreign income dividends arising in the period covered by the return. *See note 15* ... 31 £

Number of companies associated with this company in the/each financial year covered by this return *Exclude this company. See note 15* ...

	Financial year		Number of associated companies
32		33	
34		35	

Corporation tax chargeable *See note 16*

	Financial years beginning 1 April		Amounts of profit £		Rates of tax *See note 16*		Tax £ p
36		37		38	•	39	•
43		44		45	•	46	•

Total corporation tax chargeable *(box 39 plus box 46)* ... 50

Marginal small companies' relief *Attach your computation (see notes 15, 16 and 29)* ... 51 £ • p

Advance corporation tax restricted if necessary under Section 239(2) ICTA 1988 *Put an 'X' in box 53 if amounts carried back from later accounting periods are included. See note 17.* 53 54

Total of boxes 51 and 54 *Total must not be larger than entry in box 50. Restrict if necessary* ... 55

Net corporation tax chargeable *(box 50 minus box 55)* ... 56

Calculation of tax outstanding or overpaid

Income tax deducted from gross income included in return *Do not include deductions used to cover income tax for which the company was liable to account to the Inland Revenue on payments it has made. See note 18* ... 57

Corporation tax due

Box 56 minus box 57. If box 57 equals or is greater than box 56, enter '0.00' and go to box 59. Copy the figure in box 61 to the box provided in Section 1 on page 1. See note 20 ... 61

Income tax repayable to the company *(box 57 minus box 56).* *Complete Section 8 on page 8. Do not complete unless you are making a claim. See note 28...* 59

Corporation tax already paid (and not repaid). *See note 21* ... 63

Corporation tax outstanding *(box 61 minus box 63). This amount is payable to the Accounts Office. If box 63 equals or is greater than box 61, enter '0.00' and go to box 66. See note 23* ... 65

Corporation tax overpaid *(box 63 minus box 61).* *Complete Section 8 on page 8 also. See note 28* ... 66

This is the last page of the short return

Page 6

Section 4: Claims for capital allowances and details of balancing charges arising

You must complete this section if you want to claim capital allowances, whether or not those allowances are reflected elsewhere in the return. You should also show balancing charges taken into account in the short or detailed return. Show details of qualifying expenditure on which writing-down allowances may be claimed, even if you do not want to claim any allowances for this period. *See note 25*

Notice of expenditure on machinery and plant *See note 25*

Expenditure on which first year allowance is claimed £		Qualifying expenditure on long life assets on which writing down allowances may be claimed £		Qualifying expenditure on other assets on which writing down allowances may be claimed £	
68		91		69	

Charges and allowances included in calculation of trading profit or losses

		Balancing charges £		Capital allowances £
Cars *Including leased out and "expensive" cars*	70		71	
Machinery and plant *- long life assets*	92		93	
- other	72		73	
Industrial buildings and structures *Including qualifying hotels, and commercial buildings and hotels in enterprise zones*	74		75	
Other charges and allowances *For example agricultural buildings, mineral extraction, scientific research, patents*	76		77	
Charges and allowances not included in calculation of trading profit or losses	78		79	

Section 5: Particulars of advance corporation tax and surplus advance corporation tax

Complete this section if you have surplus advance corporation tax brought forward or have paid advance corporation tax (and it has not been repaid) in respect of qualifying distributions made in the period covered by this return.

	£	p
Particulars of advance corporation tax paid		
Particulars of any surplus advance corporation tax brought forward		

Section 6: Amounts claimed as group relief

Complete this section if you have claimed group relief at box 29 (see note 26). Attach a separate sheet of paper if you need more space. Attach a copy of each surrendering company's notice of consent to the claim unless a special arrangement is in force. Include claims made under the consortium provisions.

Name of surrendering company	**Accounting period** Show the start and end dates of any accounting period which is different from the one to which this return relates.	**Tax reference** Show the Tax Office number and the tax inspector's file reference. If you do not know these, supply whatever information you have that will help us to identify the company, for example the company registration number.	Amount claimed from each company
			£
			£
			£
			£
			£
			£
			£
			£
			£
			£
			£
			£
			£
		Total *This figure should be the same as the one in box 29.*	£

Page 9

Section 9: Figures brought forward and carried forward

Please complete this section if any of the following items are
- brought forward from the previous accounting period or
- available for carry forward from the period to which this return relates.

Please provide a reconciliation of any figures that are not explained elsewhere in your accounts and calculations. Attach a separate sheet of paper if you need more space.

	Total brought forward	Less amount used	Plus net amount available to carry forward from this accounting period	Total to carry forward
Trading losses *include trade charges treated as losses*	£	£	£	£
Schedule D case VI losses	£	£	£	£
Excess management expenses *Include business charges treated as management expenses*	£	£	£	£
Surplus ACT *Enter the figure net of amounts set off or repaid or surrendered to subsidiaries*	£ p	£ p	£ p	£ p
Surplus franked investment income	£ p	£ p	£ p	£ p
Losses allowable against chargeable gains	£	£	£	£
Net non-trade deficits and losses on loan relationships (including interest), exchange fluctuations, and certain financial instruments *See note 8.*	£	£	£	£
Others *Please specify*	£	£	£	£
	£	£	£	£
	£	£	£	£
	£	£	£	£

2(e)

Inland Revenue

Return of Company Payments, Distributions and Interest

Collector of Taxes
Inland Revenue Accounts Office (Shipley)
BRADFORD
West Yorkshire BD98 8AA

Telephone: Bradford (01274) 530750

4 Accounts Office ref.

1 | 2 Company regn. no. | 3 Accounting date

IMPORTANT: Please enter in these 4 boxes the details from your CT61 Notice

Advance Corporation Tax on **Qualifying Distributions**
Income Tax deducted from **Company Payments** and **Interest**
Income Tax payable on **Gilt Interest** received without deduction of tax
Tax on manufactured payments received from abroad

- Please use this form when you need to make a Return of company payments, distributions and interest. **You must give all the information asked for on this page and sign the declaration below.** But you need only fill in the other parts of the Return which are relevant to your company. Only use the CT61 Supplement if you need to make a return of Foreign Income Dividends, 'deemed FIDs' or Gilt Interest.
- You are required to make your Return, and pay any tax, within 14 days after the end of the Return Period. Send the Return back to me in the envelope provided.
- *The enclosed CT61 Notes will help you.*
- If your Return shows that tax is payable use the payslip on the enclosed form CT61 Notice.
- When you send back this Return **please also enclose the CT61 Notice**, even if no payment is enclosed.

Company details

Name of company

Address:
Enter the address you would like future CT61 Returns sent to

Postcode

Please tick if this is a change of Registered Office

Period covered by this Return

Return Periods are fixed by law. See CT61 Notes page 3 for guidance.

	Day	Month	Year		Day	Month	Year
Return period ►			19	to			19
being part of the Accounting period ►			19	to			19

Example: Distribution paid on 25 April 1997, and the accounting period is year to 31 December 1997. Enter:

Return period ►	07 04 19 97	to	30 06 19 97
being part of the Accounting period ►	01 01 19 97	to	31 12 19 97

For official use only

901

Declaration

False statements can result in prosecution

To the best of my knowledge the information given in this Return (and the Supplement, if used) is correct and complete

Signature

It would assist if you can state your daytime telephone number and extension here

Name *in CAPITALS*

State in what capacity you make this Return

Date

Please tick if CT61 Supplement is attached

21267 1/97 [illegible] Stationery & Print Limited [illegible]

1 Advance Corporation Tax (ACT) on Qualifying Distributions

Use Part 1 to calculate the ACT payable on Distributions paid.
Use Part 2 below to record Franked Investment Income received.
Franked investment income in box 23 is set-off to reduce the ACT payable in Part 1.
For further information see Notes page 2.

List separately the payments made on different dates. If you need more room please attach a schedule.

Take care to use the correct ACT rate.

	Date		Amount of distribution £	+ ACT payable £	=	Amount of franked payment £
Dividends and other qualifying distributions paid *Exclude – payments at 03* *– Foreign Income Dividends (FIDS)* *– 'deemed FIDS' (see notes page 4)*		01			02	
Dividends paid for which you wish to account for ACT despite an election under Section 247(1) ICTA 1988 *See Notes page 2*		03			04	

		Box	£
Total franked payments	02 + 04	05	
Deduct **franked investment income to be set-off** ...	From Part 2, box 23	06	
Total franked payments for which ACT is payable	05 – 06	10	
Calculate the **Advance Corporation Tax (ACT)** included in the figure at **10**	*See both examples in Notes page 2*	11	
Add the **ACT payable on Foreign Income Dividends (FIDs)**	From CT61 Supplement, boxes 67 and 72	12	
Total ACT for this return period ...	11 + 12	13	
Deduct Additional amounts paid to **non-residents** *See Notes page 4*	Enter all the additional amounts paid, and attach form 2518 Divs FD in duplicate	14	
ACT payable Carry to **Payslip** on CT61 Notice ...	13 – 14	15	

Do not enter a 'minus' figure in box 15. If 14 is greater than 13, claim repayment of the excess in Part 8

2 Franked investment income - running record for set-off or repayment

		Box	£
Amount brought forward from last Return ...		16	
Adjustment, if any, agreed with Inspector ... or a claim under Section 242 ICTA 1988 not yet agreed	*Enter 'MINUS' if appropriate*	17	
	16 + or – 17	18	

	Date	Description	Amount
Franked investment income received since last return			
		Total 19	
Adjustment, if any, agreed with Inspector		*Enter 'MINUS' if appropriate* 20	

You can include income received in earlier return periods if you did not need to submit a form for those periods. See Notes page 1.
Do not enter Foreign Income Dividends here.
If you need more room please attach a schedule.

		Box	£
Total after adjustment ...	19 + or – 20	21	
Total franked investment income now available for set-off or repayment	18 + 21	22	
Deduct **Amount set-off against franked payments in Part 1**	From 22 or 05, whichever is smaller	23	

Carry this figure to Part 1, box 06

		Box	£
Franked investment income after above set-off ...	22 – 23	24	

Repayment of ACT previously paid. Franked investment income at **24** can be set-off against franked payments of earlier return periods **for this accounting period only.**

ACT repayment now claimed		Amount of franked investment income set-off	
25		26	

Carry this figure to Part 8, line b

		Box	£
Amount to be carried forward to next Return	24 – 26	27	

3 Income Tax on Annual Payments and Interest

In boxes 28 and 29, group separately payments taxed at basic rate and payments taxed at lower rate.

If you need more room please attach a schedule.

Use Part 3 to calculate the Income Tax payable on payments made.
Use Part 4 to record Income Tax you have suffered on payments received. This can be set-off to reduce the tax due in Part 3. *For further information see Notes page 3.*

	Date	Description		Gross amount £		Income Tax £
Annual payments etc made under deduction of Income Tax at basic rate or lower rate *See Notes page 3* *Include all manufactured interest, unless entered at 30 below.*			28		29	
Annual payments etc to non-residents made under deduction of reduced rate tax under a Double Taxation Agreement *See Notes page 4.* *Ref. no. of the authority* ▶			30		31	

Income Tax on annual payments etc above	29 + 31	32	

Interest paid by deposit-takers
including distributions paid by **building societies**
Enter the Gross amount paid from which you deducted tax, and the lower rate Income Tax you deducted
See Notes page 3
***Do not** enter interest paid gross, eg TESSA interest*

		Gross amount		Income Tax
Before 6 April	33		34	
From 6 April	35		36	

When the return period does not include 6 April use boxes 35 and 36

Total Income Tax	32 + 34 + 36	37	
Less Income Tax deducted from income **received** now claimed as a **set-off**	From Part 4, box 53	38	
	37 - 38	39	
Less Income Tax on **Gilt Interest received** now claimed as a **set-off**	From CT61 Supplement, box 83	40	
Income Tax now payable Carry to **Payslip** on CT61 Notice	39 - 40	46	

4 Income Tax deducted - running record in this Accounting Period for set-off or repayment

Amount of Income Tax **brought forward** from last Return **for this accounting period**		47	
Adjustment, if any, agreed with Inspector	*Enter 'MINUS' if appropriate*	48	
	47 + or - 48	49	

Income received under deduction of tax since last Return **for this accounting period**

	Date	Description		Gross amount		Income Tax
You can include income received in earlier return periods in this accounting period if you did not need to submit a form for those periods. See Notes page 1. *If you need more room please attach a schedule.*						
		Totals	50		51	

Running total now available for set-off or repayment below	49 + 51	52		
Amount set-off against Income Tax in Part 3	From 52 or 37, whichever is smaller	53		◀ *Carry this figure to Part 3, box 38*
Repayment now claimed of tax paid on annual payments etc in Part 3 of an earlier Return **for this accounting period only**		54		◀ *Carry this figure to Part 8*
Total Income Tax now used for set-off or repayment	53 + 54	55		
Amount to be **carried forward** to next Return **for this accounting period**	52 - 55	56		

5 Certain other distributions

If you need more room please attach a schedule

	Date	Description	Amount £
a Qualifying distributions which are not money payments			
b Payments about which there is a doubt as to whether they are qualifying distributions			
c Distributions (excluding money payments) which, exceptionally, do not fall within an accounting period			

Do not account for ACT on the above payments. The Inspector will make any necessary assessment.

6 Tax on manufactured payments from abroad

See Notes page 4

a **Manufactured dividends received from abroad** *by UK resident companies* ______ (AMOUNTS RECEIVED) Tax payable - at ACT rate ______ *Carry to Payslip on CT61 Notice*

b **Manufactured interest received from abroad** *by UK resident companies and by UK branches of overseas companies* ______ (GROSS INTEREST) Income Tax payable at lower rate ______ *Carry to Payslip on CT61 Notice*

7 Income Tax on Gilt Interest received: totals from CT61 Supplement

a Income Tax **payable** on Gilt Interest received	From box 79		
b **Repayment** of excessive payment on account	78 – 77 if positive		
c **Repayment** of 'Gilts' Income Tax	From box 88		
d **Repayment** of 'other' Income Tax	From box 85		
e Total 'Gilts related' repayments ...	b + c + d		
f Net Income Tax **payable** - *Do not enter a minus figure here. If e is greater than a claim repayment of the excess in Part 8 below*	a – e		*Carry to Payslip on CT61 Notice*

8 Claim for repayment or reimbursement

Use this section to summarise any claims arising in other sections of your Return:

a *From Part 1*	Reimbursement of amounts paid to **non-residents**	14 – 13 if positive	
b *From Parts 2 and 9*	Repayment of **ACT previously paid**	From boxes 25 and 69	
c *From Part 4*	Repayment of **Income Tax previously paid**	From box 54	
d *From Part 7*	Net 'Gilts related' Income Tax repayments	7e – 7a if positive	
e	Total claimed ...	a + b + c + d	

Other forms

Please tick if you require a form to declare the following items:

- Non-qualifying distributions *Form CT2* *See Notes page 2* '✓' ☐
- Stock dividends Section 249 ICTA 1988 *Form CT101* '✓' ☐

When sending back this Return, please

- check you have filled in the blue boxes at the top of page 1
- check you have signed the declaration on page 1
- send the CT61 Notice with this Return, even if no payment is enclosed.

When we receive this Return we will send you another form for your company's next Return.

Please note If the Inspector considers that any distributions, payments, etc have been omitted from this Return, or is in any way dissatisfied with it, the Inland Revenue can issue an appropriate assessment.

PRACTICE DEVOLVED ASSESSMENT
UNIT 18 - PREPARING PERSONAL TAXATION COMPUTATIONS

Notes:

In completing this assessment:

(1) workings should be to the nearest month and to the nearest £;
(2) ignore National Insurance.

Any blank forms required in the answer will be found at the end of this assessment.

THE SITUATION

You are a qualified accounting technician, working in the personal tax department of a firm of accountants, Bond and Co. You report to the tax department manager, Roger Connery.

You are responsible for dealing with the personal tax affairs (income tax and capital gains tax) of a number of clients.

Roger has taken a long weekend and has left you a memo asking you to prepare the tax return for one of your clients, Penny Moore, and do some work on another client, Jack Fleming, ready for his return to the office on Tuesday, 8 September. His memo is reproduced beyond.

Relevant extracts from Penny's tax files are also given beyond.

MEMO

To: Accounting Technician
From: Roger Connery – Tax Department Manager
Date: 4 September 1999
Re: Penny Moore and Jack Fleming

---

(1) **Penny Moore**

I have received a bundle of papers from Penny, comprising:

- dividend vouchers
- bank interest voucher
- a copy of her P11D
- a letter from Penny with other relevant information.

(a) I would like you to prepare schedules of Penny's

(i) Schedule E earnings for 1998/99
(ii) Investment income for 1998/99
(iii) Rental income for 1998/99
(iv) Capital gains for 1998/99.

(b) Please then compute Penny's income tax and capital gains tax liabilities for 1998/99 using our standard pro-forma attached.

(c) Finally, please complete the relevant sections of Penny's self-assessment tax return (attached), and prepare a covering letter enclosing the tax computation and the self-assessment tax return, and advising her of the amount of tax to be paid and the due date(s).

(2) **Jack Fleming**

Brian Stevens, manager of the business tax department has passed to me the attached accounts of Jack's Jeans, a clothes shop which has been run by Jack Fleming for some years, and the tax computation.

Will you please complete the self employment pages of Jack's tax return for me to review before the return is finalised.

Extracts from the papers supplied by Penny Moore

Dividend Vouchers

ABC p.l.c.

1 July 1998

Number of shares	Tax Credit	Net
1,000	20.00	80.00

A. Bloggs
Company Secretary

ABC p.l.c.

1 December 1998

Number of shares	Tax Credit	Net
1,000	35.00	140.00

A. Bloggs
Company Secretary

XYZ p.l.c.

11 May 1998

Number of shares	Tax Credit	Net
2,000	17.00	68.00

J. Jones
Company Secretary

XYZ p.l.c.

31 October 1998

Number of shares	Tax Credit	Net
2,000	33.00	132.00

J. Jones
Company Secretary

LMN p.l.c.

21 June 1998

Number of shares	Tax Credit	Net
10,000	125.00	500.00

M. Smith
Company Secretary

Bank Interest Vouchers

Nat East Bank
Certificate of interest and tax deducted
Year to 5 April 1999

Account Number	After Tax	Tax Deducted	Gross
10743656	120.00	30.00	150.00
47852130	560.00	140.00	700.00

Nat North Bank
Interest Statement
Year to 5 April 1999

TESSA account No. 42359701
Gross Interest (no tax deducted) 473.00

Inland Revenue

P11D EXPENSES AND BENEFITS 1998-99

Note to employer
Complete this return for a director, or an employee who earned at a rate of £8,500 a year or more during the year 6 April 1998 to 5 April 1999. Do not include expenses and benefits covered by a dispensation or PAYE settlement agreement. Read the P11D Guide and booklet 480, Chapter 24, before you complete the form. Send the completed P11D and form P11D(b) to the Tax Office by 6 July 1999. You must give a copy of this information to the director or employee by the same date. The term employee is used to cover both directors and employees throughout the rest of this form.

Note to employee
Your employer has filled in this form. Keep it in a safe place as you may not be able to get a duplicate. You will need it for your tax records and to complete your 1998-99 Tax Return if you get one. Your tax code may need to be adjusted to take account of the information given on this P11D. The box numbers on this P11D have the same numbering as the Employment Pages of the Tax Return, for example, 1.12. Include the total figures in the corresponding box on the Tax Return, unless you think some other figure is more appropriate.

Employer's details
Employer's name: NUGGETS LTD
PAYE tax reference: 999 NIII

Employee's details
Employee's name: P MOORE
Tick here if a director: ☐
Works number or department: MIII
National Insurance number: AB123456 C

A • **Assets transferred (cars, property, goods or other assets)**

Description of asset	Cost/ Market value	− Amount made good or from which tax deducted	= 1.12 Cash equivalent
	£	£	£

B • **Payments made on behalf of employee**

Description of payment	1.12 £
Tax on notional payments not borne by employee within 30 days of receipt of each notional payment	1.12 £

C • **Vouchers or credit cards**

	Gross amount	− Amount made good or from which tax deducted	= 1.13 Cash equivalent
Value of vouchers and payments made using credit cards or tokens	£	£	£

D • **Living accommmodation**

	1.14 Cash equivalent
Cash equivalent of accommodation provided for employee, or his/ her family or household	£

E • **Mileage allowance**

	Gross amount	− Amount made good or from which tax deducted	= 1.15 Taxable payment
Car and mileage allowances paid for employee's car	£	£	£

F • **Cars and car fuel**
If more than two cars were made available, either at the same time or in succession, please give details on a separate sheet

	Car 1	Car 2
Make and Model	VAUXHALL ASTRA	
Dates first registered	01/07/97	/ /
Dates car was available (From – To)	06/04/98 – 05/04/99	/ / – / /
Business mileage used in calculation for this car. *Tick only one box for each car.* (2,499 or less / 2,500 to 17,999 / 18,000 or more)	2,500 to 17,999 ✓	☐ ☐ ☐
Enter engine size and tick type of fuel *only if there is a car fuel scale charge* (Engine size in cc / Petrol / Diesel)	1998 cc, Petrol ✓	cc

If the car was not available for part of the year, the business mileage limits are reduced proportionately.

	Car 1	Car 2
List price of car *If there is no list price, or if it is a classic car, employers see booklet 480; employees see leaflet IR133*	£ 12000	£
Price of optional accessories fitted when car was first made available to the employee	£ 200	£
Price of accessories added after the car was first made available to the employee	£	£
Capital contributions (maximum £5,000) the employee made towards the cost of car or accessories	£	£
Amount paid by employee for private use of the car	£ 180	£
Cash equivalent of each car	£ 2666	£
Total cash equivalent of all cars available in 1998-99		1.16 £ 2666
Cash equivalent of fuel for each car	£ 1,280	£
Total cash equivalent of fuel for all cars available in 1998-99		1.17 £ 1280

P11D(1999) BMSD 11/98

G • Vans

Cash equivalent of all vans made available for private use	**1.18** £

H • **Interest-free and low interest loans**

If the total amount outstanding on all loans does not exceed £5,000 at any time in the year, there is no need for details in this section.

	Loan 1	Loan 2
Purpose of loan(s) – *please use the code shown in P11D Guide for employers*		
Number of joint borrowers *(if applicable)*		
Tick the box if the loan is within MIRAS		
Amount outstanding at 5 April 1998 or at date loan was made if later	£	£
Amount outstanding at 5 April 1999 or at date loan was discharged if earlier	£	£
Maximum amount outstanding at any time in the year	£	£
Total amount of interest paid by the borrower in 1998 - 99 – *enter "NIL" if none was paid*	£	£
Date loan was made or discharged in 1998 - 99 if applicable	/ /	/ /
Cash equivalent of loans after deducting any interest paid by the borrower	**1.19** £	**1.19** £

I • **Mobile telephones**

Cash equivalent of mobile telephones provided	**1.20** £ 200

J • **Private medical treatment or insurance**

	Cost to you		Amount made good or from which tax deducted		Cash equivalent
Private medical treatment or insurance	£ 450	–	£	=	**1.21** £ 450

K • **Qualifying relocation expenses payments and benefits (non-qualifying expenses go in P below)**

Excess over £8,000 of all qualifying relocation expenses payments and benefits for each move	**1.22** £

L • **Services supplied**

	Cost to you		Amount made good or from which tax deducted		Cash equivalent
Services supplied to the employee	£	–	£	=	**1.22** £

M • **Assets placed at the employee's disposal**

		Annual value plus expenses incurred		Amount made good or from which tax deducted		Cash equivalent
Description of asset		£	–	£	=	**1.22** £

N • **Shares**

Tick the box if during the year there have been share-related benefits for the employee ☐

O • **Other items**

		Cost to you		Amount made good or from which tax deducted		Cash equivalent
Subscriptions and professional fees		£	–	£	=	**1.22** £
Description of other items		£	–	£	=	**1.22** £

	Tax paid
Income tax paid but not deducted from director's remuneration	**1.22** £

P • **Expenses payments made to, or on behalf of, the employee**

		Cost to you		Amount made good or from which tax deducted		Taxable payment
Travelling and subsistence payments		£ 595	–	£	=	**1.23** £ 595
Entertainment *(trading organisations read P11D Guide and then enter a tick or a cross as appropriate here)*	✓	£ 120	–	£	=	**1.23** £ 120
General expenses allowance for business travel		£	–	£	=	**1.23** £
Payments for use of home telephone		£	–	£	=	**1.23** £
Non-qualifying relocation expenses *(those not shown in section K)*		£	–	£	=	**1.23** £
Description of other expenses		£	–	£	=	**1.23** £

The Old Halt
High Street
Anytown
AN3 2LR

R. Connery Esq
Bond and Co
4 Church Street
Anytown
AN3 4LB

12 August 1999

Dear Roger

I have collected the papers for my tax return for the year to 5 April 1999 and am enclosing dividend and bank vouchers and my P11D.

I have lost my P60, but my payslip for the end of March showed taxable income of £28,450 and income tax deducted of £6,675. All expenses payments were incurred for business purposes.

The accountants acting for the Bullion partnership in which I have a 10% share have told me that my share of the taxable profits for the year to 31 March 1999 was £11,471. (The partnership had no other income).

I have paid £150 per month (gross) into my personal pension scheme with Norfolk Union. My cottage in Dorset was let for the whole year at £400 per month. I paid insurance of £450, but no other expenses.

I sold my LMN shares on 5 September 1998 for £22,000.

Yours sincerely

Penny Moore

Extract from Penny Moore's Tax files

Date of Birth:	11 June 1958
Marital Status:	Divorced
Employment:	Employed by Nuggets Ltd, Unit 1, Anytown Trading Estate, Anytown, AN5 4BJ.
Partnership:	10% share in Bullion partners (jewellery makers) from 1 June 1996. Accounting date, 31 March Tax reference, 67890 12345
Capital assets:	1,000 shares in ABC plc acquired 31 August 1994 for £2,500. 2,000 shares in XYZ plc acquired 17 June 1991 for £4,000. 10,000 share in LMN plc acquired 23 November 1987 for £3,000. No. 2 Farm Cottages, Tillington, Dorset, acquired 27 February 1983 for £35,000. Let to Bill Wright since May 1983. None of the above are business assets
Capital losses:	Brought forward from 1997/98 £800.
Payments on account:	Payments on account for 1998/99 of £1,000 made on 31 January 1999 and 31 July 1999.
Tax reference:	10203 04050

JACK FLEMING, TRADING AS JACK'S JEANS

ACCOUNTS YEAR TO 31 MARCH 1999

Jack's Jeans
Profit and Loss Account
Year to 31 March 1999

		1999		*1998*
	£	£	£	£
Sales		277,420		245,410
Opening stock	23,500		22,000	
Purchases	185,000		160,000	
	208,500		182,000	
Less Closing stock	25,000		23,500	
Cost of sales		(183,500)		(158,500)
Other direct costs		(11,500)		(9,000)
GROSS PROFIT		82,420		77,910
EXPENSES				
Wages and salaries	23,000		21,500	
Rent	11,000		9,000	
Repairs and maintenance	1,500		2,200	
Administration expenses	2,250		2,000	
Motor expenses	1,750		1,650	
Advertising	450		600	
Entertainment	950		1,050	
Legal fees	770		430	
Bad debts	1,200		810	
Interest paid	350		570	
Depreciation	5,500		4,750	
		48,720		44,560
NET PROFIT		33,700		33,350

Jack's Jeans
Balance Sheet
31 March 1999

		1999		*1998*
	£	£	£	£
FIXED ASSETS				
Plant and machinery		5,010		7,510
Motor vehicle		6,000		9,000
		11,010		16,510
CURRENT ASSETS				
Stock	25,000		23,500	
Debtors	12,075		11,545	
Cash at bank	2,120		1,020	
Cash in hand	153		100	
	39,348		36,165	
CURRENT LIABILITIES				
Trade creditors	14,571		12,420	
Other creditors	1,007		1,510	
	15,578		13,930	
NET CURRENT ASSETS		23,770		22,235
NET ASSETS		34,780		38,745
Represented by				
Capital Account at 1 April 1998		38,745		39,405
Net profit		33,700		33,350
Drawings		(37,665)		(34,010)
At 31 March 1999		34,780		38,745

Jack's Jeans Tax Reference 12345 67890
Schedule D Case I Computation
Year ended 31 March 1999

	£	£
Net Profit		33,700
ADD		
Motor expenses 30% x 1,750	525	
Entertainment	950	
Increase in general bad debt provision	120	
Depreciation	5,500	
		7,095
LESS		
Capital allowances		(4,050)
		36,745

Capital Allowances Computation
Year ended 31 March 1999

	General Pool £	*Expensive Car - (30% private)* £	*Allowances* £
1.4.98 Tax WDV b/f	9,200	10,000	
WDA @ 25%	(2,300)		2,300
WDA @ 25%		(2,500)	1,750
31.3.99 Tax WDV c/f	6,900	7,500	
Total allowances			4,050

JACK FLEMING
TRADING AS JACK'S JEANS
12 High Street
Anytown
AN1 1NN

BLANK FORMS

Task 1

(b) **Penny Moore**
Income and Capital Gains Tax Computation for 1998/99

Income Tax	£	£	*Tax Deducted at Source* £
Earned Income			
Schedule E			
Schedule DI			
	____		
Deductions			
	____		
		____	
Investment Income			
Savings income			
	____		
Non Savings income			
	____		
		____	
Charges on Income			
	____		
		____	
Statutory Total Income			
Less Personal allowance			
		____	____
Taxable income			
		____	____
Tax Thereon			
		____	
Less tax deducted at source			
		____	
Income tax payable			

Capital Gains

Capital gains tax thereon

Income tax and capital gains tax payable

Less payments on account

Balancing Payment

Payments on account for 1999/00

Task 1(c)

Inland Revenue

Income for the year ended 5 April 1999

EMPLOYMENT

Fill in these boxes first

Name	Tax reference

If you want help, look up the box numbers in the Notes

Details of employer

Employer's PAYE reference
1.1

Employer's name
1.2

Date employment started
(only if between 6 April 1998 and 5 April 1999)
1.3 / /

Employer's address
1.5

Postcode

Date finished (only if between 6 April 1998 and 5 April 1999)
1.4 / /

Tick box 1.6 if you were a director of the company
1.6

and, if so, tick box 1.7 if it was a close company
1.7

Income from employment

■ *Money* - *see Notes, page EN3*

		Before tax
• Payments from P60 (or P45 or pay slips)		**1.8** £
• Payments not on P60 etc.	- tips	**1.9** £
	- other payments (excluding expenses shown below and lump sums and compensation payments or benefits shown overleaf)	**1.10** £

	Tax deducted
• UK tax deducted from payments in boxes 1.8 to 1.10	**1.11** £

■ *Benefits and expenses* - *see Notes, pages EN3 to EN6. If any benefits connected with termination of employment were received, or enjoyed, after that termination and were from a* ***former*** *employer you need to complete Help Sheet IR204, available from the Orderline. Do not enter such benefits here.*

	Amount		Amount
• Assets transferred/ payments made for you	**1.12** £	• Vans	**1.18** £
• Vouchers/credit cards	**1.13** £	• Interest-free and low-interest loans	**1.19** £
• Living accommodation	**1.14** £	• Mobile telephones	**1.20** £
• Mileage allowance	**1.15** £	• Private medical or dental insurance	**1.21** £
• Company cars	**1.16** £	• Other benefits	**1.22** £
• Fuel for company cars	**1.17** £	• Expenses payments received and balancing charges	**1.23** £

Income from employment continued

■ ***Lump sums and compensation payments or benefits including such payments and benefits from a former employer***
Note that 'lump sums' here includes any contributions which your employer made to an unapproved retirement benefits scheme

*You must read page EN6 of the Notes **before** filling in boxes 1.24 to 1.30*

Reliefs

- £30,000 exemption — **1.24** £
- Foreign service and disability — **1.25** £
- Retirement and death lump sums — **1.26** £

Taxable lump sums

- From box H of *Help Sheet IR204* — **1.27** £
- From box Q of *Help Sheet IR204* — **1.28** £
- From box R of *Help Sheet IR204* — **1.29** £
- Tax deducted from payments in boxes 1.27 to 1.29 — Tax deducted **1.30** £

■ ***Foreign earnings not taxable in the UK in year ended 5 April 1999** - see Notes, page EN6* — **1.31** £

■ ***Expenses you incurred in doing your job** - see Notes, starting on page EN6*

- Travel and subsistence costs — **1.32** £
- Fixed deductions for expenses — **1.33** £
- Professional fees and subscriptions — **1.34** £
- Other expenses and capital allowances — **1.35** £
- Tick box 1.36 if the figure in box 1.32 includes travel between your home and a permanent workplace — **1.36**

■ ***Foreign Earnings Deduction*** — **1.37** £

■ ***Foreign tax for which tax credit relief not claimed*** — **1.38** £

Additional information

Now fill in any other supplementary Pages that apply to you.
Otherwise, go back to page 2 in your Tax Return and finish filling it in.

Inland Revenue

Income for the year ended 5 April 1999

PARTNERSHIP (SHORT)

Fill in these boxes first

Name

Tax reference

If you want help, look up the box numbers in the Notes

Partnership details

Partnership reference number **4.1**

Partnership trade or profession **4.2**

- Date you started being a partner (if during 1998-99) **4.3** / /
- Date you stopped being a partner (if during 1998-99) **4.4** / /

Your share of the partnership's trading or professional income

Basis period begins **4.5** / / **and ends** **4.6** / /

- Your share of the profit or loss of this year's account for tax purposes **4.7** £
- Adjustment to arrive at profit or loss for this basis period **4.8** £
- Overlap profit brought forward **4.9** £ Deduct overlap relief used this year **4.10** £
- Overlap profit carried forward **4.11** £
- Adjustment for farmers' averaging (see Notes, page PN3 if the partnership made a loss in 1998-99) or foreign tax deducted, if tax credit relief not claimed **4.12** £

Net profit for 1998-99 (if loss, enter '0' in box 4.13 and enter the loss in box 4.14) **4.13** £

Allowable loss for 1998-99 **4.14** £

- Loss offset against other income for 1998-99 **4.15** £
- Loss to carry back **4.16** £
- Loss to carry forward (that is, allowable loss not claimed in any other way) **4.17** £
- Losses brought forward from last year **4.18** £
- Losses brought forward from last year used this year **4.19** £

Taxable profit after losses brought forward box 4.13 *minus* box 4.19 **4.20** £

- Add amounts not included in the partnership accounts that are needed to calculate your taxable profit (for example, Enterprise Allowance (Business Start-up Allowance) received in 1998-99) **4.21**

Total taxable profits from this business box 4.20 + box 4.21 **4.22** £

Class 4 National Insurance Contributions

- Tick this box if exception or deferment applies **4.23**
- Adjustments to profit chargeable to Class 4 National Insurance Contributions **4.24** £

Class 4 National Insurance Contributions due **4.25** £

SA104

Your share of taxed income

- Share of taxed income (liable at 20%) **4.70** £

Your share of Partnership Trading and Professional Profits

from box 4.22

- Share of partnership profits (other than that liable at 20%) **4.73** £

Your share of tax paid

- Share of Income Tax paid **4.74** £
- Share of SC60 deductions **4.75** £
- Share of tax deducted from trading income (not SC60 deductions) **4.75A** £

boxes 4.74 + 4.75 + 4.75A

4.77 £

Additional information

Now fill in any other supplementary Pages that apply to you.
Otherwise, go back to page 2 in your Tax Return and finish filling it in

Income for the year ended 5 April 1999

Inland Revenue

LAND AND PROPERTY

Name | Tax reference

Fill in these boxes first

Are you claiming Rent a Room relief for gross rents of £4,250 or less? No | Yes

(Or £2,125 if the claim is shared?)

Read the Notes on page LN2 to find out
- **whether you can claim Rent a Room relief; and**
- **how to claim relief for gross rents over £4,250**

If 'Yes', and this is your only income from UK property, you have finished these Pages

Is your income from furnished holiday lettings? No | Yes

If 'No', turn over and fill in Page L2 to give details of your property income

If 'Yes', fill in boxes 5.1 to 5.18 before completing Page L2

Furnished holiday lettings

- Income from furnished holiday lettings — 5.1 £

■ *Expenses* (furnished holiday lettings only)

- Rent, rates, insurance, ground rents etc. — 5.2 £
- Repairs, maintenance and renewals — 5.3 £
- Finance charges, including interest — 5.4 £
- Legal and professional costs — 5.5 £
- Cost of services provided, including wages — 5.6 £
- Other expenses — 5.7 £

total of boxes 5.2 to 5.7 — 5.8 £

Net profit (put figures in brackets if a loss) — box 5.1 *minus* box 5.8 — 5.9 £

■ *Tax adjustments*

- Private use — 5.10 £
- Balancing charges — 5.11 £
- Capital allowances — 5.13 £

box 5.10 + box 5.11 — 5.12 £

Profit for the year (copy to box 5.19). If loss, enter '0' in box 5.14 and put the loss in box 5.15 — boxes 5.9 + 5.12 *minus* box 5.13 — 5.14 £

Loss for the year (if you have entered '0' in box 5.14) — boxes 5.9 + 5.12 *minus* box 5.13 — 5.15 £

- Loss offset against 1998-99 total income — 5.16 £
- Loss carried back — see Notes, page LN4 — 5.17 £
- Loss offset against other income from property (copy to box 5.38) — see Notes, page LN4 — 5.18 £

SA105

Other property income

■ ***Income***

• Furnished holiday lettings profits	copy from box 5.14 5.19 £		
• Rents and other income from land and property	5.20 £	Tax deducted 5.21 £	boxes 5.19 + 5.20 + 5.22
• Chargeable premiums	5.22 £		5.23 £

■ ***Expenses*** (do not include figures you have already put in boxes 5.2 to 5.7 on Page L1)

• Rent, rates, insurance, ground rents etc.	5.24 £		
• Repairs, maintenance and renewals	5.25 £		
• Finance charges, including interest	5.26 £		
• Legal and professional costs	5.27 £		
• Costs of services provided, including wages	5.28 £		total of boxes 5.24 to 5.29
• Other expenses	5.29 £		5.30 £
Net profit (put figures in brackets if a loss)			box 5.23 *minus* box 5.30 5.31 £

■ ***Tax adjustments***

• Private use	5.32 £		box 5.32 + box 5.33
• Balancing charges	5.33 £		5.34 £
• Rent a Room exempt amount	5.35 £		
• Capital allowances	5.36 £		
• 10% wear and tear	5.37 £		total of boxes 5.35 to 5.38
• Furnished holiday lettings losses (from box 5.18)	5.38 £		5.39 £
Adjusted profit (if loss enter '0' in box 5.40 and put the loss in box 5.41)			boxes 5.31 + 5.34 *minus* box 5.39 5.40 £
Adjusted loss (if you have entered '0' in box 5.40)		boxes 5.31 + 5.34 *minus* box 5.39 5.41 £	
• Loss brought forward from previous year			5.42 £
Profit for the year			box 5.40 *minus* box 5.42 5.43 £
• Loss offset against total income		5.44 £	
• Loss to carry forward to following year		5.45 £	
• Pooled expenses from 'one estate election' carried forward		5.46 £	
Tick box 5.47 if these Pages include details of property let jointly		5.47	

Now fill in any other supplementary Pages that apply to you.
Otherwise, go back to page 2 of your Tax Return and finish filling it in.

This page is intentionally blank so that the 2nd and 3rd pages of the Capital gains supplement are set out facing each other as would apply in practice.

For the year ended 5 April 1999

Inland Revenue

CAPITAL GAINS

Fill in these boxes first

Name	Tax reference

If you want help, look up the box numbers in the Notes.

*Please complete Pages CG2 and CG **before** filling in the rest of this Page. If you think you will need more than one copy of Pages CG2 and CG3 make photocopies before you begin filling them in.*

Your 1998-99 Capital Gains Tax liability

- Total taxable gains from Page CG3 overleaf — **8.7** £
- Your taxable gains *minus* the annual exempt amount — box 8.7 *minus* £6,800 — **8.8** £
- Additional liability in respect of non-resident or dual resident trusts — **8.9** £

Capital losses

(Remember if your loss arose on a transaction with a connected person, see Notes page CGN11, you can only set that loss agains gains you make on disposals to that same connected person)

■ ***This year's losses***

- Total from Page CG2 — **8.10** £
- Used against gains — **8.11** £
- Used against earlier years' gains (see Notes, page CGN8) — **8.12** £
- Used against income (see Notes, page CGN7) — **8.13A** £ amount claimed against income of 1998-99; **8.13B** £ amount claimed against income of 1997-98; box 8.13A + box 8.13B — **8.13** £
- This year's unused losses — box 8.10 *minus* (boxes 8.11 + 8.12 + 8.13) — **8.14** £

■ ***Earlier years' losses***

- Unused losses of 1996-97 and 1997-98 — **8.15** £
- Used this year (losses from box 8.15 are used in priority to losses from box 8.18) — **8.16** £
- Remaining unused losses of 1996-97 and 1997-98 — box 8.15 *minus* box 8.16 — **8.17** £
- Unused losses of 1995-96 and earlier years — **8.18** £
- Used this year (losses from box 8.15 are used in priority to losses from box 8.18) — box 8.6 *minus* box 8.16 — **8.19** £

■ ***Total of unused losses to carry forward***

- Carried forward losses of 1996-97 and later years — box 8.14 + box 8.17 — **8.20** £
- Carried forward losses of 1995-96 and earlier years — box 8.18 *minus* box 8.19 — **8.21** £

SA108

Please turn over

Your 1998-99 Capital Gains Tax liability

Gains (on assets without mixed use)

A Description of asset	B Tick box if unquoted shares	C Tick box if estimate or valuation used	D Tick box if asset held at 31March 1982	E Insert the later of date of acquisition and 16 March 1998	F Insert the date of disposal	G Disposal proceeds	H Tick box if relief claimed or due	I Chargeable Gains after reliefs but before losses and taper
1				/ /	/ /	£		£
2				/ /	/ /	£		£
3				/ /	/ /	£		£
4				/ /	/ /	£		£
5				/ /	/ /	£		£
6				/ /	/ /	£		£
7				/ /	/ /	£		£
8				/ /	/ /	£		£

Gains on mixed business and non-business use assets (see the notes on pages CGN2 and CGN15)

9				/ /	/ /	£		£
								£
10				/ /	/ /	£		£
								£

Total 8.1 £

Total column

Losses

Description of asset	Tick box if unquoted shares	Tick box if estimate or valuation used	Tick box if asset held at 31March 1982	Disposal proceeds	Tick box if relief claimed or due	Net losses
13				£		£
14				£		£
15				£		£
16				£		£

Total net losses of year 8.2 £

J nter r if usiness sset	K Taper rate	L Losses deducted L1 Allowable losses of the year	L2 Income losses set against gains	L3 Unused losses b/f from earlier years	M Gains after losses	N Tapered gains (gains from column M x % in column K)	O Further information
	%	£	£	£	£	£	
	%	£	£	£	£	£	
	%	£	£	£	£	£	
	%	£	£	£	£	£	
	%	£	£	£	£	£	
	%	£	£	£	£	£	
	%	£	£	£	£	£	
	%	£	£	£	£	£	
B	%	£	£	£	£	£	
	100%	£	£	£	£	£	
B	%	£	£	£	£	£	
	100%	£	£	£	£	£	
			8.5 £	8.6 £		8.3 £	
			Total column L2	*Total column L3*		*Total column N*	

1 **Attributed gains** *(enter source in right hand column)* £

2 **Attributed gains** *(enter source in right hand column)* £

Total of attributed gains 8.4 £

box 8.3 + box 8.4

Total Taxable Gains £

copy to box 8.7 on Page CG1

INCOME for the year ended 5 April 1999

Q10 **Did you receive any income from UK savings and investments?** NO ☐ YES ☐ If yes, fill in boxes 10.1 to 10.32 as appropriate. Include only your share from any joint savings and investments.

■ *Interest*

- Interest from UK banks, building societies and deposit takers
  - where **no tax** has been deducted — Taxable amount **10.1** £
  - where **tax has** been deducted — Amount after tax deducted **10.2** £ | Tax deducted **10.3** £ | Gross amount before tax **10.4** £
- Interest distributions from UK authorised unit trusts and open-ended investment companies (dividend distributions go below) — Amount after tax deducted **10.5** £ | Tax deducted **10.6** £ | Gross amount before tax **10.7** £
- National Savings (other than FIRST Option Bonds and the first £70 of interest from a National Savings Ordinary Account) — Taxable amount **10.8** £
- National Savings FIRST Option Bonds — Amount after tax deducted **10.9** £ | Tax deducted **10.10** £ | Gross amount before tax **10.11** £
- Other income from UK savings and investments (except dividends) — Amount after tax deducted **10.12** £ | Tax deducted **10.13** £ | Gross amount before tax **10.14** £

■ *Dividends*

- Dividends and other qualifying distributions from UK companies — Dividend/distribution **10.15** £ | Tax credit **10.16** £ | Dividend/distribution plus credit **10.17** £
- Dividend distributions from UK authorised unit trusts and open-ended investment companies — Dividend/distribution **10.18** £ | Tax credit **10.19** £ | Dividend/distribution plus credit **10.20** £
- Scrip dividends from UK companies — Dividend **10.21** £ | Notional tax **10.22** £ | Dividend plus notional tax **10.23** £
- Foreign income dividends from UK companies — Dividend **10.24** £ | Notional tax **10.25** £ | Dividend plus notional tax **10.26** £
- Foreign income dividend distributions from UK authorised unit trusts and open-ended investment companies — Dividend **10.27** £ | Notional tax **10.28** £ | Dividend plus notional tax **10.29** £
- Non-qualifying distributions and loans written off — **10.30** £ | Notional tax **10.31** £ | Taxable amount **10.32** £

 Please turn over

RELIEFS *for the year ended 5 April 1999*

Q14 **Do you want to claim relief for pension contributions?** NO YES — If yes, fill in boxes 14.1 to 14.17 as appropriate.

Do not include contributions deducted from your pay by your employer to their pension scheme, because tax relief is given automatically. But ***do include*** *your contributions to personal pension schemes.*

- ***Retirement annuity contracts***

Qualifying payments made in 1998-99	14.1 £	1998-99 payments used in an earlier year	14.2 £	Relief claimed box 14.1 *minus* (boxes 14.2 and 14.3, but not 14.4)
1998-99 payments now to be carried back	14.3 £	Payments brought back from 1999-2000	14.4 £	14.5 £

- ***Self-employed contributions to personal pension plans***

Qualifying payments made in 1998-99	14.6 £	1998-99 payments used in an earlier year	14.7 £	Relief claimed box 14.6 *minus* (boxes 14.7 and 14.8, but not 14.9)
1998-99 payments now to be carried back	14.8 £	Payments brought back from 1999-2000	14.9 £	14.10 £

- ***Employee contributions to personal pension plans*** *(include your gross contribution - see the note on box 14.11 in your Tax Return Guide)*

Qualifying payments made in 1998-99	14.11 £	1998-99 payments used in an earlier year	14.12 £	Relief claimed box 14.11 *minus* (boxes 14.12 and 14.13, but not 14.14)
1998-99 payments now to be carried back	14.13 £	Payments brought back from 1999-2000	14.14 £	14.15 £

- ***Contributions to other pension schemes***

• Amount of contributions to employer's schemes **not deducted** at source from pay	14.16 £
• Gross amount of free-standing additional voluntary contributions paid in 1998-99	14.17 £

Q15 **Do you want to claim any of the following reliefs?** NO YES — If yes, fill in boxes 15.1 to 15.12, as appropriate.

• Payments you made for vocational training	Amount of payment 15.1 £	
• Interest eligible for relief on loans to buy your main home (other than MIRAS)	Amount of payment 15.2 £	
• Interest eligible for relief on other qualifying loans	Amount of payment 15.3 £	
• Maintenance or alimony payments you have made under a court order, Child Support Agency assessment or legally binding order or agreement	Amount claimed under 'new' rules 15.4 £	
	Amount claimed under 'old' rules up to £1,900 15.5 £	Amount claimed under 'old' rules over £1,900 15.6 £
• Subscriptions for Venture Capital Trust shares (up to £100,000)	Amount on which relief claimed 15.7 £	
• Subscriptions under the Enterprise Investment Scheme (up to £150,000)	Amount on which relief claimed 15.8 £	
• Charitable covenants or annuities	Amount of payment 15.9 £	
• Gift Aid and Millennium Gift Aid	Amount of payment 15.10 £	
• Post-cessation expenses and losses on relevant discounted securities etc.	Amount of payment 15.11 £	
• Payments to a trade union or friendly society for death benefits	Half amount of payment 15.12 £	

Task 2

OTHER INFORMATION for the year ended 5 April 1999

Q17 **Have you already had any 1998-99 tax refunded or set off by your Tax Office or the DSS Benefits Agency?** *Read the notes for box 17.1 on page 26 of your Tax Return Guide*

NO | YES

If yes, enter the amount of the refund in box 17.1.

17.1 £

Q18 **Do you want to calculate your tax?**

NO | YES

If yes, do it now and then fill in boxes 18.1 to 18.9. Your Tax Calculation Guide will help.

- Unpaid tax for earlier years included in your tax code for 1998-99 — 18.1 £
- Tax due for 1998-99 included in your tax code for a later year — 18.2 £
- Total tax and Class 4 NIC due for 1998-99 before you made any payments on account *(put the amount in brackets if an overpayment)* — 18.3 £
- Tax due for earlier years — 18.4 £
- Tick box 18.5 if you have calculated tax overpaid for earlier years (and enter the amount in the 'Additional information' box on page 8 — 18.5
- Your first payment on account for 1999-2000 *(include the pence)* — 18.6 £

Tick box 18.7 if you are making a claim to reduce your 1999-2000 payments on account and say why in the 'Additional information' box — 18.7

Tick box 18.8 if you do not need to make 1999-2000 payments on account — 18.8

- 1999-2000 tax you are reclaiming now — 18.9 £

Q19 **Do you want to claim a repayment if you have paid too much tax?** *(If you tick 'No' or the tax you have overpaid is below £10, I will use the amount you are owed to reduce your next tax bill.)*

NO | YES

If yes, fill in boxes 19.1 to 19.12 as appropriate.

Should the repayment (or payment) be sent:

- to you? *Tick box 19.1* — 19.1

or

- to your bank or building society account or other nominee? *Tick box 19.2* — 19.2

If you ticked either box 19.2 or 19.9, fill in boxes 19.3 to 19.8, 19.11 and 19.12 as appropriate.

Your (or your nominee's) bank or building society — 19.3

Branch sort code — 19.4 – –

Account number — 19.5

Name of account — 19.6

Building society ref. — 19.7

If your nominee is your agent, *tick box 19.9 and complete boxes 19.10 to 19.12* — 19.9

Agent's ref. for you — 19.10

Name of your nominee/agent

I authorise — 19.8

Nominee's address — 19.11

Postcode

to receive on my behalf the amount due

This authority must be signed by you. A photocopy of your signature will not do. — 19.12

Signature

Q20 **Are your details on the front of the Tax Return wrong?**

NO | YES

If yes, please make any corrections on the front of the form.

Q21 **Please give other personal details in boxes 21.1 to 21.6** *This information helps us to be more efficient and effective and may support claims you have made elsewhere in your Tax Return*

Please give a daytime telephone number if convenient. It is often simpler to phone if we need to ask you about your Tax Return.

Your telephone number — 21.1

or, if you prefer, your agent's telephone number — 21.2

(also give your agent's name and reference in the 'Additional information' box on page 8)

Enter your first two forenames — 21.5

Say if you are single, married, widowed, divorced or separated — 21.3

Date of birth — 21.4 / /

Enter your date of birth if you are self-employed, or you were born before 6 April 1934, or you have ticked the 'Yes' box in Question 14, or you are claiming relief for Venture Capital Trust subscriptions

Enter your National Insurance number (if known) — 21.6

Please turn over

Inland Revenue

Income for the year ended 5April 1999

SELF-EMPLOYMENT

Name

Tax reference

Fill in these boxes first

If you want help, look up the box numbers in the Notes

Business details

Name of business **3.1**

Description of business **3.2**

Address of business **3.3**

Postcode

Accounting period - *read the Notes, page SEN2 before filling in these boxes*

Start **3.4** / /

End **3.5** / /

- Tick box 3.5A if you entered details for all relevant accounting periods on last year's Tax Return and boxes 3.11 to 3.70 will be blank **3.5A**
- Tick box 3.6 if details in boxes 3.1 or 3.3 have changed since your last Tax Return **3.6**
- Tick box 3.7 if your accounts do not cover the period from the last accounting date (explain why in the 'Additional information' box below) **3.7**
- Tick box 3.8A if your accounting date has changed (only if this is a permanent change and you want it to count for tax) **3.8A**
- Tick box 3.8B if this is the second or further change (explain why you have not used the same date as last year in the 'Additional information' box) **3.8B**
- Date of commencement if after 5 April 1996 **3.9** / /
- Date of cessation if before 6 April 1999 **3.10** / /

Additional information

Income and expenses - annual turnover below £15,000

*If your annual turnover is £15,000 or mor , **ignore** boxes 3.11 to 3.13.* ***Now fill in Page SE2***

*If your annual turnover is below £15,00 , **fill in boxes 3.11 to 3.13 instead of Page SE2**. Read the Notes, page SEN2.*

- Turnover, other business receipts and goods etc. taken for personal use (and balancing charges) **3.11** £
- Expenses allowable for tax (including capital allowances) **3.12** £

Net profit (put figure in brackets if a loss) box 3.11 minus box 3.12 **3.13** £

Now fill in Page SE3

SA103

Income and expenses - annual turnover £15,000 or more

You must fill in this Page if your annual turnover is £15,000 or more - read the Notes, page SEN2

If you were registered for VAT, do the figures in boxes 3.16 to 3.51, include VAT? **3.14** or exclude VAT? **3.15**

	Disallowable expenses included in boxes 3.33 to 3.50	Total expenses	Sales/business income (turnover)
			3.16 £
• Cost of sales	**3.17** £	**3.33** £	
• Construction industry subcontractor costs	**3.18** £	**3.34** £	
• Other direct costs	**3.19** £	**3.35** £	box 3.16 *minus* (box 3.33 + box 3.34 + box 3.35)
		Gross profit/(loss)	**3.36** £
		Other income/profits	**3.37** £
• Employee costs	**3.20** £	**3.38** £	
• Premises costs	**3.21** £	**3.39** £	
• Repairs	**3.22** £	**3.40** £	
• General administrative expenses	**3.23** £	**3.41** £	
• Motor expenses	**3.24** £	**3.42** £	
• Travel and subsistence	**3.25** £	**3.43** £	
• Advertising, promotion and entertainment	**3.26** £	**3.44** £	
• Legal and professional costs	**3.27** £	**3.45** £	
• Bad debts	**3.28** £	**3.46** £	
• Interest	**3.29** £	**3.47** £	
• Other finance charges	**3.30** £	**3.48** £	
• Depreciation and loss/(profit) on sale	**3.31** £	**3.49** £	
• Other expenses	**3.32** £	**3.50** £	total of boxes 3.38 to 3.50
	Put the total of boxes 3.17 to 3.32 in **box 3.53 below**	Total expenses	**3.51** £
			boxes 3.36 + 3.37 *minus* box 3.51
		Net profit/(loss)	**3.52** £

Tax adjustments to net profit or loss

	total of boxes 3.17 to 3.32	
• Disallowable expenses	**3.53** £	
• Goods etc. taken for personal use and other adjustments (apart from disallowable expenses) that increase profits	**3.54** £	
• Balancing charges	**3.55** £	boxes 3.53 + 3.54 + 3.55
Total additions to net profit (deduct from net loss)		**3.56** £
• Capital allowances	**3.57** £	boxes 3.57 + 3.58
• Deductions from net profit (add to net loss)	**3.58** £	**3.59** £
		boxes 3.52 + 3.56 *minus* box 3.59
Net business profit for tax purposes (put figure in brackets if a loss)		**3.60** £

You must fill in this Page (leave blank any boxes that do not apply to you)

Capital allowances - summary

	Capital allowances	Balancing charge
• Motor cars (Separate calculations must be made for each motor car costing more than £12,000 and for cars used partly for private motoring.)	3.61 £	3.62 £
• Other business plant and machinery	3.63 £	3.64 £
• Agricultural or Industrial Buildings Allowance (A separate calculation must be made for each block of expenditure.)	3.65 £	3.66 £
• Other capital allowances claimed (Separate calculations must be made.)	3.67 £	3.68 £
	total of column above	total of column above
Total capital allowances/balancing charges	3.69 £	3.70 £

Adjustments to arrive at taxable profit or loss

Basis period begins 3.71 / / and ends 3.72 / /

- Tick box 3.72A if the figure in box 3.88 is provisional 3.72A
- Tick box 3.72B if the special arrangements for certain trades detailed in the guidance notes apply 3.72B

Profit or loss of this account for tax purposes (box 3.13 or 3.60) 3.73 £

Adjustment to arrive at profit or loss for this basis period 3.74 £

- Overlap profit brought forward 3.75 £ • Deduct overlap relief used this year 3.76 £
- Overlap profit carried forward 3.77 £

Adjustment for farmers' averaging (see Notes, page SEN8 if you made a loss for 1998-99) 3.78 £

Net profit for 1998-99 (if loss, enter '0') 3.79 £

Allowable loss for 1998-99 (if you make a profit, enter '0') 3.80 £

- Loss offset against other income for 1998-99 3.81 £
- Loss to carry back 3.82 £
- Loss to carry forward (that is allowable loss not claimed in any other way) 3.83 £
- Losses brought forward from last year 3.84 £
- Losses brought forward from last year used this year 3.85 £

box 3.79 *minus* box 3.85

Taxable profit after losses brought forward 3.86 £

- Any other business income (for example, Business Start-up Allowance received in 1998-99) 3.87 £

box 3.86 + box 3.87

Total taxable profits from this business 3.88 £

Class 4 National Insurance Contributions

- Tick this box if exception or deferment applies — 3.89
- Adjustments to profit chargeable to Class 4 National Insurance Contributions — 3.90 £

Class 4 National Insurance Contributions due — 3.91 £

Subcontractors in the construction industry

- Deductions made by contractors on account of tax (you must send your SC60s to us) — 3.92 £

Summary of balance sheet

Leave these boxes blank if you do not have a balance sheet

- ***Assets***
  - Plant, machinery and motor vehicles — 3.93 £
  - Other fixed assets (premises, goodwill, investments etc.) — 3.94 £
  - Stock and work in progress — 3.95 £
  - Debtors/prepayments/other current assets — 3.96 £
  - Bank/building society balances — 3.97 £
  - Cash in hand — 3.98 £ — total of boxes 3.93 to 3.98: 3.99 £
- ***Liabilities***
  - Trade creditors/accruals — 3.100 £
  - Loans and overdrawn bank accounts — 3.101 £
  - Other liabilities — 3.102 £ — total of boxes 3.100 to 3.102: 3.103 £
- ***Net business assets*** (put the figure in brackets if you had net business liabilities) — box 3.99 *minus* box 3.103: 3.104 £
- ***Represented by***

  Capital Account
  - Balance at start of period* — 3.105 £
  - Net profit/(loss)* — 3.106 £
  - Capital introduced — 3.107 £
  - Drawings — 3.108 £
  - Balance at end of period* — total of boxes 3.105 to 3.107 *minus* box 3.108: 3.109 £

* If the Capital Account is overdrawn, or the business made a net loss, show the figure in brackets.

Tax deducted from trading income

- Any tax deducted (excluding deductions made by contractors on account of tax) from trading income. — 3.120 £

Note: box numbers 3.110 to 3.119 are not used

Additional information

Now fill in any other supplementary Pages that apply to you. Otherwise, go back to Page 2 of your Tax Return and finish filling it in.

ANSWERS

1-5 INTRODUCTION TO PERSONAL TAXATION

1 **Solution**

Calculation of property income assessable for 1998/99

Furnished house in holiday resort

	Days
Actual commercial letting in 1998/99	
April	7
May	14
June	7
July	31
September	14
	73

As this satisfies the minimum requirement of 70 days actual commercial letting and the house is available for at least 140 days a year, the net income can be calculated as if the activity was a trade.

	£	£
Rent received		1,900
Less: General expenses		
Insurance	250	
Repairs	308	
Water rates	160	
Cleaning	480	
Interest	608	
	1,806	
$^{11}/_{12}$ thereof		(1,655)
Letting expenses		
Accountancy	60	
Advertising	200	
Wear and tear 10% × £(1,900 – 160 × $^{11}/_{12}$)	175	
		(435)
Loss		190

The loss can be relieved against Arthur's other income under S380 as it arises from the letting of qualifying furnished holiday accommodation.

Letting of shops – Schedule A 1998/99

	Shop 1	*Shop 2*
	£	£
Rents accrued $\frac{3}{12} \times £3,000 + \frac{9}{12} \times 4,000$	2,750	
$£6,000 \times \frac{6}{12}$		3,000
Premium £2,000 – 2% (7 – 1) × £2,000		1,760
	£2,750	£4,760
Less: Insurance	190	300
Ground rent	10	40
Repairs and decorating	3,900	2,000
Accountancy	50	50
Advertising for tenant	100	100
	4,250	2,490
	(1,500)	2,270
		(1,500)
Profit assessable under Schedule A in 1998/99		770

Profits and losses from letting property are pooled without regard to repairing provisions in the leases.

*(**Tutorial note:*** Repairs relating to conditions present when the building is purchased are not generally allowable (dry rot in Shop 2).*)*

2 **Solution**

Task 1

Schedule A assessable for 1998/99

Upland Avenue No	*21*	*23*	*25*	*38*	*40*	*67*
	£	£	£	£	£	£
Rent due for y/e 5.4.99	2,080	1,820	2,340	1,300	1,300	520
Expenses payable						
Insurance	280	220	340	150	150	140
Gardener	200	200	200	200	200	200
Accountancy	80	80	80	80	80	80
Advertising		50			100	
Repairs	100		5,000		800	
Bad debt					350	
Interest	500	500	500	500	500	500
	1,160	1,050	6,120	930	2,180	520 (max)
Net amounts	920	770	(3,780)	370	(880)	-

Summary

	£
No 21	920
No 23	770
No 25	(3,780)
No 38	370
No 40	(880)
No 67	-
	(2,600)
Amount assessable under Schedule A for 1998/99	Nil

(*Note:* Although the question refers to a new roof for No 25 it is reasonable to assume that there was one there already and the expenditure is essentially on a repair or replacement.

As it is not necessary to consider profits and losses on each property individually the accounts could be drawn up to show the total rents etc for all the properties, instead of property by property. Care has to be taken to disallow the excess of expenses relating to the non-commercial letting.)

Task 2

The loss of £2,600 will be carried forward for offset against future Schedule A profits.

3 **Solution**

Income tax computation 1998/99

			£
Earned income			
Schedule D Case I			23,000
Less: Personal pension plan contributions lower of:			
(i)	amount paid	£6,000	
(ii)	20% × £23,000 (aged 36)	4,600	
	Add: Relief b/f 1997/98 (W)	520	
		£5,120	(5,120)
			17,880
Unearned income			
Schedule D III	- Building Society interest £1,984 × 100/80		2,480
	- War loan		3,300
			23,660
Charges -	Charitable Deed of Covenant		(3,500)
			20,160
Less:	PA		(4,195)
Taxable income			15,965

Tax borne:		
Non-savings:	4,300 × 20%	860
	5,885 × 23%	1,354
Savings:	5,780 × 20%	1,156
		3,370
Add:	Tax retained on charges	
	£3,500 × 23%	805
Tax liability		4,175
Less:	Tax suffered at source on BSI received	(496)
	Payments on account	(2,700)
Further tax payable (on 31 January 2000)		979

Note: mortgage interest within MIRAS is ignored in the income tax computation.

WORKING

Net relevant earnings for 1997/98	14,400
Relief @ 17½% (age 35 on 6.4.97)	2,520
Relief taken in 1997/98	(2,000)
Unused relief c/f for up to 6 years	520

6-7 EMOLUMENTS AND BENEFITS

1 Solution

Computation of income tax payable for 1998/99

	£	£
Earned income		
Schedule E:		
Salary		36,000
Bonus ***(note 1)***		8,000
		44,000
Benefits		
Car 20,000 × 35%	7,000	
Less: 7,000 × ⅔ ***(note 2)***	(4,667)	
Car fuel ***(note 2)***	1,890	
Scholarship paid for son	2,940	
Excess shares under profit sharing scheme ***(note 3)***	102	
		7,265
		51,265
Less: Pension contributions 7% × £36,000		2,520
		48,745
Less: Charitable deed £4,235 × 100/77		5,500
Statutory total income		43,245
Less: PA		4,195
Taxable income		39,050

£	£
4,300 @ 20%	860
22,800 @ 23%	5,244
11,950 @ 40%	4,780
Less: Tax credit re APA (1,900 × 15%) (son in full time education)	(285)
Income tax borne	10,599
Add: Tax withheld on £5,500 charitable covenant	1,265
Income tax payable	11,864

Explanation of treatment

(1) Under the receipts basis for directors under Schedule E the bonus is treated as received, and therefore taxed, when it is determined. Thus the bonus determined in May 1998 is taxable in 1998/99.

(2) The car benefit is reduced by ⅔ as Mr Darcy drives more than 18,000 business miles per year. There is no reduction in the car fuel benefit.

(3) The limit of value which may be apportioned under an approved profit sharing scheme is 10% of salary for PAYE purposes (ie, excluding benefits in kind, but after deduction of pension contributions). The higher of the current year or preceding year's remuneration may be used

1998/99 £36,000 + 8,000 – 2,520 = £41,480
1997/98 £36,000 + 4,000 – 2,520 = £37,480

	£
Value of shares allotted 1,000 × 425p	4,250
Limit 10% × £41,480 (less than the £8,000 overriding limit)	4,148
	102

2 Solution

Computation of benefits in kind 1998/99

			£
(i)	Jaguar motor car - private use 6 April to 31 July 1998 is 4 months. Business mileage is in excess of an annual rate of 18,000 charge reduced to ⅓. benefit is $^{4}/12$ × 26,700 × 35% × ⅓		1,038
(ii)	Jaguar motor car - private fuel 6 April to 31 July 1998 is 4 months. benefit is $^{4}/12$ × 1,890 (50% contribution not relevant - all private fuel must be reimbursed to avoid scale charge)		630
(iii)	Legal costs contribution		2,000
(iv)	Mercedes motor car - private use, none		Nil
(v)	Wife's BMW motor car - private use 6 April 1998 to 5 April 1999 second company car at least 4 years old at end of tax year Benefit is 15,000 × 35% × ⅔		3,500
(vi)	Wife's BMW motor car - private fuel 6 April 1998 to 5 April 1999 normal scale charge applies		1,280
(vii)	Company house Annual value	3,600	
	Additional charge (market value of £140,000 less £75,000) × 8% official rate	5,200	8,800
(viii)	Two suits - private use 20% × £800		160
Total benefits in kind assessable on Mr K for 1998/99			17,408

(Tutorial notes:

(1) The legal expenses in connection with Mr K's dangerous driving are considered to be a benefit by reason of his employment.

(2) When a car is used solely for business purposes, there is no assessable benefit.

(3) The BMW supplied to Mr K's wife is treated as a benefit provided to Mr K. It is treated as a second car, and the car benefit charge would therefore only be reduced (and only by ⅓) if business mileage exceeded 18,000 miles pa. The ⅓ reduction for age does apply.

(4) If a house is provided for first use more than 6 years after the company acquired it, the market value at first use applies instead of cost plus improvements for calculating the notional loan benefit.

(5) When an asset is provided for the use of an employee the benefit is 20% of the asset's market value when first provided.*)*

3 Solution

Task 1

The assessable benefits will be as follows:

		£	£
(i)	**Mercedes car**		
	Benefit £35,000 × 35% × ⅔		8,167
	Fuel benefit		1,890
(ii)	**BMW car**		
	Benefit for additional car £14,000 × 35% × ⅔		3,267
	Fuel benefit		1,280
(iii)	**Accommodation** - additional charge for 'expensive' house		
	(180,000 – 75,000) × official rate = £105,000 × 8.0%		8,400
	Heating and lighting		2,600
(iv)	**Suits**		
	3 × £400 × 20%		240
(v)	**Video system**		
	Original market value	3,000	
	Less: Benefits assessed 1994/95 to 1997/98 (4 × 20% × £3,000)	(2,400)	
	Less: Price paid on acquisition	(300)	
			300
			26,144

∴ Additional income tax payable is:

26,144 × 40% = £10,458

The rate used is 40% since Mr B is clearly a higher rate tax payer.

Task 2

Mr B's company will have to complete a form P11D for Mr B at the end of the tax year 1998/99 detailing the various benefits in kind provided to Mr B during the 1998/99 tax year. This form has to be sent to the company's PAYE tax district by 6 July 1999. There are monetary penalties payable by the company for sending late or incorrect P11Ds.

Mr B must include details of the benefits and expenses received in his personal tax return for 1998/99. Mr B could have minor underpayments collected by restricting his PAYE code provided he submits the return by 30 September 1999. Otherwise the tax is payable by 31 January 2000 at the latest.

The Revenue has introduced K codes which are designed to collect tax due on benefits in kind as far as possible on a current year basis via the PAYE system. Hence, some or all of the tax due on the benefits may have been collected through Mr B's PAYE deductions during 1998/99.

(Tutorial note:

1 The car benefit is calculated as 35% of the list price including accessories, delivery charges and VAT (subject to £80,000 maximum).

Reductions in the charge are as follows:

Business mileage	
2,500 to 17,999 pa	⅓
18,000 or more pa	⅔
Second car 18,000 or more pa	⅓
Then, cars 4 years old and over at end of tax year	⅓

2 When a car is provided to an employee's spouse by reason of the employee's employment, that car is also assessed on the employee as a benefit.

3 The method of calculating the fuel benefit is by scale charge.*)*

8-11 INTRODUCTION TO CGT

1 Solution

Task 1

Computation of chargeable gains

Share disposals 31 October 1998

(i) F Ltd:

	Cost	*March 1982*
	£	£
Disposal proceeds	8,000	8,000
Original cost/March 1982 value	(6,000)	(10,000)
	2,000	(2,000)
Indexation:		
10,000 × 1.062	(2,000) (max)	-
Net (loss)	Nil	(2,000)

Rebasing cannot turn a Nil result into a loss.

(ii) Q Ltd:

	Cost	*March 1982*
Disposal proceeds	21,000	21,000
Original cost/March 1982 value	(13,000)	(18,000)
	8,000	3,000
Indexation:		
18,000 × 1.062 (max)	(8,000)	(3,000)
	Nil	Nil

(iii) R Ltd:

	£	£
Disposal proceeds	38,000	38,000
Original cost/March 1982 value	(12,000)	(4,000)
	26,000	34,000
Indexation:		
12,000 × 1.062	(12,744)	(12,744)
Net gain	13,256	21,256

Chargeable gain = £13,256 since lower gain applies.

(iv) S Ltd:

	Cost	*March 1982*
Disposal proceeds	1,000	1,000
Original cost/March 1982 value	(6,000)	(5,000)
	(5,000)	(4,000)

Capital loss = £4,000 since lower loss applies. Indexation is ignored as it cannot increase a loss.

Factory lease disposal 28 February 1999

	£
Sale proceeds	600,000
Base cost for CGT purposes *:	
$400{,}000 \times \frac{76.399^1}{87.330^2}$	(349,932)
$40{,}000 \times \frac{76.399^1}{84.950^3}$	(35,974)
	214,094
Indexation:	
349,932 × 0.261	(91,332)
35,974 × 0.185	(6,655)
Chargeable gain	116,107

* Sch 8 TCGA 1992 'wasting' factors apply to restrict the original cost by the following fraction:

$$\frac{\text{\% applicable to remaining life of lease on disposal}}{\text{\% applicable to remaining life of lease on acquisition}}$$

[1] - 22 years	76.399
[2] - 30 years	87.330
[3] - 27 years 11 months	84.950

Summary of gains/(losses)

		£
Share disposals:	F Ltd	-
	Q Ltd	-
	R Ltd	13,256
	S Ltd	(4,000)
Factory lease disposal		116,107
		125,363

∴ £125,363 chargeable gain will be included in Y Ltd's corporation tax computation for the year ended 31 March 1999.

Task 2

Advice

(i) The lease sold by Y Ltd is an asset eligible for rollover relief. If the full proceeds of £600,000 are reinvested in another business asset, then the gain of £116,107 can be deferred as it is rolled over, and deducted from the replacement asset. The gain then crystallises when the replacement asset is eventually sold.

The conditions for the relief are that:

(1) the replacement asset must be a qualifying asset; and
(2) the reinvestment must be within one year before and three years after the disposal.

If the proceeds are not fully reinvested, part of the gain is chargeable immediately.

If the directors reinvest £600,000 in the factory freehold, the gain of £116,107 can be rolled over. No relief is available if an investment property is purchased as this is not a qualifying asset.

(ii) If the sale of the lease is deferred until after the company's year end (31 March 1999) the payment of any tax would be deferred for 12 months.

2 Solution

Task 1

March 1998

		£	£	£
Proceeds			880,000	
Original cost	$£500,000 \times \frac{81.10}{91.98}$	440,857		
Indexation	£440,857 × 0.472	208,085		
Addition	$£60,000 \times \frac{81.10}{91.15}$	53,384		
Indexation	£53,384 × 0.362	19,325		
			721,651	
Chargeable gain			158,349	158,349

November 1998

		£	£	£
Proceeds			260,000	
Original cost		120,000		
Indexation	£120,000 × 0.729	87,480		
Improvements		20,000		
Indexation	£20,000 × 0.676	13,520		
			241,000	
Chargeable gain			19,000	19,000
Total chargeable gains				£177,349

Task 2

Provided that the business premises were occupied by XY Ltd, rollover relief will be available on its disposal. However, there will be no such relief on the gain on the disposal of the investment property, as only business assets qualify.

When a business asset is disposed of, rollover relief is available when a qualifying asset (eg, land, buildings and fixed plant and machinery) is purchased within 12 months before or 36 months after the disposal. When all the proceeds are reinvested, the cost of the replacement is reduced by the chargeable gain. If only part of the proceeds are reinvested, the surplus will be liable to tax immediately.

(Tutorial note:

Leases

When dealing with leases it is important to differentiate between assigning (selling) a lease and granting a sublease out of an existing lease.

XY Ltd is assigning a lease, with 50 years or less to run. Such a lease is a wasting asset and subject to special rules for CGT. On the disposal of such a lease only a certain proportion of the original expenditure is allowed as a deduction from the disposal proceeds.

This is calculated as follows:

$$\text{original cost} \times \frac{\text{\% for number of years left for lease on assignment}}{\text{\% for number of years of lease on acquisition}}$$

When improvements are made which are reflected in the value of the lease, the allowable deduction is:

$$\text{improvement cost} \times \frac{\text{\% for number of years left for lease on assignment}}{\text{\% for number of years of lease at time of improvement}})$$

3 Solution

Philip

(i) January 1988.

The value of the rights sold, 200 at 70p, £140 was less than 5% of the value of the shares held, 1,000 at £3, £3,000. There was, therefore, no disposal for capital gains tax purposes at that time.

(ii) August 1998

		Original	*31.3.82 value*
		£	£
Sale proceeds		7,500	7,500
Cost (£1,500 – £140)		(1,360)	
31.3.82 value (£1,600 – £140)			(1,460)
Unindexed gain		6,140	6,040
Indexation allowance			
$£1,600 \times \frac{161.2 - 79.44}{79.44}$ (1.029)	1,646		
Less $£140 \times \frac{161.2 - 103.3}{103.3}$ (0.561)	(78)	(1,568)	(1,568)
		4,572	4,472

Chargeable gain is the lower figure, £4,472.

(Tutorial note:

When there is a sale of rights nil paid, and the sale proceeds are less than or equal to 5% of the value of the shares on which the rights are offered, there is no part disposal. (Revenue practice to treat £3,000 as *deminimis* applies from February 1997.) The proceeds are deducted from the cost of the shares.

On a subsequent disposal the indexation allowance is calculated as follows:

	£
Cost/31 March 1982 indexed from 31 March 1982 to date of disposal	X
Less: Sale proceeds of rights, indexed from date of sale of rights to date of disposal	(X)
	X

)

12-14 RETIREMENT AND REPLACEMENT

1 Solution

Task 1

(i) **Office block**

					Cost	*March 1982*
					£	£
Sale proceeds (October 1998)					520,000	520,000
Cost (pre-March 1982)					(145,000)	
March 1982 value						(160,000)
Cost (post-March 1982)					(110,000)	(110,000)
Unindexed gain					265,000	250,000
Indexation:						
March 1982	Value	1.062	×	160,000	(169,920)	(169,920)
October 1986	Addition	0.664	×	80,000	(53,120)	(53,120)
August 1990	Addition	0.279	×	30,000	(8,370)	(8,370)
					33,590	18,590

∴ Chargeable gain is the lower of the two ie, £18,590.

(ii) **Plot of land**

Original gain rolled over in February 1982:

	£
Sale proceeds (February 1982)	38,000
Cost	(30,000)
Chargeable gain rolled over	8,000

This deferred gain will escape tax because the March 1982 value, and not cost, determines the gain on the November 1998 land disposal, as indicated below:

Gain on November 1998 disposal:

	£
Sale proceeds (November 1998)	140,000
March 1982 value	(41,000)
Unindexed gain	99,000
Indexation 1.063 × £41,000	(43,583)
	55,417

(iii) **Office building**

Original gain rolled over in April 1989:

		£
Sale proceeds (April 1989)		120,000
Cost		(50,000)
Unindexed gain		70,000
Indexation 0.334 × £50,000		(16,700)
Chargeable gain rolled over		53,300

Gain on December 1998 disposal:

	£	£
Sale proceeds (December 1998)		210,000
Cost	120,000	
Less: rolled over gain	(53,300)	(66,700)
Unindexed gain		143,300
Indexation 0.436 × £66,700		(29,081)
Chargeable gain		114,219

Task 2

To: The Directors of P Ltd

From: Management accountant

Re: Roll-over of capital gains

Date: 24 May 1999

Gains on qualifying assets may be held over in full for up to ten years, against the cost of fixed machinery as long as all the net proceeds of the disposal are reinvested in qualifying assets in the period one year before to three years after the date of sale. Only gains on assets which have been used for the purposes of the trade can be held over in this way. If the machinery is sold or ceases to be used for the trade before the end of the ten year period, the held-over gain crystallises at that earlier date.

Therefore, the £210,000 proceeds of the office building could be reinvested in machinery (provided it is fixed machinery) so that the £114,219 gain is held over. In the same way, the £55,417 gain on the plot of land could be held over provided that this land was used in P Ltd's trade. The £18,590 gain on the office block could not be held over as it was an investment property for renting, and not used in P Ltd's trade.

Signed: Management accountant.

2 Solution

Task 1

Ian

		Cost	*31.3.82 value*
		£	£
Sale proceeds		250,000	250,000
Cost	(W1)	(28,571)	
31.3.82 value	(W2)		(100,000)
Unindexed gain		221,429	150,000
Indexation allowance £100,000 × $\frac{161.2-79.44}{79.44}$ (1.029)		(102,900)	(102,900)
Indexed gain		118,529	47,100
Chargeable gain is the lower figure		47,100	

WORKING

Part disposal August 1986

	Working 1 *cost*	*Working 2* *31.3.82 value*
	£	£
Cost	50,000	
31.3.82 value		175,000
Attributable to first disposal:		
$50{,}000 \times \frac{150{,}000}{(150{,}000+200{,}000)}$	(21,429)	
$175{,}000 \times \frac{150{,}000}{(150{,}000+200{,}000)}$		(75,000)
Attributable to second disposal	28,571	100,000

Task 2

Roy

	Cost	*31.3.82 value*
	£	£
Deemed disposal proceeds	500,000	500,000
Cost/31 March 1982 value	(100,000)	(80,000)
Unindexed gain	400,000	420,000
Indexation allowance $\frac{161.2-79.44}{79.44}$ = 1.029 × £100,000	(102,900)	(102,900)
	297,100	317,100

The lower gain is £297,100 and this is subject to retirement relief of:

(£250,000 × 70%) + 50% (£297,100 – £175,000) = £236,050
Upper limit of 50% relief band is £1,000,000 × 70% = £700,000

	£
Indexed gain	297,100
Retirement relief	(236,050)
Gain eligible for gift relief	61,050

No chargeable gain

Colin

Cost to set against future disposal is £500,000 – £61,050 = £438,950

3 **Solution**

Task 1

Angela
Capital gains tax computation 1998/99

(1) Scott Stockings Ltd is a 'personal' company since Angela has at least 5% of the voting rights.

(2) 'Chargeable business assets' are:

	£'000
Land and buildings	2,000
Plant and machinery	1,000
Goodwill	500
	3,500

(3) There are no 'chargeable non-business assets'.

(4) The assessable capital gain is:

		£
Chargeable gain as calculated		290,000
Less: Retirement relief:		
(i) basic relief (60% × 250,000) ***(note 1)***	150,000	
(ii) 50% × (290,000 – 150,000) ***(note 2)***	70,000	(220,000)
		70,000
Less: Taper relief (7.5%)		5,250
		64,750
Annual exemption		(6,800)
		57,950

Notes:

(1) Lower of 60% (time as full-time working officer) and 80% (time shares owned).

(2) Maximum gain eligible for relief is £600,000 (£1,000,000 × 60%).

(3) The 7.5% rate of taper relief applies as the shares are business assets which have been held for one year (the bonus year).

Task 2

Victor
Capital gains tax computation 1998/99

(i) FA 1985 pool (6.4.82 to date)

	Shares	Unindexed cost	Indexed cost
1.4.87 Bought	1,000	11,000	11,000
Indexation to September 1989			
$\frac{116.6-101.8}{101.8} \times £11,000$	-		1,599
			12,599
1.9.89 1 for 2 rights	500	3,000	3,000
	1,500	14,000	15,599
Indexation to April 1998			
$\frac{161.2-116.6}{116.6} \times £15,599$	-		5,967
	1,500	14,000	21,566
Disposal	(1,500)	(14,000)	(21,566)
	-	-	-

Sale proceeds $\frac{1,500}{2,100} \times £36,400$	26,000
Less: Unindexed cost	(14,000)
Unindexed gain	12,000
Less: Indexation allowance 21,566 – 14,000	(7,566)
	4,434

(ii) FA 1982 pool (6.4.65 - 5.4.82)

	Cost £	Cost £	Market value at 31.3.82 £	Market value at 31.3.82 £
Sale proceeds $\frac{600}{2,100} \times 36,400$		10,400		10,400
Original shares (1.8.78) 400 shares $\frac{400}{600} \times 7,200$	4,800			
Rights issue (1.9.89) 200 shares at £6	1,200	(6,000)		
Original shares (31.3.82) 400 at £8			3,200	
Rights issue (1.9.89) 200 at £6			1,200	(4,400)
Unindexed gains		4,400		6,000

Indexation allowance to April 1998 Original shares				
$\frac{161.2 - 79.44}{79.44}(1.029)$				
on 4,800 (cost greater than 31.3.82 value) restricted	4,400		4,939	
Rights issue				
$\frac{161.2 - 116.6}{116.6}(.383)$				
on 1,200 (restricted)	Nil	(4,400)	460	(5,399)
		Nil		601

As the gain over cost is nil the result is nil.

Summary

	£
FA 1985 pool	4,434
FA 1982 pool	-
Gain, before annual exemption	4,434

(Tutorial notes:

(1) Shares are matched firstly with shares acquired in the following 30 days, then with those purchased since 5 April 1998 (LIFO), then with shares from the FA 1985 pool, and then with shares from the FA 1982 pool.

(2) When a rights issue takes place, the shares purchased at different times are increased by the rights issue. Expenditure on a rights issue can only be indexed from the date of the issue, not the date of acquisition of the original holding.*)*

15 PRINCIPAL PRIVATE RESIDENCE RELIEF

1 Solution

Disposal of shares

	£
Disposal proceeds	320,000
Less: Cost	(100,000)
Less: Indexation allowance to April 1998	
$£100{,}000 \times \frac{161.2 - 79.44}{79.44} (1.029)$	(102,900)
Gain	117,100

The maximum amount that can be rolled over is the lower of:

(i) the chargeable gain (£117,100) and

(ii) the acquisition cost of the qualifying investment (£250,000)

ie, £117,100.

However, the gain rolled over can be restricted so that the CGT annual exemption is not wasted.

Adrienne would therefore rollover £110,300 (£117,100 – £6,800) leaving £6,800 to be taxed in 1998/99 which is covered by the annual exemption.

2 Solution

	£	£
Net sale proceeds		135,475
Less: MV 31.3.82 by election		35,000
Unindexed gain		100,475
Less: Indexation allowance (March 1982 - April 1998)		
$\frac{161.2 - 79.44}{79.44} (1.029) \times 35{,}000$		(36,015)
		64,460
Less: (i) Whole residence exempt for 10 years since 31.3.82: 7 years exclusive use and last 3 years in any event: $£64{,}460 \times \frac{10}{17}$	37,918	

	(ii) Two-thirds only remaining 7 years exempt while let £64,460 × $\frac{7}{17}$ × $\frac{2}{3}$	17,695	55,613
Gain (otherwise) chargeable on letting			8,847
Less:	Letting exemption, the lowest of:		
	(i) PPR exemption of £55,613		
	(ii) Gain attributable to letting period, £8,847		8,847
	(iii) the monetary limit, £40,000		
Chargeable gain			Nil

3 **Solution**

	Cost £	*MV 31.3.82* £
Net sale proceeds	86,175	86,175
Less: Cost/MV 31.3.82	6,215	35,000
Unindexed gains	79,960	51,175
Less: Indexation allowance (March 1982 - April 1998) $\frac{161.2-79.44}{79.44}$ (=1.029) × £35,000	(36,015)	(36,015)
Lower gain chargeable	43,945	15,160
Less: Exemption		
(i) Periods before 1.4.82 ignored		
(ii) 1.4.82 - 5.10.88 - occupied		
(iii) 6.10.88 - 5.10.92 - deemed occupation (4 years allowed due to location of workplace)		
(iv) 6.10.92 - 5.10.95 - deemed occupation (3 years absence allowed for any reason)		
(v) 6.10.95 - 5.11.95 - occupied		
(vi) 6.11.95 - 6.7.98 - part of last 3 years		
		15,160
Chargeable gain		Nil

16-17 PERSONAL TAX COMPUTATIONS & RETURNS

1 **Solution**

Task 1

(i) **Kevin**

Income tax liability - 1998/99

	£
Schedule D Case I	15,000
Bank interest (990 × $^{100}/_{80}$)	1,238
STI	16,238
Loss (S380)	(16,238)
Taxable income	-
Income tax on	Nil
Tax repayment	
Bank interest £1,238 × 20%	£248

Loss remaining: 20,000 – 16,238 = £3,762. This is available for relief in 1999/00 under S380 against total income or in future years under S385 against future profits from the same trade.

Capital gains liability - 1998/99	£
Agreed gain	9,100
Annual exemption	(6,800)
	2,300 at 20% = £460

(Tutorial notes:

(1) The unused personal allowance is not available to use against the capital gains tax assessment.

(2) Under S380, a loss may be relieved against the STI of the fiscal year in which the loss arises and/or the preceding year. Thus the loss of the year ended 31.12.99 may be set against the STI of 1998/99.

(3) A claim under S72 FA91 has not been considered because although it would save tax of £460 it will result in wasting the CGT exemption.)

(ii) **Susan**

Income tax liability - 1998/99

		Total	*Non-savings*	*Savings*
			£	£
Salary				
Benefits-in-kind		25,000	25,000	–
Car (W)	1,225			
Fuel (W)	505	1,730	1,730	
		26,730	26,730	
House (Note 1)	exempt			
House services	1,500			
	1,500			
(no restriction on house services - less than 10% of 26,730) (Note 2)		1,500	1,500	
		28,230	28,230	
Bank interest (10 × $^{100}/_{80}$)		12		12
		28,242	28,230	12
Personal allowance		(4,195)	(4,195)	–
Taxable income		24,047	24,035	12
Non-savings				
4,300 at 20%		860		
19,735 at 23%		4,539		
Savings 12 at 20%		2		
		5,401		
Less: Tax credit on MCA (transfer from Kevin) 1,900 × 15%		(285)		
Income tax on bank interest		(2)		
Income tax liability		5,114		

Capital gains tax liability - 1998/99

Agreed gain	3,000
Annual exemption	3,000
	-

WORKING

	£	£	
Car			
35% × £7,000	2,450		
Available for six months		1,225	$^{6}/_{12}$
Fuel			
Under 1400 cc (petrol)	1,010		
Available for six months		505	$^{6}/_{12}$

(Tutorial notes:

(1) As the occupation of the house is 'job-related' there is no charge.

(2) Where there is no charge for 'job-related' accommodation any charge for ancillary services is restricted to 10% of the other net emoluments (excluding the charge for ancillary services).*)*

Elections to be made:

(1) Under S380 for Kevin's loss arising in 1999/00 to be set against his income for 1998/99.

(2) Kevin should transfer the married couple's allowance to Susan since his own tax liability in 1998/99 is insufficient to utilise the tax credit.

(3) Since Susan pays income tax at a higher rate than Kevin, it will probably be beneficial for Kevin to be assessed on most of the joint income, say 99 : 1. They must, therefore, make a joint declaration of their actual beneficial interests in the asset and the income from it on a Revenue form to that effect. Such a declaration will be binding for all future tax years.

Task 2

A share in the land owned by Kevin might have been transferred to Susan before the sale, thereby utilising the unused balance of her annual exemption and reducing Kevin's liability. If the land was a business asset, 7.5% taper relief would be due. Alternatively rollover relief may be possible.

2 Solution

(Tutorial note: this question requires an income tax computation covering trading income for part of the tax year followed by permanent cessation of trade and income from employment, including car benefits, for the remainder of the year, together with other sources of income and charges on income and pension contributions with calculations of capital gains tax payable on net gains for the same tax year.*)*

Task 1

Income from business

(i) **Capital allowances computation**

	Plant and machinery	*Dawn car (1) (Business Use 25%)*	*Dawn car (2) (Business Use 25%)*	*Car pool*	*Total*
	£	£	£	£	£
Y/e 30.4.97					
Additions	3,200	5,600		4,000	
WDA 25%	(800)	(1,400) × 25%		(1,000)	2,150
	2,400	4,200		3,000	
Y/e 30.4.98					
Additions	1,000		7,800		
Sale	–	(3,000)			
	3,400	1,200			
Balancing allowance		(1,200) × 25%			300
WDA 25%	(850)		(1,950) × 25%	(750)	2,088
	2,550	–	5,850	2,250	2,388

P/e 30.9.98				
Additions	500			
Sales	(2,500)	(6,000)	(2,000)	
	550	(150)	250	
Balancing charge		150 × 25%		(37)
Balancing allowance	(550)		(250)	800
	-	-	-	763

(ii) **Adjusted profit**

	£
Year ended 30 April 1997	
(15,000 – 2,150)	12,850
Year ended 30 April 1998	
(12,000 - 2,388)	9,612
Period ended 30 September 1998	
(9,000 – 763)	8,237

(iii) **Case I assessments**

	£	£
1996/97 (1.5.96 - 5.4.97)		
12,850 × $^{11}/_{12}$		11,779
1997/98 (y/e 30.4.97)		12,850
1998/99 (1.5.97 - 30.9.98)		
9,612 + 8,237	17,849	
Less: overlap relief (1.5.96 - 5.4.97)	(11,779)	
		6,070

Task 2

Income tax computation 1998/99

	£	£	*Total* £	*Non savings* £	*Savings* £
Earned income					
Schedule D Case I (net)		6,070			
Schedule E $^{6}/_{12}$ × 24,000	12,000				
Benefits-in-kind					
Car (W)	569				
Fuel (W)	640				
	13,209				
17.5% PPC	(2,312)				
		10,897			
			16,967	16,967	-
Unearned income					
Barlloyd Bank					
£491 × 100/80	614				
NSB ordinary account					
Actual basis					
(199 – 70)	129				
			743	-	743
			17,710	16,967	743
Charges on income					
Deed of covenant			(100)	(100)	
Total income			17,610	16,867	743
Personal allowance			(4,195)	(4,195)	
Taxable income			13,415	12,672	743

Income tax on non savings income				
4,300 @ 20%		860		
8,372 @ 23%		1,926		
12,672		2,786		
Income tax on savings income				
743 @ 20%		149		
		2,935		
Basic rate relief retained				
Deed of covenant				
100 @ 23%	23			
Personal pension plan				
2,312 @ 23%	532			
		555		
Income tax payable		3,490		

WORKING

	£	£
Car		
35% × £9,750	3,412	
Mileage reduction	(2,275) ⅔	
	1,137	
Available for six months		569 6/12
Fuel		
1401 cc to 2000 cc (petrol)	1,280	
Available for six months		640 6/12

Tax on chargeable gains 1998/99

		£
Agreed gain		22,000
Annual exemption		(6,800)
Assessable gain		15,200
Chargeable @ 23% 27,100 – 13,415	13,685	3,147
@ 40%	1,515	606
	15,200	3,753

3 **Solution**

Task 1

Profit adjustment statement 1 May 1998 to 30 April 1999

	£
Net profit per accounts	9,250
Add: Reference books (Munby v Furlong)	300
Depreciation - car	1,600
- furniture and equipment	250
Car expenses (4,510 – 1,600) × $\frac{1}{11}$	265
Lease premium	2,500
	14,165
Less: Lease premium (W)	(205)
Adjusted profit before capital allowances	13,960

WORKING

Lease premium

	£
Premium	2,500
Less: 2% × (10 – 1)	(450)
Assessable on landlord	2,050

Allowable to Joshua at the rate of £205 (2,050 ÷ 10) for each of the 10 years of the lease. Not restricted in the first year as commenced at the start of the year.

Basis of assessment

1998/99	1.5.98 - 5.4.99
1999/00	y/e 30.4.99
2000/01	y/e 30.4.00

(Tutorial note: In the opening years, the basis of assessment for businesses is as follows:

Year 1 Actual profits from commencement to 5 April

Year 2 Either:

(i) 12 months ending with the accounting date in the year; or

(ii) 12 months from commencement date **unless** no accounting period ends in the year, in which case the fiscal year basis applies.

Year 3 12 months ending with the accounting date in the year.*)*

Capital allowances computation

	Pool	Car ($^{10}/_{11}$ business use)		Total
	£	£		£
Y/e 30.4.99				
Additions				
Car		6,500		
WDA @ 25%		(1,625)	$^{10}/_{11}$	1,477
Additions qualifying for FYA				
Reference books	300			
Furniture	1,000			
Computer	1,500			
Photocopier	920			
	3,720			
FYA @ 50%	(1,860)			1,860
	1,860	4,875		3,337
Y/e 30.4.00				
WDA @ 25%	(465)	(1,219)	$^{10}/_{11}$	1,573
Addition qualifying for FYA				
Telephone and fax	1,088			
FYA @ 40%	(435)			435
	2,048	3,656		2,008

(***Tutorial note:*** Capital allowances are a deduction in computing trading profits, and are therefore tied to a period of account. The 25% WDA is scaled down (or up) according to the length of the period of account.)

Schedule D Case II

Year ended 30 April 1999

	£
Adjusted profit	13,960
Less: Capital allowances	(3,337)
	10,623

Year ended 30 April 2000

	£
Adjusted profit	10,000
Less: Capital allowances	(2,008)
	7,992

Schedule D Case II assessments

		£
1998/99	(1.5.98 - 5.4.99) $^{11}/_{12} \times 10,623$	9,738
1999/00	(y/e 30.4.99)	10,623
2000/01	(y/e 30.4.00)	7,992

Task 2

Joshua Wrekin
Income tax computation 1998/99

	£	£
Wenlock Engineers Ltd		
Salary		2,775
Ex-gratia - cash	25,250	
- car	6,500	
	31,750	
- exemption	30,000	
		1,750
Benefits-in-kind		
- car (W1)	360	
- fuel charge (W1)	157	
- BUPA	42	
		559
Retirement pension		4,082
Own business - Net assessment		9,738
STI		18,904
Allowances: Personal (W2)		(4,195)
Taxable income		14,709
Income tax liability:		
£4,300 at 20% =		860
£10,409 at 23% =		2,394
Less: Tax credit on MCA (W3) (3,168 × 15%)		(475)
Income tax liability		2,779

WORKINGS

(W1) Benefits-in-kind

	£	£
Car		
35% × £18,500	6,475	
Age reduction		
(Over 4 years by 5 April 1999)	(2,158) ⅓	
	4,317	
Available for one month		360 ($\frac{1}{12}$)
Fuel		
2001cc and above (petrol)	1,890	
Available for one month		(157) ($\frac{1}{12}$)

(W2)	Personal allowance	£
	Total income	18,904
	Age allowance income limit	(16,200)
	Excess	2,704
	Personal allowance	5,410
	Less ½ of excess	(1,352)
		4,058

As this reduction takes the level of personal allowance below £4,195 it will be restricted to an amount (£1,215) to leave the allowance at £4,195 the basic personal allowance.

(W3) Married couple's allowance

The reduction of £1,215 in the personal allowance will be taken into consideration.

	£	£
Married couple's allowance		3,305
Less: ½ of excess	1,352	
Reduction in personal allowance	(1,215)	
		(137)
		3,168

Task 3

Brenda Wrekin
Income tax computation 1998/99

	Total £
Retirement pension	2,449
Wages from husband (£350 × 11)	3,850
Income element of annuity	600
Building society interest	2,190
	9,089
Charges on income - Deed of covenant payment	(1,200)
Total income	7,889
Personal allowance (no restriction)	(5,410)
Taxable income	2,479

Income tax liability:	£
2,479 at 20%	496
Retained on payment of charges on income 1,200 at 23%	276
Income tax liability	772

(Tutorial notes:

(1) The Revenue may treat payments on retirement (if at normal retirement age) as deriving from unapproved retirement benefit arrangements and thereby caught under Sch E by S596A ICTA88. Normal ex-gratia payments are taxed under Sch E by virtue of S148 ICTA88.

(2) The first £30,000 of an ex-gratia payment (paid in cash or in kind) is exempt but only if it is caught under S148. The question makes it clear that S148 applies in this case.

(3) Joshua's car was over four years old at 5.4.99: the benefit is therefore reduced by $\frac{1}{3}$ for 1998/99.

(4) A personal age allowance is reduced when total income is in excess of £16,200 for 1998/99. Where the reduction would take the age allowance below the normal personal allowance value, it is restricted to leave the allowance at the same level as the normal personal allowance (£4,195 for 1998/99). When calculating the age related married couple's allowance, the reduction due to the level of income is restricted by the same amount less any part of the restriction applied against the personal allowance.

(5) When an individual purchases a life annuity, the money received from the annuity is split into a capital and an income element. The income element, received net of lower rate tax, is taxable.)

18-20 INTRODUCTION TO BUSINESS TAXATION

1 Solution

Profit adjustment statement year ended 30 June 1998

	£
Profit per accounts	30,410
Entertaining overseas suppliers	750
Entertaining UK customers	2,000
General bad debt provision	1,700
Car expenses (one-quarter private)	762
Obtaining lease of premises	100
Depreciation: furniture and equipment	500
vehicles	5,000
	41,222
Less: Capital allowances (see below)	(7,031)
Adjusted profit for year to 30 June 1998	34,191

(Tutorial notes:

(1) Although a specific provision against debtors is allowable, a general provision is not.

(2) Legal expenses for obtaining a short lease are not allowable, however, they would be allowable if they were for the renewal of a short lease.)

		Capital allowances main pool	*Private use Car 25%*	*Total*
Year ended to 30 June 1998	£	£	£	£
Additions not qualifying for FYA				
(OF & E)		5,000		
(car)			9,500	
Claim WDA at 25%		(1,250)	(2,375) × ¾	3,031
		3,750		
Additions qualifying for FYA				
OF & E	1,000			
Van	7,000			
	8,000			
FYA @ 50%	(4,000)			
		4,000		4,000
WDVs carried forward		7,750	7,125	
Capital allowances				7,031

2 Solution

Roger Riviere
Profit adjustment statement year ended 30 June 1998

	+	-
	£	£
Net profit per accounts	36,000	
(1) Sales - Goods for own use $\left(500 \times {}^{400}/_{240}\right)^{\text{(Sales)}}_{\text{(Re-stated cost of sales)}} - 500$	333	
(2) Stock (difference increased by 50%)		8,000
(3) Wages - Roger's drawings	2,600	
- Roger's NIC	320	
(4) Repairs and renewals		
Capital cost of fitting covers	3,000	
(5) Miscellaneous		
Political donation	100	
Taxation	15,590	
(6) Bad debts		
Loan to former employee	250	
Reduction in general provision		150
(7) Legal expenses		
Cost in connection with lease of new and larger premises	250	
Cost in connection with tax appeal	200	
Defending Roger in connection with speeding offence	190	
Depreciation	570	
(8) Lease rental on car $8{,}400 - 8{,}400 \times \dfrac{12{,}000 + \frac{1}{2}(30{,}000 - 12{,}000)}{30{,}000}$	2,520	
Private use element on lease rental (11) $8{,}400 - 2{,}520 = 5{,}880 \times \frac{1}{3}$	1,960	
Loss on sale of office furniture	60	
(9) Deeds of covenant - Local children's hospital	50	
- Oxfam	30	
(10) Interest		
Interest on overdue tax	130	
NSB interest		160
(11) Motor car running expenses		
Fine	65	
$\frac{1}{3}$ of remaining expenses	645	
(12) Premium on lease	6,000	900
Lease premium assessable on landlord is [6,000 – 2% (6 – 1)] = 5,400		
5,400 allowable to over six years ie, 900 pa		
(13) Re-location expenditure	2,400	
	73,263	9,210
	(9,210)	
Less: Capital allowances	(480)	
Adjusted Case I profit for year to 30 June 1998	63,573	

3 Solution

Task 1

Capital Allowances - Year to 31 December 1998

	General pool £	Private use car £	Car pool £	Expensive car £	Total £
WDV b/fwd	42,000	5,400			
Purchases not qualifying for FYA					
1.3.98 car			10,000		
1.9.98 car				15,000	
Sales					
21.8.98 machine	(5,500)				
	36,500				
WDA (25%)	9,125				9,125
WDA (25%)		1,350*			945*
WDA (25%)			2,500		2,500
WDA (max)				3,000	3,000
Purchases qualifying for FYA					
10.2.98 machine	27,500				
FYA @ 50%	(13,750)				13,750
WDV c/fwd	41,125	4,050	7,500	12,000	29,320

(*70%)

Task 2

Adjusted Schedule D Case I profit for the year to 31 December 1998

Adjusted profits	85,000
Less: Capital Allowances	29,320
	55,680

21-22 BASIS PERIODS AND TRADING LOSSES

1 Solution

Schedule D Case I assessable amounts for 1995/96 to 2002/03

		£	£
1995/96	Actual (1.3.96 - 5.4.96)		
	($^1/_{14}$ × 15,000)		1,071
1996/97	Actual (6.4.96 - 5.4.97)		
	($^{12}/_{14}$ × 15,000)		12,857
1997/98	'CYB' (1.5.96 - 30.4.97)		
	($^{12}/_{14}$ × 15,000)		12,857
(overlap relief 1.5.96 - 5.4.97 $^{11}/_{14}$ × 15,000		£11,785)	
1998/99	CYB (year to 30.4.98)		17,000
1999/00	CYB (year to 30.4.99)		12,000
2000/01	CYB (year to 30.4.00)		14,000
2001/02	CYB (year to 30.4.01)		18,000
2002/03	(1.5.01 - 31.10.02)		
	Year to 30.4.02	13,000	
	Period to 31.10.02	3,000	
		16,000	
	Less overlap relief	(11,785)	4,215
Check: Total profits assessed			£92,000
Total profits (as adjusted) earned			£92,000

(Tutorial note: when the first period of account exceeds 12 months, and ends in the third tax year, as is the case with Michael, the bases of assessment for the first five years are as follows:

Tax year	*Basis period*	
1	Actual	1.3.96 - 5.4.96
2	Actual	6.4.96 - 5.4.97
3	12 months ending on the accounting date	1.5.96 - 30.4.97
4	Current year basis	1.5.97 - 30.4.98
5	Current year basis	1.5.98 - 30.4.99*)*

2 Solution

Task 1

The loss expected to be sustained in the accounting period ended 31 August 1999 will be treated as a loss for the fiscal year 1999/00. Under S380 this loss may be set off against Caren's income from all sources less charges for the year of the loss, 1999/00, and/or income from all sources less charges for the year preceding the year of loss, 1998/99. In the event that S380 claim(s) are not made or that the income available is insufficient to absorb the losses claimed under S380, a claim can be made under S385 to carry the losses forward against future trading income from the same trade.

Task 2

(i) **1998/99**

The total income for the year 1998/99 will be £4,000 being the trading profits assessed on a current year basis.

As losses are set off before personal allowances, in this case £4,195, there would be no point in claiming under S380 because the income is already covered by the personal allowance. It would also be advisable to restrict the capital allowance claim by £195 so that profits match the personal allowance.

(ii) **1999/00**

There is no trading profit expected for 1999/00 but there is building society interest of £2,000. This income would be covered by personal allowances so no additional benefit would be gained by making a claim under S380. There would in any case be a repayment of the income tax suffered, £400.

(iii) **2000/01**

The income for the year 2000/01 is expected to be £13,000 being the trading profits assessed on a current year basis.

The losses of £11,000 brought forward under S385 must be used against the first available trading profit. The assessment of £13,000 will fall to be reduced by £11,000 (S385) to £2,000. Personal allowances of £2,000 will be used to reduce the taxable income to £nil and there will be unused allowances of £2,195.

Caren should restrict her capital allowance claim for the year ended 31 August 2000 to £205 (2,400 – 2,195) to produce a further £2,195 of income and thereby avoid wasting allowances.

The reduced capital allowance claim leaves a higher balance in the expensive car 'pool' to produce a higher balancing allowance when it is eventually sold.

(Tutorial note:

If the expensive car produces £2,400 of WDA pa this must result from a £3,000 WDA with 20% private use by Caren. Until the 'pool' balance falls below £12,000, the maximum WDA is £3,000 (subject to private use restriction).*)*

3 Solution

Task

(i)

Year of assessment	*Basis period*	*Assessable profits* £
1997/98	1 January to 5 April 1998	
	$^3/_6 \times$ £18,000	9,000
1998/99	1 January to 31 December 1998	
	£18,000 + ($^6/_{12} \times$ £40,000)	38,000
1999/00	1 July 1998 to 30 June 1999	40,000

(ii) The 'overlap relief' arising is the total of the profits for the periods from 1 January 1998 to 5 April 1998 and from 1 July 1998 to 31 December 1998, which are assessed twice during the three opening years of assessment. The total profits available for overlap relief are therefore £9,000 + ($^6/_{12} \times$ £40,000) = £29,000.

These overlap relief profits will be relieved by being deducted from the assessable profits for the final year (these being the profits from the end of the previously assessed period of account to the date of cessation) or earlier if there is a change of accounting date which results in a basis period in excess of 12 months. In the second case, overlap relief can only be used to reduce the period upon which assessable profits are based to 12 months.

4 Solution

Capital allowances

Period of account	Additions/ (disposals)	General pool £	Capital allowances £
1 June 1997 - 31 August 1998			
(15 months)	Van	16,000	
	Machinery	12,000	
		28,000	
Writing down allowances			
at 25% × 15/12		(8,750)	8,750
		19,250	
1 September 1998 - 31 August 1999			
(12 months)			
Writing down allowances at 25%		(4,813)	4,813
		14,437	
1 September 1999 - 31 March 2000			
(7 months)	(Van) }		
	(Machinery) }	(12,000)	
Balancing allowance		(2,437)	2,437
		-	

Schedule D Case I amounts

Period of account	*Amount net of capital allowances* £	
1 June 1997 - 31 August 1998	27,250	(£36,000 – £8,750)
1 September 1998 - 31 August 1999	10,187	(£15,000 – £4,813)
1 September 1999 - 31 March 2000	3,163	(7 × 800 - £2,437)

Overlap profits

1 September 1997 to 5 April 1998 $\frac{7}{15} \times$ £27,250 = £12,717

Overlap profits are deductible from the profits assessable for the final year of assessment.

Fiscal year assessments

Tax year	*Basis period*	*Amount* £	*Calculation*
1997/98	1 June 1997 - 5 April 1998	18,167	$\frac{10}{15} \times$ £27,250
1998/99	1 September 1997 - 31 August 1998	21,800	$\frac{12}{15} \times$ £27,250
1999/00	1 September 1998 - 31 March 2000	633	(10,187 + 3,163 – 12,717)

23 TAXATION OF PARTNERSHIPS

1 Solution

		Total	*Dominic*	*Justin*	*Simon*
		£	£	£	£
A/cs to 30/6/97		10,000	5,000	5,000	-
A/cs to 30/6/98	$\frac{6}{12}$	6,750	3,375	3,375	-
	$\frac{6}{12}$	6,750	2,250	2,250	2,250
		13,500	5,625	5,625	2,250
A/cs to 30/6/99		18,000	6,000	6,000	6,000

Dominic and Justin will both be assessed on the following figures

		£
1996/97	£5,000 × $\frac{9}{12}$	3,750
1997/98	A/cs to 30/6/97	5,000
1998/99	A/cs to 30/6/98	5,625
1999/00	A/cs to 30/6/99	6,000

They will both be entitled to overlap relief of £3,750.

Simon will be assessed as follows:

		£
1997/98	£2,250 × $\frac{3}{6}$	1,125
1998/99	£2,250 + (£6,000 × $\frac{6}{12}$)	5,250
1999/00	A/cs to 30/6/99	6,000

Simon will be entitled to overlap relief of £4,125, which is made up as follows:

	£
1/1/98 to 5/4/98	1,125
1/7/98 to 31/12/98	3,000
	4,125

(Tutorial note: The profits must be allocated between the partners. Remember that as Simon joins the partnership part of the way through the accounting year ended 30 June 1998, the profits for that year will need to be time-apportioned prior to allocation. Once the profits have been allocated between the partners, each partner is then treated as if he is carrying on a business alone. Simon is treated as commencing trading on 1 January 1998. Simon's 1998/99 assessment is based on the profits of the first 12 months of trading as his share of the accounts to 30/6/98 does not cover a full 12 months.

2 Solution

Task 1

Time apportionment of 1998/99 Schedule DI income

The profits assessable in 1998/99 will be those for the accounts to 30 September 1998. The profit-sharing ratio was changed on 1 July 1998 which is nine months into the accounting period. The profits will therefore be time-apportioned as follows:

Old ratio	£16,500 × $\frac{9}{12}$ = £12,375
New ratio	£16,500 × $\frac{3}{12}$ = £4,125

Task 2

Allocation of 1998/99 Schedule DI income

	Total	*Bert*	*Harold*
	£	£	£
1/10/97 to 30/6/98			
Salaries ($\frac{9}{12}$)	3,750	2,250	1,500
Balance (3:2)	8,625	5,175	3,450
	12,375	7,425	4,950
1/7/98 to 30/9/98			
Salaries ($\frac{3}{12}$)	2,500	1,500	1,000
Balance (2:1)	1,625	1,083	542
	4,125	2,583	1,542
Total allocation	16,500	10,008	6,492

Task 3

Allocation of partnership loan interest

The loan interest assessable in 1998/99 will be that received in the accounts year ended 30 September 1998. As before, the income will be allocated according to the profit-sharing ratio in force during the year ended 30 September 1998:

	Total	*Bert*	*Harold*
	£	£	£
£900 × $\frac{9}{12}$ (3:2)	675	405	270
£900 × $\frac{3}{12}$ (2:1)	225	150	75
	900	555	345

This investment income will also be assessable on the partners individually.

(Tutorial note: All partnership income received gross is assessable using the case I basis period rules irrespective of its source. This means that any partnership investment income received gross is assessable on an accounts year basis rather than a tax year basis.***)***

24-25 INTRODUCTION TO CORPORATION TAX

1 Solution

Task 1

	Franked payment	*Franked investment income*	*Franked payment less franked investment income*	*ACT paid*
	£	£	£	£
Qr. to 31.3.98 (payable 14.4.98)	36,250	17,500	18,750	3,750
Qr. to 30.9.98 (payable 14.10.98)	43,750	22,500	21,250	4,250
				8,000

Task 2

	Income tax on charges on income	*Income tax on income received*		*Income tax paid/ (repaid)*
	£	£		£
Qr. to 30.6.98 (payable 14.7.98)	4,400			4,400
Qr. to 31.12.98 (re-payable)		276	(patent royalty)	
		5,400	(Deb. int.)	(4,400)
		5,676		

The balance of the income tax suffered (£1,276) will be allowed in computing the mainstream corporation tax payable.

The restriction on the income tax repaid is as a result of only this amount having been paid to the Inland Revenue in the chargeable accounting period.

Task 3

Unsurpassable Umbrellas Ltd
Corporation tax payable for year ended 31 December 1998

	£	£
Schedule D Case I profit	290,000	
Less: Trading losses b/f	(60,000)	230,000
Schedule A income		4,000
Schedule D Case III (2,000 + 27,000)		29,000
Chargeable gain		8,200
Patent royalties received ($924 \times \frac{100}{77}$)		1,200
Chargeable profits		272,400
Corporation tax payable (W1)		58,556
Advance corporation tax (W2)	8,000	
Income tax suffered	1,276	(9,276)
Mainstream corporation tax payable		49,280

WORKINGS

(1)

	£
PCTCT	272,400
'Profits' = PCTCT +	272,400
Franked investment income (17,500 + 22,500)	40,000
	312,400

The accounting period straddles FY 97 and FY 98. As the limits for FY 97 and FY 98 are the same there is no need to apportion the profits.

As 'profits' lie between £300,000 and £1,500,000 marginal relief will apply for both FYs. Again, since the tax rates and marginal relief fractions are the same for both years there is no need to apportion the profits.

	£
Corporation tax payable	
£272,400 × 31% =	84,444
Less: Marginal relief	
$\frac{1}{40} \times (1{,}500{,}000 - 312{,}400) \times \frac{272{,}400}{312{,}400}$	(25,888)
	58,556

(2) Maximum ACT set off

	£
PCTCT	272,400
Maximum set off 272,400 × 20%	54,480
ACT paid	8,000

There is, therefore, no restriction on the amount of ACT set off.

(Tutorial notes:

(1) The quarterly returns for ACT are expressed in terms of franked payments and franked investment income. The returns for taxed income received and charges paid are expressed in terms of the income tax deducted or suffered.

(2) When more income tax is suffered in a period than income tax retained on charges, the surplus is available for set off against the corporation tax payable.

2 Solution

Task 1

Elliptical Extensions Ltd
Corporation tax computation - year ended 31 March 1999

		£
Adjusted trading profit		335,000
Capital allowances -		
Industrial buildings (W1)		(4,100)
Plant and machinery (W2)		(33,625)
Schedule D Case I profit		297,275
Schedule D Case III		
Bank interest receivable	3,000	
Loan interest receivable	10,000	
		13,000
Chargeable gains	50,000	
Losses brought forward	50,000	–
Balance of capital losses £10,000 c/f		
Total profits		310,275
Charges on income paid (patent royalties)		(2,000)
PCTCT		308,275
Corporation tax payable (W3)		67,922
Advance corporation tax (W4)		(61,655)
Income tax (W5)		(1,500)
Mainstream corporation tax payable		4,767

WORKINGS

(W1) **Industrial buildings allowances**

Administration offices - 25% test.

The total cost of the original factory and extension is £110,000 and the total cost of the administration offices is £30,000. As this is more than 25% the cost of the administration offices must be excluded from the claims.

		£
(1)	Original factory and extension 4% × £80,000	3,200
(2)	New factory 4% × £22,500	900
		4,100

(W2) **Plant and machinery allowances**

	Pool	*Expensive car (1)*	*Expensive car (2)*	*Car pool*	*Short-life asset*	*Total*
	25%	*25%*	*25%*	*25%*	*25%*	
	£	£	£	£	£	£
WDV b/f	75,000	7,000		31,000	17,500	
Transfer	17,500				(17,500)	
	92,500					
Disposals	(5,000)	(6,000)				
Additions			14,000			
	87,500	1,000				
Claim						
Balancing allowance		(1,000)				1,000
Writing-down allowances	(21,875)		(3,000)	(7,750)		32,625
WDV c/f	65,625	-	11,000	23,250	-	
						33,625

The tax WDV of the short-life asset is transferred to main pool on 1 April 1998 as asset not sold within four years of end of AP in which purchased.

The maximum allowance on expensive car is £3,000.

(W3) **Corporation tax payable**

PCTCT = £308,275

'Profits' = £308,275 + FII £15,000 × $^{100}/_{80}$ = £327,025

As 'Profits' lie between the lower and upper limits (£300,000 and £1,500,000 respectively) marginal relief will apply.

		£
308,275 at 31%	=	95,565
Less: Marginal relief		
$\frac{1}{40} \times (1{,}500{,}000 - 327{,}025) \times \frac{308{,}275}{327{,}025}$	=	(27,643)
		67,922

(W4) **Advance corporation tax**

(a) Calculation

		£
Franked payment 263,420 × $^{100}/_{80}$	=	329,275
Franked investment income 15,000 × $^{100}/_{80}$	=	(18,750)
		310,525
ACT payable at 20%		62,105

(b) Set-off

Maximum set-off 308,275 at 20%	=	61,655
Surplus carried forward (62,105 – 61,655)	=	450
		62,105

(W5) **Income tax on income and charges**

		£
Income tax on interest received (9,800 at 20%)		1,960
(a)	Set-off against income tax on charges on income (2,000 at 23%)	460
(b)	Set-off against corporation tax payable	1,500
		1,960

Task 2

(i)

Manchester Models Ltd
Advance corporation tax for CAP 1 April 1998 to 31 March 1999

Period	*Franked payment*	*Franked investment income*	*Franked payment minus franked investment income*	*ACT payable/ (repayable)*
	£	£	£	£
1.4.98 - 30.6.98		60,000	(60,000)	Nil
		60,000	(60,000)	
1.7.98 - 30.9.98	240,000		240,000	
	240,000	60,000	180,000 at 20%	36,000
1.10.98 - 31.12.98		200,000	(200,000)	(36,000) *(note)*
	240,000	260,000	(20,000)	
1.1.99 - 31.3.99	120,000	40,000	80,000	
	360,000	300,000	60,000 at 20%	12,000

Note: repayments during CAP cannot exceed ACT paid or payable in the CAP to date, in the quarter to 31 December 1998 £180,000 at 20% = £36,000.

Income tax for CAP 1 April 1998 to 31 March 1999

	Tax deducted from interest paid	*Tax suffered on interest received*	*IT payable/ (repayable)*
	£	£	£
1.4.98 - 30.6.98		2,000	
		2,000	Nil *(note)*
1.7.98 - 30.9.98	800	1,200	
	800	3,200	Nil
1.10.98 - 31.12.98	2,800		
	3,600	3,200	400
1.1.99 - 31.3.99		1,600	
	3,600	4,800	(400) *(note)*
		(3,600)	
To set off against corporation tax liability		1,200	

Note: repayments during CAP cannot exceed IT paid or payable in the CAP to date.

3 Solution

Corporation tax computation - year ended 28 February 1999

	£	£
Adjusted trading profit		283,000
Capital allowances:		
Industrial buildings (W1)		(4,100)
Plant and machinery (W2)		(32,625)
Schedule D Case I profit		246,275
Schedule D Case III (3,000 + 10,000)		13,000
Chargeable gain	50,000	
Losses brought forward	(50,000)	-
(Balance of capital losses £10,000 carried forward)		
PCTCT		259,275
£259,275 × 31%		80,375
Less: Marginal relief		
$\frac{1}{40}$ (1,500,000 – 300,525) $\frac{259,275}{300,525}$		(25,871)
		54,504
Less: ACT (W4)		(38,250)
Income tax (W5)		(1,600)
Mainstream corporation tax payable		14,654

WORKINGS

(W1) **Industrial Buildings Allowances**

Administration offices - 25% test.

The total cost of the original factory and extension is £110,000 and the total cost of the administration offices is £30,000. As this is more than 25% the cost of the administration offices must be excluded from the claims.

		£
(1)	Original factory and extension 4% × £80,000	3,200
(2)	Lease on new factory 4% × £22,500	900
		4,100

(W2) **Plant and machinery allowances**

	Pool	*Expensive car (1)*	*Expensive car (2)*	*Car pool*	*Short-life asset*	*Total*
	25%	*25%*	*25%*	*25%*	*25%*	
	£	£	£	£	£	£
WDV b/f	75,000	7,000		27,000	17,500	
Transfer	17,500				(17,500)	
	92,500				-	

Disposals	(5,000)	(6,000)				
Additions			14,000			
	87,500	1,000				
Claim						
Balancing allowance		(1,000)				1,000
Writing-down allowances	(21,875)		(3,000)	(6,750)		31,625
WDV c/f	65,625	-	11,000	20,250	-	32,625

(Tutorial notes:

(1) The short life asset is transferred to main pool on 28 February 1998 as the asset was not sold within four years of end of AP in which purchased.

(2) The maximum allowance on an expensive car is £3,000.)

(W3) PCTCT = £259,275

'Profits' = £259,275 + £33,000 × $\frac{100}{80}$

= £300,525.

As 'profits' are above the lower limit (£300,000) marginal relief applies. Since the same tax rates and limits apply in FY 1998 as applied in FY 1997, there is no need to apportion the profits.

(W4) **Advance corporation tax**

(a)

		£
Franked payment March 1998	186,000 × $^{100}/_{80}$	232,500
Less: Franked investment income June 1998	33,000 × $^{100}/_{80}$	41,250
		191,250
ACT payable at 20%		38,250

(b)

		£
Set off		
Maximum set off	259,275 × 20%	51,855

(W5) **Income tax on unfranked investment income**

		£
Income tax suffered on unfranked investment income (10,000 at 20%)		2,000
(a)	Set-off against income tax on debenture interest paid (2,000 at 20%)	400
(b)	Set-off against corporation tax payable	1,600
		2,000

4 Solution

Quarterly accounting for ACT - year ended 31 March 1999

Return period ended	*FII*	*FP*	*Cumulative FII/FP*	*ACT payable/ (repayable)*	*Date of payment/ receipt*
	£	£	£	£	
30.6.1998	15,000 (a)	12,000 (b)	(3,000)	-	N/A
30.9.1998	-	50,000 (c)	47,000	9,400	14.10.1998
31.12.1998	24,000 (d)	-	23,000	(4,800)	January 1999 (note)
31.3.1999	-	24,000 (e)	47,000	4,800	14.4.99
	39,000	86,000	47,000	9,400	

Quarterly accounting for income tax - year ended 31 March 1999

Return period ended	*Income tax suffered*	*Income tax deducted*	*Cumulative income tax*	*Income tax payable/ (repayable)*	*Date of payment/ receipt*
	£	£	£	£	
30.6.1998	8,400 (f)	-	(8,400)	-	N/A
30.9.1998	4,800 (g)	9,000 (h)	(4,200)	-	N/A
31.12.1998	-	11,400 (i)	7,200	7,200	14.1.99
31.3.1999	7,200 (j)	-	-	(7,200)	April 1999 (note)
	20,400	20,400	-	-	

Note: approximate - no statutory date for repayment exists

WORKINGS

FII/(FP) - net dividend receipts/(payments) are grossed up at 100/80:

(a)	12,000 on 10/4/98	-	15,000
(b)	(9,600) on 8/5/98 -	(12,000)	
(c)	(40,000) on 15/8/98	-	(50,000)
(d)	4,800 on 12/10/98 and 14,400 on 16/11/98	-	24,000
(e)	(19,200) on 30/1/99	-	(24,000)

IT suffered (deducted) - calculated at $^{20}/_{80}$ or $^{23}/_{77}$ of net receipts/(payments):

(f)	$28,122 \times {}^{23}/_{77}$ on 10/5/98 -	8,400	
(g)	$16,070 \times {}^{23}/_{77}$ on 30/8/98 -	4,800	
(h)	$(36,000) \times {}^{20}/_{80}$ on 12/7/98	-	(9,000)
(i)	$(34,080) \times {}^{20}/_{80}$ on 24/11/98		
	and $(9,642) \times {}^{23}/_{77}$ on 30/11/98	-	(11,400)
(j)	$24,104 \times {}^{23}/_{77}$ on 15/1/1999	-	7,200

5 **Solution**

Task 1

The two accounting periods for corporation tax (CT) purposes are:

12 months ended 31 March 1998
4 months ended 31 July 1998

Capital allowances calculations

	Gen pool	*Car pool*	*Short life asset (comp)*	*Exp. car*	*Exp. car*	*Total cap. allows*
	£	£	£	£	£	£
Tax written down value at 1 April 1997	48,000	16,000	18,000	16,000		
Year ended 31 March 1998						
Purchases not qualifying for FYA						
Car 30 September 1997		7,200				
Sale proceeds:						
Plant 31 May 1997	(6,000)					
	42,000	23,200	18,000	16,000		
Capital allowances:						
At 25% pa	(10,500)	(5,800)	(4,500)			20,800
Restricted to £3,000 pa				(3,000)		3,000
Purchases qualifying for FYA						
Plant 30 January 1998	12,000					
FYA @ 50%	(6,000)					6,000
Tax written down value at 1 April 1998	37,500	17,400	13,500	13,000		29,800
4 months ended 31 July 1998						
Purchases:						
Mercedes 30 April 1998					24,000	
Sale proceeds:						
Computer 15 April 1998			(8,500)			
Jaguar 30 April 1998				(10,000)		
Balancing allowances			5,000	3,000		8,000
Capital allowances:						
At 25% pa for 4 months	(3,125)	(1,450)				4,575
Restricted to £3,000 pa for 4 months					(1,000)	1,000
Tax written down value at 31 July 1998	34,375	15,950	-	-	23,000	13,575

Task 2

Computation of chargeable profits

		12m ended 31.3.98	4m ended 31.7.98
		£	£
Schedule D Case I (W1)		996,676	328,584
Schedule A (W2)		18,000	6,000
Patent royalties (W3)		24,000	5,666
		1,038,676	340,250
Less:	Charges on income (W3)		
	Charitable covenant		(4,000)
Profits chargeable to CT		1,038,676	336,250
Add FII (W4)		7,750	30,000
'Profits' for small companies' CT rate		1,046,426	366,250

The upper limits for small companies tax rate purposes are as follows:

12 months ended 31 March 1998 £1,500,000 taper relief applies.
4 months ended 31 July 1998 £1,500,000 × $\frac{4}{12}$ = £500,000 taper relief applies.

Mainstream corporation tax (MCT) payable

12 months ended 31 March 1998:	£
1,038,676 × 31%	321,990
Less: Taper relief:	
$(1,500,000 - 1,046,426) \times \frac{1,038,676}{1,046,426} \times \frac{1}{40}$	(11,255)
	310,735
Less: ACT relief (W5)	(81,200)
Income tax suffered (W6)	(3,520)
MCT payable	226,015

4 months ended 31 July 1998:	£
336,250 × 31%	104,237
Less: Taper relief:	
$(500,000 - 366,250) \times \frac{336,250}{366,250} \times \frac{1}{40}$	(3,070)
	101,167
ACT relief (W5)	(67,250)
Income tax suffered (W6)	-
MCT payable	33,917

WORKINGS

(W1) Adjusted trading profit before capital allowances is time-apportioned between the two accounting periods, as follows:

	12m ended 31.3.98	*4m ended 31.7.98*
	£	£
Time apportioned profit	1,036,476	345,492
Less: Capital allowances per part (a)	(29,800)	(13,575)
Less: Debenture interest (10,000/10,000 × $^4/_{12}$)	(10,000)	(3,333)
Schedule D Case I	996,676	328,584

(W2) Allocated to AP for which rent is due ie, $^{12}/_{16}$ × £24,000 = £18,000 to 12m ended 31 March 1998, and $^4/_{16}$ × £24,000 = 6,000 to 4m ended 31 July 1998.

(W3) Allocated to AP in which UFII received/charges paid

(W4) Allocated to AP in which FII received

(W5) ACT relief:

12m ended 31 March 1997:

		£
Franked payments (FPs) (320,000 × $^{100}/_{80}$)		400,000
FII		(7,750)
		392,250
∴ ACT at 20% × 392,250	=	£78,450
Maximum set-off – 20% × 1,038,676	=	£207,735
ACT recoverable re current year FPs	=	£78,450
Plus: ACT carried back from 4m/e 31 July 1998	=	£2,750
Total ACT relief	=	£81,200

4m ended 31 July 1998:

		£
Franked payments (304,000 × $^{100}/_{80}$)		380,000
FII		(30,000)
		350,000
∴ ACT at 20% × 350,000	=	£70,000
∴ Maximum set-off – 20% × 336,250	=	£67,250
Surplus ACT carried back to y/e 31 March 1998	=	£2,750

(W6) Income tax suffered:

12m ended 31 March 1998	£	
On patent royalties	5,520	(23% × 24,000)
Deducted at source	(2,000)	(20% × 10,000)
Net suffered	3,520	

4m ended 31 July 1998 - Nil since tax deducted on charges and interest clearly exceeds tax suffered on income received net of tax.

Task 3

Due dates for payment of MCT are:

12 months ended 31 March 1998 - 1 January 1999
4 months ended 31 July 1998 - 1 May 1999

(Tutorial notes:

When a company has a period of account longer than 12 months, it must be split into two chargeable accounting periods of the first 12 months and the remainder.***)***

26-28

CT LOSSES, CLOSE COMPANIES & CT RETURNS

1 Solution

Task 1

(i) Trading loss for twelve months to 31 July 1998

	£
Trading loss	294,800
Capital allowances	
Industrial buildings allowance (W2)	(48,000)
Plant and machinery	24,600
	271,400

(ii) (1) The loss is to be set off against total profits (before charges on income) of the same accounting period, £40,112 Task 2).

(2) Any unrelieved loss is to be set off against total profits of previous accounting period covering a period of 12 months on a LIFO basis so as to leave trading charges on income relievable. The loss will therefore be utilised against the £67,200 of profits of the AP to 31 July 1997 ((b) below).

The summary of the utilisation of the loss sustained in the accounting period to 31 July 1998 is:

	£
CAP to 31 July 1998	40,112
CAP to 31 July 1997	67,200
Unrelieved balance c/f	164,088
	271,400

Task 2

Profits chargeable to corporation tax

	Chargeable accounting period ended 31 July	
	1997	*1998*
	£	£
Trading profit	80,000	–
Capital allowances		
Industrial buildings allowances (W2)	(4,800)	–
Plant and machinery	(20,000)	–
Schedule D Case I profit	55,200	–
Schedule D Case III bank interest	4,000	–
Loan interest	8,000	6,000
Chargeable gain (W1)	–	34,112
Total profits before non-trading charges	67,200	40,112

Less Deed of covenant	(10,000)	(8,000)
PCTCT	57,200	32,112

Task 3

Corporation tax computation after loss relief

	CAP end 31 July *1997* £	*1998* £
Total profits before non-trading charges	67,200	40,112
Loss relief	(67,200)	(40,112)
PCTCT	Nil	Nil
Mainstream corporation tax liability	Nil	Nil
Non-trading charges wasted	10,000	8,000

Task 4

(i) **Unrelieved loss to carry forward at 31 July 1998**

	£
Loss remaining (a) (ii) (2)	164,088

(ii) **Unrelieved advance corporation tax carried forward at 31 July 1998**

	£
CAP to 31 July 1997 (W3)	10,000

(iii) **Surplus franked investment income carried forward at 31 July 1998**

	£
CAP to 31 July 1998 (W6)	15,000

WORKINGS

(1) **Chargeable gains on buildings**

		£	£
Factory 1			
Disposal (May 1988)			85,000
Cost			(60,000)
Unindexed gain			25,000
Indexation allowance	$\frac{106.2 - 84.84}{84.84} = 0.252 \times 60,000$		(15,120)
Indexed gain rolled over			9,880
Factory 2			
Disposal (December 1997)			207,000
Cost (June 1987)		120,000	
Less: Gain rolled over		9,880	
			(110,120)
Unindexed gain			96,880
Indexation allowance	$\frac{160.0 - 101.9}{101.9} = 0.570 \times 110,120$		(62,768)
Chargeable gain			34,112

(2) **Industrial buildings allowances**

	£	£
Factory 2		
Cost 1 June 1987		120,000
Allowances granted		
AP to 31 July 1987		
No WDA – not in use	–	
AP to 31 July 1988 (4%)	4,800	
AP to 31 July 1989 (4%)	4,800	
AP to 31 July 1990 (4%)	4,800	
AP to 31 July 1991 (4%)	4,800	
AP to 31 July 1992 (4%)	4,800	
AP to 31 July 1993 (4%)	4,800	
AP to 31 July 1994 (4%)	4,800	
AP to 31 July 1995 (4%)	4,800	
AP to 31 July 1996 (4%)	4,800	
AP to 31 July 1997 (4%)	4,800	
		(48,000)
Residue of expenditure before sale		72,000
Sale proceeds (restricted to cost)		(120,000)
Balancing charge		48,000

(3) **Advance corporation tax - year ended 31 July 1997**

ACT payable 40,000 × $^{100}/_{80}$ = 50,000 @ 20% £10,000

(4) **Franked investment income**

CAP to 31 July 1998 12,000 × $^{100}/_{80}$ £15,000

2 Solution

Task 1

Quarterly accounting

(i) **ACT**

Year to 31 December 1997

Return period	*FP* £	*FII* £	*ACT Paid/recovered* £	*Due date*
1.1.97 – 31.3.97				
1.3.97 FII £20,000 × $^{100}/_{80}$	–	25,000		
1.4.97 – 30.6.97				
8.4.97 FP 600,000 × 18p × $^{100}/_{80}$	135,000	–	–	
ACT £(135,000 – 25,000) × 20%	–	–	22,000	14.7.97
1.7.97 – 30.9.97				
1.9.97 FII £75,000 × $^{100}/_{80}$	–	93,750		
3.9.97 FP £600,000 × 10p × $^{100}/_{80}$	75,000	–	–	
ACT recovered: £(93,750 – 75,000) × 20%	–	–	(3,750)	
1.10.97 – 31.12.97 (no return)				
	210,000	118,750	18,250	
	(118,750)			
	91,250			

9 months to 30 September 1998

Return period	*FP*	*FII*	*ACT Paid/recovered*	*Due date*
	£	£	£	
1.1.98 – 31.3.98				
10.3.98 FII (£35,000 × 100/80)	–	43,750	–	
31.3.98 FP (600,000 × 22p × 100/80	165,000	–	–	
ACT £(165,000 – 43,750) × 20%	–	–	24,250	14.4.98
1.4.98 – 30.6.98 (no return)				
1.7.98 – 30.9.98				
20.8.98 FII £70,000 × 100/80		87,500		
28.8.98 FP £600,000 × 5p × 100/80	37,500			
ACT recovered = 87,000 – 37,500				
= 50,000 × 20%	–	–	(10,000)	
	202,500	131,250	14,250	
	(131,250)			
	71,250			

(ii) **Income Tax**

Year to 31 December 1997

Return period		*IT on UFP*	*IT on UFII*	*IT Paid/(repaid)*	*Due date*
		£	£	£	
1.1.97 – 31.3.97 (no return)					
1.4.97 – 30.6.97					
30.4.97	Covenant				
	Income tax paid				
	£10,000 × 23%	2,300			
30.6.97	Debenture interest received				
	Income tax suffered £9,000 × 20%		1,800		
	Income tax paid to Collector			500	14.7.97
1.7.97 – 30.9.97 (no return)					
1.10.97 – 31.12.97					
31.12.97	Debenture interest received				
	Income tax suffered £9,000 × 20%		1,800		
	Income tax repaid by Collector			(500)	
		2,300	3,600	Nil	

Income tax to set against MCT 3,600 – 2,300 = 1,300

9 months to 30 September 1998

Return period		*IT on UFP*	*UFII*	*IT Paid/(repaid)*	*Due date*
		£	£	£	
1.1.98 – 31.3.98 (no return)					
1.4.98 – 30.6.98					
30.4.98	Covenant				
	Income tax paid £10,000 × 23%	2,300			
30.6.98	Debenture interest received				
	Income tax suffered £9,000 × 20%		1,800		
	Income tax paid to Collector			500	14.7.98
1.7.98 – 30.9.98					

30.9.98	Loan interest paid Income tax paid to Collector £12,500 × 20%	2,500		2,500	14.10.98
Net payment to Collector		4,800	1,800	3,000	

Summary

Return period	*ACT* £	*IT* £	*Total* £
1.1.97 – 31.3.97	–	–	–
1.4.97 – 30.6.97	22,000	500	22,500
1.7.97 – 30.9.97	(3,750)	–	(3,750)
1.10.97–31.12.97	–	(500)	(500)
1.1.98 – 31.3.98	24,250	–	24,250
1.4.98 – 30.6.98	–	500	500
1.7.98 – 30.9.98	(10,000)	2,500	(7,500)

Task 2

Loss relief for the nine months to 30 September 1998

	£
Loss before capital allowances	362,500
Add Capital allowances	156,000
Loss available for relief	518,500

Schedule D Case I profits for year to 31.12.97

	£
Profit before capital allowances	750,000
Less Capital allowances	(217,000)
	533,000

	Y/e 31.12.97 £	*9m to 30.9.98* £	*Loss memorandum* £
Sch D Case I/(loss)	533,000	–	518,500
Bank interest receivable	1,700	1,250	
Loan interest receivable	18,000	13,500	
Capital gain		55,500	
Total profits	552,700	70,250	
Less: *S393A* relief		(70,250)	(70,250)
S393A	(448,250)		(448,250)
			–
	104,450	–	
Less: Charges paid			
Covenanted payment	(10,000)		
Excess non-trading charge lapses			
Profits chargeable to corporation tax	94,450	–	

Task 3

Calculation of MCT for the AP to 31 December 1997

	£	£
CT liability		
FY96 94,450 × 24% × 3/12		5,667
FY97 94,450 × 21% × 9/12		14,876
		20,543
Less: ACT current (per quarterly accounting)	18,250	
ACT carried back	640	
	18,890	
Maximum set off (£94,450 × 20%)	18,890	(18,890)
Surplus ACT c/f (£14,250 – £640)	13,610	
		1,653
Less: Income tax recoverable (per quarterly accounting)		(1,300)
MCT liability		353

WORKING

	£
PCTCT	94,450
Add FII (per quarterly accounting)	118,750
'Profits'	213,200

Therefore small companies rate applies.

3 Solution

Task 1

Pay and file is the name given to the system for the payment of corporation tax and filing of corporation tax returns by companies. The system is effective for accounting periods ending on or after 1 October 1993.

Under Pay and File there are two elements:

(i) the payment of corporation tax; and
(ii) the filing of accounts and supporting computations.

Payment of corporation tax

Corporation tax is payable 9 months after the end of the chargeable accounting period, before any assessment is made. Interest on unpaid or underpaid tax runs from this 9 month date.

Filing of return

The Revenue will issue a notice to the company requiring a return to be filed.

The company must file its corporation tax return and their accounts by the end of 12 months after the end of the chargeable accounting period or 3 months after the issue of the notice if later.

If the period of account is longer than 12 months then the return must be filed within 12 months of the end of the period of account or 3 months after the issue of the notice if later.

There are penalties for the late filing of returns.

Task 2

Assessments

On receipt of the return the Revenue will issue a corporation tax assessment. If too little tax has been paid provisionally the company will be liable to interest on the tax overdue from the due date and if it has paid too much tax the company will receive interest on the excess from the due date or the date paid, if later.

If the company does not agree with the assessment, it may, within 30 days, appeal against the assessment to the Revenue in writing. If the company and the Revenue can resolve the points at issue, the appeal may be settled by agreement. Failing this, the appeal will be heard by the General or Special Commissioners. Their decision may be appealed to the High Court, and further appeals may then be made to the Court of Appeal and the House of Lords

PRACTICE
ASSESSMENT ACTIVITIES

ANSWERS

AAT Assessments

AAT June 1996

Task	1	Unit	17
	2		17 & 18
	3		18
	4		17
	5		17

AAT December 1996

Section 1

Task	1.1	Unit	17
	1.2		17

Section 2

Task	2.1	Unit	18

Section 3

Task	3.1	Unit	18
	3.2		18

AAT June 1997

Section 1

Task	1.1	Unit	17
	1.2		17
	1.3		17

Section 2

Task	2.1	Unit	18
	2.2		18

Section 3

Task	3.1	Unit	17

AAT December 1997

Section 1

Task	1.1	Unit	18
	1.2		18
	1.3		18

Section 2

Task	2.1	Unit	17
	2.2		17

Section 3

Task	3.1	Unit	18
	3.2		18

PREPARING TAXATION COMPUTATIONS

ANSWERS - JUNE 1996

Task 1

Miss Kitty Bennet
Calculation of Schedule D Case I
Adjusted profits for year ended 30 April 1998

	£	£
Net profit per the accounts		28,842
Add:		
Depreciation	3,715	
Parking fine	30	
Oxfam donation	100	
Telephone (10% × £305)	31	
Motor expenses (40% × £1,229)	492	
		4,368
Less:		
Profit on disposal of fixed assets	1,158	
Bank interest	190	
		(1,348)
		31,862

Calculation of capital allowances
for year ended 30 April 1998

	General Pool	*Private use assets* 205		405		*Total allowances*
	£	£		£		£
Tax written down value (TWDV) b/fwd	6,500	-		7,985		
Additions not qualifying for FYA		7,431				
Disposals	(4,113)			(2,107		
	2,387	7,431		5,878		
WDA @ 25%	(597)	(1,858)	× 60%			1,712
Balancing adjustments				(5,878	× 60%	3,527
Additions qualifying for FYA	1,060					
FYA @ 50%	(530)					530
TWDV C/FWD	2,320	5,573		nil		£5,769

Adjusted profit	31,862
Less: Capital allowances	(5,769)
	£26,093

Task 2

Miss Kitty Bennet
Income tax computation 1998/99

	£	£
Earned income		
Schedule D Case 1	26,093	
		26,093
Investment income		
Schedule A (W1)	850	
Dividends	6,000	
Building Society interest	4,600	
Bank interest	1,990	
		13,440
Statutory total income		39,533
Less: Personal allowance		(4,195)
Taxable income		35,338
Tax thereon:	£	
Tax on non savings income		
£4,300 × 20%	860	
£18,448 × 23%	4,243	
£22,748		
Tax on savings income:		
£4,352 × 20%	870	
£8,238 × 40%	3,295	
£12,590		
Less ACA (£1,900 × 15%)	(285)	
TOTAL INCOME TAX LIABILITY		8,983
Less: Tax paid at source:		
Dividends (20% × £6,000)	1,200	
Building society interest (20% × £4,600)	920	
Bank interest (20% × £1,990)	398	
		(2,518)
Tax due under self-assessment		£6,465
Payments on account due for 1999/00 ½ × £6,465		£3,233

(W1) Schedule A Income: 1998/99

	£
6.4.98-30.9.98 (£4,000 × $^6/_{12}$)	2,000
1.9.98-5.4.99 (5,000 × $^6/_{12}$)	2,500
	4,500
Less Property management fees	(800)
Repairs to flat roof	(400)
Loan interest	(2,450)
	£850

Note: The question did not state whether the rented property was let furnished or unfurnished. The above calculation is for an unfurnished property. A calculation for a furnished property using a wear and tear allowance would have been equally acceptable.

Inland Revenue

Income for the year ended 5April 1999

SELF-EMPLOYMENT

Fill in these boxes first

Name: KITTY BENNET

Tax reference:

If you want help, look up the box numbers in the Notes

Business details

Name of business

3.1 LONGBOURN GIFT SHOP

Description of business

3.2 GIFT SHOP

Address of business

3.3 LONGBOURN HOUSE
MERYTON
HERTS

Postcode

Accounting period - *read the Notes, page SEN2 before filling in these boxes*

Start **3.4** 01 / 05 / 97

End **3.5** 30 / 04 / 98

- Tick box 3.5A if you entered details for all relevant accounting periods on last year's Tax Return and boxes 3.11 to 3.70 will be blank **3.5A**
- Tick box 3.6 if details in boxes 3.1 or 3.3 have changed since your last Tax Return **3.6**
- Tick box 3.7 if your accounts do not cover the period from the last accounting date (explain why in the 'Additional information' box below) **3.7**
- Tick box 3.8A if your accounting date has changed (only if this is a permanent change and you want it to count for tax) **3.8A**
- Tick box 3.8B if this is the second or further change (explain why you have not used the same date as last year in the 'Additional information' box) **3.8B**
- Date of commencement if after 5 April 1996 **3.9** / /
- Date of cessation if before 6 April 1999 **3.10** / /

Additional information

Income and expenses - annual turnover below £15,000

If your annual turnover is £15,000 or more, ***ignore*** *boxes 3.11 to 3.13.* *Now fill in Page SE2*

If your annual turnover is below £15,000, ***fill in boxes 3.11 to 3.13 instead of Page SE2****. Read the Notes, page SEN2.*

- Turnover, other business receipts and goods etc. taken for personal use (and balancing charges) **3.11** £
- Expenses allowable for tax (including capital allowances) **3.12** £

box 3.11 minus box 3.12

Net profit (put figure in brackets if a loss) **3.13** £

Now fill in Page SE3

SA103

Income and expenses - annual turnover £15,000 or more

You must fill in this Page if your annual turnover is £15,000 or more - read the Notes, page SEN2

If you were registered for VAT, do the figures in boxes 3.16 to 3.51, include VAT? **3.14** [ ] or exclude VAT? **3.15** ✓

Sales/business income (turnover) — **3.16** £ 137,450

	Disallowable expenses included in boxes 3.33 to 3.50	Total expenses	
• Cost of sales	**3.17** £	**3.33** £ 58,659	
• Construction industry subcontractor costs	**3.18** £	**3.34** £	
• Other direct costs	**3.19** £	**3.35** £ 617	box 3.16 *minus* (box 3.33 + box 3.34 + box 3.35)
		Gross profit/(loss)	**3.36** £ 78,174
		Other income/profits	**3.37** £ 190
• Employee costs	**3.20** £	**3.38** £ 25,394	
• Premises costs	**3.21** £	**3.39** £ 10,111	
• Repairs	**3.22** £	**3.40** £ 1,586	
• General administrative expenses	**3.23** £ 31	**3.41** £ 1,955	
• Motor expenses	**3.24** £ 492	**3.42** £ 1,954	
• Travel and subsistence	**3.25** £	**3.43** £	
• Advertising, promotion and entertainment	**3.26** £	**3.44** £	
• Legal and professional costs	**3.27** £	**3.45** £ 3,980	
• Bad debts	**3.28** £	**3.46** £	
• Interest	**3.29** £	**3.47** £ 1,481	
• Other finance charges	**3.30** £	**3.48** £	
• Depreciation and loss/(profit) on sale	**3.31** £ 2557	**3.49** £ 2,557	
• Other expenses	**3.32** £ 130	**3.50** £ 204	total of boxes 3.38 to 3.50
	Put the total of boxes 3.17 to 3.32 in **box 3.53 below**	Total expenses	**3.51** £ 49,522
			boxes 3.36 + 3.37 *minus* box 3.51
		Net profit/(loss)	**3.52** £ 28,842

Tax adjustments to net profit or loss

• Disallowable expenses	total of boxes 3.17 to 3.32 **3.53** £ 3,210	
• Goods etc. taken for personal use and other adjustments (apart from disallowable expenses) that increase profits	**3.54** £	
• Balancing charges	**3.55** £	boxes 3.53 + 3.54 + 3.55
Total additions to net profit (deduct from net loss)		**3.56** £ 3210
• Capital allowances	**3.57** £ 5769	boxes 3.57 + 3.58
• Deductions from net profit (add to net loss)	**3.58** £ 190	**3.59** £ 5959
		boxes 3.52 + 3.56 *minus* box 3.59
Net business profit for tax purposes (put figure in brackets if a loss)		**3.60** £ 26093

Now fill in Page SE3

You must fill in this Page (leave blank any boxes that do not apply to you)

Capital allowances - summary

	Capital allowances	Balancing charge
• Motor cars (Separate calculations must be made for each motor car costing more than £12,000 and for cars used partly for private motoring.)	3.61 £ 4,642	3.62 £
• Other business plant and machinery	3.63 £ 1,127	3.64 £
• Agricultural or Industrial Buildings Allowance (A separate calculation must be made for each block of expenditure.)	3.65 £	3.66 £
• Other capital allowances claimed (Separate calculations must be made.)	3.67 £	3.68 £
	total of column above	total of column above
Total capital allowances/balancing charges	3.69 £ 5,769	3.70 £

Adjustments to arrive at taxable profit or loss

Basis period begins 3.71 01 / 05 / 97 and ends 3.72 30 / 04 / 98

- Tick box 3.72A if the figure in box 3.88 is provisional — 3.72A
- Tick box 3.72B if the special arrangements for certain trades detailed in the guidance notes apply — 3.72B

Profit or loss of this account for tax purposes (box 3.13 or 3.60) — 3.73 £ 26,093

Adjustment to arrive at profit or loss for this basis period — 3.74 £

- Overlap profit brought forward — 3.75 £
- Deduct overlap relief used this year — 3.76 £
- Overlap profit carried forward — 3.77 £

Adjustment for farmers' averaging (see Notes, page SEN8 if you made a loss for 1998-99) — 3.78 £

Net profit for 1998-99 (if loss, enter '0') — 3.79 £ 26,093

Allowable loss for 1998-99 (if you make a profit, enter '0') — 3.80 £

- Loss offset against other income for 1998-99 — 3.81 £
- Loss to carry back — 3.82 £
- Loss to carry forward (that is allowable loss not claimed in any other way) — 3.83 £
- Losses brought forward from last year — 3.84 £
- Losses brought forward from last year used this year — 3.85 £

Taxable profit after losses brought forward — box 3.79 *minus* box 3.85 — 3.86 £ 26,093

- Any other business income (for example, Business Start-up Allowance received in 1998-99) — 3.87 £

Total taxable profits from this business — box 3.86 + box 3.87 — 3.88 £ 26,093

Class 4 National Insurance Contributions

- Tick this box if exception or deferment applies **3.89**
- Adjustments to profit chargeable to Class 4 National Insurance Contributions **3.90** £

Class 4 National Insurance Contributions due **3.91** £

Subcontractors in the construction industry

- Deductions made by contractors on account of tax (you must send your SC60s to us) **3.92** £

Summary of balance sheet

Leave these boxes blank if you do not have a balance sheet

		Box	£	Total
■ *Assets*	• Plant, machinery and motor vehicles	3.93	23,629	
	• Other fixed assets (premises, goodwill, investments etc.)	3.94	75,625	
	• Stock and work in progress	3.95	7,550	
	• Debtors/prepayments/other current assets	3.96	276	
	• Bank/building society balances	3.97	3,458	total of boxes 3.93 to 3.98
	• Cash in hand	3.98	4,321	3.99 £ 115,059
■ *Liabilities*	• Trade creditors/accruals	3.100	8,149	
	• Loans and overdrawn bank accounts	3.101	5,332	total of boxes 3.100 to 3.102
	• Other liabilities	3.102		3.103 £ 13,481

■ ***Net business assets*** (put the figure in brackets if you had net business liabilities) — box 3.99 *minus* box 3.103 — **3.104** £ 101,578

■ ***Represented by***

Capital Account

	Box	£	Total
• Balance at start of period*	3.105	99,516	
• Net profit/(loss)*	3.106	28,842	
• Capital introduced	3.107		
• Drawings	3.108	26,780	total of boxes 3.105 to 3.107 *minus* box 3.108
• Balance at end of period*			3.109 £ 101,578

* If the Capital Account is overdrawn, or the business made a net loss, show the figure in brackets.

Tax deducted from trading income

- Any tax deducted (excluding deductions made by contractors on account of tax) from trading income. **3.120** £

Note: box numbers 3.110 to 3.119 are not used

Additional information

Now fill in any other supplementary Pages that apply to you.
Otherwise, go back to Page 2 of your Tax Return and finish filling it in.

Inland Revenue

Income for the year ended 5 April 1999

LAND AND PROPERTY

Fill in these boxes first

Name: KITTY BENNET

Tax reference:

Are you claiming Rent a Room relief for gross rents of £4,250 or less? No ✓ Yes

(Or £2,125 if the claim is shared?)

Read the Notes on page LN2 to find out

- whether you can claim Rent a Room relief; and
- how to claim relief for gross rents over £4,250

If 'Yes', and this is your only income from UK property, you have finished these Pages

Is your income from furnished holiday lettings? No ✓ Yes

If 'No', turn over and fill in Page L2 to give details of your property income

If 'Yes', fill in boxes 5.1 to 5.18 before completing Page L2

Furnished holiday lettings

- Income from furnished holiday lettings — 5.1 £

■ *Expenses* (furnished holiday lettings only)

- Rent, rates, insurance, ground rents etc. — 5.2 £
- Repairs, maintenance and renewals — 5.3 £
- Finance charges, including interest — 5.4 £
- Legal and professional costs — 5.5 £
- Cost of services provided, including wages — 5.6 £
- Other expenses — 5.7 £ — total of boxes 5.2 to 5.7: 5.8 £

Net profit (put figures in brackets if a loss) — box 5.1 *minus* box 5.8: 5.9 £

■ *Tax adjustments*

- Private use — 5.10 £
- Balancing charges — 5.11 £ — box 5.10 + box 5.11: 5.12 £
- Capital allowances — 5.13 £

Profit for the year (copy to box 5.19). If loss, enter '0' in box 5.14 and put the loss in box 5.15 — boxes 5.9 + 5.12 *minus* box 5.13: 5.14 £

Loss for the year (if you have entered '0' in box 5.14) — boxes 5.9 + 5.12 *minus* box 5.13: 5.15 £

- Loss offset against 1998-99 total income — 5.16 £
- Loss carried back — see Notes, page LN4: 5.17 £
- Loss offset against other income from property (copy to box 5.38) — see Notes, page LN4: 5.18 £

SA105

Other property income

■ *Income*

	copy from box 5.14	Tax deducted	boxes 5.19 + 5.20 + 5.22
• Furnished holiday lettings profits	5.19 £		
• Rents and other income from land and property	5.20 £ 4,500	5.21 £	5.23 £ 4,500
• Chargeable premiums	5.22 £		

■ *Expenses* (do not include figures you have already put in boxes 5.2 to 5.7 on Page L1)

• Rent, rates, insurance, ground rents etc.	5.24 £	
• Repairs, maintenance and renewals	5.25 £ 400	
• Finance charges, including interest	5.26 £ 2,450	
• Legal and professional costs	5.27 £ 800	
• Costs of services provided, including wages	5.28 £	total of boxes 5.24 to 5.29
• Other expenses	5.29 £	5.30 £ 3,650
		box 5.23 *minus* box 5.30
Net profit (put figures in brackets if a loss)		5.31 £ 850

■ *Tax adjustments*

• Private use	5.32 £	box 5.32 + box 5.33
• Balancing charges	5.33 £	5.34 £
• Rent a Room exempt amount	5.35 £	
• Capital allowances	5.36 £	
• 10% wear and tear	5.37 £	total of boxes 5.35 to 5.38
• Furnished holiday lettings losses (from box 5.18)	5.38 £	5.39 £

		boxes 5.31 + 5.34 *minus* box 5.39
Adjusted profit (if loss enter '0' in box 5.40 and put the loss in box 5.41)	boxes 5.31 + 5.34 *minus* box 5.39	5.40 £ 850
Adjusted loss (if you have entered '0' in box 5.40)	5.41 £	
• Loss brought forward from previous year		5.42 £
		box 5.40 *minus* box 5.42
Profit for the year		5.43 £ 850
• Loss offset against total income	5.44 £	
• Loss to carry forward to following year	5.45 £	
• Pooled expenses from 'one estate election' carried forward	5.46 £	

Tick box 5.47 if these Pages include details of property let jointly 5.47

Now fill in any other supplementary Pages that apply to you. Otherwise, go back to page 2 of your Tax Return and finish filling it in.

INCOME *for the year ended 5 April 1999*

Q10 Did you receive any income from UK savings and investments? NO [ ] YES [✓]

If yes, fill in boxes 10.1 to 10.32 as appropriate. Include only your share from any joint savings and investments.

■ ***Interest***

• Interest from UK banks, building societies and deposit takers			
- where **no tax** has been deducted			Taxable amount **10.1** £
- where **tax has** been deducted	Amount after tax deducted **10.2** £ 5,272	Tax deducted **10.3** £ 1,318	Gross amount before tax **10.4** £ 6,590
• Interest distributions from UK authorised unit trusts and open-ended investment companies (dividend distributions go below)	Amount after tax deducted **10.5** £	Tax deducted **10.6** £	Gross amount before tax **10.7** £
• National Savings (other than FIRST Option Bonds and the first £70 of interest from a National Savings Ordinary Account)			Taxable amount **10.8** £
• National Savings FIRST Option Bonds	Amount after tax deducted **10.9** £	Tax deducted **10.10** £	Gross amount before tax **10.11** £
• Other income from UK savings and investments (except dividends)	Amount after tax deducted **10.12** £	Tax deducted **10.13** £	Gross amount before tax **10.14** £

■ ***Dividends***

• Dividends and other qualifying distributions from UK companies	Dividend/distribution **10.15** £ 4800	Tax credit **10.16** £ 1200	Dividend/distribution plus credit **10.17** £ 6000
• Dividend distributions from UK authorised unit trusts and open-ended investment companies	Dividend/distribution **10.18** £	Tax credit **10.19** £	Dividend/distribution plus credit **10.20** £
• Scrip dividends from UK companies	Dividend **10.21** £	Notional tax **10.22** £	Dividend plus notional tax **10.23** £
• Foreign income dividends from UK companies	Dividend **10.24** £	Notional tax **10.25** £	Dividend plus notional tax **10.26** £
• Foreign income dividend distributions from UK authorised unit trusts and open-ended investment companies	Dividend **10.27** £	Notional tax **10.28** £	Dividend plus notional tax **10.29** £
• Non-qualifying distributions and loans written off	**10.30** £	Notional tax **10.31** £	Taxable amount **10.32** £

ALLOWANCES *for the year ended 5 April 1999*

Q16

You get your personal allowance of £4,195 automatically. ***If you were born before 6 April 1934, enter your date of birth in box 21.4*** *- you may get higher age-related allowances.*

Do you want to claim any of the following allowances? NO | YES ✓ If yes, please read pages 23 to 26 of your Tax Return Guide and then fill in boxes 16.1 to 16.28 as appropriate.

■ *Blind person's allowance* — Date of registration (if first year of claim) 16.1 / / — Local authority (or other register) 16.2

■ *Transitional allowance* (for some wives with husbands on low income if received in earlier years).

- Tick to claim and give details in the 'Additional information' box on page 8 *(please see page 23 of your Tax Return Guide for what is needed)* 16.3
- If you want to calculate your tax, enter the amount of transitional allowance you can have in box 16.4 — 16.4 £

■ *Married couple's allowance for a married man* - *see page 24 of your Tax Return Guide.*

- Wife's full name 16.5
- Date of marriage (if after 5 April 1998) 16.6 / /
- Wife's date of birth (if before 6 April 1934) 16.7 / /
- Tick box 16.8 if you or your wife have allocated **half** the allowance to her 16.8

box number 16.9 is not used

- Tick box 16.10 if you and your wife have allocated **all** the allowance to her 16.10

■ *Married couple's allowance for a married woman* - *see page 24 of your Tax Return Guide.*

- Date of marriage (if after 5 April 1998) 16.11 / /
- Husband's full name 16.12
- Tick box 16.13 if you or your husband have allocated **half** the allowance to you 16.13

box number 16.14 is not used

- Tick box 16.15 if you and your husband have allocated **all** the allowance to you 16.15

■ *Additional personal allowance* *(available in some circumstances if you have a child living with you - see page 25 of your Tax Return Guide).*

- Tick box 16.16A if you are claiming the married couple's allowance **and** additional personal allowance because your spouse was unable to work, because of illness or disablement, throughout the year ended 5 April 1999 16.16A
- Name of the child claimed for 16.16 GEORGE BENNET
- Child's date of birth 16.17 18 / 02 / 96
- Tick if child lives with you 16.18 ✓
- Name of university etc/type of training if the child is 16 or over on 6 April 1998 and in full time education or training 16.19

Sharing a claim

Name and address of other person claiming

16.20

Postcode

- Enter your share as a percentage 16.21 %
- If share not agreed, enter the number of days in the year ended 5 April 1999 that the child lived with
  - you 16.22 days
  - other person 16.23 days

■ *Widow's bereavement allowance* — Date of your husband's death 16.24 / /

■ *Transfer of surplus allowances* - *see page 26 of your Tax Return Guide before you fill in boxes 16.25 to 16.28.*

- Tick if you want your spouse to have your unused allowances 16.25
- Tick if you want to have your spouse's unused allowances 16.26

Please give details in the 'Additional information' box on page 8 - *see page 26 of your Tax Return Guide for what is needed.*

If you want to calculate your tax, enter the amount of the surplus allowance you can have.

- Blind person's surplus allowance 16.27 £
- Married couple's surplus allowance 16.28 £

OTHER INFORMATION *for the year ended 5 April 1999*

Q17 Have you already had any 1998-99 tax refunded or set off by your Tax Office or the DSS Benefits Agency? *Read the notes for box 17.1 on page 26 of your Tax Return Guide*

NO ✓ YES

If yes, enter the amount of the refund in box 17.1.

17.1 £

Q18 Do you want to calculate your tax?

NO YES ✓

If yes, do it now and then fill in boxes 18.1 to 18.9. Your Tax Calculation Guide will help.

- Unpaid tax for earlier years included in your tax code for 1998-99 — 18.1 £
- Tax due for 1998-99 included in your tax code for a later year — 18.2 £
- Total tax and Class 4 NIC due for 1998-99 **before** you made any payments on account *(put the amount in brackets if an overpayment)* — 18.3 £ 6,465
- Tax due for earlier years — 18.4 £
- Tick box 18.5 if you have calculated tax overpaid for earlier years (and enter the amount in the 'Additional information' box on page 8 — 18.5
- Your first payment on account for 1999-2000 *(include the pence)* — 18.6 £ 3,233

Tick box 18.7 if you are making a claim to reduce your 1999-2000 payments on account and say why in the 'Additional information' box — 18.7

Tick box 18.8 if you do **not** need to make 1999-2000 payments on account — 18.8

- 1999-2000 tax you are reclaiming now — 18.9 £

Q19 Do you want to claim a repayment if you have paid too much tax? *(If you tick 'No' or the tax you have overpaid is below £10, I will use the amount you are owed to reduce your next tax bill.)*

NO ✓ YES

If yes, fill in boxes 19.1 to 19.12 as appropriate.

Should the repayment (or payment) be sent:

- to you? *Tick box 19.1* — 19.1

or

- to your bank or building society account or other nominee? *Tick box 19.2* — 19.2

If you ticked either box 19.2 or 19.9, fill in boxes 19.3 to 19.8, 19.11 and 19.12 as appropriate.

Your (or your nominee's) bank or building society — 19.3

Branch sort code — 19.4 – –

Account number — 19.5

Name of account — 19.6

Building society ref. — 19.7

If your nominee is your agent, *tick box 19.9 and complete boxes 19.10 to 19.12* — 19.9

Agent's ref. for you — 19.10

I authorise — 19.8 Name of your nominee/agent

Nominee's address — 19.11

Postcode

to receive on my behalf the amount due

This authority must be signed by you. A photocopy of your signature will not do. — 19.12 Signature

Q20 Are your details on the front of the Tax Return wrong?

NO ✓ YES

If yes, please make any corrections on the front of the form.

Q21 Please give other personal details in boxes 21.1 to 21.6 *This information helps us to be more efficient and effective and may support claims you have made elsewhere in your Tax Return*

Please give a daytime telephone number if convenient. It is often simpler to phone if we need to ask you about your Tax Return.

Your telephone number — 21.1

or, if you prefer, your agent's telephone number — 21.2

(also give your agent's name and reference in the 'Additional information' box on page 8)

Enter your first two forenames — 21.5 KITTY

Say if you are single, married, widowed, divorced or separated — 21.3 SINGLE

Date of birth — 21.4 31/03/65

Enter your date of birth if you are self-employed, or you were born before 6 April 1934, or you have ticked the 'Yes' box in Question 14, or you are claiming relief for Venture Capital Trust subscriptions

Enter your National Insurance number (if known) — 21.6 NB 61 72 21 F

Task 3

Lucas and Collins
Accountants
Barrack Road
Meryton
Hertfordshire

Miss Kitty Bennet
Longbourn House
Meryton
Hertfordshire

Dear Miss Bennet 21 June 1999

Offer of Employment

Further to your letter of 10 June 1999 containing queries concerning the income tax effect of accepting an offer of employment with Darcy's Derbyshire Delights, I set out my answers to your queries below:

1. *Net Pay After Tax:*
If we assume that your salary from Darcy's Derbyshire Delights will be received on top of your existing income you will effectively suffer 40% tax on any additional income, because your current self employed earnings exceed your personal allowances and are already partially taxed at 40%.

The value of your taxable income from employment for the rest of 1999/00 will be as follows:

	£
Salary £29,250 × 8/12	19,500
Commission £100 × 8	800
Car benefit:	
£26,000 × 35% × 2/3 × 8/12	4,044
Fuel benefit:	
£1,890 × 8/12	1,260
	25,604

(I will explain how I have calculated the car and fuel benefit figures later in the letter in answer to one of your later questions.)

Tax thereon at 40% £10,242

Monthly take home pay:

	£		£
Salary	19,500		
Commission	800		
	20,300	÷ 8 =	2,538
Less: Tax:	10,242	÷ 8 =	(1,280)
			1,258

2. *Car and Fuel Benefit:*
In the above calculations I have valued the car and fuel the company will provide you with, for income tax purposes.

These valuations have been made in accordance with legislation. Basically, if an employer provides an employee with a car and/or fuel for private (that is, non-business) use, then the employee is being provided with additional remuneration as a benefit-in-kind. The valuation of this benefit for income tax purposes is as follows:

Car:
- Each tax year the benefit is valued as 35% × manufacturer's list price of the car.
- This benefit is reduced for high mileage on business (≥2,500 but <18,000 business miles—1/3 reduction) (≥ 18,000 business miles—2/3 reduction).
  This business mileage is logged by the employer and employee during the course of the tax year.
- The benefit is also reduced by contributions by the employee towards private use and if the car is not available for the full tax year.

Fuel:
- Each tax year the benefit is valued according to the cc of the car and whether petrol or diesel is used.
- There is no reduction in the benefit for contributions towards private use (reimbursing the employer for the cost of all private fuel will wipe out the benefit, but partial contributions will not bring about a reduction).
- There is no reduction in the benefit for high business mileage.
- Again, the benefit is reduced if the car is not available for the full tax year.

3. *Explanation of the PAYE System*
As the proprietor of the Longbourn Gift Shop, you are classed as self-employed and the profits are taxed under Schedule D Case 1. This means you receive payments from your business gross of tax. Tax on these payments is paid in two instalments on 31 January in the tax year and 31 July following the tax year, based on the previous year's tax liability, with any balance of tax being due on 31 January following the tax year.

Your self-employed income will continue to be taxed on this basis. Your employment income is taxed under Schedule E. Tax under Schedule E is usually deducted from your gross pay at source under the Pay-As-You-Earn (PAYE) scheme. The PAYE scheme is used by the Inland Revenue to deduct income tax from your pay each month. The pay you receive from your employers will be net of income tax and your employers will remit the income tax deducted to the Inland Revenue on your behalf.

The amount of tax you pay will be calculated using tax tables provided by the Inland Revenue. You will receive an Inland Revenue notice of coding, which enables your employer to work out how much tax you will pay (using tax tables) and deduct this amount from your gross pay.

I hope that this has answered your questions satisfactorily, but if you would like to discuss any aspect of the letter please contact me.

Yours Sincerely

J Smith

J Smith
Tax Department Manager

Note:
Specific knowledge of National Insurance is outside the scope of this unit and has been ignored in the above answer.

Task 4

Chargeable gains

			Cost	MV82
Property		£	£	£
Proceeds	1 July 1998		419,539	419,539
Disposal costs			(4,000)	(4,000)
Cost	17 January 1970	2,000		
Enhancements				(125,000)
	3 April 1976	9,500		
	31 October 1992	85,000		(85,000)
		96,500		
March 1982 Indexation $1.047 \left(\frac{162.6-79.44}{79.44}\right)$ × £125,000		130,875		(130,875)
Oct 1992 $0.162 \left(\frac{162.6-139.9}{139.9}\right)$ × £85,000		13,770		(13,770)
			(241,145)	
			£174,394	£60,894 NOTE 1

Lower gain taken	£60,894
Shares	
Proceeds	325,000
Less: Cost	(127,224)
Unindexed gain	197,776
Less: indexation allowance (153,326 – 127,224)	(26,102)
	171,674
Summary	
Property	60,894
Shares	171,674
Rolls Royce Car	Exempt
Total	232,568

NOTE 1: The cost of the temporary warehouse has been ignored in this computation because it did not exist at the date of sale.

Finance Act 1985 Pool

	No of shares	*Cost*	*Cost & indexation*
	£	£	£
Acquisition 13.8.82	100	100	100
5.4.85 Pool starts			
Indexed rise			
$100 \times \frac{94.80-81.90}{81.90}$ (0.158)			16
			116
7.11.87 Acquisition			
Indexed rise			
$116 \times \frac{103.4-94.80}{94.80}$			11
Acquisition	20,000	25,000	25,000
	20,100	25,100	25,127
12.12.89 Bonus			
(no need to do indexed rise)	20,100	-	-
	40,200	25,100	25,127
13.2.93 Acquisition			
Indexed rise			
$25{,}127 \times \frac{138.8-103.4}{103.4}$			8,603
Acquisition	160,300	275,000	275,000
	200,500	300,100	308,730
Disposal 21.7.98			
Indexed rise			
$308{,}730 \times \frac{162.6-138.8}{138.8}$			52,938
			361,668
Disposal	(85,000)	(127,224)	(153,326)
	115,500	172,876	208,342

Task 5

Plantagenet Limited
Abbreviated corporation tax computations

	Year ended 31/12/95	*Year ended 31/12/95*	*Year ended 31/12/96*	*Year ended 31/12/97*	*Year ended 31/12/98*
	£	£	£	£	£
Sch D Case 1 per computations	1,111,337	1,113,059	504,325	159,095	663,143
Capital gains	372,836	142,517	136,477	0	232,568
Capital allowances	(97,493)	(82,435)	(85,059)	(96,566)	(99,614)
Net charges	(148,537)	(10,132)	(241,619)	(199,570)	(217,497)
Profits chargeable to tax	1,238,143	1,163,009	314,124	Nil	578,600
Corporation tax	408,587	383,793	94,127	0	175,081
Less ACT–original deduction	0	(100,000)	(10,000)	0	0
Less ACT: deduction 31/12/98 year end					(115,720)
carry back of surplus ACT		(26,445)	(52,825)		
Corporation tax payable	408,587	257,338	(31,302)	Nil	59,361

ACT paid	£
Gross dividends paid	1,000,000
Less gross dividends received	(25,000)
	975,000
ACT paid 975,000 × 20% =	195,000

Use of ACT paid	*Year ended 31/12/94*	*Year ended 31/12/95*	*Year ended 31/12/96*	*Year ended 31/12/97*	*Year ended 31/12/98*	
	£	£	£	£	£	
PCTCT	1,238,143	1,163,009	314,124	-	578,600	
ACT rate	$^3/_{12}$ × 22.5%					
	$^9/_{12}$ × 20%	20%	20%		20%	
Max. ACT set off	255,367	232,602	62,825	-	115,720	
Less: already set off in original comps		(100,000)	(10,000)			
Surplus capacity to use ACT	255,367	132,602	52,825		115,720	Total
Less: use of ACT paid of £195,000		(26,455) [3]	(52,825) [2]		[1] (115,720)	195,000
Surplus capacity to use ACT @ 1/1/99	255,367	106,147	Nil		Nil	

Calculation of CT liability year ended 31.12.98

PCTCT £578,600

No dividends to add in to create 'profits' as all dividends received are from group companies

Upper limit $\frac{£1,500,000}{2}$ = £750,000

Lower limited $\frac{£300,000}{2}$ = £150,000

∴ Company to receive marginal relief

	£
£578,600 × 31%	179,366
Less: marginal relief	
$\frac{1}{40}$ × (750,000 – 578,600)	(4,285)
	175,081

PREPARING TAXATION COMPUTATIONS

ANSWERS - DECEMBER 1996

Answer to Section 1, Task 1.1

Cole Limited
Corporation tax Computation for the year ended 31 March 1999

	£	£
Schedule D Case I (WI)	22,665	
Schedule D Case III	5,000	
Patent Royalties received	10,000	
		37,665
Less: Charges on income		
Gift Aid payment	5,000	(5,000)
PCTCT		£32,665

Corporation Tax Payable:
Profits are less than £300,000 therefore the company is a small company

Corporation tax payable £32,665 @ 21%	6,860
Less: ACT set off (W2)	(6,533)
	327
Less: Income tax suffered (W3)	(1,150)
Repayment due	£(823)

Workings for Section 1, Task 1.1

Cole Limited
Adjustment of Profit for the purposes of Schedule D Case I

	£	£
Net Profit per accounts		36,728
Add:		
Depreciation	9,133	
Entertaining customers	3,483	
Non trade loan written off	250	
Legal fees re tax appeal	324	
Gift aid payment	5,000	
		18,190
Less:		54,918
Profit on sale of fixed assets	9,900	
Capital Allowances (see below)	7,313	
Reduction in general bad debt provision	40	
Bank interest receivable	5,000	
Patent royalties received	10,000	
		(32,253)
Schedule D Case I profit		£22,665

Capital Allowance Computation

	General Pool	*FA80 Pool*	*Expensive Car Land Rover Discovery*	*Total Allowances*
	£	£	£	£
TWDV at 1 April 1998	11,250	2,500	23,600	
Additions not qualifying for FYA		6,000		
Disposals	(10,000)	(2,500)		
	1,250	6,000	23,600	
WDA @ 25%	(313)	(1,500)		1,813
WDA Restricted			(3,000)	3,000
Balancing allowance/charge				
Additions qualifying for FYA	5,000			
FYA @ 50%	(2,500)			2,500
TWDV at 31 March 1999	£3,437	£4,500	£20,600	£7,313

Workings for Section 1, Task 1.1

(W2) Advance Corporation Tax
Per form CT61 Paid £8,250
Maximum set off £32,665 (PCTCT) @ 20% = £6,533

Income Tax
Per form CT61 Income tax available for offset £1,150

Inland Revenue

Page 1

Corporation Tax Return
Version 3

This form, or an approved substitute version of it, must be used whenever a company is required to do so, by a *Notice to deliver a Corporation Tax Return (form CT203)*. This return sets out the information we need and provides a standard format for calculations.

You should read this return form along with your *Notice to deliver a Corporation Tax Return (form CT203)* and *Filling in your Corporation Tax Return (leaflet CT200 Notes)* which you should have received with this form. The notes referred to throughout can be found in the leaflet *CT200 Notes*. You should contact your Tax Office if you need more help.

'Company' means any body chargeable to corporation tax, whether incorporated or not. This definition includes clubs, associations and voluntary organisations.

Sections to be completed
Members' clubs, associations and voluntary organisations - It is likely that you will only have to complete Sections 1 and 2. For further guidance see note 1 in the *Notes*.

All companies - including clubs, etc. - You will not need to complete every Section, but you **must** complete the Declaration and Section 1 on this page. The *Notes* will help you decide whether you should complete the mutually exclusive *Short return* at Section 2 or the *Detailed return* at Section 3. Sections 9 and 10 are optional but you are asked to complete them if they are relevant to the company.

It is important that you read the *Notes* before completing any part of this form.

What to do when you have completed the return

- Make sure you have completed and signed the Declaration, then
- staple together the pages you have completed and attach any supporting calculations
- send these together with the relevant company accounts and, where prepared, directors' and auditors' reports, to your Tax Office using the envelope provided (see Note 3 for the date by which you should do this)
- pay any outstanding corporation tax (as you have shown at box box 65), as advised on the payslip attached to your *Notice to deliver a Corporation Tax Return (form CT203)*. Interest is charged on tax paid later than nine months and one day after the end of an accounting period. Tax is due without the making of an assessment.

Remember - ***Your tax return is not complete unless you send relevant accounts and documentation with this form. Penalties may be charged if your return, or any part of it, is late or incorrect.***

As soon as your figures are agreed

- we will send you an assessment setting out the tax position for the accounting period - unless there are no figures to assess
- we will issue an amended assessment if you have already received an estimated assessment and you have appealed against it.

Section 1: Summary

The company name

COLE LIMITED

The company address - only if changed since last return made.
Enter the UK registered office address, or the UK address if the company does not have a registered office. If the company does not have premises in the UK show the address of the person making the return.

Company registration number *(if registered)*

223421

Reference
Enter the reference number shown on the *Notice to deliver a Corporation Tax Return (form CT203)*

313 / 42679 / 00013

Corporation tax accounting period covered by this return
Cannot exceed 12 months. Enter start and end dates.

From 01 / 04 / 98 To 31 / 03 / 99

If this period is not an accounting period of the company for corporation tax purposes (see note 2) put an 'X' in the box below, complete the Declaration to the right and return this form to your Tax Office. You do not need to complete the rest of this Section or other Sections of this form in these circumstances. ☐

Profits chargeable *(Enter the firgure from box 30). If there are none enter '0'.*

£ 32,665

Corporation tax due *(Enter the figure from box 61 minus any entry in box 64). If none is due enter '0.00'.*

£ 0 . p 00

Put an X in the appropriate box

Have you completed Section 8 (Repayments)? Yes ☑ No ☐

Is the company name different from that shown in the *Notice (form CT203)*? Yes ☐ No ☑

Declaration

Enter here the page numbers you are attaching

2,3,6,8,9

Put an 'X' in the appropriate boxes to show the documents you are enclosing

- a copy of the accounts for the period to which this return relates ☒
- a copy of the company accounts for a different period ☐
- no accounts ☐
- say why not
- calculations showing how the entries in the return form have been arrived at. ☒

I declare that to the best of my knowledge and belief the return on this page and the pages attached is correct and complete.

Signature

Except where a liquidator has been appointed, the company secretary, treasurer, or any other person who is authorised to do so may sign this declaration on behalf of the company. A photocopy of a signature is not acceptable.

Date / /

Name *(in capital letters)*

Status *(company secretary, treasurer, liquidator etc.)*

Page 2

Section 2: Short return

You may complete this section if

- it covers all the entries you need to make and
- each entry, including the company's total income and deductions, is less than £10 million.

In all other cases, or if you prefer, complete Section 3 instead. You should enclose an explanation and calculations of any figures which you have estimated or which are not immediately recognisable from the company's accounts.

The figures to be entered are those adjusted for tax purposes, after deducting capital allowances and adding balancing charges where appropriate. Section 4 should also be completed if capital allowances are claimed.

Please do not enter '0's where the company did not have the source specified in the return form.

	Box	£	Box	£
Trading profits *See note 5*	1	22665		
Trading losses brought forward *Only include losses made in the same trade. Include charges treated as losses.* ***Do not enter an amount larger than is needed to cover the profits in box 1.*** *See note 6*	2			
Net trading profit *(box 1 minus box 2). If box 2 equals box 1, enter '0'. Leave this box blank if there are no trading profits in box 1*			3	22665
Trading losses of this accounting period *Where there is more than one trade give total for all trades. Do not set box 4 losses against box 1 profits, claim at box 22 against total profits.*	4			
Profits and gains from non-trading loan relationships and other Schedule D Case III income *Include interest and other profits and gains from non-trading loan relationships even if tax has been deducted. Complete box 57 to claim credit for income tax deducted. You will need to complete the* **Detailed return** *at Section 3 if you have deficits on non-trading loan relationships from this, earlier or later accounting periods to include. See note 8*			6	5000
Income within Schedule D Case VI - for example furnished lettings *Enter the figure net of allowable losses brought forward. Exclude income you enter in box 12. See note 7*			9	
Income from which income tax has been deducted - for example building society interest *Enter the gross amount before tax. Exclude any amount included in box 6 above. Complete box 57 to claim credit for income tax deducted. See note 9*			10	10,000
Income from UK land and buildings *Enter the amount net of allowable expenses brought forward. Exclude income in box 9 above. See note 10*			12	
Chargeable gains *See note 11*				
Gross gains	13			
Allowable losses *Include any losses brought forward but do not enter an amount larger than the amount of gross gains in box 13 above.*	14			
Net chargeable gains *(box 13 minus box 14) If box 14 equals box 13, enter '0'*			15	
Profits *(total of boxes 3, 6, 9, 10, 12 and 15)*			17	37665
Relief for trading losses of this or of a later period *Put an 'X' in box 21 if amounts carried back from later accounting periods are included in box 22. See note 12*	21	☐	22	
Profits before charges *(box 17 minus box 22)*			26	37665
Charges paid *Do not enter an amount larger than is needed to cover profits in box 26. See note13*			27	5000
Profits chargeable to corporation tax *(box 26 minus box 27)* *Copy this figure into the box provided in Section 1 on page 1, and also into the box at the top of page 3*			30	32665

The short return is continued on page 3

Page 3

Profits chargeable to corporation tax

Enter the figure brought forward from page 2, box 30 ... £ 32665

If you claim tax is chargeable at the small companies' rate, or if you are claiming marginal small companies' relief, complete boxes 31 - 35. If there are no associated companies please enter '0' against the relevant financial year. *See note 15*

Franked investment income and foreign income dividends arising in the period covered by the return. *See note 15* ... 31 £

Number of companies associated with this company in the/each financial year covered by this return
Exclude this company. See note 15 ...

	Financial year		Number of associated companies
32	1998	33	0
34	19	35	

Corporation tax chargeable *See note 16*

	Financial years beginning 1 April		Amounts of profit £		Rates of tax *See note 16*		Tax £	p
36	1998	37	32665	38	21 • 00	39	6860	00
43	19	44		45	•	46		

Total corporation tax chargeable *(box 39 plus box 46)* ... 50 6860 • 00

Marginal small companies' relief
Attach your computation (see notes 15, 16 and 29) ... 51 £ • p

Advance corporation tax restricted if necessary
under Section 239(2) ICTA 1988
Put an 'X' in box 53 if amounts carried back from later accounting periods are included. See note 17. 53 [ ] 54 6533 • 00

Total of boxes 51 and 54
Total must not be larger than entry in box 50. Restrict if necessary ... 55 6533 • 00

Net corporation tax chargeable *(box 50 minus box 55)* ... 56 327 • 00

Calculation of tax outstanding or overpaid

Income tax deducted from gross income included in return
Do not include deductions used to cover income tax for which the company was liable to account to the Inland Revenue on payments it has made. See note 18 ... 57 1150 • 00

Corporation tax due

Box 56 minus box 57. If box 57 equals or is greater than box 56, enter '0.00' and go to box 59.
Copy the figure in box 61 to the box provided in Section 1 on page 1. *See note 20* ... 61 0 • 00

Income tax repayable to the company *(box 57 minus box 56).*
Complete Section 8 on page 8. Do not complete unless you are making a claim. *See note 28*... 59 823 • 00

Corporation tax already paid (and not repaid). *See note 21* ... 63 1000 • 00

Corporation tax outstanding *(box 61 minus box 63). This amount is payable to the Accounts Office.*
If box 63 equals or is greater than box 61, enter '0.00' and go to box 66. *See note 23* ... 65 0 • 00

Corporation tax overpaid *(box 63 minus box 61).*
Complete Section 8 on page 8 also. *See note 28* ... 66 1000 • 00

This is the last page of the short return

Page 6

Section 4: Claims for capital allowances and details of balancing charges arising

You must complete this section if you want to claim capital allowances, whether or not those allowances are reflected elsewhere in the return. You should also show balancing charges taken into account in the short or detailed return. Show details of qualifying expenditure on which writing-down allowances may be claimed, even if you do not want to claim any allowances for this period. *See note 25*

Notice of expenditure on machinery and plant *See note 25*

Expenditure on which first year allowance is claimed £	Qualifying expenditure on long life assets on which writing down allowances may be claimed £	Qualifying expenditure on other assets on which writing down allowances may be claimed £
68: 5000	91:	69: 6000

Charges and allowances included in calculation of trading profit or losses

	Balancing charges £	Capital allowances £
Cars *Including leased out and "expensive" cars*	70	71: 4500
Machinery and plant - *long life assets*	92	93
- *other*	72	73: 2813
Industrial buildings and structures *Including qualifying hotels, and commercial buildings and hotels in enterprise zones*	74	75
Other charges and allowances *For example agricultural buildings, mineral extraction, scientific research, patents*	76	77
Charges and allowances not included in calculation of trading profit or losses	78	79

Section 5: Particulars of advance corporation tax and surplus advance corporation tax

Complete this section if you have surplus advance corporation tax brought forward or have paid advance corporation tax (and it has not been repaid) in respect of qualifying distributions made in the period covered by this return.

	£	p
Particulars of advance corporation tax paid	8250	00
Particulars of any surplus advance corporation tax brought forward		

Section 6: Amounts claimed as group relief

Complete this section if you have claimed group relief at box 29 (see note 26). Attach a separate sheet of paper if you need more space. Attach a copy of each surrendering company's notice of consent to the claim unless a special arrangement is in force. Include claims made under the consortium provisions.

Name of surrendering company	**Accounting period** Show the start and end dates of any accounting period which is different from the one to which this return relates.	**Tax reference** Show the Tax Office number and the tax inspector's file reference. If you do not know these, supply whatever information you have that will help us to identify the company, for example the company registration number.	Amount claimed from each company
			£
			£
			£
			£
			£
			£
			£
			£
			£
			£
			£
			£
			£
		Total *This figure should be the same as the one in box 29.*	£

Page 8

Section 8: Overpayments and repayment claims

Complete this section if you are claiming a repayment (including a payment of tax credits). *See note 28* Attach your calculations unless you have already done so in Section 2 or 3.

	£	p
Repayment of corporation tax *Include construction industry deductions repayable*	1000	00
Repayment of income tax *Enclose vouchers to cover the amount of repayment claimed*	823	00
Payment of tax credits *Enclose vouchers to cover the amount of payment claimed*		
Repayment of advance corporation tax *See note 27*		
Total		

Bank details (for person to whom the repayment is to be made)

Repayments of corporation tax (but not income tax, tax credits, advance corporation tax or construction industry deductions) for accounting periods ending after 30 September 1993 are made by direct credit to a bank or building society account. You should provide the following details of the account to which the repayment is to be made.

Bank (or building society)

Branch sort code

Account number

Name of account

Building society reference

Other repayments will be made by payable order.

How total overpayment is to be dealt with

Please show how you want the overpayment to be dealt with.

To be repaid ... 1823 | 00

- **to the company** '✓' [✓]
- **to the nominee shown in the following authority** '✓' [ ]

Surrendered under S102 Finance Act 1989 ...

Note that a repayment of advance corporation tax cannot be surrendered

The required joint notice

- **is attached** [ ]
- **will follow, where an amount is not final.** The Inspector is asked to stop repayment of [ ] until the Notice is received

Payments to a person other than the company

Complete the authority below if you want the repayment to be made to a person other than the company. The Revenue reserves the right not to make a repayment to a nominee and will not normally make a repayment to an overseas nominee.

I, as *(enter status - Company Secretary, Treasurer etc.)*

of

authorise

Name

Address

Postcode

Nominee reference

to receive on the company's behalf the amount due **Signed**

Name in capital letters

Except where a liquidator has been appointed, any person who is authorised to do so may sign this authority on behalf of the company. A photocopy of a signature is not acceptable.

This is the last section of the statutory return form, but it would be helpful if you would complete Sections 9 and 10 if they are applicable.

Page 9

Section 9: Figures brought forward and carried forward

Please complete this section if any of the following items are
- brought forward from the previous accounting period *or*
- available for carry forward from the period to which this return relates.

Please provide a reconciliation of any figures that are not explained elsewhere in your accounts and calculations. Attach a separate sheet of paper if you need more space.

	Total brought forward	Less amount used	Plus net amount available to carry forward from this accounting period	Total to carry forward
Trading losses *include trade charges treated as losses*	£	£	£	£
Schedule D case VI losses	£	£	£	£
Excess management expenses *Include business charges treated as management expenses*	£	£	£	£
Surplus ACT *Enter the figure net of amounts set off or repaid or surrendered to subsidiaries*	£ p	£ p	£ 1717 p 00	£ 1717 p 00
Surplus franked investment income	£ p	£ p	£ p	£ p
Losses allowable against chargeable gains	£	£	£	£
Net non-trade deficits and losses on loan relationships (including interest), exchange fluctuations, and certain financial instruments *See note 8.*	£	£	£	£
Others *Please specify*	£	£	£	£
	£	£	£	£
	£	£	£	£
	£	£	£	£

Answer to Section 2, Task 2.1

Mr Nathaniel King
Income Tax Computation 1998/99

		£	£	£ Tax deducted At Source
Earned Income				
Schedule E (WI)		22,167		2,973
Pension contributions (£600 × 100/77)		(779)		
			21,388	
Investment Income				
Dividends (W2)		41,050		8,210
Building Society Interest (TESSA interest exempt)		13,333		2,667
		54,383		
Less Charges on income				
Deed of Covenant to Oxfam (£154 × 100/77)	200			
Gift Aid Payment to RSPCA (£500 × 100/ 77)	649			
		(849)		
			53,534	
Statutory Total income			74,922	
Less Personal allowance			(4,195)	
Taxable income			£70,727	
				£13,850
Tax Thereon:				
On non savings income:				
4,300 @ 20%			860	
12,044 @ 23%			2,770	
16,344			3,630	
On savings income:				
10,756 @ 20%			2,151	
43,627 @ 40%			17,451	
70,727			23,232	
Less: MCA £1,900 @ 15%			(285)	
Add: tax on charges paid net (£849 × 23%)			195	
Add: tax on pension contributions paid net (£779 × 23%)			179	
			23,321	
Less: tax deducted at source			(13,850)	
Tax due by self-assessment			£9,471	

Workings for Section 2, Task 2.1

(Wl) Schedule E

	£
Salary	12,530
Benefits in Kind	
Car £26,600 × 35% × 2/3	6,207
Fuel> 2,000cc Diesel	1,890
Private medical insurance	625
Business entertaining	1,550
Telephone Rental	100
Telephone calls	500
Institute of Directors fees	120
Computer 20% × £3,650 × 6/12	365
	23,887
Less S198 Claim:	
Telephone calls £500 @ 10%	(50)
Business entertaining	(1,550)
Less Professional subscriptions:	
Institute of Directors fees	(120)
	£22,167

(W2) Dividends

	Net	*Tax Credit*	*Gross*
	£	£	£
Cole Limited	32,340	8,085	40,425
James Brown Limited	500	125	625
	£32,840	£8,210	£41,050

INCOME *for the year ended 5 April 1999*

Q10 **Did you receive any income from UK savings and investments?** NO ☐ YES ✓ — If yes, fill in boxes 10.1 to 10.32 as appropriate. Include only your share from any joint savings and investments.

■ *Interest*

• Interest from UK banks, building societies and deposit takers			
- where **no tax** has been deducted			Taxable amount: 10.1 £
	Amount after tax deducted	Tax deducted	Gross amount before tax
- where **tax has** been deducted	10.2 £ 10,666	10.3 £ 2,667	10.4 £ 13,333
	Amount after tax deducted	Tax deducted	Gross amount before tax
• Interest distributions from UK authorised unit trusts and open-ended investment companies (dividend distributions go below)	10.5 £	10.6 £	10.7 £
• National Savings (other than FIRST Option Bonds and the first £70 of interest from a National Savings Ordinary Account)			Taxable amount: 10.8 £
	Amount after tax deducted	Tax deducted	Gross amount before tax
• National Savings FIRST Option Bonds	10.9 £	10.10 £	10.11 £
	Amount after tax deducted	Tax deducted	Gross amount before tax
• Other income from UK savings and investments (except dividends)	10.12 £	10.13 £	10.14 £

■ *Dividends*

	Dividend/distribution	Tax credit	Dividend/distribution plus credit
• Dividends and other qualifying distributions from UK companies	10.15 £ 32,840	10.16 £ 8,210	10.17 £ 41,050
	Dividend/distribution	Tax credit	Dividend/distribution plus credit
• Dividend distributions from UK authorised unit trusts and open-ended investment companies	10.18 £	10.19 £	10.20 £
	Dividend	Notional tax	Dividend plus notional tax
• Scrip dividends from UK companies	10.21 £	10.22 £	10.23 £
	Dividend	Notional tax	Dividend plus notional tax
• Foreign income dividends from UK companies	10.24 £	10.25 £	10.26 £
	Dividend	Notional tax	Dividend plus notional tax
• Foreign income dividend distributions from UK authorised unit trusts and open-ended investment companies	10.27 £	10.28 £	10.29 £
		Notional tax	Taxable amount
• Non-qualifying distributions and loans written off	10.30 £	10.31 £	10.32 £

RELIEFS *for the year ended 5 April 1999*

Q14 Do you want to claim relief for pension contributions? NO [ ] YES [✓] If yes, fill in boxes 14.1 to 14.17 as appropriate.

Do not include contributions deducted from your pay by your employer to their pension scheme, because tax relief is given automatically. But ***do include*** *your contributions to personal pension schemes.*

■ ***Retirement annuity contracts***

Qualifying payments made in 1998-99	14.1 £	1998-99 payments used in an earlier year	14.2 £	Relief claimed box 14.1 *minus* (boxes 14.2 and 14.3, but not 14.4)
1998-99 payments now to be carried back	14.3 £	Payments brought back from 1999-2000	14.4 £	14.5 £

■ ***Self-employed contributions to personal pension plans***

Qualifying payments made in 1998-99	14.6 £	1998-99 payments used in an earlier year	14.7 £	Relief claimed box 14.6 *minus* (boxes 14.7 and 14.8, but not 14.9)
1998-99 payments now to be carried back	14.8 £	Payments brought back from 1999-2000	14.9 £	14.10 £

■ ***Employee contributions to personal pension plans*** *(include your gross contribution - see the note on box 14.11 in your Tax Return Guide)*

Qualifying payments made in 1998-99	14.11 £ 779	1998-99 payments used in an earlier year	14.12 £	Relief claimed box 14.11 *minus* (boxes 14.12 and 14.13, but not 14.14)
1998-99 payments now to be carried back	14.13 £	Payments brought back from 1999-2000	14.14 £	14.15 £ 779

■ ***Contributions to other pension schemes***

- Amount of contributions to employer's schemes **not deducted** at source from pay — 14.16 £
- Gross amount of free-standing additional voluntary contributions paid in 1998-99 — 14.17 £

Q15 Do you want to claim any of the following reliefs? NO [ ] YES [✓] If yes, fill in boxes 15.1 to 15.12, as appropriate.

Payments you made for vocational training	Amount of payment 15.1 £	
Interest eligible for relief on loans to buy your main home (other than MIRAS)	Amount of payment 15.2 £	
Interest eligible for relief on other qualifying loans	Amount of payment 15.3 £	
Maintenance or alimony payments you have made under a court order, Child Support Agency assessment or legally binding order or agreement	Amount claimed under 'new' rules 15.4 £	
	Amount claimed under 'old' rules up to £1,900 15.5 £	Amount claimed under 'old' rules over £1,900 15.6 £
Subscriptions for Venture Capital Trust shares (up to £100,000)	Amount on which relief claimed 15.7 £	
Subscriptions under the Enterprise Investment Scheme (up to £150,000)	Amount on which relief claimed 15.8 £	
Charitable covenants or annuities	Amount of payment 15.9 £ 154	
Gift Aid and Millennium Gift Aid	Amount of payment 15.10 £ 500	
Post-cessation expenses and losses on relevant discounted securities etc.	Amount of payment 15.11 £	
Payments to a trade union or friendly society for death benefits	Half amount of payment 15.12 £	

ALLOWANCES *for the year ended 5 April 1999*

Q16 *You get your personal allowance of £4,195 automatically.* ***If you were born before 6 April 1934, enter your date of birth in box 21.4*** *- you may get higher age-related allowances.*

Do you want to claim any of the following allowances? NO [ ] YES [✓] If yes, please read pages 23 to 26 of your Tax Return Guide and then fill in boxes 16.1 to 16.28 as appropriate.

- *Blind person's allowance* — Date of registration (if first year of claim) **16.1** / / — Local authority (or other register) **16.2**
- *Transitional allowance* (for some wives with husbands on low income if received in earlier years).
  - Tick to claim and give details in the 'Additional information' box on page 8 *(please see page 23 of your Tax Return Guide for what is needed)* **16.3**
  - If you want to calculate your tax, enter the amount of transitional allowance you can have in box 16.4 **16.4** £
- ***Married couple's allowance for a married man*** *- see page 24 of your Tax Return Guide.*
  - Wife's full name **16.5** PEGGY KING
  - Date of marriage (if after 5 April 1998) **16.6** / /
  - Wife's date of birth (if before 6 April 1934) **16.7** / /
  - Tick box 16.8 if you or your wife have allocated **half** the allowance to her **16.8**
  - *box number 16.9 is not used*
  - Tick box 16.10 if you and your wife have allocated **all** the allowance to her **16.10**
- ***Married couple's allowance for a married woman*** *- see page 24 of your Tax Return Guide.*
  - Date of marriage (if after 5 April 1998) **16.11** / /
  - Husband's full name **16.12**
  - Tick box 16.13 if you or your husband have allocated **half** the allowance to you **16.13**
  - *box number 16.14 is not used*
  - Tick box 16.15 if you and your husband have allocated **all** the allowance to you **16.15**
- ***Additional personal allowance*** *(available in some circumstances if you have a child living with you - see page 25 of your Tax Return Guide).*
  - Tick box 16.16A if you are claiming the married couple's allowance **and** additional personal allowance because your spouse was unable to work, because of illness or disablement, throughout the year ended 5 April 1999 **16.16A**
  - Name of the child claimed for **16.16**
  - Child's date of birth **16.17** / /
  - Tick if child lives with you **16.18**
  - Name of university etc/type of training if the child is 16 or over on 6 April 1998 and in full time education or training **16.19**

Sharing a claim

Name and address of other person claiming **16.20**

Postcode

- Enter your share as a percentage **16.21** %
- If share not agreed, enter the number of days in the year ended 5 April 1999 that the child lived with
  - you **16.22** days
  - other person **16.23** days

- *Widow's bereavement allowance* — Date of your husband's death **16.24** / /
- ***Transfer of surplus allowances*** *- see page 26 of your Tax Return Guide before you fill in boxes 16.25 to 16.28.*
  - Tick if you want your spouse to have your unused allowances **16.25**
  - Tick if you want to have your spouse's unused allowances **16.26**

***Please give details in the 'Additional information' box on page 8** - see page 26 of your Tax Return Guide for what is needed.*

If you want to calculate your tax, enter the amount of the surplus allowance you can have.

- Blind person's **surplus allowance** **16.27** £
- Married couple's **surplus allowance** **16.28** £

OTHER INFORMATION *for the year ended 5 April 1999*

Q17 **Have you already had any 1998-99 tax refunded or set off by your Tax Office or the DSS Benefits Agency?** *Read the notes for box 17.1 on page 26 of your Tax Return Guide*

NO ✓ | YES | If yes, enter the amount of the refund in box 17.1.

17.1 £

Q18 **Do you want to calculate your tax?**

NO | YES ✓ | If yes, do it now and then fill in boxes 18.1 to 18.9. Your Tax Calculation Guide will help.

- Unpaid tax for earlier years included in your tax code for 1998-99 — 18.1 £
- Tax due for 1998-99 included in your tax code for a later year — 18.2 £
- Total tax and Class 4 NIC due for 1998-99 before you made any payments on account *(put the amount in brackets if an overpayment)* — 18.3 £ 9,471
- Tax due for earlier years — 18.4 £
- Tick box 18.5 if you have calculated tax overpaid for earlier years (and enter the amount in the 'Additional information' box on page 8) — 18.5
- Your first payment on account for 1999-2000 *(include the pence)* — 18.6 £ 4,736
- Tick box 18.7 if you are making a claim to reduce your 1999-2000 payments on account and say why in the 'Additional information' box — 18.7

  Tick box 18.8 if you do not need to make 1999-2000 payments on account — 18.8
- 1999-2000 tax you are reclaiming now — 18.9 £

Q19 **Do you want to claim a repayment if you have paid too much tax?** *(If you tick 'No' or the tax you have overpaid is below £10, I will use the amount you are owed to reduce your next tax bill.)*

NO | YES | If yes, fill in boxes 19.1 to 19.12 as appropriate.

Should the repayment (or payment) be sent:

- to you? *Tick box 19.1* — 19.1

or

- to your bank or building society account or other nominee? *Tick box 19.2* — 19.2

If you ticked either box 19.2 or 19.9, fill in boxes 19.3 to 19.8, 19.11 and 19.12 as appropriate.

Your (or your nominee's) bank or building society — 19.3

Branch sort code — 19.4 – –

Account number — 19.5

Name of account — 19.6

Building society ref. — 19.7

If your nominee is your agent, *tick box 19.9 and complete boxes 19.10 to 19.12* — 19.9

Agent's ref. for you — 19.10

I authorise — 19.8 Name of your nominee/agent

Nominee's address — 19.11

Postcode

to receive on my behalf the amount due

This authority must be signed by you. A photocopy of your signature will not do. — 19.12 Signature

Q20 **Are your details on the front of the Tax Return wrong?**

NO ✓ | YES | If yes, please make any corrections on the front of the form.

Q21 **Please give other personal details in boxes 21.1 to 21.6** *This information helps us to be more efficient and effective and may support claims you have made elsewhere in your Tax Return*

Please give a daytime telephone number if convenient. It is often simpler to phone if we need to ask you about your Tax Return.

Your telephone number — 21.1

or, if you prefer, your agent's telephone number — 21.2

(also give your agent's name and reference in the 'Additional information' box on page 8)

Enter your first two forenames — 21.5 NATHANIEL

Say if you are single, married, widowed, divorced or separated — 21.3 MARRIED

Date of birth — 21.4 / /

Enter your date of birth if you are self-employed, or you were born before 6 April 1934, or you have ticked the 'Yes' box in Question 14, or you are claiming relief for Venture Capital Trust subscriptions

Enter your National Insurance number (if known) — 21.6 NB 52 26 79 C

Inland Revenue

Income for the year ended 5 April 1999

EMPLOYMENT

Fill in these boxes first

Name: NATHANIEL KING

Tax reference:

If you want help, look up the box numbers in the Notes

Details of employer

Employer's PAYE reference **1.1** 299 IC21

Employer's name **1.2** COLE LTD

Date employment started (only if between 6 April 1998 and 5 April 1999) **1.3** / /

Date finished (only if between 6 April 1998 and 5 April 1999) **1.4** / /

Employer's address **1.5** UNIT 1, BARCHESTER TRADING ESTATE, BARCHESTER

Postcode

Tick box 1.6 if you were a director of the company **1.6** ✓

and, if so, tick box 1.7 if it was a close company **1.7**

Income from employment

- ***Money*** *- see Notes, page EN3*

		Before tax
• Payments from P60 (or P45 or pay slips)		**1.8** £ 12,350
• Payments not on P60 etc.	- tips	**1.9** £
	- other payments (excluding expenses shown below and lump sums and compensation payments or benefits shown overleaf)	**1.10** £

	Tax deducted
• UK tax deducted from payments in boxes 1.8 to 1.10	**1.11** £ 2973

- ***Benefits and expenses*** *- see Notes, pages EN3 to EN6. If any benefits connected with termination of employment were received, or enjoyed, after that termination and were from a **former** employer you need to complete Help Sheet IR204, available from the Orderline. Do not enter such benefits here.*

	Amount		Amount
• Assets transferred/payments made for you	**1.12** £	• Vans	**1.18** £
• Vouchers/credit cards	**1.13** £	• Interest-free and low-interest loans	**1.19** £
• Living accommodation	**1.14** £	• Mobile telephones	**1.20** £
• Mileage allowance	**1.15** £	• Private medical or dental insurance	**1.21** £ 625
• Company cars	**1.16** £ 6207	• Other benefits	**1.22** £ 485
• Fuel for company cars	**1.17** £ 1890	• Expenses payments received and balancing charges	**1.23** £ 2150

SA101

Income from employment continued

■ ***Lump sums and compensation payments or benefits including such payments and benefits from a former employer***
Note that 'lump sums' here includes any contributions which your employer made to an unapproved retirement benefits scheme

*You must read page EN6 of the Notes **before** filling in boxes 1.24 to 1.30*

Reliefs

- £30,000 exemption — **1.24** £
- Foreign service and disability — **1.25** £
- Retirement and death lump sums — **1.26** £

Taxable lump sums

- From box H of *Help Sheet IR204* — **1.27** £
- From box Q of *Help Sheet IR204* — **1.28** £
- From box R of *Help Sheet IR204* — **1.29** £
- Tax deducted from payments in boxes 1.27 to 1.29 — Tax deducted **1.30** £

■ ***Foreign earnings not taxable in the UK in year ended 5 April 1999** - see Notes, page EN6* — **1.31** £

■ ***Expenses you incurred in doing your job** - see Notes, starting on page EN6*

- Travel and subsistence costs — **1.32** £
- Fixed deductions for expenses — **1.33** £
- Professional fees and subscriptions — **1.34** £ 120
- Other expenses and capital allowances — **1.35** £ 1600
- Tick box 1.36 if the figure in box 1.32 includes travel between your home and a permanent workplace — **1.36**

■ ***Foreign Earnings Deduction*** — **1.37** £

■ ***Foreign tax for which tax credit relief not claimed*** — **1.38** £

Additional information

Now fill in any other supplementary Pages that apply to you.
Otherwise, go back to page 2 in your Tax Return and finish filling it in.

Answer to Section 3, Task 3.1

Capital Gains Tax Payable by Mrs Peggy King

	£
Shares in Morse plc (W1)	1,407
London Flat (W2)	13,550
Painting (W3)	(2,120)
Desk	Small chattels exemption
Sports car	Exempt
Total net gains	12,837
Less Annual exemption 1998/99	(6,800)
Taxable gains	£6,037
Tax thereon	
£4,300 × 20%	860
£1,737 × 23%	400
CGT Payable	£1,260

Workings for Section 3, Task 3.1

(W1) Shares in Morse plc
Gain on 1985 pool shares

		Total Gain
		£
Proceeds $\frac{1,250}{1,375} \times £8,250$	7,500	
Less cost	(5,000)	
Unindexed gain	2,500	
Less Indexation allowance	(1,234)	
Net gain	£1,266	1,266

Gain on 1982 Pool shares

	Cost	MV82	
	£	£	
Proceeds $\frac{125}{1,375} \times £8,250$	750	750	
Less Cost/MV82	(200)	(300)	
Unindexed gain	550	450	
Less Indexation allowance			
$£300 \times (1.029) \left(\frac{161.2 - 79.44}{79.44}\right)$	(309)	(309)	
Net Gain	£241	£141	
Take lower gain = £141			141
Total gain on sale of shares			£1,407

1985 Pool working

Date	No	Cost	Cost plus indexation
		£	£
15.9.90	1,000	5,000	5,000
Bonus 1:4 (21.6.94)	250	nil	nil
	1,250		
Disposal:			
Indexed Rise			
$£5,000 \times \frac{161.2 - 129.3}{129.3}$			1,234
		5,000	6,234
Disposal January 1999	(1,250)	(5,000)	(6,234)

1982 Pool working

Date	No	Cost	MV82
		£	£
10.1.72	100	200	300
Bonus (21.6.94) 1:4	25	nil	nil
	125	£200	£300

Workings for Section 3, Task 3.1

(W2) London flat

	£
Proceeds	120,000
Less Costs of sale (no indexation)	(5,000)
Acquisition cost	(50,000)
Unindexed gain	65,000
Less Indexation allowance	
$£50{,}000 \times (1{,}029) \left(\frac{161.2 - 79.44}{79.44}\right) =$	(51,450)
Net gain	£13,550

(W3) Painting by E Costello

	£
Proceeds	10,000
Less: Costs of acquisition	(120)
Acquisition cost	(12,000)
Unindexed loss	£(2,120)

No indexation allowance available, because a loss cannot be increased by indexation.

Answer to Section 3, Task 3.2

(a) The answer is to be in letter format, as requested in the assessment memorandum. Marks will therefore be allocated for communication skills.

A Handel
Garrett, Turner & Co
Debit Street
Barchester

6 December 1999

Mrs P King
King House
Queen Street
Barchester

Dear Peggy

Investment of sale proceeds

Further to your letter of 25 November 1999, concerning your investment plans, I set out below my advice concerning:

—reduction of the CGT bill for 1998/99;
—Income tax implications;
—Capital gains tax implications, for each of the proposed investments

(1) Reduction in CGT due for 1998/99

In order to reduce the CGT due the reinvestments made would have to be eligible for some form of CGT relief. The eligibility for the relief will come from either the subject matter of the sale or the subject matter of the reinvestment property, or both.

Items sold:
None of the items sold specifically entitle you to a particular relief. However all of the items sold entitle you to receive EIS deferral relief, if you subscribe for new ordinary shares in an unquoted trading company.

Items Purchased:
Of the items purchased, the shares in Cole Limited, an unquoted trading company, are eligible for EIS deferral relief. The reinvestment should be made within the period of 12 months before and up to three years after making the gain. The effect of the relief is to defer the gain until the shares are sold, or cease to qualify. You can limit the claim, so that only gains in excess of your annual exemption are deferred. Please note the relief is not available if you buy shares from another shareholder.

(2) Income tax implications:

All possible investments would yield income. As you have no income and are not using your personal allowance, the first £4,195 (less the small amount of dividend income you receive on your shares in Cole Limited) would be tax free as covered by the personal allowance, and income would then be taxed at 20% (for the next £4,300) and then at 23% (for the next £22,800) and thereafter at 40%.

(a) Long term lets of UK property:
Rental profit, assessable as Schedule A, is calculated as rents less eligible expenses on an accruals basis. All profits and losses on different properties would be pooled. If property is let furnished than additional expenses may be available and capital allowances or a wear and tear allowance (10% gross rent less water rates) may be claimed.

(b) Holiday lets:
Income assessed as above and taxed under Schedule A. Criteria need to be met for the rents to be classed as furnished holiday accommodation, namely:

UK, furnished property, let on a commercial basis for 70 days a tax year, during a period of at least 140 days for which the property was available for let.

The property is not normally let for more than 31 consecutive days to the same person during any seven month period.

The advantages of being furnished holiday accommodation are that:

- profits are earned income for pensions purposes
- losses are deductible as trading losses
- CGT reliefs are available, see below.

(c) Cole Limited shares:
Income received will be in the form of dividends. They are received net of a 20% tax credit. To the extent that dividends fall within your personal allowance, you will be able to reclaim the tax credit. If the income falls within your lower and basic rate bands (the 20% and 23% bands) you will have no more tax to pay as dividends in these bands are taxed at 20%. If any of the dividends fall within your 40% band then an additional 20% tax will be payable, as dividends falling within the 40% band are taxable at 40%.

(3) CGT on sale

Sale proceeds, less original cost (reduced by any gain deferred by EIS deferral relief for shares, if claimed) will produce the net chargeable gain. The first £6,800 (1998/99 rate) of gains will be tax free due to the annual exemption. Taper relief is available at 5% per annum after 3 years, except that a higher rate of taper rellief would be available on any gains on furnished holiday lettings.

If you have invested in furnished holiday lettings you may be able to claim rollover relief if you acquire a new business asset, or retirement relief if you are over 50 at the date of sale.

Bed and Breakfast accommodation

If you rent out part of your own home in the form of furnished accommodation, and the gross rents received do not exceed £4,250, the rents and expenses are ignored under 'rent a room' relief. There is no taxable income and no allowable loss.

If you need any further advice, or clarification of any of the above points, please do not hesitate to contact me.

Yours sincerely

Alison

Alison Handel
Partner
Garrett, Turner & Co

PREPARING TAXATION COMPUTATIONS

ANSWERS - JUNE 1997

SECTION 1

Task 1.1

Nuts and Bolts Limited
Calculation of capital gains for the year ended 31 March 1999

1. Sale of Manchester factory

		Cost		*MV'82*
		£		£
Sale Proceeds (April 1998)		500,000		500,000
Less: costs of sale		(1,500)		(1,500)
Less: original cost		(100,000)		(125,000)
Unindexed gain		398,500		373,500
Less: Indexation allowance				
$£125{,}000 \times \frac{161.2 - 79.44}{79.44}$ (1.029)		(128,625)		(128,625)
Gain		£269,875		£244,875
Lower gain taken			£244,875	

2. Part disposal of plot of land at Wigan

	£
Sale Proceeds (December 1998)	100,200
Less: original cost	
$£50{,}000 \times \frac{A}{A+B}$	
Where A = the value of the part sold	
and B = the value of the part retained	
Therefore:	
$£50{,}000 \times \frac{100{,}200}{100{,}200 + 50{,}000}$	(33,356)
Unindexed gain	66,844
Less: Indexation allowance	
$33{,}356 \times \frac{164.1 - 153.0}{153.0}$ (0.073)	(2,435)
Gain	£64,409

Total Gains chargeable to corporation tax:	
Sale of Manchester factory	244,875
Sale of half of land at Wigan	64,409
	£309,284

Task 1.2

Nuts and Bolts Limited
Corporation tax Computation for the year ended 31 March 1999

		£	£
Schedule D Case I (see Working)		285,758	
Less: S 393(1) trading losses brought forward		(5,000)	
		280,758	
Schedule A		12,000	
Chargeable gains (Task 1.1)	309,284		
Less: capital losses brought forward of	(10,000)		
		299,284	
			592,042
Less: Charges on income			
Deed of covenant to The Red Cross			(10,000)
PCTCT			582,042

Corporation Tax Payable:

The PCTCT lies above the lower limit and below the upper limit for small companies rate purposes and the company is therefore taxable at the marginal rate:

	£
FY 1998:	
£582,042 @ 31%	180,433
Less: Marginal relief 1/40 × [£750,000 – £582,042]	(4,199)
	176,234
Less: ACT paid (£2,000 @ 20%)	(400)
Mainstream Corporation tax payable	175,834

Workings for Section 1 Task 1.2

Nuts and Bolts Limited
Adjustment of Profit for the purposes of Schedule D Case I

	£	£
Net profit per accounts		646,533
Add:		
Depreciation	47,450	
Balancing charge on sale of Manchester factory	64,800	
Entertaining customers	15,500	
Gifts of alcohol to customers	7,200	
Increase in general bad debt provision (25,000 - 2,400)	22,600	
Legal fees re sale of Manchester factory	1,500	
Charge on income: deed of covenant	10,000	
		169,050
		815,583

Less:		
Profit on sale of fixed assets	493,000	
Capital Allowances (below)	24,825	
Rental Income	12,000	
		529,825
Schedule D Case I profit		285,758

Capital Allowance Computation

		General Pool	*FA80/ Cheap Car Pool*	*Expensive Cars Vauxhall Cavalier*	*Expensive Cars Ford Mondeo*	*Total Allowances*
	£	£	£	£	£	£
TWDV at 1 April 1998		3,400	6,000	7,500	nil	
Additions			8,000		15,000	
Disposals		(500) (1,000)	(1,000)	(5,000)		
		1,900	13,000	2,500	15,000	
WDA @ 25%		(475)	(3,250)			3,725
WDA Restricted					(3,000)	3,000
Balancing (allowance) /charge				(2,500)		2,500
Additions qualifying for FYA (25,000 + 14,000)	39,000					
FYA (40%)	(15,600)					15,600
		23,400				
TWDV at 31 March 1999		24,825	9,750	£nil	12,000	24,825

Balancing Allowance/Charge on disposal of Manchester factory

The building has been sold for more than its original cost of £90,000, and had been in industrial use throughout its period of ownership. The result of the sale is therefore a balancing charge of £64,800 (the amount of industrial buildings allowance already given (£90,000 – TWDV of £25,200)).

Limits for small companies rate purposes:

As Nuts and Bolts Limited has one associated company the limits for small companies rate purposes need to be divided by two.

Upper limit = £1,500,000/2 = £750,000

Lower limit = £300,000/2 = £150,000

Profits are £582,042, and fall between the above upper and lower limits, therefore the company is taxed at full rate with marginal relief.

Inland Revenue

Page 1

Corporation Tax Return
Version 3

This form, or an approved substitute version of it, must be used whenever a company is required to do so, by a *Notice to deliver a Corporation Tax Return (form CT203)*. This return sets out the information we need and provides a standard format for calculations.

You should read this return form along with your *Notice to deliver a Corporation Tax Return (form CT203)* and *Filling in your Corporation Tax Return (leaflet CT200 Notes)* which you should have received with this form. The notes referred to throughout can be found in the leaflet *CT200 Notes*. You should contact your Tax Office if you need more help.

'Company' means any body chargeable to corporation tax, whether incorporated or not. This definition includes clubs, associations and voluntary organisations.

Sections to be completed
Members' clubs, associations and voluntary organisations - It is likely that you will only have to complete Sections 1 and 2. For further guidance see note 1 in the *Notes*.

All companies - including clubs, etc. - You will not need to complete every Section, but you **must** complete the Declaration and Section 1 on this page. The *Notes* will help you decide whether you should complete the mutually exclusive *Short return* at Section 2 or the *Detailed return* at Section 3. Sections 9 and 10 are optional but you are asked to complete them if they are relevant to the company.

It is important that you read the *Notes* before completing any part of this form.

What to do when you have completed the return
- Make sure you have completed and signed the Declaration, then
- staple together the pages you have completed and attach any supporting calculations
- send these together with the relevant company accounts and, where prepared, directors' and auditors' reports, to your Tax Office using the envelope provided (see Note 3 for the date by which you should do this)
- pay any outstanding corporation tax (as you have shown at box box 65), as advised on the payslip attached to your *Notice to deliver a Corporation Tax Return (form CT203)*. Interest is charged on tax paid later than nine months and one day after the end of an accounting period. Tax is due without the making of an assessment.

Remember - *Your tax return is not complete unless you send relevant accounts and documentation with this form. Penalties may be charged if your return, or any part of it, is late or incorrect.*

As soon as your figures are agreed
- we will send you an assessment setting out the tax position for the accounting period - unless there are no figures to assess
- we will issue an amended assessment if you have already received an estimated assessment and you have appealed against it.

Section 1: Summary

The company name

NUTS AND BOLTS LIMITED

The company address - only if changed since last return made.
Enter the UK registered office address, or the UK address if the company does not have a registered office. If the company does not have premises in the UK show the address of the person making the return.

Company registration number *(if registered)*

0987654

Reference
Enter the reference number shown on the *Notice to deliver a Corporation Tax Return (form CT203)*

XXX / 12345 / 91011

Corporation tax accounting period covered by this return
Cannot exceed 12 months. Enter start and end dates.

From 01 / 04 / 98 To 31 / 03 / 99

If this period is not an accounting period of the company for corporation tax purposes (see note 2) put an 'X' in the box below, complete the Declaration to the right and return this form to your Tax Office. You do not need to complete the rest of this Section or other Sections of this form in these circumstances. ☐

Profits chargeable *(Enter the firgure from box 30). If there are none enter '0'.*

£ 582,042

Corporation tax due
(Enter the figure from box 61 minus any entry in box 64). If none is due enter '0.00'.

£ 175,834 p 00

Put an X in the appropriate box

Have you completed Section 8 (Repayments)? Yes ☐ No ☒

Is the company name different from that shown in the *Notice (form CT203)*? Yes ☐ No ☒

Declaration

Enter here the page numbers you are attaching

2, 3, 6, 9

Put an 'X' in the appropriate boxes to show the documents you are enclosing
- a copy of the accounts for the period to which this return relates ☒
- a copy of the company accounts for a different period ☐
- no accounts ☐
- say why not
- calculations showing how the entries in the return form have been arrived at. ☒

I declare that to the best of my knowledge and belief the return on this page and the pages attached is correct and complete.

Signature

Except where a liquidator has been appointed, the company secretary, treasurer, or any other person who is authorised to do so may sign this declaration on behalf of the company. A photocopy of a signature is not acceptable.

Date / /

Name *(in capital letters)*

Status *(company secretary, treasurer, liquidator etc.)*

Section 2: Short return

You may complete this section if
- it covers all the entries you need to make and
- each entry, including the company's total income and deductions, is less than £10 million.

In all other cases, or if you prefer, complete Section 3 instead. You should enclose an explanation and calculations of any figures which you have estimated or which are not immediately recognisable from the company's accounts.

The figures to be entered are those adjusted for tax purposes, after deducting capital allowances and adding balancing charges where appropriate. Section 4 should also be completed if capital allowances are claimed.
Please do not enter '0's where the company did not have the source specified in the return form.

	Box	£	Box	£
Trading profits *See note 5*	1	285,758		
Trading losses brought forward *Only include losses made in the same trade. Include charges treated as losses.* ***Do not enter an amount larger than is needed to cover the profits in box 1.*** *See note 6*	2	5000		
Net trading profit *(box 1 minus box 2). If box 2 equals box 1, enter '0'. Leave this box blank if there are no trading profits in box 1*			3	280,758
Trading losses of this accounting period *Where there is more than one trade give total for all trades. Do not set box 4 losses against box 1 profits, claim at box 22 against total profits.*	4			
Profits and gains from non-trading loan relationships and other Schedule D Case III income *Include interest and other profits and gains from non-trading loan relationships even if tax has been deducted. Complete box 57 to claim credit for income tax deducted. You will need to complete the* **Detailed return** *at Section 3 if you have deficits on non-trading loan relationships from this, earlier or later accounting periods to include. See note 8*			6	
Income within Schedule D Case VI - for example furnished lettings *Enter the figure net of allowable losses brought forward. Exclude income you enter in box 12. See note 7*			9	
Income from which income tax has been deducted - for example building society interest *Enter the gross amount before tax. Exclude any amount included in box 6 above. Complete box 57 to claim credit for income tax deducted. See note 9*			10	
Income from UK land and buildings *Enter the amount net of allowable expenses brought forward. Exclude income in box 9 above. See note 10*			12	12000
Chargeable gains *See note 11*				
Gross gains	13	309,284		
Allowable losses *Include any losses brought forward but do not enter an amount larger than the amount of gross gains in box 13 above.*	14	10,000		
Net chargeable gains *(box 13 minus box 14) If box 14 equals box 13, enter '0'*			15	299,284
Profits *(total of boxes 3, 6, 9, 10, 12 and 15)*			17	590042
Relief for trading losses of this or of a later period *Put an 'X' in box 21 if amounts carried back from later accounting periods are included in box 22. See note 12*	21	☐	22	
Profits before charges *(box 17 minus box 22)*			26	590,042
Charges paid *Do not enter an amount larger than is needed to cover profits in box 26. See note 13*			27	10,000
Profits chargeable to corporation tax *(box 26 minus box 27)* ***Copy this figure into the box provided in Section 1 on page 1, and also into the box at the top of page 3***			30	580,042

The short return is continued on page 3

Page 3

Profits chargeable to corporation tax

Enter the figure brought forward from page 2, box 30 ... £ 582,042

If you claim tax is chargeable at the small companies' rate, or if you are claiming marginal small companies' relief, complete boxes 31 - 35. If there are no associated companies please enter '0' against the relevant financial year. *See note 15*

Franked investment income and foreign income dividends arising in the period covered by the return. *See note 15* ... 31 £

Number of companies associated with this company in the/each financial year covered by this return
Exclude this company. See note 15 ...

	Financial year		Number of associated companies
32	1998	33	1
34	19	35	

Corporation tax chargeable *See note 16*

	Financial years beginning 1 April		Amounts of profit £		Rates of tax *See note 16*		Tax £	p
36	1998	37	582042	38	31 • 00	39	180433	00
43	19	44		45	•	46		

Total corporation tax chargeable *(box 39 plus box 46)* ... 50 180,433 • 00

Marginal small companies' relief
Attach your computation (see notes 15, 16 and 29) ... 51 £ 4199 • p 00

Advance corporation tax restricted if necessary under **Section 239(2) ICTA 1988**
Put an 'X' in box 53 if amounts carried back from later accounting periods are included. See note 17. 53 [ ] 54 400 • 00

Total of boxes 51 and 54
Total must not be larger than entry in box 50. Restrict if necessary ... 55 4599 • 00

Net corporation tax chargeable *(box 50 minus box 55)* ... 56 175,834 • 00

Calculation of tax outstanding or overpaid

Income tax deducted from gross income included in return
Do not include deductions used to cover income tax for which the company was liable to account to the Inland Revenue on payments it has made. See note 18 ... 57

Corporation tax due

Box 56 minus box 57. If box 57 equals or is greater than box 56, enter '0.00' and go to box 59. Copy the figure in box 61 to the box provided in Section 1 on page 1. See note 20 ... 61 175,834 • 00

Income tax repayable to the company *(box 57 minus box 56). Complete Section 8 on page 8. Do not complete unless you are making a claim. See note 28*... 59

Corporation tax already paid (and not repaid). *See note 21* ... 63

Corporation tax outstanding *(box 61 minus box 63). This amount is payable to the Accounts Office. If box 63 equals or is greater than box 61, enter '0.00' and go to box 66. See note 23* ... 65 175,834 • 00

Corporation tax overpaid *(box 63 minus box 61). Complete Section 8 on page 8 also. See note 28* ... 66

This is the last page of the short return

Section 4: Claims for capital allowances and details of balancing charges arising

You must complete this section if you want to claim capital allowances, whether or not those allowances are reflected elsewhere in the return. You should also show balancing charges taken into account in the short or detailed return. Show details of qualifying expenditure on which writing-down allowances may be claimed, even if you do not want to claim any allowances for this period. *See note 25*

Notice of expenditure on machinery and plant *See note 25*

Expenditure on which first year allowance is claimed £		Qualifying expenditure on long life assets on which writing down allowances may be claimed £		Qualifying expenditure on other assets on which writing down allowances may be claimed £	
68	39000	91		69	23,000

Charges and allowances included in calculation of trading profit or losses

		Balancing charges £		Capital allowances £
Cars *Including leased out and "expensive" cars*	70		71	8,750
Machinery and plant *- long life assets*	92		93	
- other	72		73	16,075
Industrial buildings and structures *Including qualifying hotels, and commercial buildings and hotels in enterprise zones*	74	64,500	75	
Other charges and allowances *For example agricultural buildings, mineral extraction, scientific research, patents*	76		77	
Charges and allowances not included in calculation of trading profit or losses	78		79	

Section 5: Particulars of advance corporation tax and surplus advance corporation tax

Complete this section if you have surplus advance corporation tax brought forward or have paid advance corporation tax (and it has not been repaid) in respect of qualifying distributions made in the period covered by this return.

	£	p
Particulars of advance corporation tax paid	400	00
Particulars of any surplus advance corporation tax brought forward		

Section 6: Amounts claimed as group relief

Complete this section if you have claimed group relief at box 29 (see note 26). Attach a separate sheet of paper if you need more space. Attach a copy of each surrendering company's notice of consent to the claim unless a special arrangement is in force. Include claims made under the consortium provisions.

Name of surrendering company	**Accounting period** Show the start and end dates of any accounting period which is different from the one to which this return relates.	**Tax reference** Show the Tax Office number and the tax inspector's file reference. If you do not know these, supply whatever information you have that will help us to identify the company, for example the company registration number.	Amount claimed from each company
			£
			£
			£
			£
			£
			£
			£
			£
			£
			£
			£
			£
			£
		Total	£

This figure should be the same as the one in box 29.

Page 9

Section 9: Figures brought forward and carried forward

Please complete this section if any of the following items are
- brought forward from the previous accounting period *or*
- available for carry forward from the period to which this return relates.

Please provide a reconciliation of any figures that are not explained elsewhere in your accounts and calculations. Attach a separate sheet of paper if you need more space.

	Total brought forward	Less amount used	Plus net amount available to carry forward from this accounting period	Total to carry forward
Trading losses *include trade charges treated as losses*	£ 5000	£ 5000	£	£ NIL
Schedule D case VI losses	£	£	£	£
Excess management expenses *Include business charges treated as management expenses*	£	£	£	£
Surplus ACT *Enter the figure net of amounts set off or repaid or surrendered to subsidiaries*	£ p	£ p	£ p	£ p
Surplus franked investment income	£ p	£ p	£ p	£ p
Losses allowable against chargeable gains	£ 10000	£ 10000	£	£ NIL
Net non-trade deficits and losses on loan relationships (including interest), exchange fluctuations, and certain financial instruments *See note 8.*	£	£	£	£
Others *Please specify*	£	£	£	£
	£	£	£	£
	£	£	£	£
	£	£	£	£

SECTION 2

Task 2.1

1. (a) **Calculation of Schedule E Earnings for Mr Frederick Fuse for 1998/99**

	£
Salary	41,000
Car benefit	
Vauxhall Cavalier £14,003 x 35% = 4,901 × 2/3	3,267
Fuel Benefit	
Vauxhall Cavalier Petrol 1,401cc – 2,000cc = 1,280	1,280
Private medical insurance	865
Entertainment	3,000
Home telephone Rental	100
Calls	600
Mobile Telephone	200
Asset made available for private use (computer)	
£10,000 × 20% = £2,000 × 4/12 =	667
	50,979
Less S 198 claim for expenses incurred wholly, exclusively and necessarily in the course of employment	
Telephone calls (£600 x 50%)	(300)
Entertaining costs	(2,900)
Schedule E Earnings	47,779

Task 2.1 (continued)

1. (b) **Explanation of the calculation of Mr Fuse's benefits in kind**

Car benefit:
If a company car is available for private use to an employee the employee is taxed on 35% of the manufacturer's list price of the car per fiscal year.

If the employee has a reasonable level of business mileage the benefit is reduced:

2,500 to 17,999 business miles per tax year—reduce the car benefit figure by one third
18,000 or more business miles per annum—reduce the car benefit figure by two thirds

If a car is only available for part of the tax year, then the car benefit figure is proportionately reduced.

Fuel Benefit
If an employer pays for an employee's private fuel costs the employee is taxed on a flat rate benefit depending on the cc of the car's engine and the type of fuel provided (petrol or diesel). The benefit tables are determined for each tax year.

Again if fuel is only available for part of the fiscal year the benefit is reduced proportionately.

Expenses reimbursed (e.g. entertaining and home telephone)
The employee is taxed on the amount of expense reimbursed subject to a deduction under S198 ICTA 1988 for expenses incurred wholly, exclusively and necessarily in the course of the employment.

As far as home telephone expenses are concerned, the S198 claim can only extend to the cost of the telephone calls. The rental of the phone line is not deemed to be exclusively for business purposes.

Private medical insurance
Where there are no specific rates for benefits, e.g. medical insurance cover, the employee is taxed on the cost to the employer of providing the benefit.

Mobile telephone
Regardless of the actual private telephone costs incurred there is a flat rate benefit for mobile telephones available for private use, of £200 per fiscal year.

Assets made available for private use
Any asset made available for private use is assessed on 20% of its market value, when first made available, each fiscal year.

2. **Explanation of the effect of contributions towards private use of a company car and car fuel**

Partial contributions towards the private use of a company car reduce the car benefit chargeable. Therefore if a contribution of £100 x 12 months of £1,200 per annum would lead to a deduction of £1,200 from the 1999/00 car benefit figure. Partial contributions towards the cost of private fuel do not reduce the value of the fuel benefit assessable. Only making good the costs of all private fuel would reduce the benefit (to £nil).

Task 2.2

Mr Frederick Fuse
Income Tax Computation 1998/99

	£	£	*Tax deducted At Source* £
Earned Income			
Schedule E (see Task 2.1)	47,779		15,300
Less: Personal pension contributions			
(£165 × 12=£1,980 × 100/77)	(2,571)		
		45,208	
Investment Income			
Savings Income			
Dividends (1,000 + 2,625)	3,625		725
Building society interest	5,625		1,125
Bank interest	1,375		275
National Savings Bank interest (£165 – £70)	95		nil
Non Savings income			
		10,720	
Less Charges on income			
Statutory Total income		55,928	
Less Personal allowance		(4,195)	
Taxable income		51,733	17,425

Tax Thereon:

Note tax should be calculated separately on savings and non savings income, but as all savings income is in the 40% band there is no need to do so as it will all be taxed at 40%.

4,300 @ 20%	860
22,800 @ 23%	5,244
24,633 @ 40%	9,853
£51,733	15,957
Less: married couples allowance £1,900 @ 15%	(285)
Add: basic rate tax deducted on pension contributions paid net (£2,571 @ 23%)	591
	16,263
Less: tax paid at source (above)	(17,425)
Tax repayable	(1,162)

Note: interest on TESSAs is free of income tax

Income for the year ended 5April 1999

Inland Revenue **SELF-EMPLOYMENT**

Fill in these boxes first

Name: MRS FIONA FUSE

Tax reference: FF 205

If you want help, look up the box numbers in the Notes

Business details

Name of business
3.1 FUSE'S FURRY ANIMALS

Description of business
3.2 MANUFACTURE AND DISTRIBUTION OF SOFT TOYS

Address of business
3.3 25 TOWN ROAD
LANCHESTER

Postcode

Accounting period - *read the Notes, page SEN2 before filling in these boxes*

Start 3.4 01 / 01 / 98

End 3.5 31 / 12 / 98

- Tick box 3.5A if you entered details for all relevant accounting periods on last year's Tax Return and boxes 3.11 to 3.70 will be blank — 3.5A
- Tick box 3.6 if details in boxes 3.1 or 3.3 have changed since your last Tax Return — 3.6
- Tick box 3.7 if your accounts do not cover the period from the last accounting date (explain why in the 'Additional information' box below) — 3.7
- Tick box 3.8A if your accounting date has changed (only if this is a permanent change and you want it to count for tax) — 3.8A
- Tick box 3.8B if this is the second or further change (explain why you have not used the same date as last year in the 'Additional information' box) — 3.8B
- Date of commencement if after 5 April 1996 — 3.9 10 / 04 / 96
- Date of cessation if before 6 April 1999 — 3.10 / /

Additional information

Income and expenses - annual turnover below £15,000

If your annual turnover is £15,000 or more, ***ignore*** *boxes 3.11 to 3.13.* *Now fill in Page SE2*

If your annual turnover is below £15,000, ***fill in boxes 3.11 to 3.13 instead of Page SE2****. Read the Notes, page SEN2.*

- Turnover, other business receipts and goods etc. taken for personal use (and balancing charges) — 3.11 £
- Expenses allowable for tax (including capital allowances) — 3.12 £

Net profit (put figure in brackets if a loss) — box 3.11 minus box 3.12 — 3.13 £

Now fill in Page SE3

SA103

Income and expenses - annual turnover £15,000 or more

You must fill in this Page if your annual turnover is £15,000 or more - read the Notes, page SEN2

If you were registered for VAT, do the figures in boxes 3.16 to 3.51, include VAT? **3.14** [ ] or exclude VAT? **3.15** [ ]

Sales/business income (turnover) **3.16** £ 19,396

	Disallowable expenses included in boxes 3.33 to 3.50	Total expenses	
• Cost of sales	3.17 £	3.33 £ 577	
• Construction industry subcontractor costs	3.18 £	3.34 £	
• Other direct costs	3.19 £	3.35 £	box 3.16 *minus* (box 3.33 + box 3.34 + box 3.35)
Gross profit/(loss)			3.36 £ 18,819
Other income/profits			3.37 £
• Employee costs	3.20 £	3.38 £ 3673	
• Premises costs	3.21 £	3.39 £ 3970	
• Repairs	3.22 £	3.40 £ 31	
• General administrative expenses	3.23 £ 204	3.41 £ 366	
• Motor expenses	3.24 £ 308	3.42 £ 770	
• Travel and subsistence	3.25 £	3.43 £	
• Advertising, promotion and entertainment	3.26 £	3.44 £ 36	
• Legal and professional costs	3.27 £	3.45 £	
• Bad debts	3.28 £	3.46 £	
• Interest	3.29 £	3.47 £	
• Other finance charges	3.30 £	3.48 £	
• Depreciation and loss/(profit) on sale	3.31 £ 2739	3.49 £ 2739	
• Other expenses	3.32 £ 140	3.50 £ 425	total of boxes 3.38 to 3.50
	Put the total of boxes 3.17 to 3.32 in **box 3.53 below**	Total expenses	3.51 £ 12010
			boxes 3.36 + 3.37 *minus* box 3.51
Net profit/(loss)			3.52 £ 6809

Tax adjustments to net profit or loss

	total of boxes 3.17 to 3.32	
• Disallowable expenses	3.53 £ 3391	
• Goods etc. taken for personal use and other adjustments (apart from disallowable expenses) that increase profits	3.54 £	
• Balancing charges	3.55 £	boxes 3.53 + 3.54 + 3.55
Total additions to net profit (deduct from net loss)		3.56 £ 3391
• Capital allowances	3.57 £ 2500	boxes 3.57 + 3.58
• Deductions from net profit (add to net loss)	3.58 £	3.59 £ 2500
		boxes 3.52 + 3.56 *minus* box 3.59
Net business profit for tax purposes (put figure in brackets if a loss)		3.60 £ 7700

You must fill in this Page (leave blank any boxes that do not apply to you)

Capital allowances - summary

	Capital allowances	Balancing charge
• Motor cars (Separate calculations must be made for each motor car costing more than £12,000 and for cars used partly for private motoring.)	3.61 £ 1000	3.62 £
• Other business plant and machinery	3.63 £ 1500	3.64 £
• Agricultural or Industrial Buildings Allowance (A separate calculation must be made for each block of expenditure.)	3.65 £	3.66 £
• Other capital allowances claimed (Separate calculations must be made.)	3.67 £	3.68 £
	total of column above	total of column above
Total capital allowances/balancing charges	3.69 £ 2500	3.70 £

Adjustments to arrive at taxable profit or loss

Basis period begins 3.71 01 / 01 / 98 and ends 3.72 31/ 12 / 98

- Tick box 3.72A if the figure in box 3.88 is provisional 3.72A
- Tick box 3.72B if the special arrangements for certain trades detailed in the guidance notes apply 3.72B

Profit or loss of this account for tax purposes (box 3.13 or 3.60) 3.73 £ 7700

Adjustment to arrive at profit or loss for this basis period 3.74 £

- Overlap profit brought forward 3.75 £ 2301 • Deduct overlap relief used this year 3.76 £
- Overlap profit carried forward 3.77 £ 2301

Adjustment for farmers' averaging (see Notes, page SEN8 if you made a loss for 1998-99) 3.78 £

Net profit for 1998-99 (if loss, enter '0') 3.79 £ 7700

Allowable loss for 1998-99 (if you make a profit, enter '0') 3.80 £

- Loss offset against other income for 1998-99 3.81 £
- Loss to carry back 3.82 £
- Loss to carry forward (that is allowable loss not claimed in any other way) 3.83 £
- Losses brought forward from last year 3.84 £
- Losses brought forward from last year used this year 3.85 £

box 3.79 *minus* box 3.85

Taxable profit after losses brought forward 3.86 £ 7700

- Any other business income (for example, Business Start-up Allowance received in 1998-99) 3.87 £

box 3.86 + box 3.87

Total taxable profits from this business 3.88 £ 7700

Class 4 National Insurance Contributions

- Tick this box if exception or deferment applies — 3.89
- Adjustments to profit chargeable to Class 4 National Insurance Contributions — 3.90 £

Class 4 National Insurance Contributions due — 3.91 £

Subcontractors in the construction industry

- Deductions made by contractors on account of tax (you must send your SC60s to us) — 3.92 £

Summary of balance sheet

Leave these boxes blank if you do not have a balance sheet

- ***Assets***
  - Plant, machinery and motor vehicles — 3.93 £
  - Other fixed assets (premises, goodwill, investments etc.) — 3.94 £
  - Stock and work in progress — 3.95 £
  - Debtors/prepayments/other current assets — 3.96 £
  - Bank/building society balances — 3.97 £
  - Cash in hand — 3.98 £

  total of boxes 3.93 to 3.98 — 3.99 £

- ***Liabilities***
  - Trade creditors/accruals — 3.100 £
  - Loans and overdrawn bank accounts — 3.101 £
  - Other liabilities — 3.102 £

  total of boxes 3.100 to 3.102 — 3.103 £

- ***Net business assets*** (put the figure in brackets if you had net business liabilities) — box 3.99 *minus* box 3.103 — 3.104 £
- ***Represented by***

  Capital Account
  - Balance at start of period* — 3.105 £
  - Net profit/(loss)* — 3.106 £
  - Capital introduced — 3.107 £
  - Drawings — 3.108 £
  - Balance at end of period* — total of boxes 3.105 to 3.107 *minus* box 3.108 — 3.109 £

* If the Capital Account is overdrawn, or the business made a net loss, show the figure in brackets.

Tax deducted from trading income

- Any tax deducted (excluding deductions made by contractors on account of tax) from trading income. — 3.120 £

Note: box numbers 3.110 to 3.119 are not used

Additional information

Now fill in any other supplementary Pages that apply to you.
Otherwise, go back to Page 2 of your Tax Return and finish filling it in.

PREPARING TAXATION COMPUTATIONS

ANSWERS - DECEMBER 1997

SECTION 1

Task 1.1(a)

Calculation of Schedule A rental income for 1998/99

	Flat 1	*Flat 2*	*Flat 3*	*Flat 4*
	£	£	£	£
Rental income	2,000		4,000	
6 April 1998 to 31 October 1998 (7/12 × £3,000)		1,750		
6 April 1998 to 31 December 1998 (£5,000 × 9/12)				3,750
January 1999 to 5April 1999 (£6,000 × 3/12)				1,500
Expenditure				
Advertising		(1,000)		(500)
Management fees	(1,000)	(1,000)	(1,000)	(1,000)
Buildings insurance	(250)	(250)	(250)	(250)
Repairs	(100)	(500)	(nil)	(200)
Schedule A profit /(loss)	£650	£(1,000)	£2,750	£3,300

Total Schedule A profit (£650 + £(1,000) + £2,750 + £3,300) = £5,700

The kitchen extension was capital in nature and is therefore not an allowable Schedule A expense for income tax purposes.

Task 1.1(b)

Schedule E computation

Schedule E earnings

Salary	25,000
Benefits in kind	
Car	
£24,600 — £1,000 = £23,600 × 35% × 1/3 × 5/12	1,147
Less: contribution	(500)
Car fuel	
Petrol £1,890 × 5/12	787
Private medical insurance (550 – 100)	450
Use of colour television (1,000 × 20%)	200
Travelling and subsistence	5,000
Entertaining	3,500
Telephone	100
	35,684
Less: S 198 claims	
Travelling and subsistence	(2,500)
Entertaining (excluding golf club subscription)	(3,000)
Telephone	(100)
Schedule E earnings	£30,084

Income for the year ended 5 April 1999

Inland Revenue

LAND AND PROPERTY

Fill in these boxes first

Name: HARRIET ASHDOWN

Tax reference:

Are you claiming Rent a Room relief for gross rents of £4,250 or less? No ✓ Yes

(Or £2,125 if the claim is shared?)

Read the Notes on page LN2 to find out

- **whether you can claim Rent a Room relief; and**
- **how to claim relief for gross rents over £4,250**

If 'Yes', and this is your only income from UK property, you have finished these Pages

Is your income from furnished holiday lettings? No ✓ Yes

If 'No', turn over and fill in Page L2 to give details of your property income

If 'Yes', fill in boxes 5.1 to 5.18 before completing Page L2

Furnished holiday lettings

- Income from furnished holiday lettings **5.1** £

■ *Expenses* (furnished holiday lettings only)

- Rent, rates, insurance, ground rents etc. **5.2** £
- Repairs, maintenance and renewals **5.3** £
- Finance charges, including interest **5.4** £
- Legal and professional costs **5.5** £
- Cost of services provided, including wages **5.6** £
- Other expenses **5.7** £

total of boxes 5.2 to 5.7 **5.8** £

Net profit (put figures in brackets if a loss) box 5.1 *minus* box 5.8 **5.9** £

■ *Tax adjustments*

- Private use **5.10** £
- Balancing charges **5.11** £

box 5.10 + box 5.11 **5.12** £

- Capital allowances **5.13** £

Profit for the year (copy to box 5.19). If loss, enter '0' in box 5.14 and put the loss in box 5.15 — boxes 5.9 + 5.12 *minus* box 5.13 **5.14** £

Loss for the year (if you have entered '0' in box 5.14) — boxes 5.9 + 5.12 *minus* box 5.13 **5.15** £

- Loss offset against 1998-99 total income **5.16** £
- Loss carried back — see Notes, page LN4 **5.17** £
- Loss offset against other income from property (copy to box 5.38) — see Notes, page LN4 **5.18** £

SA105

Other property income

■ ***Income***

• Furnished holiday lettings profits	5.19 £ (copy from box 5.14)		
• Rents and other income from land and property	5.20 £ 13,000	5.21 £ NIL (Tax deducted)	5.23 £ 13000 (boxes 5.19 + 5.20 + 5.22)
• Chargeable premiums	5.22 £		

■ ***Expenses*** (do not include figures you have already put in boxes 5.2 to 5.7 on Page L1)

• Rent, rates, insurance, ground rents etc.	5.24 £ 1000	
• Repairs, maintenance and renewals	5.25 £ 800	
• Finance charges, including interest	5.26 £	
• Legal and professional costs	5.27 £ 4000	
• Costs of services provided, including wages	5.28 £	
• Other expenses	5.29 £ 1500	5.30 £ 7300 (total of boxes 5.24 to 5.29)

Net profit (put figures in brackets if a loss)	5.31 £ 5700 (box 5.23 *minus* box 5.30)

■ ***Tax adjustments***

• Private use	5.32 £	
• Balancing charges	5.33 £	5.34 £ (box 5.32 + box 5.33)
• Rent a Room exempt amount	5.35 £	
• Capital allowances	5.36 £	
• 10% wear and tear	5.37 £	
• Furnished holiday lettings losses (from box 5.18)	5.38 £	5.39 £ (total of boxes 5.35 to 5.38)

Adjusted profit (if loss enter '0' in box 5.40 and put the loss in box 5.41)		5.40 £ 5700 (boxes 5.31 + 5.34 *minus* box 5.39)
Adjusted loss (if you have entered '0' in box 5.40)	5.41 £ (boxes 5.31 + 5.34 *minus* box 5.39)	
• Loss brought forward from previous year		5.42 £
Profit for the year		5.43 £ 5700 (box 5.40 *minus* box 5.42)
• Loss offset against total income	5.44 £	
• Loss to carry forward to following year	5.45 £	
• Pooled expenses from 'one estate election' carried forward	5.46 £	

Tick box 5.47 if these Pages include details of property let jointly 5.47 ☐

Now fill in any other supplementary Pages that apply to you.
Otherwise, go back to page 2 of your Tax Return and finish filling it in.

Income for the year ended 5 April 1999

Inland Revenue

EMPLOYMENT

Fill in these boxes first

Name: HARRIET ASHDOWN

Tax reference:

If you want help, look up the box numbers in the Notes

Details of employer

Employer's PAYE reference
1.1 3491 AS3

Employer's name
1.2 ASHDOWN LTD

Date employment started (only if between 6 April 1998 and 5 April 1999)
1.3 / /

Employer's address
1.5 TIN LANE
ST LINTON
DEVON

Postcode

Date finished (only if between 6 April 1998 and 5 April 1999)
1.4 / /

Tick box 1.6 if you were a director of the company
1.6 ✓

and, if so, tick box 1.7 if it was a close company
1.7

Income from employment

■ *Money* - *see Notes, page EN3*

		Before tax
• Payments from P60 (or P45 or pay slips)	**1.8**	£ 25 000
• Payments not on P60 etc. - tips	**1.9**	£
- other payments (excluding expenses shown below and lump sums and compensation payments or benefits shown overleaf)	**1.10**	£

		Tax deducted
• UK tax deducted from payments in boxes 1.8 to 1.10	**1.11**	£ 6055

■ *Benefits and expenses* - *see Notes, pages EN3 to EN6. If any benefits connected with termination of employment were received, or enjoyed, after that termination and were from a* **former** *employer you need to complete Help Sheet IR204, available from the Orderline. Do not enter such benefits here.*

		Amount			Amount
• Assets transferred/ payments made for you	**1.12**	£	• Vans	**1.18**	£
• Vouchers/credit cards	**1.13**	£	• Interest-free and low-interest loans	**1.19**	£
• Living accommodation	**1.14**	£	• Mobile telephones	**1.20**	£
• Mileage allowance	**1.15**	£	• Private medical or dental insurance	**1.21**	£ 450
• Company cars	**1.16**	£ 647	• Other benefits	**1.22**	£ 200
• Fuel for company cars	**1.17**	£ 787	• Expenses payments received and balancing charges	**1.23**	£ 8600

SA101

Income from employment continued

■ ***Lump sums and compensation payments or benefits including such payments and benefits from a former employer***
Note that 'lump sums' here includes any contributions which your employer made to an unapproved retirement benefits scheme

*You must read page EN6 of the Notes **before** filling in boxes 1.24 to 1.30*

Reliefs

- £30,000 exemption — **1.24** £
- Foreign service and disability — **1.25** £
- Retirement and death lump sums — **1.26** £

Taxable lump sums

- From box H of *Help Sheet IR204* — **1.27** £
- From box Q of *Help Sheet IR204* — **1.28** £
- From box R of *Help Sheet IR204* — **1.29** £
- Tax deducted from payments in boxes 1.27 to 1.29 — Tax deducted **1.30** £

■ ***Foreign earnings not taxable in the UK in year ended 5 April 1999** - see Notes, page EN6* — **1.31** £

■ ***Expenses you incurred in doing your job** - see Notes, starting on page EN6*

- Travel and subsistence costs — **1.32** £ 2 500
- Fixed deductions for expenses — **1.33** £
- Professional fees and subscriptions — **1.34** £
- Other expenses and capital allowances — **1.35** £ 3,100
- Tick box 1.36 if the figure in box 1.32 includes travel between your home and a permanent workplace — **1.36**

■ ***Foreign Earnings Deduction*** — **1.37** £

■ ***Foreign tax for which tax credit relief not claimed*** — **1.38** £

Additional information

Now fill in any other supplementary Pages that apply to you.
Otherwise, go back to page 2 in your Tax Return and finish filling it in.

Task 1.3

Income tax computation 1998/99

Harriet Ashdown

Income Tax Computation 1998/99

	£	£	*Tax deducted at source* £
Earned income			
Schedule E	30,084		6,055
		30,084	
Investment income:			
1. Savings income			
2. Non savings income			
Schedule A	5,700	5,700	
Less: Charges on income			
Statutory total income		35,784	
Less: Personal allowance		(4,195)	
Taxable income		31,589	
Tax thereon:			
£4,300 × 20%		860	
£22,800 × 23%		5,244	
£4,489 × 40%		1,796	
£31,589			
Total income tax liability		7,900	
Less: Tax deducted under PAYE		(6,055)	
		1,845	

Calculating your tax bill - continued

If any of the sums on this page result in a negative amount, enter a zero in the appropriate box

Total income from: **(copy figures from your Tax Return)**

- *Employment* including benefits and *minus* expenses for each employment

Add income in:
- boxes 1.8 to 1.10, and
- boxes 1.12 to 1.23, and
- boxes 1.27 and 1.28

	First employment	Other employments	
Add income in boxes 1.8 to 1.10, 1.12 to 1.23, 1.27 and 1.28	£ 35684	£	
Deduct any figures in boxes 1.31 to 1.38	£ 5600	£	
Total taxable income	£ 30084	£	W1 £ 30084

• *Share schemes* (from box 2.31)	W2 £
• *Self-employment* (from box 3.88)	W3 £
• *Partnerships* (from boxes 4.35, 4.70 and 4.73)	W4 £
• *UK land and property* (from box 5.43)	W5 £ 5700
• *Foreign income* (from boxes 6.2, 6.4 and 6.5)	W6 £
• *Trusts, settlements or estates of deceased persons* (add together any figures in the 'right hand' column of the Trusts etc. Pages and deduct any figure in box 7.19)	W7 £
• *UK savings and investments* (total any figures in the 'right hand' column on page 3 of your Tax Return)	W8 £
• *UK pensions, retirement annuities and benefits* (add together any figures in the 'right hand' column of Question 11 on page 4 of your Tax Return *minus* any deduction in box 11.13)	W9 £
• *Maintenance or alimony received* (from box 12.3)	W10 £
• *Other income* (copy the figure in box 13.3 *minus* any figure in box 13.5)	W11 £
Total income total boxes W1 to W11	W12 £ 35784

Deductions for

• *Personal pension* (add together any figures in boxes 14.5, 14.10, 14.15, 14.16 and 14.17)	W13 £
• *Vocational training* (multiply any figure in box 15.1 by $^{100}/_{77}$)	W14 £
• *Interest on qualifying loans* (from box 15.3)	W15 £
• *Maintenance or alimony paid* (see the notes on page 2 of this Guide)	W16 £
• *Charitable covenants, annuities, Gift Aid and Millennium Gift Aid payments* (multiply any figures in boxes 15.9 and 15.10 by $^{100}/_{77}$)	W17 £
• *Losses and post-cessation expenses* (from boxes 3.81, 4.15, 4.61, 5.16, 5.44, 8.13A and 15.11)	W18 £
• *Trade union and friendly society death benefit payments* (from box 15.12)	W19 £
Total deductions total boxes W13 to W19	W20 £
Total income minus deductions (box W12 *minus* box W20)	W21 £ 35784

now copy the figure in box W21 to box W22 on page 6

Calculating your tax bill - continued

Reliefs
- you get basic rate relief automatically - further relief will be due if you are liable to higher rate tax.

from box W21
W22 £ 35784

If any of the sums on this page result in a negative amount, enter a zero in the appropriate box

- *Pension payments* (from boxes 14.15 and 14.17) — W23.1 £
- *Vocational training* (from box W14) — W23.2 £

box W23.1 + box W23.2
W23 £

box W22 + box W23
W24 £ 35784

Allowances given as a deduction from your income
- you may need to check your entitlement - see notes starting on page 3 of this Guide.

- *Personal allowance* - normally £4,195 unless you are non-resident and not claiming allowances — W25.1 £ 4195 +
- *Age-related personal allowance* - see notes page 3 — W25.2 £ +
- *Blind person's allowance* - enter £1,330 — W25.3 £ +
- *Transitional allowance* (from box 16.4) — W25.4 £
- *Blind person's surplus allowance from your spouse* (from box 16.27) — W25.5 £

total boxes W25.1 to W25.5
W25 £ 4195

If the figure in box W26 is £4,300 or less, do not fill in boxes W28 to W38

box W24 *minus* box W25
W26 £ 31589

box W26 x 20%
W27 £ 6,318

Savings income taxable at the lower (20%) rate

- *Partnership savings* (from boxes 4.35 and 4.70) — W28.1 £ +
- *UK savings* (from box W8) — W28.2 £ +
- *Foreign savings* (from box 6.2) — W28.3 £
- *Trusts, settlements and estate income* (from boxes 7.6, 7.12 and 7.15) — W28.4 £

total boxes W28.1 to W28.4
W28 £

box W26 *minus* box W28
W29 £ 31589

W30 £ *4,300*

box W29 *minus* box W30
W31 £ 27289

box W31 x 3%
W32 £ 819

If the figure in box W33 is £27,100 or less, do not fill in boxes W35 to W38

box W26 *minus* box W23 *minus* box 12.9
W33 £ 31589

W34 £ *27,100*

box W33 *minus* box W34
W35 £ 4489

box W35 x 17%
W36 £ 763

lower of box W28 *or* box W35
W37 £

box W37 x 3%
W38 £

boxes W27 + W32 + W36 + W38
Income Tax due W39 £ 7900

Copy box W39 to top of page 7

Calculating your tax bill - continued

If any of the sums on this page result in a negative amount, enter a zero in the appropriate box

from page 6

W39 £ 7900

- *Venture Capital Trust and Enterprise Investment Scheme subscriptions*

box 15.7 + box 15.8 — W40 £ → box W40 x 20% — W41 £

box 15.2 x 10% — W42 £

Allowances and reliefs given in terms of tax
- these reduce your tax bill - you may need to use the Question 16 notes on pages 23 to 26 of the Tax Return Guide and starting on page 4 of this Guide.

- *Married couple's allowance*
  - see notes on pages 4 and 9 of this Guide — W43.1 £
  +
- *Married couple's surplus allowance*
  (from box 16.28) — W43.2 £
  +
- *Additional personal allowance*
  - usually £1,900, may be split with another person - see the notes — W43.3 £
  +
- *Widow's bereavement allowance - £1,900*
  (if your husband died in 1997-98 or 1998-99 and you have not remarried) — W43.4 £
- *Maintenance and alimony*
  (boxes 15.4 and 15.5 - see the notes for box W16 on page 2 of this Guide) — W43.5 £

total boxes W43.1 to W43.5 — W43.6 £ → box W43.6 x 15% — W43 £

Notional tax is not repayable and so has to be calculated as an allowance given in terms of tax rather than being regarded as tax deducted at source.

- *Partnership notional tax*
  (from box 4.78) — W44.1 £
  +
- *Notional tax on UK scrip dividends and FIDs*
  (from boxes 10.22, 10.25, 10.28 and 10.31) — W44.2 £
- *Notional tax on estate income*
  (from box 7.14) — W44.3 £

total boxes W44.1 to W44.3 — W44 £

- *Tax credit relief on foreign income and treaty relief on UK income*
  (and see the notes on page 9 of this Guide) — from boxes 6.9 and 9.35 — W45 £

boxes W41 to W45 — W46 £

Income Tax due, after allowances and reliefs — box W39 *minus* box W46 — W47 £ 7900
If the figure in box W46 is more than the figure in box W39, enter a zero

- *Recoverable tax on charitable covenants, annuities, Gift Aid and Millennium Gift Aid payments* (box W17 x 23%) — W48 £
- *Class 4 National Insurance Contributions*
  (from box 3.91 or box 4.25) — W49 £

Income Tax and Class 4 National Insurance Contributions — boxes W47 + W48 + W49 — W50 £ 7900

Copy the figure in box W50 to box W50 on page 8

Calculating your tax bill - continued

(copy figure from box W50 on page 7) **Income Tax and Class 4 NIC due** — W50 £ 7900

- *Unpaid tax for earlier years included in PAYE code for 1998-99* — W51 £

Copy the figure in box W51 to box 18.1 in your Tax Return

box W50 + box W51 — W52 £ 7900

Tax paid at source

Employment (from boxes 1.11 and 1.30)	W53.1	£ 6055
Self-employment (from boxes 3.92 and 3.120)	W53.2	£
Partnerships (from box 4.77)	W53.3	£
UK land and property (from box 5.21)	W53.4	£
Foreign income (from boxes 6.1 and 6.3)	W53.5	£
Trusts, settlements or estate income (from boxes 7.2, 7.5, 7.8 and 7.11)	W53.6	£
UK savings (from boxes 10.3, 10.6, 10.10, 10.13, 10.16 and 10.19)	W53.7	£
UK pensions, retirement annuities and benefits (from boxes 11.8 and 11.11)	W53.8	£
Other income (from box 13.2)	W53.9	£

total boxes W53.1 to W53.9 — W53 £ 6055

- *Tax due for 1998-99 included in 1999-2000 PAYE tax code* — W54 £

Copy the figure in box W54 to box 18.2 in your Tax Return

box W53 + box W54 — W55 £ 6055

Total tax and Class 4 NIC due for 1998-99 (overpayment in brackets) — box W52 *minus* box W55 — W56 £ 1845

Copy the figure in box W56 to box 18.3 in your Tax Return

Tax owed or overpaid in 1998-99

- *1998-99 tax already refunded* (from box 17.1) — W57A £
- *Tax due for earlier years* — W57 £

  Copy the figure in box W57 to box 18.4 in your Tax Return

boxes W56 + W57A + W57 — W58 £ 1845

- *Tax overpaid for earlier years* — W59 £

  Tick box 18.5 and copy the figure in box W59 to the 'Additional information' box on page 8 of your Tax Return

- *Payments already made* (from your Statements of Account) — W60 £

box W59 + box W60 — W61 £

Tax you owe for 1998-99 — box W58 *minus* box W61 — W62 £ 1545

OR

Tax you have overpaid for 1998-99 — box W61 *minus* box W58 — W63 £

Payments on account for 1999-2000

If there is a figure in box W62, add it to any figure in box W59. If the total is less than £1,000 and you would like the amount you owe collected through your 2000 2001 tax code, copy W62 to W64. Otherwise enter zero — W64 £

If W65 is ***less than £500****, you do not need to make payments on account. Leave box 18.6 blank and tick box 18.8.* ***If W65 is equal to or more than £500****, carry on* — box W56 *minus* box W64 — W65 £ 1845

- *Income Tax due, after allowances and reliefs* — from boxes W44 + W47 + W48 — W66 £ 7900
- *Class 4 National Insurance Contributions* — from box W49 — W67 £

box W66 + box W67 — W68 £ 7900

box W68 x 20% — W69 £ 1550

If W65 is ***less than*** *W69, you do not need to make payments on account. Leave box 18.6 blank and tick box 18.8.*
If W65 is ***equal to or more than*** *W69,* ***you do have to make payments on account. Fill in box W70***

This is the amount of each payment on account for 1999-2000 — box W65 x 50% — W70 £ 923

Copy the figure in box W70 ***(including pence)*** *to box 18.6 in your Tax Return*

SECTION 2

Task 2.1

Ashdown Limited

Corporation tax computations

	Years ended 31 March 1998	1999	2000 (estimated)
	£	£	£
Schedule D Case I	58,000	nil	32,000
Less: S393 (1) loss relief	-	-	(32,000)
Other income	15,000	6,000	11,000
Capital Gains	2,000	20,000	nil
	75,000	26,000	11,000
Less: S393A losses of loss making accounting period	-	(26,000)	-
Less: Trade/business charges on income 1999 - unrelieved - see below	(4,000)	(8,000)	(6,000)
Less: S393A losses carried back	(71,000)	-	-
Less: Non trade/non business charges on income	(1,000)*	(1,000)*	(1,000)
Profits chargeable to corporation tax (PCTCT)	£nil	£nil	£4,000

Loss working	
Total loss available for the year ended 31 March 1999	170,000
Less:	
S393A 31 March 1999	(26,000)
S393A 31 March 1998	(71,000)
Loss left to carry forward under S393(1)	73,000
Add: trade charges unrelieved year ended 31 March 1999	8,000
Total loss to carry forward	173,000
Less: S393(1) 31 March 2000	(32,000)
Loss carried forward at 1 April 2000	141,000

* Non-trade/non business charges on income unrelieved and lost.

Inland Revenue

Page 1

Corporation Tax Return
Version 3

This form, or an approved substitute version of it, must be used whenever a company is required to do so, by a *Notice to deliver a Corporation Tax Return (form CT203)*. This return sets out the information we need and provides a standard format for calculations.

You should read this return form along with your *Notice to deliver a Corporation Tax Return (form CT203)* and *Filling in your Corporation Tax Return (leaflet CT200 Notes)* which you should have received with this form. The notes referred to throughout can be found in the leaflet *CT200 Notes*. You should contact your Tax Office if you need more help.

'Company' means any body chargeable to corporation tax, whether incorporated or not. This definition includes clubs, associations and voluntary organisations.

Sections to be completed
Members' clubs, associations and voluntary organisations - It is likely that you will only have to complete Sections 1 and 2. For further guidance see note 1 in the *Notes*.

All companies - including clubs, etc. - You will not need to complete every Section, but you **must** complete the Declaration and Section 1 on this page. The *Notes* will help you decide whether you should complete the mutually exclusive *Short return* at Section 2 or the *Detailed return* at Section 3. Sections 9 and 10 are optional but you are asked to complete them if they are relevant to the company.

It is important that you read the *Notes* before completing any part of this form.

What to do when you have completed the return
- Make sure you have completed and signed the Declaration, then
- staple together the pages you have completed and attach any supporting calculations
- send these together with the relevant company accounts and, where prepared, directors' and auditors' reports, to your Tax Office using the envelope provided (see Note 3 for the date by which you should do this)
- pay any outstanding corporation tax (as you have shown at box box 65), as advised on the payslip attached to your *Notice to deliver a Corporation Tax Return (form CT203)*. Interest is charged on tax paid later than nine months and one day after the end of an accounting period. Tax is due without the making of an assessment.

Remember - ***Your tax return is not complete unless you send relevant accounts and documentation with this form. Penalties may be charged if your return, or any part of it, is late or incorrect.***

As soon as your figures are agreed
- we will send you an assessment setting out the tax position for the accounting period - unless there are no figures to assess
- we will issue an amended assessment if you have already received an estimated assessment and you have appealed against it.

Section 1: Summary

The company name

ASHDOWN LIMITED

The company address - only if changed since last return made.
Enter the UK registered office address, or the UK address if the company does not have a registered office. If the company does not have premises in the UK show the address of the person making the return.

Company registration number *(if registered)*

Reference
Enter the reference number shown on the *Notice to deliver a Corporation Tax Return (form CT203)*

XXX / 12345 / 6789

Corporation tax accounting period covered by this return
Cannot exceed 12 months. Enter start and end dates.

From 01/04/98 To 31/03/99

If this period is not an accounting period of the company for corporation tax purposes (see note 2) put an 'X' in the box below, complete the Declaration to the right and return this form to your Tax Office. You do not need to complete the rest of this Section or other Sections of this form in these circumstances. ☐

Profits chargeable *(Enter the firgure from box 30). If there are none enter '0'.*

£ 0

Corporation tax due £ 0 . p 00
(Enter the figure from box 61 minus any entry in box 64). If none is due enter '0.00'.

Put an X in the appropriate box

Have you completed Section 8 (Repayments)? Yes ☐ No ☒

Is the company name different from that shown in the *Notice (form CT203)*? Yes ☐ No ☒

Declaration

Enter here the page numbers you are attaching

2, 3

Put an 'X' in the appropriate boxes to show the documents you are enclosing
- a copy of the accounts for the period to which this return relates ☒
- a copy of the company accounts for a different period ☐
- no accounts ☐
- say why not
- calculations showing how the entries in the return form have been arrived at. ☐

I declare that to the best of my knowledge and belief the return on this page and the pages attached is correct and complete.

Signature

Except where a liquidator has been appointed, the company secretary, treasurer, or any other person who is authorised to do so may sign this declaration on behalf of the company. A photocopy of a signature is not acceptable.

Date / /

Name *(in capital letters)*

Status *(company secretary, treasurer, liquidator etc.)*

Page 2

Section 2: Short return

You may complete this section if
- it covers all the entries you need to make and
- each entry, including the company's total income and deductions, is less than £10 million.

In all other cases, or if you prefer, complete Section 3 instead. You should enclose an explanation and calculations of any figures which you have estimated or which are not immediately recognisable from the company's accounts.

The figures to be entered are those adjusted for tax purposes, after deducting capital allowances and adding balancing charges where appropriate. Section 4 should also be completed if capital allowances are claimed.

Please do not enter '0's where the company did not have the source specified in the return form.

	Box	£	Box	£
Trading profits *See note 5*	1			
Trading losses brought forward *Only include losses made in the same trade. Include charges treated as losses.* ***Do not enter an amount larger than is needed to cover the profits in box 1.*** *See note 6*	2			
Net trading profit *(box 1 minus box 2). If box 2 equals box 1, enter '0'. Leave this box blank if there are no trading profits in box 1*			3	
Trading losses of this accounting period *Where there is more than one trade give total for all trades. Do not set box 4 losses against box 1 profits, claim at box 22 against total profits.*	4	170,000		
Profits and gains from non-trading loan relationships and other Schedule D Case III income *Include interest and other profits and gains from non-trading loan relationships even if tax has been deducted. Complete box 57 to claim credit for income tax deducted. You will need to complete the* **Detailed return** *at Section 3 if you have deficits on non-trading loan relationships from this, earlier or later accounting periods to include. See note 8*			6	
Income within Schedule D Case VI - for example furnished lettings *Enter the figure net of allowable losses brought forward. Exclude income you enter in box 12. See note 7*			9	
Income from which income tax has been deducted - for example building society interest *Enter the gross amount before tax. Exclude any amount included in box 6 above. Complete box 57 to claim credit for income tax deducted. See note 9*			10	6,000
Income from UK land and buildings *Enter the amount net of allowable expenses brought forward. Exclude income in box 9 above. See note 10*			12	
Chargeable gains *See note 11*				
Gross gains	13	20,000		
Allowable losses *Include any losses brought forward but do not enter an amount larger than the amount of gross gains in box 13 above.*	14	NIL		
Net chargeable gains *(box 13 minus box 14) If box 14 equals box 13, enter '0'*			15	20,000
Profits *(total of boxes 3, 6, 9, 10, 12 and 15)*			17	26,000
Relief for trading losses of this or of a later period *Put an 'X' in box 21 if amounts carried back from later accounting periods are included in box 22. See note 12*	21	☐	22	26,000
Profits before charges *(box 17 minus box 22)*			26	NIL
Charges paid *Do not enter an amount larger than is needed to cover profits in box 26. See note 13*			27	–
Profits chargeable to corporation tax *(box 26 minus box 27)* ***Copy this figure into the box provided in Section 1 on page 1, and also into the box at the top of page 3***			30	NIL

The short return is continued on page 3

Page 3

Profits chargeable to corporation tax

Enter the figure brought forward from page 2, box 30 ... £ NIL

If you claim tax is chargeable at the small companies' rate, or if you are claiming marginal small companies' relief, complete boxes 31 - 35. If there are no associated companies please enter '0' against the relevant financial year. *See note 15*

Franked investment income and foreign income dividends arising in the period covered by the return. *See note 15* ... 31 £

Number of companies associated with this company in the/each financial year covered by this return *Exclude this company. See note 15* ...

	Financial year		Number of associated companies
32		33	
34		35	

Corporation tax chargeable *See note 16*

	Financial years beginning 1 April		Amounts of profit £		Rates of tax *See note 16*		Tax £ p
36		37		38	•	39	•
43		44		45	•	46	•

Total corporation tax chargeable *(box 39 plus box 46)* ... 50 •

Marginal small companies' relief
Attach your computation (see notes 15, 16 and 29) ... 51 £ • p

Advance corporation tax restricted if necessary under Section 239(2) ICTA 1988
Put an 'X' in box 53 if amounts carried back from later accounting periods are included. See note 17. 53 54 •

Total of boxes 51 and 54
Total must not be larger than entry in box 50. Restrict if necessary ... 55 •

Net corporation tax chargeable *(box 50 minus box 55)* ... 56 NIL •

Calculation of tax outstanding or overpaid

Income tax deducted from gross income included in return
Do not include deductions used to cover income tax for which the company was liable to account to the Inland Revenue on payments it has made. See note 18 ... 57 •

Corporation tax due

Box 56 minus box 57. If box 57 equals or is greater than box 56, enter '0.00' and go to box 59. Copy the figure in box 61 to the box provided in Section 1 on page 1. See note 20 ... 61 0 • 00

Income tax repayable to the company *(box 57 minus box 56).*
Complete Section 8 on page 8. Do not complete unless you are making a claim. See note 28... 59 •

Corporation tax already paid (and not repaid). *See note 21* ... 63 •

Corporation tax outstanding *(box 61 minus box 63). This amount is payable to the Accounts Office.*
If box 63 equals or is greater than box 61, enter '0.00' and go to box 66. See note 23 ... 65 0 • 00

Corporation tax overpaid *(box 63 minus box 61).*
Complete Section 8 on page 8 also. See note 28 ... 66 •

This is the last page of the short return

SECTION 3

Task 3.1

	£	*Cost* £		*MV82* £
Sale proceeds		150,000		150,000
Less: costs of sale				
Estate agents' fees	1,500			
Solicitors' fees	2,500			
		(4,000)		(4,000)
		146,000		146,000
Less: Cost (June 1981)		(25,000)		
Kitchen extension (August 1981)		(15,000)	MV 31.3.82	(35,000)
Bedroom extension (September 1991)		(3,500)		(3,500)
Unindexed gain		102,500		107,500
Less: Indexation Allowance				
$£40,000 \times \frac{161.2 - 79.44}{79.44} = (1.029)$		(41,160)		(41,160)
(£40,000 = costs of £25,000 and £15,000 incurred up to March 1982 and greater than MV 1982 of £35,000)				
$£3,500 \times \frac{161.2 - 134.6}{134.6} = (0.198)$		(693)		(693)
		60,647		65,647
The lower gain is taken of			60,647	

		£
Capital gains tax liability:		
Gains of 1998/99		60,647
Less Annual exemption 1998/99		(6,800)
Less capital losses brought forward		(10,000)
Chargeable gains		43,847

		£
Tax thereon:		
£27,100 – £10,000	= £17,100 × 23% =	3,933
Balance	= £26,747 × 40% =	10,699
	£43,847	
Total Capital Gains Tax Due on 31 January 2000		14,632

Task 3.2

MEMO

To: Harold Heath

From: An Accounting Technician

Note to Harold Heath concerning capital gains tax computation for Patrick Ashdown:

Date: 5 December 1999

Please find attached my computation of the gain on the sale of Patrick Ashdown's house.

As requested I have set out below the basis of my computation, so that you can test my understanding of the computational procedure.

Because the asset was owned on 31 March 1982 the gain had to be calculated in two ways. One gain was computed by reference to the original costs of the asset and one gain by reference to the value of the asset on 31 March 1982.

Allowable incidental expenses of sale were deducted from the sale proceeds, in this case these expenses were the solicitors and estate agents fees incurred.

The deductions in the cost column were the original cost of the property and the costs of any capital improvement expenditure incurred.

The amounts deducted in the March 1982 column were the value of the property on 31 March 1982 and the improvement expenditure incurred after 31 March 1982. The value on 31 March 1982, is of the property, as it stood on that date and does not include the value of any subsequent improvements.

An allowance for inflation is given using the movement in the retail prices index to show the inflationary effects up to April 1998. The indexation allowance is deducted from the capital gain.

The indexation allowance in this computation is calculated separately on the expenditure incurred up to March 1982 and the post-March 1982 expenditure. This is because you can only allow for the effects of inflation from the date expenditure is incurred, or March 1982, if later.

Once the net gains have been calculated in both the cost and MV 1982 columns the lower of the two gains is taxed.

This net gain is then taxed in the fiscal year of disposal. For Patrick this was 1998/99. The gains, net of current fiscal year capital losses, annual exemption for the 1998/99 fiscal year (of £6,800) and brought forward capital losses are then taxed on Patrick. Taper relef would be deducted before the annual exemption, but since the house is not a business asset the rate of taper relief is nil.

The rate of tax applied is determined by treating the gains as the top slice of Patrick's income, in order to determine the rate of 20%, 23% or 40% applicable to the gains. In this case, as the £4,300 20% band had been used and £5,700 of the 23% band had been used there was £17,100 of the 23% band left and the balance of the gains was taxed at 40%.

Note: *This answer is longer than would be required from a competent student. It encompasses all the points that could have gained credit.*

BUSINESS TAXATION
PRACTICE DEVOLVED ASSESSMENT

SUGGESTED SOLUTIONS

Task 1

Jack's Novelties

(a) Schedule D Case I taxable profits for 1997/98, 1998/99 and 1999/00

1997/98

Basis of assessment is the profits of the period 1 December 1997 to 5 April 1998

ie $^4/_7 \times$ £14,000 = £8,000

1998/99

As there is no accounting date in 1998/99 which falls at least twelve months after commencement the basis of assessment is the profits of the first twelve months of trading, ie, the twelve months to 30 November 1998

ie, £14,000 + $^5/_{12} \times$ £25,980 £24,825

The profits of the period 1 December 1997 to 5 April 1998 have been taxed twice, and are overlap profits

ie, $^4/_7 \times$ £14,000 = £8,000

1999/00

The basis of assessment is the profits of the period from the end of the previous basis period (1 December 1998) to cessation (31 March 2000), less overlap relief.

ie, $^7/_{12} \times$ £25,980 + £30,000 - £8,000 = £37,155

(b) Mitigation of capital gain of £100,000

(i) *Retirement relief*

Jack is over 50 years old and will be entitled to retirement relief. He has traded for 28 months and the retirement relief will be:

$^{28}/_{120} \times$ £200,000	46,667
½ × (100,000 – 46,667)	26,667
	73,334

The capital gain remaining after retirement relief would be £26,666. This will be eligible for taper relief at the rate of 15% (two years ownership since 5 April 1998, including the bonus year).

(ii) *EIS deferral relief*

If Jack subscribes for unquoted shares he may elect to defer the gain. This relief will be applied after retirement relief, and Jack needs to reinvest 26,666 to fully relieve the gain.

If Jack's annual capital gains tax exemption for 1999/00 is unused, he should hold over only £26,666 – $\left(£6,800 \times {}^{100}/_{85}\right)$ = £18,666. (Check £(26,666 – 18,666) × 85% = £6,800).

(iii) If Jack were to commence a new trade within three years of the disposal, acquiring land and buildings, fixed plant and machinery, or goodwill, he could claim rollover relief for the replacement of business assets. The gain would then be rolled over against the cost of the new assets.

Task 2

(a) **Wooden Toys (UK) Limited**
Capital allowances computation
Year ended 31 December 1998

	General Pool	FA1980 Pool	Expensive Car (BMW)	Allowances
	£	£	£	£
1.1.98 Tax WDV b/f	14,500	5,625	9,000	
Additions not qualifying for FYA		10,000		
Disposals	(8,000)	(2,500)		
	6,500	13,125	9,000	
WDA @ 25%	(1,625)	(3,281)	(2,250)	7,156
Additions qualifying for FYA	12,000			
FYA @ 50%	(6,000)			6,000
31.12.98 Tax WDV c/f	10,875	9,844	6,750	13,156
Industrial Building Cost	75,000			
Architects' fees	2,000			
	77,000			
WDA @ 4%	3,080			3,080
Tax WDV c/f	73,920			
Total capital allowances				16,236

(b) **Wooden Toys (UK) Limited**
Schedule D Case I Computation
Year ended 31 December 1998

	£	£
Profit on ordinary activities		28,900
ADD		
Depreciation	20,500	
Loss on sale of fixed assets	1,500	
Entertaining (1,724 + 462)	2,186	
Architects fees	2,000	
		26,186
LESS		
Capital allowances	16,236	
Interest receivable and similar income	12,460	
Reduction in general bad debt provision	225	
		(28,921)
Schedule D Case I profit		26,165

(c) Wooden Toys (UK) Limited
Corporation Tax Computation
Year ended 31 December 1998

	£
Schedule D Case I	26,165
less trading loss brought forward	(3,726)
	22,439
Schedule D Case III	3,460
Patent Royalties received	8,000
Profits chargeable to corporation tax (PCTCT)	33,899
Corporation tax payable	
£33,899 × 21%	7,119
Less ACT set-off (per CT61) (max 20% × £33,899 = £6,780)	(3,750)
Less Income tax suffered (per CT61)	(1,840)
Mainstream corporation tax payable (due 1 October 1999)	1,529

Task 2 (d)

Inland Revenue

Page 1

Corporation Tax Return Version 3

This form, or an approved substitute version of it, must be used whenever a company is required to do so, by a *Notice to deliver a Corporation Tax Return (form CT203)*. This return sets out the information we need and provides a standard format for calculations.

You should read this return form along with your *Notice to deliver a Corporation Tax Return (form CT203)* and *Filling in your Corporation Tax Return (leaflet CT200 Notes)* which you should have received with this form. The notes referred to throughout can be found in the leaflet *CT200 Notes*. You should contact your Tax Office if you need more help.

'Company' means any body chargeable to corporation tax, whether incorporated or not. This definition includes clubs, associations and voluntary organisations.

Sections to be completed
Members' clubs, associations and voluntary organisations - It is likely that you will only have to complete Sections 1 and 2. For further guidance see note 1 in the *Notes*.

All companies - including clubs, etc. - You will not need to complete every Section, but you **must** complete the Declaration and Section 1 on this page. The *Notes* will help you decide whether you should complete the mutually exclusive *Short return* at Section 2 or the *Detailed return* at Section 3. Sections 9 and 10 are optional but you are asked to complete them if they are relevant to the company.

It is important that you read the *Notes* before completing any part of this form.

What to do when you have completed the return

- Make sure you have completed and signed the Declaration, then
- staple together the pages you have completed and attach any supporting calculations
- send these together with the relevant company accounts and, where prepared, directors' and auditors' reports, to your Tax Office using the envelope provided (see Note 3 for the date by which you should do this)
- pay any outstanding corporation tax (as you have shown at box box 65), as advised on the payslip attached to your *Notice to deliver a Corporation Tax Return (form CT203)*. Interest is charged on tax paid later than nine months and one day after the end of an accounting period. Tax is due without the making of an assessment.

Remember - ***Your tax return is not complete unless you send relevant accounts and documentation with this form. Penalties may be charged if your return, or any part of it, is late or incorrect.***

As soon as your figures are agreed
- we will send you an assessment setting out the tax position for the accounting period - unless there are no figures to assess
- we will issue an amended assessment if you have already received an estimated assessment and you have appealed against it.

Section 1: Summary

The company name

WOODEN TOYS (UK) LIMITED

The company address - only if changed since last return made.
Enter the UK registered office address, or the UK address if the company does not have a registered office. If the company does not have premises in the UK show the address of the person making the return.

Company registration number *(if registered)*

100000

Reference
Enter the reference number shown on the *Notice to deliver a Corporation Tax Return (form CT203)*

721 / 14973 / 80

Corporation tax accounting period covered by this return
Cannot exceed 12 months. Enter start and end dates.

From 01 / 01 / 98 To 31 / 12 / 98

If this period is not an accounting period of the company for corporation tax purposes (see note 2) put an 'X' in the box below, complete the Declaration to the right and return this form to your Tax Office. You do not need to complete the rest of this Section or other Sections of this form in these circumstances. ☐

Profits chargeable *(Enter the firgure from box 30). If there are none enter '0'.*

£ 33899

Corporation tax due £ 1529 . 00 p
(Enter the figure from box 61 minus any entry in box 64). If none is due enter '0.00'.

Put an X in the appropriate box

Have you completed Section 8 (Repayments)? Yes ☐ No ☑

Is the company name different from that shown in the *Notice (form CT203)*? Yes ☐ No ☑

Declaration

Enter here the page numbers you are attaching

2, 3, 6, 9

Put an 'X' in the appropriate boxes to show the documents you are enclosing

- a copy of the accounts for the period to which this return relates ☒
- a copy of the company accounts for a different period ☐
- no accounts ☐
- say why not
- calculations showing how the entries in the return form have been arrived at. ☐

I declare that to the best of my knowledge and belief the return on this page and the pages attached is correct and complete.

Signature

Except where a liquidator has been appointed, the company secretary, treasurer, or any other person who is authorised to do so may sign this declaration on behalf of the company. A photocopy of a signature is not acceptable.

Date / /

Name *(in capital letters)*

Status *(company secretary, treasurer, liquidator etc.)*

Page 2

Section 2: Short return

You may complete this section if
- it covers all the entries you need to make and
- each entry, including the company's total income and deductions, is less than £10 million.

In all other cases, or if you prefer, complete Section 3 instead. You should enclose an explanation and calculations of any figures which you have estimated or which are not immediately recognisable from the company's accounts.

The figures to be entered are those adjusted for tax purposes, after deducting capital allowances and adding balancing charges where appropriate. Section 4 should also be completed if capital allowances are claimed.
Please do not enter '0's where the company did not have the source specified in the return form.

	Box	£	Box	£
Trading profits *See note 5*	1	26 165		
Trading losses brought forward *Only include losses made in the same trade. Include charges treated as losses.* ***Do not enter an amount larger than is needed to cover the profits in box 1.*** *See note 6*	2	3726		
Net trading profit *(box 1 minus box 2). If box 2 equals box 1, enter '0'. Leave this box blank if there are no trading profits in box 1*			3	22439
Trading losses of this accounting period *Where there is more than one trade give total for all trades. Do not set box 4 losses against box 1 profits, claim at box 22 against total profits.*	4			
Profits and gains from non-trading loan relationships and other Schedule D Case III income *Include interest and other profits and gains from non-trading loan relationships even if tax has been deducted. Complete box 57 to claim credit for income tax deducted. You will need to complete the* **Detailed return** *at Section 3 if you have deficits on non-trading loan relationships from this, earlier or later accounting periods to include. See note 8*			6	3460
Income within Schedule D Case VI - for example furnished lettings *Enter the figure net of allowable losses brought forward. Exclude income you enter in box 12. See note 7*			9	
Income from which income tax has been deducted - for example building society interest *Enter the gross amount before tax. Exclude any amount included in box 6 above. Complete box 57 to claim credit for income tax deducted. See note 9*			10	8000
Income from UK land and buildings *Enter the amount net of allowable expenses brought forward. Exclude income in box 9 above. See note 10*			12	
Chargeable gains *See note 11*				
Gross gains	13			
Allowable losses *Include any losses brought forward but do not enter an amount larger than the amount of gross gains in box 13 above.*	14			
Net chargeable gains *(box 13 minus box 14) If box 14 equals box 13, enter '0'*			15	
Profits *(total of boxes 3, 6, 9, 10, 12 and 15)*			17	33899
Relief for trading losses of this or of a later period *Put an 'X' in box 21 if amounts carried back from later accounting periods are included in box 22. See note 12*	21		22	
Profits before charges *(box 17 minus box 22)*			26	33899
Charges paid *Do not enter an amount larger than is needed to cover profits in box 26. See note13*			27	
Profits chargeable to corporation tax *(box 26 minus box 27)* ***Copy this figure into the box provided in Section 1 on page 1, and also into the box at the top of page 3***			30	33899

The short return is continued on page 3

Page 3

Profits chargeable to corporation tax

Enter the figure brought forward from page 2, box 30 ... ... £ 33899

If you claim tax is chargeable at the small companies' rate, or if you are claiming marginal small companies' relief, complete boxes 31 - 35. If there are no associated companies please enter '0' against the relevant financial year. *See note 15*

Franked investment income and foreign income dividends arising in the period covered by the return. *See note 15* ... 31 £ [ ]

Number of companies associated with this company in the/each financial year covered by this return *Exclude this company. See note 15* ...	Financial year		Number of associated companies
32	1997	33	0
34	1998	35	0

Corporation tax chargeable *See note 16*

	Financial years beginning 1 April		Amounts of profit £		Rates of tax *See note 16*		Tax £ p
36	1997	37	8475	38	21 · 00	39	1780 · 00
43	1998	44	25424	45	21 · 00	46	5339 · 00

Total corporation tax chargeable *(box 39 plus box 46)* ... ... 50 7119 · 00

Marginal small companies' relief
Attach your computation (see notes 15, 16 and 29) ... 51 £ [ ] · p [ ]

Advance corporation tax restricted if necessary under Section 239(2) ICTA 1988
Put an 'X' in box 53 if amounts carried back from later accounting periods are included. See note 17. 53 [ ] 54 3750 · 00

Total of boxes 51 and 54
Total must not be larger than entry in box 50. Restrict if necessary ... ... 55 3750 · 00

Net corporation tax chargeable *(box 50 minus box 55)* ... ... 56 3369 · 00

Calculation of tax outstanding or overpaid

Income tax deducted from gross income included in return
Do not include deductions used to cover income tax for which the company was liable to account to the Inland Revenue on payments it has made. See note 18 ... ... 57 1840 · 00

Corporation tax due

Box 56 minus box 57. If box 57 equals or is greater than box 56, enter '0.00' and go to box 59.
Copy the figure in box 61 to the box provided in Section 1 on page 1. *See note 20* ... ... 61 1529 · 00

Income tax repayable to the company *(box 57 minus box 56).*
Complete Section 8 on page 8. Do not complete unless you are making a claim. *See note 28...* ... 59 [ ] · [ ]

Corporation tax already paid (and not repaid). *See note 21* ... ... 63 [ ] · [ ]

Corporation tax outstanding *(box 61 minus box 63). This amount is payable to the Accounts Office.*
If box 63 equals or is greater than box 61, enter '0.00' and go to box 66. See note 23 ... ... 65 1529 · 00

Corporation tax overpaid *(box 63 minus box 61).*
Complete Section 8 on page 8 also. See note 28 ... ... 66 [ ] · [ ]

This is the last page of the short return

Section 4: Claims for capital allowances and details of balancing charges arising

You must complete this section if you want to claim capital allowances, whether or not those allowances are reflected elsewhere in the return. You should also show balancing charges taken into account in the short or detailed return. Show details of qualifying expenditure on which writing-down allowances may be claimed, even if you do not want to claim any allowances for this period. *See note 25*

Notice of expenditure on machinery and plant *See note 25*

Expenditure on which first year allowance is claimed £	Qualifying expenditure on long life assets on which writing down allowances may be claimed £	Qualifying expenditure on other assets on which writing down allowances may be claimed £
68 12000	91	69 10000

Charges and allowances included in calculation of trading profit or losses

	Balancing charges £	Capital allowances £
Cars *Including leased out and "expensive" cars*	70	71 5531
Machinery and plant - *long life assets*	92	93
- *other*	72	73 7625
Industrial buildings and structures *Including qualifying hotels, and commercial buildings and hotels in enterprise zones*	74	75 3080
Other charges and allowances *For example agricultural buildings, mineral extraction, scientific research, patents*	76	77
Charges and allowances not included in calculation of trading profit or losses	78	79

Section 5: Particulars of advance corporation tax and surplus advance corporation tax

Complete this section if you have surplus advance corporation tax brought forward or have paid advance corporation tax (and it has not been repaid) in respect of qualifying distributions made in the period covered by this return.

	£	p
Particulars of advance corporation tax paid ...	3750	00
Particulars of any surplus advance corporation tax brought forward ...		

Section 6: Amounts claimed as group relief

Complete this section if you have claimed group relief at box 29 (see note 26). Attach a separate sheet of paper if you need more space. Attach a copy of each surrendering company's notice of consent to the claim unless a special arrangement is in force. Include claims made under the consortium provisions.

Name of surrendering company	**Accounting period** Show the start and end dates of any accounting period which is different from the one to which this return relates.	**Tax reference** Show the Tax Office number and the tax inspector's file reference. If you do not know these, supply whatever information you have that will help us to identify the company, for example the company registration number.	**Amount claimed from each company**
			£
			£
			£
			£
			£
			£
			£
			£
			£
			£
			£
			£
			£

Total £

This figure should be the same as the one in box 29.

Page 9

Section 9: Figures brought forward and carried forward

Please complete this section if any of the following items are

- brought forward from the previous accounting period or
- available for carry forward from the period to which this return relates.

Please provide a reconciliation of any figures that are not explained elsewhere in your accounts and calculations. Attach a separate sheet of paper if you need more space.

	Total brought forward	Less amount used	Plus net amount available to carry forward from this accounting period	Total to carry forward
Trading losses *include trade charges treated as losses*	£ 3,726	£ 3,726	£	£
Schedule D case VI losses	£	£	£	£
Excess management expenses *Include business charges treated as management expenses*	£	£	£	£
Surplus ACT *Enter the figure net of amounts set off or repaid or surrendered to subsidiaries*	£ p	£ p	£ p	£ p
Surplus franked investment income	£ p	£ p	£ p	£ p
Losses allowable against chargeable gains	£	£	£	£
Net non-trade deficits and losses on loan relationships (including interest), exchange fluctuations, and certain financial instruments *See note 8.*	£	£	£	£
Others *Please specify*	£	£	£	£
	£	£	£	£
	£	£	£	£
	£	£	£	£

Task 2(e)

Inland Revenue

Return of
Company Payments, Distributions and Interest

Collector of Taxes
Inland Revenue Accounts Office (Shipley)
BRADFORD
West Yorkshire BD98 8AA
Telephone: Bradford (01274) 530750

1	2 Company regn. no.	3 Accounting date	4 Accounts Office ref.

IMPORTANT: Please enter in these 4 boxes the details from your CT61 Notice

Advance Corporation Tax on **Qualifying Distributions**
Income Tax deducted from **Company Payments** and **Interest**
Income Tax payable on **Gilt Interest** received without deduction of tax
Tax on manufactured payments received from abroad

- Please use this form when you need to make a Return of company payments, distributions and interest. **You must give all the information asked for on this page and sign the declaration below.** But you need only fill in the other parts of the Return which are relevant to your company. Only use the CT61 Supplement if you need to make a return of Foreign Income Dividends, 'deemed FIDs' or Gilt Interest.
- You are required to make your Return, and pay any tax, within 14 days after the end of the Return Period. Send the Return back to me in the envelope provided.
- *The enclosed CT61 Notes will help you.*
- If your Return shows that tax is payable use the payslip on the enclosed form CT61 Notice.
- When you send back this Return **please also enclose the CT61 Notice**, even if no payment is enclosed.

Company details

Name of company: WOODEN TOYS (UK) LIMITED

Address:
Enter the address you would like future CT61 Returns sent to

UNIT 3
THE INDUSTRIAL ESTATE
CASTER BRIDGE
WESSEX Postcode CA11 2RQ

Please tick if this is a change of Registered Office '✓' [ ]

Period covered by this Return

Return Periods are fixed by law. See CT61 Notes page 3 for guidance.

	Day	Month	Year		Day	Month	Year
Return period ►	01	04	19 99	to	30	06	19 99
being part of the **Accounting period** ►	01	01	19 99	to	31	12	19 99

Example: Distribution paid on 25 April 1997, and the accounting period is year to 31 December 1997. Enter:

Return period ►	01	04	19 97	to	30	06	19 97
being part of the Accounting period ►	01	01	19 97	to	31	12	19 97

For official use only
901

Declaration *False statements can result in prosecution*

To the best of my knowledge the information given in this Return (and the Supplement, if used) is correct and complete

Signature

It would assist if you can state your daytime telephone number and extension here

Name *in CAPITALS*

State in what capacity you make this Return

Date

Please tick if CT61 Supplement is attached '✓' [ ]

21267 4.97 Niceday Stationery & Print Limited BMSD4/97 W0H7003

1 Advance Corporation Tax (ACT) on Qualifying Distributions

Use Part 1 to calculate the ACT payable on Distributions paid.
Use Part 2 below to record Franked Investment Income received.
Franked investment income in box 23 is set-off to reduce the ACT payable in Part 1.
For further information see Notes page 2.

List separately the payments made on different dates. If you need more room please attach a schedule.

Take care to use the correct ACT rate.

	Date		Amount of distribution £	+ ACT payable £	=	Amount of franked payment £
Dividends and other qualifying distributions paid *Exclude – payments at* **03** *– Foreign Income Dividends (FIDS)* *– 'deemed FIDS' (see notes page 4)*		01			02	
Dividends paid for which you wish to account for ACT despite an election under Section 247(1) ICTA 1988 *See Notes page 2*		03			04	

Total **franked payments**	02 + 04	05	
Deduct **franked investment income to be set-off**	From Part 2, box 23	06	
Total **franked payments** for which ACT is payable	05 – 06	10	
Calculate the **Advance Corporation Tax (ACT)** included in the figure at **10**	*See both examples in Notes page 2*	11	
Add the **ACT payable on Foreign Income Dividends (FIDs)**	From CT61 Supplement, boxes 67 and 72	12	
Total ACT for this return period	11 + 12	13	
Deduct Additional amounts paid to **non-residents** *See Notes page 4*	**Enter all the additional amounts paid, and attach form 251B Divs FD in duplicate**	14	
ACT payable Carry to **Payslip** on CT61 Notice	13 – 14	15	

Do not enter a 'minus' figure in box 15. If 14 is greater than 13, claim repayment of the excess in Part 8

2 Franked investment income - running record for set-off or repayment

Amount **brought forward** from last Return		16	
Adjustment, if any, agreed with Inspector ... ... or a claim under Section 242 ICTA 1988 not yet agreed	*Enter 'MINUS' if appropriate*	17	
	16 + or – 17	18	

	Date	Description	Amount
Franked investment income received since last return			
		Total 19	

You can include income received in earlier return periods if you did not need to submit a form for those periods. See Notes page 1.
Do not enter Foreign Income Dividends here.
If you need more room please attach a schedule.

Adjustment, if any, agreed with Inspector	*Enter 'MINUS' if appropriate*	20	
Total after adjustment	19 + or – 20	21	
Total franked investment income now available for set-off or repayment	18 + 21	22	
Deduct **Amount set-off against franked payments in Part 1**	From 22 or 05, whichever is smaller	23	*Carry this figure to Part 1, box 06*
Franked investment income after above set-off	22 – 23	24	
Repayment of ACT previously paid. Franked investment income at 24 can be set-off against franked payments of earlier return periods **for this accounting period only.**	25 **ACT repayment now claimed** *Carry this figure to Part 8, line b*	26	**Amount of franked investment income set-off**
Amount to be carried forward to next Return	24 – 26	27	

3 Income Tax on Annual Payments and Interest

In boxes 28 and 29, group separately payments taxed at basic rate and payments taxed at lower rate.
If you need more room please attach a schedule.

Use Part 3 to calculate the Income Tax payable on payments made.
Use Part 4 to record Income Tax you have suffered on payments received. This can be set-off to reduce the tax due in Part 3. *For further information see Notes page 3.*

	Date	Description		Gross amount £		Income Tax £
Annual payments etc made under deduction of Income Tax at basic rate or lower rate *See Notes page 3* *Include all manufactured interest, unless entered at 30 below.*	02.06.99	GIFT AID	28	12987 : 00	29	2987 : 00
Annual payments etc to non-residents made under deduction of reduced rate tax under a Double Taxation Agreement *See Notes page 4.* *Ref. no. of the authority* ▶			30		31	
Income Tax on annual payments etc above ... 29 + 31					32	2987 : 00

Interest paid by deposit-takers including distributions paid by building societies *Enter the Gross amount paid from which you deducted tax, and the lower rate Income Tax you deducted* *See Notes page 3* *Do not enter interest paid gross, eg TESSA interest*			Gross amount		Income Tax
	Before 6 April	33		34	
	From 6 April	35		36	
			When the return period does not include 6 April use boxes 35 and 36		

Total Income Tax	32 + 34 + 36	37	2987 : 00
Less Income Tax deducted from income **received** now claimed as a set-off	From Part 4, box 53	38	2300 : 00
	37 – 38	39	687 : 00
Less Income Tax on Gilt Interest received now claimed as a set-off	From CT61 Supplement, box 83	40	
Income Tax now payable Carry to **Payslip** on CT61 Notice	39 – 40	46	687 : 00

4 Income Tax deducted - running record in this Accounting Period for set-off or repayment

Amount of Income Tax **brought forward** from last Return for this accounting period		47	
Adjustment, if any, agreed with Inspector ...	*Enter 'MINUS' if appropriate*	48	
	47 + or – 48	49	

Income received under deduction of tax since last Return for this accounting period

	Date	Description		Gross amount		Income Tax
You can include income received in earlier return periods in this accounting period if you did not need to submit a form for those periods. See Notes page 1. *If you need more room please attach a schedule.*	01.04.99	PATENT ROYALTIES		10000 : 00		2300 : 00
		Totals	50	10000 : 00	51	2300 : 00

Running total now available for set-off or repayment below	49 + 51	52	2300 : 00
Amount set-off against Income Tax in Part 3	From 52 or 37, whichever is smaller	53	2300 : 00 ◀ *Carry this figure to Part 3, box 38*
Repayment now claimed of tax paid on annual payments etc in Part 3 of an earlier Return **for this accounting period only**		54	◀ *Carry this figure to Part 8*
Total Income Tax now used for set-off or repayment ...	53 + 54	55	2300 : 00
Amount to be **carried forward** to next Return for **this accounting period**	52 – 55	56	NIL

5 Certain other distributions

If you need more room please attach a schedule

	Date	Description	Amount £
a Qualifying distributions which are not money payments			
b Payments about which there is a doubt as to whether they are qualifying distributions			
c Distributions (excluding money payments) which, exceptionally, do not fall within an accounting period			

Do not account for ACT on the above payments. The Inspector will make any necessary assessment.

6 Tax on manufactured payments from abroad

See Notes page 4

a **Manufactured dividends received from abroad** *by UK resident companies* *(AMOUNTS RECEIVED)* Tax payable - *at ACT rate* *Carry to Payslip on CT61 Notice*

b **Manufactured interest received from abroad** *by UK resident companies and by UK branches of overseas companies* *(GROSS INTEREST)* Income Tax payable at lower rate *Carry to Payslip on CT61 Notice*

7 Income Tax on Gilt Interest received: totals from CT61 Supplement

a Income Tax **payable** on Gilt Interest received — From box 79

b **Repayment** of excessive payment on account — 78 – 77 if positive

c **Repayment** of 'Gilts' Income Tax — From box 88

d **Repayment** of 'other' Income Tax — From box 85

e Total 'Gilts related' repayments ... ... b + c + d

f Net Income Tax **payable** · *Do not enter a minus figure here. If e is greater than a claim repayment of the excess in Part 8 below* a – e *Carry to Payslip on CT61 Notice*

8 Claim for repayment or reimbursement

Use this section to summarise any claims arising in other sections of your Return:

a *From Part 1*	Reimbursement of amounts paid to **non-residents**	14 – 13 if positive	
b *From Parts 2 and 9*	Repayment of **ACT previously paid**	From boxes 25 and 69	
c *From Part 4*	Repayment of **Income Tax previously paid**	From box 54	
d *From Part 7*	Net 'Gilts related' Income Tax repayments	7e – 7a if positive	
e	**Total claimed**	a + b + c + d	

Other forms

Please tick if you require a form to declare the following items:

Non-qualifying distributions *Form CT2* *See Notes page 2* '√' ☐

Stock dividends Section 249 ICTA 1988 *Form CT101* '√' ☐

When sending back this Return, please

- check you have filled in the blue boxes at the top of page 1
- check you have signed the declaration on page 1
- send the CT61 Notice with this Return, even if no payment is enclosed.

When we receive this Return we will send you another form for your company's next Return.

Please note If the Inspector considers that any distributions, payments, etc have been omitted from this Return, or is in any way dissatisfied with it, the Inland Revenue can issue an appropriate assessment.

(f)

Templar and Co
23 Back Lane
Casterbridge
Wessex
CA11 2RT

Mr R. Wood
Wooden Toys (UK) Limited
Unit 3
The Industrial Estate
Casterbridge
Wessex
CA11 2RQ

Dear Mr Wood

Wooden Toys (UK) Limited
Corporation Tax Computation and Return, year ended 31 December 1998
CT61, Quarter Ended 30 June 1999.

I have pleasure in enclosing the corporation tax computation and the corporation tax return form CT200 for the year to 31 December 1998, together with a copy for your retention.

Will you please look through the computation and the return, and if you are happy that they are both complete and correct will you sign and date each and return them to me for submission to the Inland Revenue.

The computation shows that corporation tax of £1,529 is due, and this should be paid by 1 October 1999 to avoid a charge to interest. You should have received a payslip attached to the notice to file the corporation tax return, but if you would like any assistance with making the payment, please let me know.

I am also enclosing the form CT61 in respect of the income tax payable on the Gift Aid payment as reduced by the income tax deducted from the patent royalties received.

Will you please read through the form, and if you are happy that it is complete and correct please sign it on the front and return it to me. A further copy is enclosed for your retention.

The income tax now due is £687. This must be paid by 14 July 1999, so will you please let me have a cheque for this amount (payable to "Inland Revenue") so that I can forward it with the return.

Please do not hesitate to contact me if you have any queries.

Yours sincerely

Jane Simons
Tax Department Manager
Templar & Co.

PERSONAL TAXATION
PRACTICE DEVOLVED ASSESSMENT

SUGGESTED SOLUTIONS

TASK 1

(a) (i) **Penny Moore**
Schedule E Earnings for 1998/99

	£	£
Salary (PAYE £6,675)		28,450
Benefits in kind		
Car benefit	2,666	
Fuel for company car	1,280	
Mobile telephone	200	
Private medical or dental insurance	450	
Expenses payments	715	5,311
		33,761
Allowable expenses		
Travel and subsistence	595	
Entertaining	120	(715)
Schedule E earnings		33,046

(ii) **Penny Moore**
Investment Income for 1998/99

		Dividend £	*Tax Credit* £	*Dividend plus Tax credit* £
1,000 ABC plc	1.7.98	80.00	20.00	100.00
1,000 ABC plc	1.12.98	140.00	35.00	175.00
2,000 XYZ plc	11.5.98	68.00	17.00	85.00
2,000 XYZ plc	31.10.98	132.00	33.00	165.00
10,000 LMN plc	21.6.98	500.00	125.00	625.00
		920.00	230.00	1,150.00

Bank Interest	*After Tax* £	*Tax Deducted* £	*Gross* £
Nat East Bank			
10743656	120.00	30.00	150.00
47852130	560.00	140.00	700.00
	680.00	170.00	850.00

Nat North Bank
TESSA Exempt

(iii) **Penny Moore**
Rental income for 1998/99

	£
No.2 Farm Cottages	
Rent receivable	
12 × 400	4,800
Less Insurance	(450)
Schedule A income	4,350

(iv) **Penny Moore**
Capital Gains for 1998/99

				£
5.9.98	10,000	LMN plc Shares	proceeds	22,000
23.11.87		Cost		(3,000)
				19,000
	Less indexation allowance			
	$\frac{161.2 - 103.4}{103.4} \times 3,000$			(1,677)
				17,323
	Less capital losses brought forward			(800)
				16,523
	Less annual exemption			(6,800)
	Capital gains			9,723

(b) **Penny Moore - Income and Capital Gains Tax Computation for 1998/99**

Income tax			*Tax deducted at source*
Earned income	£	£	£
Schedule E	33,046		6,675
Schedule D Case I	11,471		
		44,517	
Deductions			
Personal pension 12 × 150	1,800		
		(1,800)	
		42,717	
Investment income			
Savings income			
Dividends	1,150		230
Bank interest	850	2,000	170
Non Savings income			
Rental income	4,350		
		4,350	
		49,067	
Charges on income		-	
Statutory Total Income		49,067	
Less personal allowance		(4,195)	
Taxable income		44,872	7,075
Tax thereon			
4,300 @ 20%		860	
22,800 @ 23%		5,244	
17,772 @ 40%		7,109	
		13,213	
Less tax deducted at source		(7,075)	
Income tax payable		6,138	
Capital gains	9,723		
Capital gains tax thereon			
9,723 @ 40%	3,889		
		3,889	
Income tax and capital gains tax payable		10,027	
Less payments on account			
31 January 1999	1,000		
31 July 1999	1,000		
		(2,000)	
Balancing Payment		8,027	
Payments on account for 1999/00 ½ × 6,138		3,069	

Task 1(c)

Income for the year ended 5 April 1999

Inland Revenue

EMPLOYMENT

Fill in these boxes first

Name: PENNY MOORE

Tax reference: 1020304050

If you want help, look up the box numbers in the Notes

Details of employer

Employer's PAYE reference — 1.1	999 1N111
Employer's name — 1.2	NUGGETS LTD
Date employment started (only if between 6 April 1998 and 5 April 1999) — 1.3	/ /
Date finished (only if between 6 April 1998 and 5 April 1999) — 1.4	/ /
Employer's address — 1.5	UNIT 1 ANYTOWN TRADING ESTATE ANYTOWN Postcode AN5 4BJ
Tick box 1.6 if you were a director of the company — 1.6	
and, if so, tick box 1.7 if it was a close company — 1.7	

Income from employment

- ***Money*** - see Notes, page EN3

	Box	Before tax
Payments from P60 (or P45 or pay slips)	1.8	£ 28,450
Payments not on P60 etc. - tips	1.9	£
- other payments (excluding expenses shown below and lump sums and compensation payments or benefits shown overleaf)	1.10	£

	Box	Tax deducted
UK tax deducted from payments in boxes 1.8 to 1.10	1.11	£ 6675

- ***Benefits and expenses*** *- see Notes, pages EN3 to EN6. If any benefits connected with termination of employment were received, or enjoyed, after that termination and were from a **former** employer you need to complete Help Sheet IR204, available from the Orderline. Do not enter such benefits here.*

	Box	Amount		Box	Amount
Assets transferred/ payments made for you	1.12	£	Vans	1.18	£
Vouchers/credit cards	1.13	£	Interest-free and low-interest loans	1.19	£
Living accommodation	1.14	£	Mobile telephones	1.20	£ 200
Mileage allowance	1.15	£	Private medical or dental insurance	1.21	£ 450
Company cars	1.16	£ 2666	Other benefits	1.22	£
Fuel for company cars	1.17	£ 1280	Expenses payments received and balancing charges	1.23	£ 715

SA101

Income from employment continued

■ *Lump sums and compensation payments or benefits including such payments and benefits from a former employer*
Note that 'lump sums' here includes any contributions which your employer made to an unapproved retirement benefits scheme

*You must read page EN6 of the Notes **before** filling in boxes 1.24 to 1.30*

Reliefs

- £30,000 exemption — **1.24** £
- Foreign service and disability — **1.25** £
- Retirement and death lump sums — **1.26** £

Taxable lump sums

- From box H of *Help Sheet IR204* — **1.27** £
- From box Q of *Help Sheet IR204* — **1.28** £
- From box R of *Help Sheet IR204* — **1.29** £
- Tax deducted from payments in boxes 1.27 to 1.29 — Tax deducted **1.30** £

■ *Foreign earnings not taxable in the UK in year ended 5 April 1999* - *see Notes, page EN6* — **1.31** £

■ *Expenses you incurred in doing your job* - *see Notes, starting on page EN6*

- Travel and subsistence costs — **1.32** £ 595
- Fixed deductions for expenses — **1.33** £
- Professional fees and subscriptions — **1.34** £
- Other expenses and capital allowances — **1.35** £ 120
- Tick box 1.36 if the figure in box 1.32 includes travel between your home and a permanent workplace — **1.36**

■ *Foreign Earnings Deduction* — **1.37** £

■ *Foreign tax for which tax credit relief not claimed* — **1.38** £

Additional information

Now fill in any other supplementary Pages that apply to you.
Otherwise, go back to page 2 in your Tax Return and finish filling it in.

Income for the year ended 5 April 1999

Inland Revenue

PARTNERSHIP (SHORT)

Fill in these boxes first

Name: PENNY MOORE

Tax reference: 10203 04050

If you want help, look up the box numbers in the Notes

Partnership details

Partnership reference number **4.1** 67890 12345

Partnership trade or profession **4.2** JEWELLERS

- Date you started being a partner (if during 1998-99) **4.3** / /
- Date you stopped being a partner (if during 1998-99) **4.4** / /

Your share of the partnership's trading or professional income

Basis period begins **4.5** 01/04/98 and ends **4.6** 31/03/99

• Your share of the profit or loss of this year's account for tax purposes			**4.7** £ 11471
• Adjustment to arrive at profit or loss for this basis period			**4.8** £
• Overlap profit brought forward	**4.9** £	Deduct overlap relief used this year	**4.10** £
• Overlap profit carried forward	**4.11** £		
• Adjustment for farmers' averaging (see Notes, page PN3 if the partnership made a loss in 1998-99) or foreign tax deducted, if tax credit relief not claimed			**4.12** £
Net profit for 1998-99 (if loss, enter '0' in box 4.13 and enter the loss in box 4.14)			**4.13** £ 11471
Allowable loss for 1998-99		**4.14** £	
• Loss offset against other income for 1998-99		**4.15** £	
• Loss to carry back		**4.16** £	
• Loss to carry forward (that is, allowable loss not claimed in any other way)		**4.17** £	
• Losses brought forward from last year		**4.18** £	
• Losses brought forward from last year used this year			**4.19** £
Taxable profit after losses brought forward			box 4.13 *minus* box 4.19 **4.20** £ 11471
• Add amounts **not** included in the partnership accounts that are needed to calculate your taxable profit (for example, Enterprise Allowance (Business Start-up Allowance) received in 1998-99)			**4.21**
Total taxable profits from this business			box 4.20 + box 4.21 **4.22** £ 11471

Class 4 National Insurance Contributions

• Tick this box if exception or deferment applies	**4.23**
• Adjustments to profit chargeable to Class 4 National Insurance Contributions	**4.24** £
Class 4 National Insurance Contributions due	**4.25** £

SA104

Your share of taxed income

- Share of taxed income (liable at 20%) — **4.70** £

Your share of Partnership Trading and Professional Profits

- Share of partnership profits (other than that liable at 20%) — from box 4.22 — **4.73** £ 11471

Your share of tax paid

- Share of Income Tax paid — **4.74** £
- Share of SC60 deductions — **4.75** £
- Share of tax deducted from trading income (not SC60 deductions) — **4.75A** £

boxes 4.74 + 4.75 + 4.75A — **4.77** £

Additional information

Now fill in any other supplementary Pages that apply to you.
Otherwise, go back to page 2 in your Tax Return and finish filling it in

Income for the year ended 5 April 1999

Inland Revenue

LAND AND PROPERTY

Fill in these boxes first

Name: PENNY MOORE

Tax reference: 10203 04050

Are you claiming Rent a Room relief for gross rents of £4,250 or less? No ✓ Yes

(Or £2,125 if the claim is shared?)

Read the Notes on page LN2 to find out

- **whether you can claim Rent a Room relief; and**
- **how to claim relief for gross rents over £4,250**

If 'Yes', and this is your only income from UK property, you have finished these Pages

Is your income from furnished holiday lettings? No ✓ Yes

If 'No', turn over and fill in Page L2 to give details of your property income

If 'Yes', fill in boxes 5.1 to 5.18 before completing Page L2

Furnished holiday lettings

- Income from furnished holiday lettings — 5.1 £

■ *Expenses* (furnished holiday lettings only)

- Rent, rates, insurance, ground rents etc. — 5.2 £
- Repairs, maintenance and renewals — 5.3 £
- Finance charges, including interest — 5.4 £
- Legal and professional costs — 5.5 £
- Cost of services provided, including wages — 5.6 £
- Other expenses — 5.7 £

total of boxes 5.2 to 5.7 — 5.8 £

Net profit (put figures in brackets if a loss) — box 5.1 *minus* box 5.8 — 5.9 £

■ *Tax adjustments*

- Private use — 5.10 £
- Balancing charges — 5.11 £
- Capital allowances — 5.13 £

box 5.10 + box 5.11 — 5.12 £

Profit for the year (copy to box 5.19). If loss, enter '0' in box 5.14 and put the loss in box 5.15 — boxes 5.9 + 5.12 *minus* box 5.13 — 5.14 £

Loss for the year (if you have entered '0' in box 5.14) — boxes 5.9 + 5.12 *minus* box 5.13 — 5.15 £

- Loss offset against 1998-99 total income — 5.16 £
- Loss carried back — see Notes, page LN4 — 5.17 £
- Loss offset against other income from property (copy to box 5.38) — see Notes, page LN4 — 5.18 £

SA105

Other property income

■ *Income*

• Furnished holiday lettings profits	copy from box 5.14 **5.19** £				
• Rents and other income from land and property	**5.20** £ 4800	Tax deducted **5.21** £			
• Chargeable premiums	**5.22** £			boxes 5.19 + 5.20 + 5.22 **5.23** £ 4800	

■ ***Expenses*** (do not include figures you have already put in boxes 5.2 to 5.7 on Page L1)

• Rent, rates, insurance, ground rents etc.	**5.24** £ 450		
• Repairs, maintenance and renewals	**5.25** £		
• Finance charges, including interest	**5.26** £		
• Legal and professional costs	**5.27** £		
• Costs of services provided, including wages	**5.28** £		
• Other expenses	**5.29** £		total of boxes 5.24 to 5.29 **5.30** £ 450
Net profit (put figures in brackets if a loss)			box 5.23 *minus* box 5.30 **5.31** £ 4350

■ ***Tax adjustments***

• Private use	**5.32** £		
• Balancing charges	**5.33** £		box 5.32 + box 5.33 **5.34** £
• Rent a Room exempt amount	**5.35** £		
• Capital allowances	**5.36** £		
• 10% wear and tear	**5.37** £		
• Furnished holiday lettings losses (from box 5.18)	**5.38** £		total of boxes 5.35 to 5.38 **5.39** £
Adjusted profit (if loss enter '0' in box 5.40 and put the loss in box 5.41)			boxes 5.31 + 5.34 *minus* box 5.39 **5.40** £ 4350
Adjusted loss (if you have entered '0' in box 5.40)		boxes 5.31 + 5.34 *minus* box 5.39 **5.41** £	
• Loss brought forward from previous year			**5.42** £
Profit for the year			box 5.40 *minus* box 5.42 **5.43** £ 4350
• Loss offset against total income		**5.44** £	
• Loss to carry forward to following year		**5.45** £	
• Pooled expenses from 'one estate election' carried forward		**5.46** £	
Tick box 5.47 if these Pages include details of property let jointly		**5.47**	

Now fill in any other supplementary Pages that apply to you.
Otherwise, go back to page 2 of your Tax Return and finish filling it in.

Inland Revenue

For the year ended 5 April 1999

CAPITAL GAINS

Fill in these boxes first

Name	Tax reference
PENNY MOORE	10203 04050

If you want help, look up the box numbers in the Notes.

*Please complete Pages CG2 and CG **before** filling in the rest of this Page. If you think you will need more than one copy of Pages CG2 and CG3 make photocopies before you begin filling them in.*

Your 1998-99 Capital Gains Tax liability

• Total taxable gains from Page CG3 overleaf	8.7	£ 16523
• Your taxable gains *minus* the annual exempt amount	8.8 (box 8.7 *minus* £6,800)	£ 9723
• Additional liability in respect of non-resident or dual resident trusts	8.9	£

Capital losses

(Remember if your loss arose on a transaction with a connected person, see Notes page CGN11, you can only set that loss agains gains you make on disposals to that same connected person)

■ ***This year's losses***

• Total from Page CG2	8.10	£
• Used against gains	8.11	£
• Used against earlier years' gains (see Notes, page CGN8)	8.12	£
• Used against income (see Notes, page CGN7): 8.13A £ amount claimed against income of 1998-99; 8.13B £ amount claimed against income of 1997-98	8.13 (box 8.13A + box 8.13B)	£
• This year's unused losses	8.14 (box 8.10 *minus* (boxes 8.11 + 8.12 + 8.13))	£

■ ***Earlier years' losses***

• Unused losses of 1996-97 and 1997-98	8.15	£ 800
• Used this year (losses from box 8.15 are used in priority to losses from box 8.18)	8.16	£ 800
• Remaining unused losses of 1996-97 and 1997-98	8.17 (box 8.15 *minu* box 8.16)	£
• Unused losses of 1995-96 and earlier years	8.18	£
• Used this year (losses from box 8.15 are used in priority to losses from box 8.18)	8.19 (box 8.6 *minu* box 8.16)	£

■ ***Total of unused losses to carry forward***

• Carried forward losses of 1996-97 and later years	8.20 (box 8.14 + box 8.17)	£
• Carried forward losses of 1995-96 and earlier years	8.21 (box 8.18 *minu* box 8.19)	£

Your 1998-99 Capital Gains Tax liability

Gains (on assets without mixed use)

	A Description of asset	B Tick box if unquoted shares	C Tick box if estimate or valuation used	D Tick box if asset held at 31March 1982	E Insert the later of date of acquisition and 16 March 1998	F Insert the date of disposal	G Disposal proceeds	H Tick box if relief claimed or due	I Chargeable Gains after reliefs but before loss and taper
1	LMN plc shares				16/03/98	5/09/98	£ 22,000		£17,32[illegible]
2					/ /	/ /	£		£
3					/ /	/ /	£		£
4					/ /	/ /	£		£
5					/ /	/ /	£		£
6					/ /	/ /	£		£
7					/ /	/ /	£		£
8					/ /	/ /	£		£

Gains on mixed business and non-business use assets (see the notes on pages CGN2 and CGN15)

9					/ /	/ /	£		£
									£
10					/ /	/ /	£		£
									£

Total **8.1** £17,323

Total column

Losses

	Description of asset	Tick box if unquoted shares	Tick box if estimate or valuation used	Tick box if asset held at 31March 1982	Disposal proceeds	Tick box if relief claimed or due	Net losses
13					£		£
14					£		£
15					£		£
16					£		£

Total net losses of year **8.2** £

J	K	L			M	N	O
...ater, ...r if ...usiness ...set	Taper rate	Losses deducted			Gains after losses	Tapered gains (gains from column M x % in column K)	Further information
		L1 Allowable losses of the year	L2 Income losses set against gains	L3 Unused losses b/f from earlier years			
	100%	£	£	£ 800	£ 16523	£ 16523	
	%	£	£	£	£	£	
	%	£	£	£	£	£	
	%	£	£	£	£	£	
	%	£	£	£	£	£	
	%	£	£	£	£	£	
	%	£	£	£	£	£	
	%	£	£	£	£	£	
B	%	£	£	£	£	£	
	100%	£	£	£	£	£	
B	%	£	£	£	£	£	
	100%	£	£	£	£	£	
			8.5 £	**8.6** £ 800		**8.3** £ 16523	
			Total column L2	*Total column L3*		*Total column N*	

1 **Attributed gains** *(enter source in right hand column)* £

2 **Attributed gains** *(enter source in right hand column)* £

Total of attributed gains **8.4** £

box 8.3 + box 8.4

Total Taxable Gains £16523

copy to box 8.7 on Page CG1

INCOME for the year ended 5 April 1999

Q10 Did you receive any income from UK savings and investments? NO [ ] YES [✓]

If yes, fill in boxes 10.1 to 10.32 as appropriate. Include only your share from any joint savings and investments.

■ *Interest*

	Amount after tax deducted	Tax deducted	Gross amount before tax / Taxable amount
• Interest from UK banks, building societies and deposit takers			
- where **no tax** has been deducted			Taxable amount **10.1** £
- where **tax has** been deducted	**10.2** £ 680	**10.3** £ 170	**10.4** £ 850
• Interest distributions from UK authorised unit trusts and open-ended investment companies (dividend distributions go below)	**10.5** £	**10.6** £	**10.7** £
• National Savings (other than FIRST Option Bonds and the first £70 of interest from a National Savings Ordinary Account)			Taxable amount **10.8** £
• National Savings FIRST Option Bonds	**10.9** £	**10.10** £	**10.11** £
• Other income from UK savings and investments (except dividends)	**10.12** £	**10.13** £	**10.14** £

■ *Dividends*

• Dividends and other qualifying distributions from UK companies	Dividend/distribution **10.15** £ 920	Tax credit **10.16** £ 230	Dividend/distribution plus credit **10.17** £ 1150
• Dividend distributions from UK authorised unit trusts and open-ended investment companies	Dividend/distribution **10.18** £	Tax credit **10.19** £	Dividend/distribution plus credit **10.20** £
• Scrip dividends from UK companies	Dividend **10.21** £	Notional tax **10.22** £	Dividend plus notional tax **10.23** £
• Foreign income dividends from UK companies	Dividend **10.24** £	Notional tax **10.25** £	Dividend plus notional tax **10.26** £
• Foreign income dividend distributions from UK authorised unit trusts and open-ended investment companies	Dividend **10.27** £	Notional tax **10.28** £	Dividend plus notional tax **10.29** £
• Non-qualifying distributions and loans written off	**10.30** £	Notional tax **10.31** £	Taxable amount **10.32** £

RELIEFS *for the year ended 5 April 1999*

Q14 Do you want to claim relief for pension contributions? NO YES ✓ — If yes, fill in boxes 14.1 to 14.17 as appropriate.

Do not include contributions deducted from your pay by your employer to their pension scheme, because tax relief is given automatically. But do include your contributions to personal pension schemes.

■ ***Retirement annuity contracts***

Qualifying payments made in 1998-99	14.1 £	1998-99 payments used in an earlier year	14.2 £	Relief claimed box 14.1 *minus* (boxes 14.2 and 14.3, but not 14.4)
1998-99 payments now to be carried back	14.3 £	Payments brought back from 1999-2000	14.4 £	14.5 £

■ ***Self-employed contributions to personal pension plans***

Qualifying payments made in 1998-99	14.6 £ 1800	1998-99 payments used in an earlier year	14.7 £	Relief claimed box 14.6 *minus* (boxes 14.7 and 14.8, but not 14.9)
1998-99 payments now to be carried back	14.8 £	Payments brought back from 1999-2000	14.9 £	14.10 £ 1800

■ ***Employee contributions to personal pension plans*** *(include your gross contribution - see the note on box 14.11 in your Tax Return Guide)*

Qualifying payments made in 1998-99	14.11 £	1998-99 payments used in an earlier year	14.12 £	Relief claimed box 14.11 *minus* (boxes 14.12 and 14.13, but not 14.14)
1998-99 payments now to be carried back	14.13 £	Payments brought back from 1999-2000	14.14 £	14.15 £

■ ***Contributions to other pension schemes***

- Amount of contributions to employer's schemes **not deducted** at source from pay — 14.16 £
- Gross amount of free-standing additional voluntary contributions paid in 1998-99 — 14.17 £

Q15 Do you want to claim any of the following reliefs? NO ✓ YES — If yes, fill in boxes 15.1 to 15.12, as appropriate.

• Payments you made for vocational training	Amount of payment 15.1 £	
• Interest eligible for relief on loans to buy your main home (other than MIRAS)	Amount of payment 15.2 £	
• Interest eligible for relief on other qualifying loans	Amount of payment 15.3 £	
• Maintenance or alimony payments you have made under a court order, Child Support Agency assessment or legally binding order or agreement	Amount claimed under 'new' rules 15.4 £	
	Amount claimed under 'old' rules up to £1,900 15.5 £	Amount claimed under 'old' rules over £1,900 15.6 £
• Subscriptions for Venture Capital Trust shares (up to £100,000)	Amount on which relief claimed 15.7 £	
• Subscriptions under the Enterprise Investment Scheme (up to £150,000)	Amount on which relief claimed 15.8 £	
• Charitable covenants or annuities	Amount of payment 15.9 £	
• Gift Aid and Millennium Gift Aid	Amount of payment 15.10 £	
• Post-cessation expenses and losses on relevant discounted securities etc.	Amount of payment 15.11 £	
• Payments to a trade union or friendly society for death benefits	Half amount of payment 15.12 £	

Please turn over

OTHER INFORMATION *for the year ended 5 April 1999*

Q17 **Have you already had any 1998-99 tax refunded or set off by your Tax Office or the DSS Benefits Agency?** *Read the notes for box 17.1 on page 26 of your Tax Return Guide*

NO ✓ YES

If yes, enter the amount of the refund in box 17.1.

17.1 £

Q18 **Do you want to calculate your tax?**

NO YES ✓

If yes, do it now and then fill in boxes 18.1 to 18.9. Your Tax Calculation Guide will help.

- Unpaid tax for earlier years included in your tax code for 1998-99 — 18.1 £
- Tax due for 1998-99 included in your tax code for a later year — 18.2 £
- Total tax and Class 4 NIC due for 1998-99 **before** you made any payments on account *(put the amount in brackets if an overpayment)* — 18.3 £ 10027
- Tax due for earlier years — 18.4 £
- Tick box 18.5 if you have calculated tax overpaid for earlier years (and enter the amount in the 'Additional information' box on page 8) — 18.5
- Your first payment on account for 1999-2000 *(include the pence)* — 18.6 £ 3069

Tick box 18.7 if you are making a claim to reduce your 1999-2000 payments on account and say why in the 'Additional information' box — 18.7

Tick box 18.8 if you do **not** need to make 1999-2000 payments on account — 18.8

- 1999-2000 tax you are reclaiming now — 18.9 £

Q19 **Do you want to claim a repayment if you have paid too much tax?** *(If you tick 'No' or the tax you have overpaid is below £10, I will use the amount you are owed to reduce your next tax bill.)*

NO ✓ YES

If yes, fill in boxes 19.1 to 19.12 as appropriate.

Should the repayment (or payment) be sent:

- to you? *Tick box 19.1* — 19.1

or

- to your bank or building society account or other nominee? *Tick box 19.2* — 19.2

If you ticked either box 19.2 or 19.9, fill in boxes 19.3 to 19.8, 19.11 and 19.12 as appropriate.

Your (or your nominee's) bank or building society — 19.3

Branch sort code — 19.4 – –

Account number — 19.5

Name of account — 19.6

Building society ref. — 19.7

If your nominee is your agent, *tick box 19.9 and complete boxes 19.10 to 19.12* — 19.9

Agent's ref. for you — 19.10

I authorise — 19.8 Name of your nominee/agent

Nominee's address — 19.11 Postcode

to receive on my behalf the amount due

This authority must be signed by you. A photocopy of your signature will not do. — 19.12 Signature

Q20 **Are your details on the front of the Tax Return wrong?**

NO ✓ YES

If yes, please make any corrections on the front of the form.

Q21 **Please give other personal details in boxes 21.1 to 21.6** *This information helps us to be more efficient and effective and may support claims you have made elsewhere in your Tax Return*

Please give a **daytime telephone number if convenient.** It is often simpler to phone if we need to ask you about your Tax Return.

Your telephone number — 21.1

or, if you prefer, your agent's telephone number — 21.2

(also give your agent's name and reference in the 'Additional information' box on page 8)

Say if you are single, married, widowed, divorced or separated — 21.3 DIVORCED

Date of birth — 21.4 11 / 06 / 58

Enter your date of birth if you are self-employed, or you were born before 6 April 1934, or you have ticked the 'Yes' box in Question 14, or you are claiming relief for Venture Capital Trust subscriptions

Enter your first two forenames — 21.5 PENNY

Enter your National Insurance number (if known) — 21.6 AB 12 34 56 C

Bond and Co.
4 Church Street
Anytown
AN3 4LB

Penny Moore
The Old Halt
Anytown High Street
AN3 2LR

8 September 1999

Dear Penny

Self Assessment Tax Return and Tax Payable

I enclose a copy of your income tax and capital gains tax computation for 1998/99, together with your completed self assessment tax return. A further copy of the return is enclosed for your retention.

Will you please look through the computation and the self assessment tax return, and if you are happy with them both, please sign and date the return and return it to me for submission to the Inland Revenue.

The computation shows that there is a balancing payment of tax due of £8,027 (income tax £4,138 capital gains tax £3,889). This amount should be paid to the Collector of Taxes before 31 January 2000.

You are also due to make payments on account for 1999/00 of £3,069 each, by 31 January 2000 and 31 July 2000.

You should receive a statement of account before 31 January 2000 showing the tax due, together with a payslip. If you require any assistance in making the payment, please contact me.

If you need any further help or information please telephone me.

Yours sincerely

Roger Connery
Tax Department Manager

Task 2

Income for the year ended 5April 1999

Inland Revenue **SELF-EMPLOYMENT**

Fill in these boxes first

Name: JACK FLEMING

Tax reference: 12345 67890

If you want help, look up the box numbers in the Notes

Business details

Name of business
3.1 JACK'S JEANS

Description of business
3.2 CLOTHES SHOP

Address of business
3.3 12 HIGH STREET
ANY TOWN

Postcode AN1 1NN

Accounting period - *read the Notes, page SEN2 before filling in these boxes*

Start
3.4 01 / 04 / 98

End
3.5 31 / 03 / 99

- Tick box 3.5A if you entered details for all relevant accounting periods on last year's Tax Return and boxes 3.11 to 3.70 will be blank — 3.5A
- Tick box 3.6 if details in boxes 3.1 or 3.3 have changed since your last Tax Return — 3.6
- Tick box 3.7 if your accounts do not cover the period from the last accounting date (explain why in the 'Additional information' box below) — 3.7
- Tick box 3.8A if your accounting date has changed (only if this is a permanent change and you want it to count for tax) — 3.8A
- Tick box 3.8B if this is the second or further change (explain why you have not used the same date as last year in the 'Additional information' box) — 3.8B
- Date of commencement if after 5 April 1996 — 3.9 / /
- Date of cessation if before 6 April 1999 — 3.10 / /

Additional information

Income and expenses - annual turnover below £15,000

If your annual turnover is £15,000 or more, ***ignore*** *boxes 3.11 to 3.13.* — *Now fill in Page SE2*

If your annual turnover is below £15,000, ***fill in boxes 3.11 to 3.13 instead of Page SE2.*** *Read the Notes, page SEN2.*

- Turnover, other business receipts and goods etc. taken for personal use (and balancing charges) — 3.11 £
- Expenses allowable for tax (including capital allowances) — 3.12 £

Net profit (put figure in brackets if a loss) — box 3.11 minus box 3.12 — 3.13 £

Now fill in Page SE3

Income and expenses - annual turnover £15,000 or more

You must fill in this Page if your annual turnover is £15,000 or more - read the Notes, page SEN2

If you were registered for VAT, do the figures in boxes 3.16 to 3.51, include VAT? **3.14** [ ] or exclude VAT? **3.15** [ ]

Sales/business income (turnover) **3.16** £ 277420

	Disallowable expenses included in boxes 3.33 to 3.50	Total expenses	
• Cost of sales	**3.17** £	**3.33** £ 183500	
• Construction industry subcontractor costs	**3.18** £	**3.34** £	
• Other direct costs	**3.19** £	**3.35** £ 11500	box 3.16 *minus* (box 3.33 + box 3.34 + box 3.35)
		Gross profit/(loss)	**3.36** £ 82420
		Other income/profits	**3.37** £
• Employee costs	**3.20** £	**3.38** £ 23000	
• Premises costs	**3.21** £	**3.39** £ 11000	
• Repairs	**3.22** £	**3.40** £ 1500	
• General administrative expenses	**3.23** £	**3.41** £ 2250	
• Motor expenses	**3.24** £ 525	**3.42** £ 1750	
• Travel and subsistence	**3.25** £	**3.43** £	
• Advertising, promotion and entertainment	**3.26** £ 950	**3.44** £ 1400	
• Legal and professional costs	**3.27** £	**3.45** £ 770	
• Bad debts	**3.28** £ 120	**3.46** £ 1200	
• Interest	**3.29** £	**3.47** £ 350	
• Other finance charges	**3.30** £	**3.48** £	
• Depreciation and loss/(profit) on sale	**3.31** £ 5500	**3.49** £ 5500	
• Other expenses	**3.32** £	**3.50** £	total of boxes 3.38 to 3.50
	Put the total of boxes 3.17 to 3.32 in **box 3.53 below**	Total expenses	**3.51** £48,720
			boxes 3.36 + 3.37 *minus* box 3.51
		Net profit/(loss)	**3.52** £ 33,700

Tax adjustments to net profit or loss

	total of boxes 3.17 to 3.32	
• Disallowable expenses	**3.53** £ 7095	
• Goods etc. taken for personal use and other adjustments (apart from disallowable expenses) that increase profits	**3.54** £	
• Balancing charges	**3.55** £	boxes 3.53 + 3.54 + 3.55
Total additions to net profit (deduct from net loss)		**3.56** £ 7095
• Capital allowances	**3.57** £ 4050	boxes 3.57 + 3.58
• Deductions from net profit (add to net loss)	**3.58** £	**3.59** £ 4050
		boxes 3.52 + 3.56 *minus* box 3.59
Net business profit for tax purposes (put figure in brackets if a loss)		**3.60** £ 36,745

You must fill in this Page (leave blank any boxes that do not apply to you)

Capital allowances - summary

		Capital allowances		Balancing charge
• Motor cars (Separate calculations must be made for each motor car costing more than £12,000 and for cars used partly for private motoring.)	3.61	£ 1750	3.62	£
• Other business plant and machinery	3.63	£ 2300	3.64	£
• Agricultural or Industrial Buildings Allowance (A separate calculation must be made for each block of expenditure.)	3.65	£	3.66	£
• Other capital allowances claimed (Separate calculations must be made.)	3.67	£	3.68	£
		total of column above		total of column above
Total capital allowances/balancing charges	3.69	£ 4050	3.70	£

Adjustments to arrive at taxable profit or loss

Basis period begins **3.71** 01/04/98 and ends **3.72** 31/03/99

- Tick box 3.72A if the figure in box 3.88 is provisional **3.72A** ☐
- Tick box 3.72B if the special arrangements for certain trades detailed in the guidance notes apply **3.72B** ☐

Profit or loss of this account for tax purposes (box 3.13 or 3.60) **3.73** £ 36745

Adjustment to arrive at profit or loss for this basis period **3.74** £

- Overlap profit brought forward **3.75** £
- Deduct overlap relief used this year **3.76** £
- Overlap profit carried forward **3.77** £

Adjustment for farmers' averaging (see Notes, page SEN8 if you made a loss for 1998-99) **3.78** £

Net profit for 1998-99 (if loss, enter '0') **3.79** £ 36745

Allowable loss for 1998-99 (if you make a profit, enter '0') **3.80** £

- Loss offset against other income for 1998-99 **3.81** £
- Loss to carry back **3.82** £
- Loss to carry forward (that is allowable loss not claimed in any other way) **3.83** £
- Losses brought forward from last year **3.84** £
- Losses brought forward from last year used this year **3.85** £

box 3.79 *minus* box 3.85

Taxable profit after losses brought forward **3.86** £ 36745

- Any other business income (for example, Business Start-up Allowance received in 1998-99) **3.87** £

box 3.86 + box 3.87

Total taxable profits from this business **3.88** £ 36745

Class 4 National Insurance Contributions

- Tick this box if exception or deferment applies — 3.89
- Adjustments to profit chargeable to Class 4 National Insurance Contributions — 3.90 £

Class 4 National Insurance Contributions due — 3.91 £

Subcontractors in the construction industry

- Deductions made by contractors on account of tax (you must send your SC60s to us) — 3.92 £

Summary of balance sheet

Leave these boxes blank if you do not have a balance sheet

■ ***Assets***

	Box	£	Total
• Plant, machinery and motor vehicles	3.93	11010	
• Other fixed assets (premises, goodwill, investments etc.)	3.94		
• Stock and work in progress	3.95	25000	
• Debtors/prepayments/other current assets	3.96	12075	
• Bank/building society balances	3.97	2120	total of boxes 3.93 to 3.98
• Cash in hand	3.98	153	3.99 £ 50358

■ ***Liabilities***

	Box	£	Total
• Trade creditors/accruals	3.100	14571	
• Loans and overdrawn bank accounts	3.101		total of boxes 3.100 to 3.102
• Other liabilities	3.102	1007	3.103 £ 15578

■ ***Net business assets*** (put the figure in brackets if you had net business liabilities) — box 3.99 *minus* box 3.103 — 3.104 £ 34780

■ ***Represented by***

Capital Account

	Box	£	Total
• Balance at start of period*	3.105	38745	
• Net profit/(loss)*	3.106	33700	
• Capital introduced	3.107		
• Drawings	3.108	37665	total of boxes 3.105 to 3.107 *minus* box 3.108
• Balance at end of period*			3.109 £ 34780

* If the Capital Account is overdrawn, or the business made a net loss, show the figure in brackets.

Tax deducted from trading income

- Any tax deducted (excluding deductions made by contractors on account of tax) from trading income. — 3.120 £

Note: box numbers 3.110 to 3.119 are not used

Additional information

Now fill in any other supplementary Pages that apply to you.
Otherwise, go back to Page 2 of your Tax Return and finish filling it in.

CLASS ACTIVITIES

QUESTIONS

1-5 INTRODUCTION TO PERSONAL TAXATION

1 **Activity**

Task

State when the following allowances are available:

(a) Married couple's allowance

(b) Widow's bereavement allowance

(c) Additional personal allowance

(d) Personal and married couple's age allowance

6-7 EMOLUMENTS AND BENEFITS

1 Activity

(a) Emoluments from an office or employment are taxable under Schedule E.

Task 1

Explain the basis of assessment for Schedule E.

(b) **Task 2**

State how the taxable value of goods and services provided for employees is determined:

(i) for employees earning less than £8,500 pa;
(ii) for employees earning £8,500 pa and over.

(c) Alexander and Sonia, a married couple, permanently separated on 5 April 1998 and were divorced on 5 August 1998. They had one child, Nicholas. The court ordered Alexander to pay maintenance payments to both Sonia and Nicholas.

Task 3

State the income tax treatment of such maintenance payments on the payer and on the recipient.

8-11 INTRODUCTION TO CGT

1 Activity

Evelyn purchased shares in Dassau plc, a quoted company, as follows:

	No. of shares	*Cost £*
December 1974	2,000	3,000
December 1984	1,000	2,000
April 1987 1 for 2 rights issue		£2 per share

In November 1998 Evelyn sold 4,000 shares for £16,000.

The market value of the shares on 31 March 1982 was £1.75 each.

No election has been, or will be made, under S35(5), TCGA 1992, to have all pre-31 March 1982 acquisitions re-based to 31 March 1982.

Task

Calculate Evelyn's capital gain for 1998/99 (before annual exemption). The shares are not business assets for taper relief.

2 Activity

Monica Day sold two oil paintings at auction on 1 November 1998, the auctioneer deducting 10% commission, details of which were as follows:

	Painting 1 £	*Painting 2* £
Purchase price (May 1968)	500	6,800
Expenses of acquisition	100	200
Market value 31 March 1982	3,000	4,000
Sale proceeds	7,200	2,000

Task

Calculate the chargeable gain/allowable loss arising on the sale of each painting.

3 **Activity**

Mr and Mrs Steel had the following transactions in assets in the year ended 5 April 1999

Mr Steel

(a) A house, which had been bought for £4,000 on 3 April 1983 and let to tenants thereafter, was sold on 1 July 1998. On 2 April 1984 an extension costing £2,000 was built, and on 12 June 1986 the loft was converted into a bedroom at a cost of £3,000. The net proceeds of sale were £62,750.

(b) Sold a piece of sculpture for £6,500 on 30 August 1998 which he had bought for £3,900. Indexation factor is 0.424 to April 1998.

(c) Sold a one-tenth share in a racehorse on 31 August 1998 for £6,200. The interest had cost £1,340 in November 1989.

(d) Sold a vintage Alfa Romeo motor car for £76,500 on 19 December 1998. The car had cost £17,400 on 31 March 1983. During his period of ownership Steel had never actually used the car on the road.

Mrs Steel

(e) Sold a rare Russian icon on 24 May 1998 for £5,600 which had cost £6,300. Indexation factor is 0.618 to April 1998.

(f) Sold three acres out of a twelve acre plot of land on 14 December 1998 for £8,000. The whole plot had been purchased for £2,000. On 14 December 1998 the unsold acres had an agreed market value of £20,000. Indexation factor is 0.682 to April 1998.

(g) Sold a piece of Chinese jade for £13,800 on 1 September 1998. This was purchased at auction in May 1970 for £4,100. The market value on 31 March 1982 was £6,500.

Mr Steel had capital losses brought forward at 6 April 1998 of £3,024. His taxable income for 1998/99 is £22,400. Mrs Steel has no income. None of the above assets qualify as 'business' assets for taper relief purposes.

Task 1

Calculate Mr Steel's tax liability on chargeable gains for 1998/99 if any.

Task 2

Calculate Mrs Steel's tax liability on chargeable gains for 1998/99 if any.

12-14 RETIREMENT AND REPLACEMENT

1 Activity

(a) In October 1998 Kathleen had her 57th birthday and decided to retire immediately from her 'personal' company. She had two children, Corinne and Stephen, to whom she gave all her shares in the company in equal shares. In October 1998 the total value of the shares was £1,050,000. The shares had cost £250,000 in September 1981 and were valued at £200,000 in March 1983. Kathleen had been a full-time working director in the company since October 1993. The company did not own any 'non-business' chargeable assets.

No election has been made or will be made, to have all pre-31 March 1982 acquisitions re-based to 31 March 1982: S35(5) TCGA 1992.

Task 1

(i) Calculate the capital gain (before annual exemption) assessable on Kathleen for 1998/99; and

(ii) explain the present and future consequences of a joint election made by Kathleen, Corinne and Stephen to 'hold-over' any capital gain.

(b) Ranek Innovators Ltd sold a factory in November 1998 for £200,000 and moved into rented premises. The factory had been purchased in April 1987 for £100,000. The company purchased fixed plant in December 1997 costing £180,000 and elected to 'hold-over' any gain on the sale of the building against the cost of the plant.

Task 2

(i) Calculate the chargeable gain on the sale of the factory and the effect of the 'hold-over' claim on the chargeable gain; and

(ii) state the earliest time the 'hold-over' would cease to be effective.

2 Activity

Your client, Medway, has been offered £160,000 for a freehold factory he owns and is considering disposing of it in early October 1998. He acquired the factory in early October 1966 for £10,000, and it was valued at £60,000 in March 1982. The factory has always been used for business purposes.

Task 1

Compute the chargeable gain which will arise if Medway disposes of the factory.

Task 2

Indicate to Medway the capital gains consequences of each of the following alternative courses of action he is considering taking, following the sale, and give any advice you consider to be relevant.

(i) acquiring a larger freehold factory in 1999 for £172,000.

(ii) acquiring a smaller freehold factory in 1999 for £155,500 and using the remainder of the proceeds as working capital.

(iii) using the proceeds to pay a premium of £180,000 for a 40-year lease of a new factory (it is possible that a freehold warehouse will be bought in the next two or three years for an estimated cost of £200,000).

15 PRINCIPAL PRIVATE RESIDENCE RELIEF

1 Activity

On 30 September 1998 Jane Smith made a gift of a house to her grandson Norman. The house had been bought by Jane on 1 September 1981 for £32,800, and was extended at a cost of £10,600 during June 1987. Market values of £45,000 at 31 March 1982 and £140,000 at 30 September 1998 have been agreed by the Inland Revenue.

Jane occupied the house as her main residence until 30 September 1989 when she went to live with her sister. The house remained empty for four years, but has been rented out continuously since then.

Calculate the chargeable gain.

16-17 PERSONAL TAX COMPUTATIONS & RETURNS

1 Activity

Vernon Alexander is the manager of the local office of an insurance company. His wife Pamela is a self-employed doctor in general practice.

Information provided is:

(1) Vernon's salary for 1998/99 was £25,500.

(2) Vernon was provided with a new company car (1500cc) on 1 January 1994 which cost £10,200 when new. His mileage in 1998/99 was 22,000, of which one-quarter was private. The running costs of the car including all petrol were paid for by the company and amounted of £2,200.

(3) Dividend income from UK companies in 1998/99 was:

Vernon	£350
Pamela	£1,200

(4) Pamela has had a deposit account with the Midwest Bank plc since May 1995, the interest credited to which was:

Year ended 5 April 1998	£1,000
Year ended 5 April 1999	£1,200

(5) Vernon and Pamela opened a joint ordinary account with National Savings Bank on 17 April 1996. Interest has been credited.

31 December 1996	£150
31 December 1997	£190
31 December 1998	£180

(6) Both Vernon and Pamela realised capital gains in 1998/99, Vernon £7,000 and Pamela £11,000 both after indexation allowance and taper relief (where available).

(7) Mortgage interest payments of £3,000 (gross) were made to the Lloydminster Bank plc in 1998/99 on the outstanding mortgage of £28,000. These interest payments which relate to the family's only residence were divided equally between Vernon and Pamela and paid under the MIRAS arrangements.

(8) Pamela pays £1,520 (net) each year under a four year charitable covenant to Oxfam which started on 1 January 1997.

(9) Pamela commenced self-employment on 1 May 1996 and decided to retire from general practice on 31 March 1999, prior to taking up an appointment with the local hospital. Her adjusted profits are:

	£
Year ended 30.4.97	48,000
Year ended 30.4.98	30,000
Period ended 31.3.99	46,000

The following purchases were made:

1 May 1996	Rover car	£10,667
10 May 1996	Medical equipment	£5,400
2 June 1997	Waiting-room chairs	£200

There was one third private use of the car.

Upon retirement from the practice the assets in the pool were sold for £3,500 (all less than cost) and the car was valued at £3,000.

Task 1

Calculate Case II assessments in respect of Pamela's practice for 1996/97, 1997/98 and 1998/99.

Task 2

Calculate the income tax and capital gains tax liability for 1997/98 in respect of both Vernon and Pamela Alexander.

18-20 INTRODUCTION TO BUSINESS TAXATION

1 **Activity**

In May 1997 Bernard, a self-employed plumber, and his son Gerald, a self-employed electrician, purchased 1,000 empty barrels from a Scottish whisky distillery. The barrels were over 100 years old and of no further use to the distillery. Bernard and Gerald sawed the barrels into halves and sold them to several local garden centres for use as ornamental flower tubs. Bernard and Gerald paid £10 for a full barrel to the distillery and sold a half barrel for £8. Three-quarters of the barrels were sold by Bernard and Gerald in the summer of 1997 and the remainder in the summer of 1998.

Task

Prepare a list of points for consideration prior to writing a report to Bernard and Gerald on the liability to income tax of the profit generated by the venture.

21-22 BASIS PERIODS AND TRADING LOSSES

1 Activity

Sigmund, a single man, began trading on 1 January 1998. He prepares accounts to 31 December annually, with results as follows.

	Schedule D Case I
	£
Year ended 31 December 1998 Loss	(12,000)
Year ended 31 December 1999 Loss (estimated)	(4,000)
Year ended 31 December 2000 Profit (estimated)	8,000
Year ended 31 December 2001 Profit (estimated)	11,500

Details of the amounts of other income and payments for the years 1994/95 to 1997/98 were as follows

	Salary from employment	*Dividends received (incl tax credit)*	*Gross loan interest paid*
	£	£	£
1994/95	9,000	3,000	2,800
1995/96	12,500	3,400	2,600
1996/97	8,800	3,800	2,500
1997/98	3,300	700	2,600

From 1 January 1998 the business is Sigmund's only source of income. The gross loan interest paid is eligible loan interest which qualifies to be treated as a charge on income. Gross interest paid after 1997/98 can be taken at £2,300 a year.

Sigmund wishes to obtain relief for his initial trading losses as soon as possible.

Task 1

Calculate the Schedule D Case I assessments for 1997/98 to 2001/02 before giving relief for any losses under S380 or S381 ICTA 1988.

Task 2

Show how the losses incurred in the first two years of trading are to be relieved so as to provide earliest relief.

23 TAXATION OF PARTNERSHIPS

1 **Activity**

Edward commenced a retail business as a sole trader on 1 February 1997. Six months later Arnold joined him as a partner. Edward is a part-qualified accountant and has produced a draft balance sheet for the 18 month period from the date of commencement, 1 February 1997 to 31 July 1998. He has asked you to prepare computations showing the amounts assessable on himself and Arnold for all tax years in which the above profits are assessable.

Edward and Arnold
Balance sheet at 31 July 1998

	£	£	£
Edward			
Capital account			20,000
Current account:			
Salary at £12,000 pa from 1 August 1997		12,000	
Interest on capital at 8% from 1 May 1998		400	
Share of profit - to 31 July 1997	9,000		
- from 1 August 1997 (⅔)	12,000		
		21,000	
		33,400	
Drawings		10,500	
			22,900
Arnold			
Capital account			10,000
Current account:			
Salary at £6,000 pa from 1 January 1998		3,500	
Interest on capital at 8% from 1 May 1998		200	
Share of profit from 1 August 1997 (⅓)		6,000	
		9,700	
Drawings		(6,500)	
			3,200
			56,100

Fixed assets			
Leasehold premises:			
Premium on 10 year lease on retail premises taken out on 1 February 1997		20,000	
Less: Amortisation		(3,000)	
			17,000
Equipment and fittings:			
Acquired - 1 February 1997		8,400	
- 15 June 1997		4,800	
		13,200	
Disposal - 20 April 1998		(800)	
		12,400	
Depreciation		(3,100)	
			9,300
Motor cars			
Acquired - 1 February 1997		11,200	
- 1 August 1997		7,400	
		18,600	
Depreciation		(5,580)	
			13,020
			39,320
Current assets			
Stocks, less a 10% contingency provision		9,180	
Debtors, less a 5% bad debt provision		11,970	
Cash in hand		128	
		21,278	
Creditors	3,258		
Bank overdraft	1,240		
		(4,498)	
			16,780
			56,100

Edward has provided you with the following additional information:

(1) the proceeds of the equipment sold on 20 April 1998, amounted to £910;

(2) the new 2000cc Rover car acquired on 1 February 1997, has private use of 10%;

the new 1994cc Montego car acquired on 1 August 1997, has the following typical annual mileage

- home to business premises	6,000
- visiting customers	7,000
- visiting suppliers	2,000
- attendance at trade conference, whilst visiting family	1,000
- travel overseas to establish retail networks	4,000
Total annual mileage	20,000

Motor car expenses are:

	£
Rover (including fuel £860)	1,980
Montego (including fuel £640)	1,400

(3) the expenditure charged in the profit and loss account includes:

Legal fees in drawing up a partnership agreement	420
Legal fees re lease	280
Fee for negotiating loan to finance the lease	250
Redecoration of premises - which were in a bad condition - though useable - when acquired	538
Gifts of business diaries to customers - cost £12 each	720
Entertaining French supplier	282
Subscription to Retail Trade Association	80

(4) in June 1998 Arnold provided retail advice to his nephew for which he would normally charge a fee of £200. No charge was made;

Task

Prepare the necessary computations to show the amounts assessable on each partner for *all tax years* in which the above profit will be assessed, and to compute the overlap profits for each partner.

(You can assume no further changes in salaries, interest on capital or profit sharing ratio. All calculations can be made to the nearest £.)

24-25 INTRODUCTION TO CORPORATION TAX

1 Activity

Pat Ltd, a company with no associated companies, was incorporated in 1980.

The following information relates to its financial accounting period of twelve months ended on 31 December 1998:

	£	
Income:		
Schedule DI profits as adjusted for taxation	980,000	
Bank interest	8,000	
Loan interest (gross)	6,000	- 10.4.1998
Capital gains	32,000	
(There were also capital losses b/f 1.1.1998 - £12,000)		
Rents receivable	10,000	
Dividends from UK companies (including tax credits):		
received 13 April 1998	12,000	
received 20 August 1998	8,000	
Charge paid:		
Patent royalties (gross)	10,000	- 10.2.1998
Covenant to cancer research (gross)	2,000	- 31.7.1998
Dividends paid:		
28 March 1998	96,000	
13 October 1998	25,600	

Additional information

The bank interest and loan interest received were the same as the amounts calculated on an accruals basis for the year.

The mainstream corporation tax liability for the year ended 31 December 1997 has been agreed at £126,000.

The company has surplus ACT brought forward at 1 January 1998 amounting to £24,000.

Task 1

Compute the MCT payable for the above chargeable accounting period, showing clearly your treatment of income tax and ACT.

Task 2

For budget purposes, prepare a schedule of the dates on which each of the various amounts of corporation tax and income tax will fall to be paid or refunded as a result of the above information.

2 **Activity**

The following is the operating profit and loss account of BJD Ltd for its first year of trading ending on 31 March 1999.

			£	*Note*
Gross profit			764,000	
Add:	Discounts received		5,400	
	Bank interest received		8,500	(1)
	Dividends from UK companies (including tax credit)		7,000	
	Gain on sale of factory		108,000	(2)
			892,900	
Less:	Distribution costs	270,000		(3)
	Administration expenses	196,000		(4)
			(466,000)	
			426,900	
Less:	Patent royalties (gross)		(8,000)	(5)
NET PROFIT			£418,900	

Notes

(1) The amount of bank interest received is the same as the amount receivable on an accruals basis for the year.

(2) The gain on sale represents the difference between the book value of the factory and the disposal value of £158,000.

It had cost £60,000 in 1978 and its market value, for capital gains tax purposes, at 31 March 1982 was agreed at £60,000.

You may assume an indexation allowance of £63,000. Thus the total input cost for capital gains is £123,000.

(3) Distribution costs include:

	£	£
Depreciation of motor vans		9,500
Parking fines paid on behalf of staff using own cars (amounts assessed on staff)		850
Salary of sales director		34,000
Legal fees:		
Defending action for poor workmanship	840	
Defending breach of Factory Act: Verdict - Guilty	650	1,490

(4) Administration expenses include:

	£	£
Redundancy payment to works manager in branch where trade involved ceased entirely (his statutory entitlement was £3,000)		12,000
Finance director's salary		24,000
Covenant to Heart Foundation (gross)		3,000
Legal fees:		
Bad debt recovery	3,200	
Recovery of loans to employees	600	3,800
General expenses including:		
Costs of staff canteen used by ALL staff	2,940	
Cost of Staff Dance for staff members	2,600	5,540

(5) Patent royalties:

	£	£
Paid in year	6,000	
Accrued at 31 March 1999	2,000	8,000

In addition to the above, the company incurred the following expenditure in the two years prior to 1 April 1998:

	£
Training costs of staff	2,900
Rates of factory and office	4,800
Legal fees re new lease of premises	2,800

These items have NOT been reflected in the above profit and loss account.

Capital allowances have been agreed at £24,000.

Task 1

Compute the Schedule D Case I profit for the above accounting period, explaining your treatment of EACH item shown above.

Task 2

Compute the company's profits for corporation tax purposes.

Note: You are NOT required to compute the corporation tax payable.

3 **Activity**

Longwood plc, a UK trading company with no associates, has the following income and outgoings for the year to 31 March 1999.

Income	£
Sch D Case I Profits	880,000
Building Society Interest Receivable	20,000
Debenture Interest Receivable	19,200
Capital Gains (after indexation)	36,500
UK Dividends Received	16,000
Outgoings	
Patent royalties paid	123,200
Dividend Paid	96,000

Task

Compute the Mainstream Corporation Tax payable for the year to 31 March 1999.

4 **Activity**

Malaga Ltd prepares accounts to 31 March annually. During the year ended 31 March 1999 the following transactions took place:

1998			£
May	20	Dividend received	5,600
June	1	Debenture interest paid (gross)	16,000
August	10	Dividend paid	28,000
September	5	Royalties received (gross)	11,200
November	23	Dividend received	7,000
December	8	Loan interest received (gross)	5,720
1999			
January	14	Dividend received	1,400
February	28	Dividend paid	28,000

All dividends paid and received are shown before addition of ACT or tax credit.

Task

Show the quarterly accounting for ACT and income tax with relevant dates and the relief available for any tax unrelieved at the end of the accounting period.

26-28 CT LOSSES, CLOSE COMPANIES & CT RETURNS

1 Activity

The recent results of Segovia Ltd are as follows:

	Years ending			*9 months ended*
	31.3.96	*31.3.97*	*31.3.98*	*31.12.98*
	£	£	£	£
Schedule D Case I	40,800	61,200	342,720	
Trading loss				(325,500)
Schedule A	7,750	6,800	7,100	5,440
Bank interest receivable	2,440	1,350	2,170	2,050
Schedule D Case V	680	880	800	275
Capital (loss)/gain	-	(3,200)	7,280	7,860
Patent royalties (gross)	(2,750)	(2,750)	(2,750)	(2,750)

Segovia Ltd had trading losses to carry forward of £7,000 at 1 April 1995.

Task

Calculate the corporation tax liability for all four periods, assuming that all beneficial claims are made.

2 Activity

Loser Ltd made up its accounts to 31 March 1998 but has since changed to a 30 September accounting date. The company has suffered declining results in recent years, and is therefore planning to restructure its business operations during September 1999 by closing three branches of its business, and disposing of the related assets. (You should assume that today's date is 1 August 1999.)

Loser Ltd forecasts a substantial tax adjusted Schedule DI trading loss for the current year to 30 September 1999. A small trading profit is forecast for the following year to 30 September 2000, with steadily increasing profits thereafter.

The company's tax adjusted Schedule DI trading profits for recent years have been as follows:

	£
Year ended 31 March 1998	550,000
Period ended 30 September 1998	70,000

Task 1

Advise Loser Ltd as to which loss relief claims would be the most beneficial.

Task 2

Advise Loser Ltd as to when it would be beneficial for tax purposes to delay certain aspects of its restructuring until after 30 September 1999.

Task 3

Advise Loser Ltd as to whether the delaying of certain aspects of its restructuring until after 30 September 1999 would be considered to be tax avoidance or tax evasion.

AAT

AT FOULKS LYNCH

HOTLINES

Telephone: 0181 844 0667
Enquiries: 0181 831 9990
Fax: 0181 831 9991

AT FOULKS LYNCH LTD

Number 4, The Griffin Centre
Staines Road, Feltham
Middlesex TW14 0HS

Intended Examination Date: Dec 99 ☐ June 2000 ☐	Textbooks	Workbooks	Distance Learning (UK MAINLAND ONLY)
Foundation	* Combined textbook and workbook		
Unit 1 Cash Transactions	£9.95 ☐	£9.95 ☐	£85 ☐
Unit 2 Credit Transactions	£9.95 ☐	£9.95 ☐	£85 ☐
Unit 3 Payroll	£9.95 ☐	£9.95 ☐	£85 ☐
Unit 19 Data Processing	£9.95 ☐*		£85 ☐
Units 21 - 25 The Business Background	£9.95 ☐*		£40 ☐
Foundation Level Distance Learning Course			£360 ☐
Intermediate			
Unit 4 Financial Records & Preparing Accounts	£9.95 ☐	£9.95 ☐	£95 ☐
Unit 5 Recording Cost Information	£9.95 ☐	£9.95 ☐	£95 ☐
Unit 6 Preparing Reports and Returns	£9.95 ☐	£9.95 ☐	£95 ☐
Unit 20 Using Information Technology	£9.95 ☐*		£95 ☐
Unit 22 Health and Safety	£3.95 ☐*		Option-FOC** ☐
Intermediate Level Distance Learning Course		** When any other AAT DLC is purchased	£380 ☐
Technician *Notes:* Units 7, 8 and 9 are compulsory	Students choose 1 out of Units 10, 11, 12, 13 (only 10 available)		Students choose 3 out of Units 14, 15, 16, 17, 18
Units 7, 8 & 15 Cost Management, Resource Allocation and Evaluating Activities	£9.95 ☐	£9.95 ☐	Please contact us regarding availability
Unit 9 Managing Accounting Systems	£9.95 ☐	£9.95 ☐	
Unit 10 Drafting Financial Statements	£9.95 ☐	£9.95 ☐	
Unit 14 Cash Management and Credit Control	£9.95 ☐	£9.95 ☐	
Unit 16 Implementing Auditing Procedures	£9.95 ☐	£9.95 ☐	
Units 17 & 18 Business and Personal Taxation	£9.95 ☐	£9.95 ☐	
Technician Level Distance Learning Course (See notes above)			
P & P + Delivery UK Mainland	£2.00/book	£2.00/book	Post Free
NI, ROI & EU Countries	£5.00/book	£5.00/book	UK Mainland Only
Rest of world standard air service	£10.00/book	£10.00/book	
Rest of world courier service (tel number essential)	£22.00/book	£22.00/book	

SINGLE ITEM SUPPLEMENT: If you only order 1 item, INCREASE postage costs by £2.50 for UK, NI & EU Countries or by £15.00 for Rest of World Service

TOTAL	Textbooks	Workbooks	Distance Learning
Sub Total £			
Less 23% tax relief for Distance Learning paid for by student only £			
Post & Packing £			
Total £			

Payments in Sterling in London **Order Total £**

DELIVERY DETAILS

☐ Mr ☐ Miss ☐ Mrs ☐ Ms Other

Initials Surname

Address

Postcode

Telephone Deliver to home ☐

Company name

Address

Postcode

Telephone Fax

Monthly report to go to employer ☐ Deliver to work ☐

PAYMENT

1 I enclose Cheque/PO/Bankers Draft for £__________
Please make cheques payable to AT Foulks Lynch Ltd.

2 Charge Mastercard/Visa/Switch A/C No:

Valid from: Expiry Date:

Issue No: (Switch only)

Signature Date

DECLARATION

I agree to pay as indicated on this form and understand that AT Foulks Lynch Terms and Conditions apply (available on request). I understand that AT Foulks Lynch Ltd are not liable for non-delivery if the rest of world standard air service is used.

Signature Date

Please Allow:

UK mainland	- 5-10 w/days
NI, ROI & EU Countries	- 1-3 weeks
Rest of world standard air service	- 6 weeks
Rest of world courier service	- 10 w/days

Notes: All delivery times subject to stock availability. Signature required on receipt (except rest of world standard air service). Please give both addresses for Distance Learning students where possible.

Form effective at Jul 99 *All details correct at time of printing* *Source: AATTXT99*